MOTHER OF CHRIST, MOTHER OF THE CHURCH

MOTHER OF CHRIST, MOTHER OF THE CHURCH

Documents on the Blessed Virgin Mary

Introductions by
M. Jean Frisk, S.T.L.

General Editor
Marianne Lorraine Trouvé, FSP

Pauline
BOOKS & MEDIA
· BOSTON

Nihil Obstat (for the introductions)
Reverend Edward J. Gratsch

Imprimatur
Most Reverend Carl K. Moeddel, Vicar General and Auxiliary Bishop of the Archdiocese of Cincinnati, on April 3, 2000.

Library of Congress Cataloging-in-Publication Data

Mother of Christ, Mother of the Church : documents on the Blessed Virgin Mary / introductions by M. Jean Frisk ; general editor, Marianne Lorraine Trouvé.
    p. cm. — (Ecclesial classics)
Includes bibliographical references and index.
  ISBN 0-8198-4808-5
  1. Mary, Blessed Virgin, Saint—Theology. 2. Mary, Blessed Virgin, Saint—Papal documents. 3. Catholic Church—Doctrines. I. Frisk, M. Jean. II. Trouvé, Marianne Lorraine. III. Series.
  BT613 .M68 2000
  232.91—dc21

00-008306

Cover design: Helen Rita Lane, FSP

The Vatican translation is used for all documents except *Ineffabilis Deus, Munificentissimus Deus, Lumen Gentium* and all excerpts from Vatican II, for which the N.C.W.C. translation is used.

English translation of the *Catechism of the Catholic Church* for the United States of America copyright © 1994, United States Catholic Conference, Inc.—*Libreria Editrice Vaticana.* Used with permission.

Printed and published in the U.S.A. by Pauline Books & Media, 50 Saint Pauls Avenue, Boston MA 02130-3491.

www.pauline.org

Pauline Books & Media is the publishing house of the Daughters of St. Paul, an international congregation of women religious serving the Church with the communications media.

1 2 3 4 5 6 7 8   05 04 03 02 01 00

CONTENTS

THE MONTH OF MAY
Mense Maio
Pope Paul VI

THE GREAT SIGN
Signum Magnum
Pope Paul VI

FOR THE RIGHT ORDERING AND DEVELOPMENT OF DEVOTION TO THE BLESSED VIRGIN MARY
Marialis Cultus
Pope Paul VI

ON CHRISTIAN JOY
Gaudete in Domino
Pope Paul VI

THE SPLENDOR OF TRUTH
Veritatis Splendor
Pope John Paul II

ON PREPARATION FOR THE JUBILEE OF THE YEAR 2000
Tertio Millennio Adveniente
Pope John Paul II

ABOUT THE AUTHOR
OF THE INTRODUCTIONS

M. Jean Frisk is a member of the secular institute of the Schoenstatt Sisters of Mary. With a background in education and educational administration, she spent several years in the United States and in Europe working as coordinator of retreats, education, pilgrimages and activities for the Schoenstatt Movement, a Marian and apostolic lay foundation of the Church. Upon returning from Germany, she completed a Masters in Theology with a Marian concentration (MA) at the University of Dayton and a Licentiate in Sacred Theology (STL) at the International Marian Research Institute in Dayton, Ohio. For her STL thesis Sister Jean researched 2000 catechetical texts to discover what has been taught about Mary since Vatican II in the United States. She currently holds a position at the Marian Library/International Marian Research Institute in Dayton, which has the most extensive collection in the world devoted to the Blessed Virgin Mary. Sister Jean assists in a variety of research projects and is part of a team that produces the Mary Page, an Internet site devoted to Marian research (Mary Page: www.udayton.edu/mary).

EDITOR'S NOTE

The *Ecclesial Classics* series presents essential documents on topics of vital importance to the life of the Church today. This volume contains the full text of major Church documents on the Blessed Virgin Mary, as well as excerpts from selected documents that contain significant sections on Marian doctrine.

While the series focuses on Vatican II and post-conciliar documents, this volume contains two documents predating the Council because of their doctrinal importance: the apostolic constitution of Pius IX defining the dogma of the Immaculate Conception, and that of Pius XII defining the dogma of the Assumption.

The translation used for the documents on the Immaculate Conception, the Assumption, chapter eight of *Lumen Gentium* and other quotations from Vatican II is that of the National Catholic Welfare Conference (N.C.W.C.), the precursor of the National Council of Catholic Bishops. The translation of the other documents is the Vatican translation obtained from the Holy See.

GENERAL INTRODUCTION

This volume gathers together a selection of major documents published by the Magisterium of the Catholic Church concerning teachings on the Blessed Virgin Mary, Mother of Jesus Christ. Arranged by date of publication, the book begins with the dogmatic definitions of the Immaculate Conception in 1854 and of the Assumption in 1950. Then it presents chapter eight of *Lumen Gentium* and various post-conciliar statements, focusing on papal teachings since Vatican II.

Thus it does not include every magisterial document on Mary during the time frame indicated above. Pope Leo XIII, for instance, pontiff from 1873–1903, published sixteen Marian documents. Other Marian material not included in this volume is available in the *Catechism of the Catholic Church,* which integrates Marian teachings in each of its four sections, referring to her in 143 paragraphs. For liturgical celebrations, forty-six new Mass formularies have been published in *A Collection of Masses of the Blessed Virgin Mary.*[1] From 1995 to 1997, Pope John Paul II presented an overview of Marian teaching in a series of seventy general audiences.[2]

This compendium includes those teachings which, to quote the doctrinal commentary issued together with the statement *Ad Tuendam Fidem,* are essential to our Catholic faith:

---

1. *Collection of Masses of the Blessed Virgin Mary* (New York: Catholic Book Publishers, 1992).

2. These are available in a volume entitled *Theotókos—Woman, Mother, Disciple: A Catechesis on Mary, Mother of God* (Boston: Pauline Books & Media, 2000).

In the case of a *defining* act, a truth is solemnly defined by an *ex cathedra* pronouncement by the Roman Pontiff or by the action of an ecumenical council. In the case of a *non-defining* act, a doctrine is taught *infallibly* by the ordinary and universal Magisterium of the bishops dispersed throughout the world who are in communion with the Successor of Peter. *Such a doctrine can be confirmed or reaffirmed by the Roman Pontiff, even without recourse to a solemn definition,* by declaring explicitly that it belongs to the teaching of the ordinary and universal Magisterium as a truth that is divinely revealed or as a truth of Catholic doctrine.[3]

As we have seen, in the century and a half following the definition of the Immaculate Conception in 1854, a rich tapestry of teachings has been woven in papal writings and in theological studies. Vatican II and the pontiffs thereafter have drawn on this wealth in formulating the Church's teaching about Mary.

The documents on Mary do not stand in isolation. They are supported by the long history of the Church's constant teaching and are interwoven with the cultural contexts of the times in which they were published. The teachings, faithfully guarded by the Church, "to be sure always with the same meaning and the same content — must be transmitted to people in a manner that is alive and appropriate to the exigencies of the day."[4]

Marian teaching today

Studies on Mary continue beyond the magisterial context. In 1991 René Laurentin, the renowned Marian theologian, documented in his work *La question mariale* eighty-nine Marian congresses held on local, national and international levels since 1900. Currently, theologians gather every four years at an international Marian congress, and several countries have Mariological societies that meet annually. The members study various topics concerning Mary, including the development of papal teachings about her. From Pope Leo XIII to John Paul II, the Church has enjoyed a rich growth of Marian doctrine. In 1954, the first Marian

---

3. Joseph Cardinal Ratzinger, *Commentary on the Concluding Formula of the Professio Fidei*—Appendix to the document *Ad Tuendam Fidem* (Boston: Pauline Books & Media, 1998).

4. International Theological Commission, "On the Interpretation of Dogmas," *Origins* 20 (May 17, 1990): 6–7.

Year proclaimed by the Church, Pope Pius XII established the liturgical Feast of the Queenship of Mary (August 22) to complement the dogmas of 1854 and 1950.

A decade later, Vatican II presented its teaching on the Blessed Virgin Mary, more extensive than that of any previous council. Since Vatican II, major documents from Pope Paul VI and Pope John Paul II have brought out Mary's role in salvation history. The catechetical documents of the Church require that doctrine about Mary be taught in conjunction with doctrine concerning Christ and the Church. Mary appears in the basic outline of truths essential for knowing the faith. In 1987, in anticipation of the millennial celebration of Christ's birth, Pope John Paul II proclaimed a second Marian Year to honor the woman who gave Jesus Christ human life.

Mary's place in Christian life

What is the Catholic Church's teaching about Mary, the Mother of Jesus Christ? What do these teachings signify regarding Jesus Christ? What do they matter to the Christian Churches or to the world at large? The documents in this volume will help to answer these questions. The introduction to each document will briefly establish the historical context of the particular document, describe its major content, and suggest the relevance of its teaching to situations today. Taken together, the documents give a complete overview of Marian theology.

Recognizing that the many facets of the "Marian question" require careful study, the Council fathers did not attempt to cover every aspect of Marian doctrine (*LG* 54). But that was the strength of Vatican II. Soon after it began, the bishops discerned that the pressing concern of the Church today was not only knowing doctrine but knowing how to *live* it. The pastoral perspective that prevailed at the Council made the bishops ask: What would help the people of God to live according to a Christian world view? Furthermore, where did Mary fit into this scheme of things? Knowing this will help one understand Church teachings about her prior to and following the Council, up to our own day.

What do these teachings signify regarding Jesus Christ? The documents amply answer that query. Mary has everything to do with our Lord and Savior, Jesus Christ. Without Christ, the young woman of Nazareth would be forgotten dust blown away by the winds of time. Because of him, people still know and honor Mary today.

What do teachings on Mary matter to the Christian? Marian teachings show us how to put Christ at the center of our lives. In Mary the Church finds the fulfillment of the baptismal promise of the fully redeemed person, the person at harmony with heaven and earth, in whom God dwells. For the newly baptized, perhaps the best time to study Mary is *after* initiation during the period of mystagogy, when the neophyte looks to the community of believers to discover where life in Christ is evident and fruitful.

From its earliest foundations the Christian community has gathered together in prayer with Mary. The early churches began to see her as a model of life lived as an intimate associate of the Savior, as one who believed in him from the first moment of his Incarnation.

In our own discovery of Jesus Christ, we sense that the Lord who is our Savior did not establish his reign in isolation. He did so in the context of family and society, of fellowship and community, of Mystical Body and People of God, the Church born of his heart. Even in the isolation of his redemptive death, a death he alone suffered, he was not alone. A few disciples stood with him, including his mother. Ultimately, to speak about Mary is to tell the story of one who believed.

Mary was the first to believe in him, the first to learn of him as the Savior and Lord who would save his people from their sins. She was the first to enter his school of faith; she who instructed her child was also educated by him. She remained faithful to him at his death and beyond. She lived among the first disciples, offering her prayerful presence as the early Church began to grow.

Mary grew in faith, hope and love on her daily pilgrimage. The lives of Christians are meant to be radically different after their baptism. But the initiation process leading to baptism and the outpouring of transforming grace is not some kind of magic wand transforming pumpkins into royal carriages. Instead, the *seeds* of faith, hope and love, nurtured by the faith community, must take root and grow to maturity, very much as they did in Mary who pondered all things in her heart.

But when newly baptized persons have entered the faith community of the Church can they be left alone to discover all there is to know about the Lord? Even with eyes fixed on the Master, does the Christian not gather *in community* to listen to him? Is not the Lord evident in our midst? Believers look to the Lord and one another to discern how to continue the journey of faith. This is the communion we share—the communion of saints. We gather in church communities sustained by hope, confident of the Lord's return.

As we wait, we also work to build the kingdom on earth. Jesus teaches us how to master life. He tells us what to do. St. Paul summed up Christ's teaching by telling us that our lives hinge on how we love. "In the end three things remain: faith, hope and love; and the greatest of these is love" (1 Cor 13:13). How does Mary fit into this context? As Christ teaches us to love one another, so Mary teaches us how to faithfully love, accompany and serve Christ.

Sacred Scripture provides a basis for insight into Mary's identity and purpose. We find in every Mary-passage a story of love. Her whole being reaches out to Jesus Christ and to others. She shows motherly love, love of neighbor, and love of God whose servant she desires to be. The rich Mary-images always show her relating to others. We see her with the child in her womb and in her arms. We see the concerned woman searching, the strong woman standing, the silent woman praying. We see the woman listening, asking, pondering, responding, the woman hurrying to serve another. Through it all, she never isolates herself, for as much as she belongs to God, God wills her to share family life with Joseph in the context of their society. True, we see the family fleeing, suffering, searching, but all of this has a redemptive purpose according to God's plan.

For this reason the early Christian communities not only welcomed her, but also gathered around her in prayer and fellowship. The early Church remembered her, told stories about her, and recorded these memories for our benefit. Each glimpse that the sacred text gives us of Mary teaches us how to live by love. We may call her our mother for by her influence and intercession she does what mothers do: she educates us in our faith. Mary is not divine, but in her, divinity and humanity can find a home.

LIST OF ABBREVIATIONS

1. Church documents

BYM	*Behold Your Mother: Mary in the Life of the Priest*
DM	*Dives in Misericordia* (The Mercy of God)
GS	*Gaudium et Spes* (Pastoral Constitution on the Church in the Modern World)
ISF	The Virgin Mary in Intellectual and Spiritual Formation
LG	*Lumen Gentium* (Dogmatic Constitution on the Church)
MC	*Marialis Cultus* (For the Right Ordering and Development of Devotion to the Blessed Virgin Mary)
MD	*Mulieris Dignitatem* (On the Dignity and Vocation of Women)
MM	*Mense Maio* (The Month of Mary)
NA	*Nostra Aetate* (Declaration on the Relation of the Church to Non-Christian Religions)
RC	*Redemptoris Custos* (Guardian of the Redeemer)
RM	*Redemptoris Mater* (Mother of the Redeemer)
SC	*Sacrosanctam Concilium* (Constitution on the Sacred Liturgy)
SM	*Signum Magnam* (The Great Sign)

TM	*Tertio Millennio Adveniente* (On Preparation for the Jubilee of the Year 2000)
VS	*Veritatis Splendor* (The Splendor of Truth)

2. Other sources

AAS	*Acta Apostolicae Sedis* (Official acts of the Holy See)
CCL	*Corpus Christianorum Latina* (Writings of Church Fathers in Latin)
CSCO	*Corpus Scriptorum Christianorum Orientalium* (Writings of Eastern Church Fathers)
CSEL	*Corpus Scriptorum Ecclesiasticorum Latinorum* (Collection of writings of Latin Fathers of the Church)
Denz.	H. Denzinger, *Enchiridion Symbolorum* (Collection of Church documents)
DS	*Denzinger-Schönmetzer* (New edition of Denzinger)
PG	*Patrologia Graeca* (Collection of writings of Greek Fathers of the Church)
PL	*Patrologia Latina* (Collection of writings of Latin Fathers of the Church)
SCh	*Sources chrétiennes* (Another collection of writings of the Church Fathers)

DEFINING THE DOGMA OF THE IMMACULATE CONCEPTION

Ineffabilis Deus

Apostolic Constitution
of Pope Pius IX
December 8, 1854

INTRODUCTION[1]

In reading this document on Mary's Immaculate Conception we need to recall that because it was written in 1854, its language could ensnare or distract us from the document's essential doctrine. The flowery writing, filled with superlatives praising Mary, indicates the *language* style of the mid-1800s. But compared to other literature of this age, the document's style is actually conservative.

Historical Perspectives

The teaching on the Immaculate Conception is backed by centuries of belief, liturgical practice, and veneration of the pure and sinless Virgin, although theologians had long debated the question.[2] Around 1060, an English monk named Eadmer wrote a treatise entitled *On the Conception of the Blessed Mary* defending the teaching. But St. Bernard opposed the doctrine. He also opposed the establishment of a liturgical feast celebrating Mary's conception that had come to Europe from the East. Medieval theologians and saints such as Bonaventure, Albert the Great and Thomas Aquinas also countered the doctrine. These theologians "believed that her sanctification took place as soon as possible after animation (conception), but were unable to see how she could have been redeemed by Christ unless Mary actually incurred original sin, at

---

1. The Latin text can be found in: *Pii IX Pontificis Maximi Acta* (Rome: Vatican Press, I, 1: 597–619). Pius XII repeated the text in *Fulgens Corona* (September 8, 1953): *AAS* 45 (1953), 577–592. Referenced in *LG* 59.

2. For an overview of the arguments pertaining to the development of the dogma, see: René Laurentin, *A Short Treatise on the Virgin Mary* (Washington, NJ: AMI Press, 1991); International Theological Commission, "On the Interpretation of Dogmas," *Origins* 20 (May 17, 1990): 1, 3–14.

least for an instant."[3] The Franciscan theologian John Duns Scotus proposed a solution by introducing the idea of a preservative redemption. That is, Mary was fully redeemed by Christ beforehand, preserved from original sin in view of his merits. This insight paved the way for the full acceptance of the teaching, although that would still take centuries.

On December 8, 1661, Pope Alexander VII issued the bull *Sollicitudo* which approved the Immaculate Conception as a pious belief. In 1708, the liturgical feast was extended to the universal Church. Pius IX borrowed from the language of Alexander VII's bull, but went beyond it to define the dogma:

> We declare, pronounce and define that the doctrine which holds that the most Blessed Virgin Mary, in the first instant of her conception, by a singular grace and privilege granted by Almighty God, in view of the merits of Jesus Christ, the Savior of the human race, was preserved free from all stain of original sin, is a doctrine revealed by God and therefore to be believed firmly and constantly by all the faithful.

The Teaching

The Immaculate Conception is often confused with the virgin birth. The dogma of the Immaculate Conception teaches that *Mary* was free of sin. From the first instant of her existence God's grace filled her. This favor of God's divine life dwelling within her left no absence of his divine indwelling and hence no "place" for a lack of holiness. Mary was preserved from *original sin*. This is not to be confused with the virgin birth, when Mary virginally conceived and gave birth to Jesus Christ, the God-man, who was never subject to sin and its consequences.

Ineffabilis Deus begins by pointing out that God in his inexpressible mystery can freely grant privileges as he desires. He included Mary of Nazareth in his plan of salvation. The God who chose her to be the mother of his Son also prepared her for this privilege. He preredeemed her by the merits of the redemption he intended for the human race. In his favor he created her already filled with grace. Her role as Mother of God *(Theotókos)* points out her "wonderful sanctity and preeminent dignity."

---

3. Frederick M. Jelly, O.P., *Madonna: Mary in the Catholic Tradition* (Huntington, IN: Our Sunday Visitor, 1986), 112.

In the document the pope addresses some aspects of the theological debate concerning the teaching. To be sinless is to be holy. From the first instant of her existence, Mary is the holy one, worthy to become the dwelling place of the Savior. The Scriptural basis for this is found in the annunciation message, which addresses Mary with a greeting found nowhere else in the sacred texts. She is "highly favored, full of grace." Because of her holiness she was never under the power of the evil one.

Readers well tuned to Scripture will note as aspect in *Ineffabilis Deus* that may need clarification. The document was written before the contemporary Scripture studies on Genesis 3:15 that have pointed out a long-standing mistranslation. In this sacred text, God is speaking to the serpent who had tempted the first woman to disobey God's command. The text reads: "I will put enmity between you and the woman, and between your offspring and hers; he will strike your head, and you will strike his heel." In the Vulgate, St. Jerome or a later manuscript writer had mistranslated this *ipsa* as "*she* will strike your head." This translation influenced exegetes to see Mary as the one obtaining the victory over the serpent. But the woman will not crush the serpent; the child in her arms will do so. This error in no way alters or diminishes the doctrine of the Immaculate Conception. Such a centuries-old error does not diminish faith that Mary has conquered evil, if the full teaching is kept in mind: Mary receives her dignity and her full strength from the redemption of her divine Son. According to the plan of the eternal Father, she is inseparable from him and cannot be imagined apart from him.

Today

Pius IX calls Mary the "crown and joy of all the saints…the safest refuge and the most trustworthy helper of all who are in danger." In the mid-19th century, the Church saw its lands confiscated, many of its institutions assaulted, and its dignity questioned. Industrialization crowded people together in cities, often in slums. Poverty and materialism eroded the dignity of families and individuals. The Catholic Church hoped that Mary could stand out as an eminent example of a fully redeemed person. Because Mary was such a sign, the Church was convinced that Mary could "remove spiritual blindness from all who are in error, so that they may return to the path of truth and justice, and that there may be one flock and one shepherd."

The *Catechism of the Catholic Church* treats the Immaculate Conception in paragraphs 490–493. The teaching relies on the explanation given at Vatican II and cannot be stated more clearly or eloquently:

492 The "splendor of an entirely unique holiness" by which Mary is "enriched from the first instant of her conception" comes wholly from Christ: she is "redeemed, in a more exalted fashion, by reason of the merits of her Son" (*LG* 53, 56). The Father blessed Mary more than any other created person "in Christ with every spiritual blessing in the heavenly places" and chose her "in Christ before the foundation of the world, to be holy and blameless before him in love" (cf. Eph 1:3–4).

493 The Fathers of the Eastern tradition call the Mother of God "the All-Holy" *(Panagia)* and celebrate her as "free from any stain of sin, as though fashioned by the Holy Spirit and formed as a new creature" (*LG* 56). By the grace of God Mary remained free of every personal sin her whole life long.

The splendor of holiness is offered to each Christian. As *Lumen Gentium* teaches, "All the faithful of Christ, of whatever rank or status, are called to the fullness of Christian life and to the perfection of charity" (*LG* 40). All may share intimate union with Christ. To look to Mary is to see this intimacy in its full human beauty, harmony and radiance.

TOPICAL OUTLINE

1. Introduction: Mary in God's plan of salvation

2. Theological reasons in favor of the definition

    A. Mary's divine maternity

    B. Liturgical celebrations of the feast of Mary's conception

    C. The ordinary teaching of the Church

        1. Veneration of Mary Immaculate

        2. Teachings of previous popes

    D. Testimonies of the Catholic world

        1. The Council of Trent

        2. Testimonies from tradition

        3. The Fathers' commentaries on Scripture

        4. The Eve-Mary parallel

        5. Other teachings about Mary's holiness

3. The definition of the Immaculate Conception

    A. Preparation for the definition

    B. The consultation of the bishops

    C. The definition stated

    D. Fruits of the dogma

DEFINING THE DOGMA
OF THE IMMACULATE CONCEPTION

Ineffabilis Deus

Promulgated by His Holiness Pope Pius IX
On December 8, 1854

Introduction

God Ineffable—whose ways are mercy and truth, whose will is omnipotence itself, and whose wisdom "reaches from end to end mightily, and orders all things sweetly"—having foreseen from all eternity the lamentable wretchedness of the entire human race which would result from the sin of Adam, decreed, by a plan hidden from the centuries, to complete the first work of his goodness by a mystery yet more wondrously sublime through the Incarnation of the Word. This he decreed in order that man who, contrary to the plan of divine mercy had been led into sin by the cunning malice of Satan, should not perish; and in order that what had been lost in the first Adam would be gloriously restored in the second Adam. From the very beginning, and before time began, the eternal Father chose and prepared for his only-begotten Son a Mother in whom the Son of God would become incarnate and from whom, in the blessed fullness of time, he would be born into this world. Above all creatures did God so love her that truly in her was the Father well pleased with singular delight. Therefore, far above all the angels and all the saints, so wondrously did God endow her with the abundance of all heavenly gifts poured from the treasury of his divinity that this mother, ever absolutely free of all stain of sin, all fair and perfect, would possess that fullness of holy innocence and sanctity than which, under God, one cannot even imagine anything greater, and which, outside of God, no mind can succeed in comprehending fully.

Supreme Reason for the Privilege: The Divine Maternity

And indeed it was wholly fitting that so wonderful a mother should be ever resplendent with the glory of most sublime holiness, and so completely free from all taint of original sin that she would triumph utterly over the ancient serpent. To her did the Father will to give his only-begotten Son—the Son whom, equal to the Father and begotten by him, the Father loves from his heart—and to give this Son in such a way that he would be the one and the same common Son of God the Father and of the Blessed Virgin Mary. It was she whom the Son himself chose to make his Mother, and it was from her that the Holy Spirit willed and brought it about that he should be conceived and born from whom he himself proceeds.[1]

Liturgical Argument

The Catholic Church, directed by the Holy Spirit of God, is the pillar and base of truth, and has ever held as divinely revealed and as contained in the deposit of heavenly revelation this doctrine concerning the original innocence of the august Virgin—a doctrine which is so perfectly in harmony with her wonderful sanctity and preeminent dignity as Mother of God—and thus has never ceased to explain, to teach and to foster this doctrine age after age, in many ways and by solemn acts. For this very doctrine, flourishing and wondrously propagated in the Catholic world through the efforts and zeal of the bishops, was made very clear by the Church when she did not hesitate to present for the public devotion and veneration of the faithful the Feast of the Conception of the Blessed Virgin.[2] By this most significant fact, the Church made it clear indeed that the conception of Mary is to be venerated as something extraordinary, wonderful, eminently holy, and different from the conception of all other human beings—for the Church celebrates only the feast days of the saints.

---

1. *Et quidem decebat omnino, ut perfectissimae sanctitatis splendoribus semper ornata fulgeret, ac vel ab ipsa originalis culpae labe plane immunis amplissimum de antiquo serpente triumphum referret tam venerabilis mater, cui Deus Pater unicum Filium suum, quem de corde suo aequalem sibi genitum tamquam seipsum diligit, ita dare disposuit, ut naturaliter esset unus idemque communis Dei Patris et Virginis Filius, et quam ipse Filius, Filius substantialiter facere sibi matrem elegit, et de qua Spiritus Sanctus voluit et operatus est, ut conciperetur et nasceretur ille, de quo ipse procedit.*

2. Cf. Gregory XVI, Letter *Summa Quidem Animi*, April 23, 1845.

And hence the very words with which the Sacred Scriptures speak of Uncreated Wisdom and set forth his eternal origin, the Church, both in its ecclesiastical offices and in its liturgy, has been wont to apply likewise to the origin of the Blessed Virgin, inasmuch as God, by one and the same decree, had established the origin of Mary and the Incarnation of Divine Wisdom.

Ordinary Teaching of the Roman Church

These truths, so generally accepted and put into practice by the faithful, indicate how zealously the Roman Church, mother and teacher of all Churches, has continued to teach this doctrine of the Immaculate Conception of the Virgin. Yet the more important actions of the Church deserve to be mentioned in detail. For such dignity and authority belong to the Church that she alone is the center of truth and of Catholic unity. It is the Church in which alone religion has been inviolably preserved and from which all other Churches must receive the tradition of the Faith.[3]

The same Roman Church, therefore, desired nothing more than by the most persuasive means to state, to protect, to promote and to defend the doctrine of the Immaculate Conception. This fact is most clearly shown to the whole world by numerous and significant acts of the Roman Pontiffs, our predecessors. To them, in the person of the Prince of the Apostles, were divinely entrusted by Christ our Lord, the charge and supreme care and the power of feeding the lambs and sheep, in particular, of confirming their brethren, and of ruling and governing the universal Church.

Veneration of the Immaculate

Our predecessors, indeed, by virtue of their apostolic authority, gloried in instituting the Feast of the Conception in the Roman Church. They did so to enhance its importance and dignity by a suitable Office and Mass, whereby the prerogative of the Virgin, her exception from the hereditary taint, was most distinctly affirmed. As to the homage already instituted, they spared no effort to promote and to extend it either by the granting of indulgences, or by allowing cities, provinces and kingdoms

---

3. Cf. St. Irenaeus, *Adv. Haereses,* III, 3, 2.

to choose as their patroness God's own Mother, under the title of "The Immaculate Conception." Again, our predecessors approved confraternities, congregations and religious communities founded in honor of the Immaculate Conception, monasteries, hospitals, altars, or churches; they praised persons who vowed to uphold with all their ability the doctrine of the Immaculate Conception of the Mother of God. Besides, it afforded the greatest joy to our predecessors to ordain that the Feast of the Conception should be celebrated in every church with the very same honor as the Feast of the Nativity, that it should be celebrated with an octave by the whole Church, that it should be reverently and generally observed as a holy day of obligation, and that a pontifical *Capella* should be held in our Liberian pontifical basilica on the day dedicated to the conception of the Virgin. Finally, in their desire to impress this doctrine of the Immaculate Conception of the Mother of God upon the hearts of the faithful, and to intensify the people's piety and enthusiasm for the homage and the veneration of the Virgin conceived without the stain of original sin, they delighted to grant, with the greatest pleasure, permission to proclaim the Immaculate Conception of the Virgin in the Litany of Loreto, and in the preface of the Mass, so that the rule of prayer might thus serve to illustrate the rule of belief. Therefore, we ourselves, following the procedure of our predecessors, have not only approved and accepted what had already been established, but bearing in mind, moreover, the decree of Sixtus IV,[4] have confirmed by our authority a proper Office in honor of the Immaculate Conception, and have with exceeding joy extended its use to the universal Church.[5]

The Roman Doctrine

Now inasmuch as whatever pertains to sacred worship is intimately connected with its object and cannot have either consistency or durability if this object is vague or uncertain, our predecessors, the Roman Pontiffs, therefore, while directing all their efforts toward an increase of devotion to the conception, made it their aim not only to emphasize the

---

4. Apostolic Constitution *Cum Praeexcelsa,* February 28, 1476; Denz., 734.
5. Decree of the Sacred Congregation of Rites, September 30, 1847.

object with the utmost zeal, but also to enunciate the exact doctrine.[6] Definitely and clearly they taught that the feast was held in honor of the conception of the Virgin. They denounced as false and absolutely foreign to the mind of the Church the opinion of those who held and affirmed that it was not the conception of the Virgin but her sanctification that was honored by the Church. They never thought that greater leniency should be extended toward those who, attempting to disprove the doctrine of the Immaculate Conception of the Virgin, devised a distinction between the first and second instance of conception and inferred that the conception which the Church celebrates was not that of the first instance of conception but the second. In fact, they held it was their duty not only to uphold and defend with all their power the Feast of the Conception of the Blessed Virgin, but also to assert that the true object of this veneration was her conception considered in its first instant. Hence the words of one of our predecessors, Alexander VII, who authoritatively and decisively declared the mind of the Church: "Concerning the most Blessed Virgin Mary, Mother of God, ancient indeed is that devotion of the faithful based on the belief that her soul, in the first instant of its creation and in the first instant of the soul's infusion into the body, was, by a special grace and privilege of God, in view of the merits of Jesus Christ, her Son and the Redeemer of the human race, preserved free from all stain of original sin. And in this sense have the faithful ever solemnized and celebrated the Feast of the Conception."[7]

Moreover, our predecessors considered it their special solemn duty with all diligence, zeal and effort to preserve intact the doctrine of the Immaculate Conception of the Mother of God. For not only have they in no way ever allowed this doctrine to be censured or changed, but they have gone much further, and by clear statements repeatedly asserted that the doctrine by which we profess the Immaculate Conception of the Virgin is on its own merits entirely in harmony with the ecclesiastical ven-

---

6. This has been the constant care of the popes, as is shown by the condemnation of one of the propositions of Anthony de Rosmini-Serbati (cf. Denz., 1891–1930). This is how the 34th proposition runs (Denz., 1924): *"Ad praeservandam B. V. Mariam a labe originis, satis erat, ut incorruptum maneret minimum semen in homine, neglectum forte ab ipso demone, e quo incorrupto semine de generatione in generationem transfuso, suo tempore oriretur Virgo Maria."* Decree of the Holy Office, December 14, 1887 (*AAS* 20, 393), Denz., 1924.

7. Apostolic Constitution *Sollicitudo Omnium Ecclesiarum,* December 8, 1661.

eration, that it is ancient and widespread, and of the same nature as that which the Roman Church has undertaken to promote and to protect, and that it is entirely worthy to be used in the sacred liturgy and solemn prayers. Not content with this, they most strictly prohibited any opinion contrary to this doctrine to be defended in public or private in order that the doctrine of the Immaculate Conception of the Virgin might remain inviolate. By repeated blows they wished to put an end to such an opinion. And lest these oft-repeated and clearest statements seem useless, they added a sanction to them.

Papal Sanctions

All these things our illustrious predecessor, Alexander VII, summed up in these words: "We have in mind the fact that the Holy Roman Church solemnly celebrated the Feast of the Conception of the undefiled and ever Virgin Mary, and has long ago appointed for this a special and proper Office according to the pious, devout and laudable instruction which was given by our predecessor, Sixtus IV. Likewise, we were desirous, after the example of our predecessors, to favor this praiseworthy piety, devotion, feast and veneration—a veneration which is in keeping with the piety unchanged in the Roman Church from the day it was instituted. We also desired to protect this piety and devotion of venerating and extolling the most Blessed Virgin preserved from original sin by the grace of the Holy Spirit. Moreover, we were anxious to preserve the unity of the Spirit in the bond of peace in the flock of Christ by putting down arguments and controversies and by removing scandals. So at the instance and request of the bishops mentioned above, with the chapters of the churches, and of King Philip and his kingdoms, we renew the constitutions and decrees issued by the Roman Pontiffs, our predecessors, especially Sixtus IV,[8] Paul V[9] and Gregory XV,[10] in favor of the doctrine asserting that the soul of the Blessed Virgin, in its creation and infusion into the body, was endowed with the grace of the Holy Spirit and preserved from original sin; and also in favor of the feast and veneration

---

8. Apostolic Constitution *Cum Praeexcelsa,* February 28, 1476; *Grave Nemis,* September 4, 1483; Denz., 734, 735.

9. Apostolic Constitution *Sanctissimus,* September 12, 1617.

10. Apostolic Constitution *Sanctissimus,* June 4, 1622.

of the conception of the Virgin Mother of God, which, as is manifest, was instituted in keeping with that pious belief. So we command this feast to be observed under the censures and penalties contained in the same constitutions.

"And therefore, against all and everyone of those who shall continue to construe the said constitutions and decrees in a manner apt to frustrate the favor which is thereby given to the said doctrine, and to the feast and relative veneration, or who shall dare to call into question the said sentence, feast and worship, or in any way whatever, directly or indirectly, shall declare themselves opposed to it under any pretext whatsoever, were it but only to the extent of examining the possibilities of effecting the definition, or who shall comment upon and interpret the Sacred Scripture, or the Fathers or Doctors in connection therewith, or finally, for any reason, or on any occasion, shall dare, either in writing or verbally, to speak, preach, treat, dispute or determine upon, or assert whatsoever against the foregoing matters, or who shall adduce any arguments against them, while leaving them unresolved, or who shall disagree therewith in any other conceivable manner, we hereby declare that in addition to the penalties and censures contained in the constitutions issued by Sixtus IV, to which we want them to be subjected and to which we subject them by the present constitution, we hereby decree that they be deprived of the authority of preaching, reading in public, that is to say teaching and interpreting, and that they be also deprived *ipso facto* of the power of voting, either actively or passively, in all elections, without the need for any further declaration, and that also, *ipso facto,* without any further declaration, they shall incur the penalty of perpetual disability from preaching, reading in public, teaching and interpreting, and that it shall not be possible to absolve them from such penalty, or remove it, save through ourselves, or the Roman Pontiffs who shall succeed us.

"We also require that the same shall remain subject to any other penalties which by us, of our own free will—or by the Roman Pontiffs, our successors (according as they may decree)—shall be deemed advisable to establish, and by the present constitution we declare them subject thereto, and hereby renew the above decrees and constitutions of Paul V and Gregory XV.

"Moreover, as regards those books in which the said sentence, feast and relative veneration are called into question or are contradicted in any way whatsoever, according to what has already been stated, either in writing or verbally, in discourses, sermons, lectures, treatises and de-bates—that may have been printed after the above-praised Decree of Paul V, or may be printed hereafter, we hereby prohibit them, subject to the penalties and censures established by the Index of prohibited books, and *ipso facto,* without any further declaration, we desire and command that they be held as expressly prohibited."[11]

Testimonies of the Catholic World

All are aware with how much diligence this doctrine of the Immacu-late Conception of the Mother of God has been handed down, proposed and defended by the most outstanding religious orders, by the more cel-ebrated theological academies, and by very eminent doctors in the sci-ences of theology. All know, likewise, how eager the bishops have been to profess openly and publicly, even in ecclesiastical assemblies, that Mary, the most holy Mother of God, by virtue of the foreseen merits of Christ, our Lord and Redeemer, was never subject to original sin, but was completely preserved from the original taint, and hence she was re-deemed in a manner more sublime.

The Council of Trent

Besides, we must note a fact of the greatest importance indeed. Even the Council of Trent itself, when it promulgated the dogmatic decree concerning original sin, following the testimonies of the Sacred Scrip-tures, of the Holy Fathers and of the renowned Council, decreed and defined that all men are born infected by original sin; nevertheless, it solemnly declared that it had no intention of including the blessed and immaculate Virgin Mary, the Mother of God, in this decree and in the general extension of its definition. Indeed, considering the times and cir-cumstances, the Fathers of Trent sufficiently intimated by this declara-tion that the Blessed Virgin Mary was free from the original stain; and thus they clearly signified that nothing could be reasonably cited from the Sacred Scriptures, from Tradition, or from the authority of the Fa-

---

11. Alexander VIII, Apostolic Constitution *Sollicitudo Omnium Ecclesiarum,* Decem-ber 8, 1661.

thers, which would in any way be opposed to so great a prerogative of the Blessed Virgin.[12]

Testimonies of Tradition

And indeed, illustrious documents of venerable antiquity, of both the Eastern and the Western Church, very forcibly testify that this doctrine of the Immaculate Conception of the most Blessed Virgin, which was daily more and more splendidly explained, stated and confirmed by the highest authority, teaching, zeal, knowledge and wisdom of the Church, and which was disseminated among all peoples and nations of the Catholic world in a marvelous manner—this doctrine always existed in the Church as a doctrine that has been received from our ancestors, and that has been stamped with the character of revealed doctrine. For the Church of Christ, watchful guardian that she is, and defender of the dogmas deposited with her, never changes anything, never diminishes anything, never adds anything to them, but with all diligence she treats the ancient documents faithfully and wisely. If they really are of ancient origin and if the faith of the Fathers has transmitted them, she strives to investigate and explain them in such a way that the ancient dogmas of heavenly doctrine will be made evident and clear, but will retain their full, integral and proper nature, and will grow only within their own genus— that is, within the same dogma, in the same sense and the same meaning.

Interpreters of Sacred Scripture

The Fathers and writers of the Church, well versed in the heavenly Scriptures, had nothing more at heart than to vie with one another in preaching and teaching in many wonderful ways the Virgin's supreme sanctity, dignity and immunity from all stain of sin, and her renowned victory over the most foul enemy of the human race. This they did in the books they wrote to explain the Scriptures, to vindicate the dogmas, and to instruct the faithful. These ecclesiastical writers, in quoting the words by which at the beginning of the world God announced his merciful

---

12. Sess. V, Can. 6; Denz., 792. *Declarat tamen haec ipsa sancta Synodus, non esse suae intentionis, comprehendere in hoc decreto, ubi de peccato originali agitur, beatam et immaculatam Virginem Mariam Dei genitricem, sed observandas esse constitutiones felicis recordationis Sixti Papae IV, sub poenis in eis constitutionibus contentis, quas innovat.*

remedies prepared for the regeneration of mankind—words by which he crushed the audacity of the deceitful serpent and wondrously raised up the hope of our race, saying, "I will put enmities between you and the woman, between your seed and her seed" (Gn 3:15)—taught that by this divine prophecy the merciful Redeemer of mankind, Jesus Christ, the only begotten Son of God, was clearly foretold: That his most Blessed Mother, the Virgin Mary, was prophetically indicated, and, at the same time, the very enmity of both against the evil one was significantly expressed. Hence, just as Christ, the Mediator between God and man, assumed human nature, blotted the handwriting of the decree that stood against us, and fastened it triumphantly to the cross, so the most holy Virgin, united with him by a most intimate and indissoluble bond, was, with him and through him, eternally at enmity with the evil serpent, and most completely triumphed over him, and thus crushed his head with her immaculate foot.[13]

This sublime and singular privilege of the Blessed Virgin, together with her most excellent innocence, purity, holiness and freedom from every stain of sin, as well as the unspeakable abundance and greatness of all heavenly graces, virtues and privileges—these the Fathers beheld in that ark of Noah, which was built by divine command and escaped entirely safe and sound from the common shipwreck of the whole world (cf. Gn 6:9); in the ladder which Jacob saw reaching from the earth to heaven, by whose rungs the angels of God ascended and descended, and on whose top the Lord himself leaned (cf. Gn 28:12); in that bush which Moses saw in the holy place burning on all sides, which was not consumed or injured in any way but grew green and blossomed beautifully (cf. Ex 3:2); in that impregnable tower before the enemy, from which hung a thousand bucklers and all the armor of the strong (cf. Sg 4:4); in that garden enclosed on all sides, which cannot be violated or corrupted by any deceitful plots (cf. Sg 4:12); as in that resplendent city of God, which has its foundations on the holy mountains (cf. Ps 87:1); in that most august temple of God, which, radiant with divine splendors, is full of the glory of God (cf. Is 6:1–4); and in very many other biblical types

---

13. *Quo circa sicut Christus Dei hominumque mediator, humana assumpta natura, delens quod adversus nos erat chirographum decretia, illud cruci triumphator affixit; sic Sanctissima Virgo, arctissimo et indissolubili vinculo cum eo conjuncta, una cum illo et per illum, sempiternas contra venenosum serpentem inimicitias exercens, ac de ipso plenissime triumphans, illus caput immaculato pede contrivit.*

of this kind. In such allusions the Fathers taught that the exalted dignity of the Mother of God, her spotless innocence and her sanctity unstained by any fault, had been prophesied in a wonderful manner.

In like manner did they use the words of the prophets to describe this wondrous abundance of divine gifts and the original innocence of the Virgin of whom Jesus was born. They celebrated the august Virgin as the spotless dove, as the holy Jerusalem, as the exalted throne of God, as the ark and house of holiness which Eternal Wisdom built, and as that Queen who, abounding in delights and leaning on her Beloved, came forth from the mouth of the Most High, entirely perfect, beautiful, most dear to God and never stained with the least blemish.

The Annunciation

When the Fathers and writers of the Church meditated on the fact that the most Blessed Virgin was, in the name and by order of God himself, proclaimed full of grace (cf. Lk 1:28) by the Angel Gabriel when he announced her most sublime dignity of Mother of God, they thought that this singular and solemn salutation, never heard before, showed that the Mother of God is the seat of all divine graces and is adorned with all gifts of the Holy Spirit. To them Mary is an almost infinite treasury, an inexhaustible abyss of these gifts, to such an extent that she was never subject to the curse and was, together with her Son, the only partaker of perpetual benediction. Hence she was worthy to hear Elizabeth, inspired by the Holy Spirit, exclaim: "Blessed are you among women, and blessed is the fruit of your womb" (Lk 1:42).

Mary Compared with Eve

Hence, it is the clear and unanimous opinion of the Fathers that the most glorious Virgin, for whom "he who is mighty has done great things," was resplendent with such an abundance of heavenly gifts, with such a fullness of grace and with such innocence, that she is an unspeakable miracle of God—indeed, the crown of all miracles and truly the Mother of God; that she approaches as near to God himself as is possible for a created being; and that she is above all men and angels in glory. Hence, to demonstrate the original innocence and sanctity of the Mother of God, not only did they frequently compare her to Eve while yet a virgin, while yet innocent, while yet incorrupt, while not yet deceived by the deadly snares of the most treacherous serpent, but they have also exalted her above Eve with a wonderful variety of expressions. Eve listened to the serpent with lamentable consequences; she fell from original innocence and became his slave. The most Blessed Virgin, on the contrary, ever increased her original gift, and not only never lent an ear to the serpent, but by divinely given power she utterly destroyed the force and dominion of the evil one.

Biblical Figures

Accordingly, the Fathers have never ceased to call the Mother of God the lily among thorns, the land entirely intact, the Virgin undefiled, immaculate, ever blessed, and free from all contagion of sin, she from whom was formed the new Adam, the flawless, brightest and most beautiful paradise of innocence, immortality and delights planted by God himself and protected against all the snares of the poisonous serpent, the incorruptible wood that the worm of sin had never corrupted, the fountain ever clear and sealed with the power of the Holy Spirit, the most holy temple, the treasure of immortality, the one and only daughter of life—not of death—the plant not of anger but of grace, through the singular providence of God growing ever green contrary to the common law, coming as it does from a corrupted and tainted root.

Explicit Affirmation...

As if these splendid eulogies and tributes were not sufficient, the Fathers proclaimed with particular and definite statements that when one treats of sin, the holy Virgin Mary is not even to be mentioned; for to her more grace was given than was necessary to conquer sin completely.[14] They also declared that the most glorious Virgin was Reparatrix of the first parents, the giver of life to posterity; that she was chosen before the ages, prepared for himself by the Most High, foretold by God when he said to the serpent, "I will put enmities between you and the woman" (Gn 3:15)—unmistakable evidence that she has crushed the poisonous head of the serpent. And hence they affirmed that the Blessed Virgin was, through grace, entirely free from every stain of sin, and from all corruption of body, soul and mind; that she was always united with God and joined to

---

14. Cf. St. Augustine, *De Natura et Gratia*, 36.

him by an eternal covenant; that she was never in darkness but always in light; and that, therefore, she was entirely a fit habitation for Christ, not because of the state of her body, but because of her original grace.

...Of a Supereminent Sanctity

To these praises they have added very noble words. Speaking of the conception of the Virgin, they testified that nature yielded to grace and, unable to go on, stood trembling. The Virgin Mother of God would not be conceived by Anna before grace would bear its fruits; it was proper that she be conceived as the first-born, by whom "the first-born of every creature" would be conceived. They testified, too, that the flesh of the Virgin, although derived from Adam, did not contract the stains of Adam, and that on this account the most Blessed Virgin was the tabernacle created by God himself and formed by the Holy Spirit, truly a work in royal purple, adorned and woven with gold, which that new Beseleel (cf. Ex 31:2) made. They affirmed that the same Virgin is, and is deservedly, the first and especial work of God, escaping the fiery arrows of the evil one; that she is beautiful by nature and entirely free from all stain; that at her Immaculate Conception she came into the world all radiant like the dawn. For it was certainly not fitting that this vessel of election should be wounded by the common injuries, since she, differing so much from the others, had only nature in common with them, not sin. In fact, it was quite fitting that, as the Only-Begotten has a Father in heaven, whom the seraphim extol as thrice holy, so he should have a Mother on earth who would never be without the splendor of holiness.

This doctrine so filled the minds and souls of our ancestors in the faith that a singular and truly marvelous style of speech came into vogue among them. They have frequently addressed the Mother of God as immaculate, as immaculate in every respect; innocent, and verily most innocent; spotless, and entirely spotless; holy and removed from every stain of sin; all pure, all stainless, the very model of purity and innocence; more beautiful than beauty, more lovely than loveliness; more holy than holiness, singularly holy and most pure in soul and body; the one who surpassed all integrity and virginity; the only one who has become the dwelling place of all the graces of the most Holy Spirit. God alone excepted, Mary is more excellent than all, and by nature fair and beautiful, and more holy than the cherubim and seraphim. To praise her all the tongues of heaven and earth do not suffice.

Everyone is cognizant that this style of speech has passed almost spontaneously into the books of the most holy liturgy and the Offices of the Church, in which they occur so often and abundantly. In them, the Mother of God is invoked and praised as the one spotless and most beautiful dove, as a rose ever blooming, as perfectly pure, ever immaculate, and ever blessed. She is celebrated as innocence never sullied and as the second Eve who brought forth the Emmanuel.

Preparation for the Definition

No wonder, then, that the pastors of the Church and the faithful gloried daily more and more in professing with so much piety, religion and love this doctrine of the Immaculate Conception of the Virgin Mother of God, which, as the Fathers discerned, was recorded in the divine Scriptures, which was handed down in so many of their most important writings, which was expressed and celebrated in so many illustrious monuments of venerable antiquity, which was proposed and confirmed by the official and authoritative teaching of the Church. Hence, nothing was dearer, nothing more pleasing to these pastors than to venerate, invoke and proclaim with most ardent affection the Virgin Mother of God conceived without original stain. Accordingly, from ancient times the bishops of the Church, ecclesiastics, religious orders and even emperors and kings, have earnestly petitioned this Apostolic See to define as a dogma of the Catholic Faith the Immaculate Conception of the most holy Mother of God. These petitions were renewed in these our own times; they were especially brought to the attention of Gregory XVI, our predecessor of happy memory, and to ourselves, not only by bishops, but by the secular clergy and religious orders, by sovereign rulers and by the faithful.

Mindful, indeed, of all these things and considering them most attentively with particular joy in our heart, as soon as we, by the inscrutable design of Providence, had been raised to the sublime Chair of St. Peter—in spite of our unworthiness—and had begun to govern the universal Church, nothing have we had more at heart—a heart which from our tenderest years has overflowed with devoted veneration and love for the most Blessed Virgin—than to show forth her prerogatives in resplendent light.

That we might proceed with great prudence, we established a special congregation of our venerable brethren, the cardinals of the holy Roman

Church, illustrious for their piety, wisdom and knowledge of the Sacred Scriptures. We also selected priests, both secular and regular, well trained in the theological sciences, that they should most carefully consider all matters pertaining to the Immaculate Conception of the Virgin and make known to us their opinion.

The Mind of the Bishops

Although we knew the mind of the bishops from the petitions which we had received from them, namely, that the Immaculate Conception of the Blessed Virgin be finally defined, nevertheless, on February 2, 1849,[15] we sent an encyclical letter from Gaeta to all our venerable brethren, the bishops of the Catholic world, that they should offer prayers to God and then tell us in writing what the piety and devotion of their faithful was in regard to the Immaculate Conception of the Mother of God. We likewise inquired what the bishops themselves thought about defining this doctrine, and what their wishes were in regard to making known with all possible solemnity our supreme judgment.

We were certainly filled with the greatest consolation when the replies of our venerable brethren came to us. For, replying to us with a most enthusiastic joy, exultation and zeal, they not only again confirmed their own singular piety toward the Immaculate Conception of the most Blessed Virgin, and that of the secular and religious clergy and of the faithful, but with one voice they even entreated us to define with our supreme judgment and authority the Immaculate Conception of the Virgin. In the meantime we were indeed filled with no less joy when, after a diligent examination, our venerable brethren, the cardinals of the special congregation and the theologians chosen by us as counselors (whom we mentioned above), asked with the same enthusiasm and fervor for the definition of the Immaculate Conception of the Mother of God.

Consequently, following the examples of our predecessors, and desiring to proceed in the traditional manner, we announced and held a consistory, in which we addressed our brethren, the cardinals of the holy Roman Church. It was the greatest spiritual joy for us when we heard them ask us to promulgate the dogmatic definition of the Immaculate Conception of the Virgin Mother of God.[16]

---

15. Cf. Pius IX, Encyclical Letter *Ubi Primum,* February 2, 1849.
16. Cf. Pius IX, *Allocution to the Consistory,* December 1, 1854.

Therefore, having full trust in the Lord that the opportune time had come for defining the Immaculate Conception of the Blessed Virgin Mary, Mother of God, which Holy Scripture, venerable Tradition, the constant mind of the Church, the desire of Catholic bishops and the faithful, and the memorable acts and constitutions of our predecessors wonderfully illustrate and proclaim, and having most diligently considered all things, as we poured forth to God ceaseless and fervent prayers, we concluded that we should no longer delay in decreeing and defining by our supreme authority the Immaculate Conception of the Blessed Virgin. And thus, we can satisfy the most holy desire of the Catholic world as well as our own devotion toward the most holy Virgin, and at the same time honor more and more the only-begotten Son, Jesus Christ our Lord, through his holy Mother—since whatever honor and praise are bestowed on the Mother redound to the Son.

The Definition

Wherefore, in humility and fasting, we unceasingly offered our private prayers as well as the public prayers of the Church to God the Father through his Son, that he would deign to direct and strengthen our mind by the power of the Holy Spirit. In like manner did we implore the help of the entire heavenly host as we ardently invoked the Paraclete. Accordingly, by the inspiration of the Holy Spirit, for the honor of the holy and undivided Trinity, for the glory and adornment of the Virgin Mother of God, for the exaltation of the Catholic Faith, and for the furtherance of the Catholic religion, by the authority of Jesus Christ our Lord, of the Blessed Apostles Peter and Paul, and by our own: "We declare, pronounce and define that the doctrine which holds that the most Blessed Virgin Mary, in the first instant of her conception, by a singular grace and privilege granted by Almighty God, in view of the merits of Jesus Christ, the Savior of the human race, was preserved free from all stain of original sin, is a doctrine revealed by God and therefore to be believed firmly and constantly by all the faithful."[17]

---

17. *Declaramus, pronuntiamus et definimus doctrinam quae tenet beatissimam Virginem Mariam in primo instanti suae conceptionis fuisse singulari Omnipotentis Dei gratia et privilegio, intuitu meritorum Christi Jesu Salvatoris humani generis, ab omni originalis culpae labe praeservatam immunem, esse a Deo revelatam, atque idcirco ab omnibus fidelibus firmiter constanterque credendam.* Cf. Denz., 1641.

Hence, if anyone shall dare—which God forbid!—to think otherwise than as has been defined by us, let him know and understand that he is condemned by his own judgment, that he has suffered shipwreck in the faith, that he has separated from the unity of the Church, and that, furthermore, by his own action he incurs the penalties established by law if he should dare to express in words or writing or by any other outward means the errors he think in his heart.

Hoped-For Results

Our soul overflows with joy and our tongue with exultation. We give, and we shall continue to give, the humblest and deepest thanks to Jesus Christ, our Lord, because through his singular grace he has granted to us, unworthy though we be, to decree and offer this honor and glory and praise to his most holy Mother. All our hope do we repose in the most Blessed Virgin—in the all fair and immaculate one who has crushed the poisonous head of the most cruel serpent and brought salvation to the world: in she who is the glory of the prophets and apostles, the honor of the martyrs, the crown and joy of all the saints, in she who is the safest refuge and the most trustworthy helper of all who are in danger, in she who, with her only-begotten Son, is the most powerful Mediatrix and Conciliatrix in the whole world, in she who is the most excellent glory, ornament and impregnable stronghold of the holy Church, in she who has destroyed all heresies and snatched the faithful people and nations from all kinds of direst calamities, in her do we hope, who has delivered us from so many threatening dangers. We have, therefore, a very certain hope and complete confidence that the most Blessed Virgin will ensure by her most powerful patronage that all difficulties be removed and all errors dissipated, so that our Holy Mother the Catholic Church may flourish daily more and more throughout all the nations and countries, and may reign "from sea to sea and from the river to the ends of the earth," and may enjoy genuine peace, tranquility and liberty. We are firm in our confidence that she will obtain pardon for the sinner, health for the sick, strength of heart for the weak, consolation for the afflicted, help for those in danger, that she will remove spiritual blindness from all who are in error, so that they may return to the path of truth and justice, and that there may be one flock and one shepherd.

Let all the children of the Catholic Church, who are so very dear to us, hear these words of ours. With a still more ardent zeal for piety, religion and love, let them continue to venerate, invoke and pray to the most Blessed Virgin Mary, Mother of God, conceived without original sin. Let them fly with utter confidence to this most sweet Mother of mercy and grace in all dangers, difficulties, needs, doubts and fears. Under her guidance, under her patronage, under her kindness and protection, nothing is to be feared; nothing is hopeless. Because, while bearing toward us a truly motherly affection and having in her care the work of our salvation, she is solicitous about the whole human race. And since she has been appointed by God to be the Queen of heaven and earth, and is exalted above all the choirs of angels and saints, and even stands at the right hand of her only-begotten Son, Jesus Christ our Lord, she presents our petitions in a most efficacious manner. What she asks, she obtains. Her pleas can never be unheard.

Given at St. Peter's in Rome, the eighth day of December, 1854, in the eighth year of our pontificate.

Pius IX

THE ASSUMPTION OF THE BLESSED VIRGIN MARY

Munificentissimus Deus

Apostolic Constitution of Pope Pius XII
November 1, 1950

INTRODUCTION[1]

Nearly a century after the definitive teaching on the Immaculate Conception was promulgated, Mary's Assumption was confirmed as a divinely revealed dogma.

Historical Perspectives

In *Munificentissimus Deus* Pope Pius XII briefly traces the historical process that led to confirming belief in the Assumption. He mentions the churches dedicated to it, the works of art depicting it and ways the faithful have honored Mary under this title. The liturgy and liturgical books testify to its ancient character. In the East, the feast developed in the fifth and sixth centuries under the title of Mary's Dormition, or falling asleep, to indicate her passing from this world. In the West, it was celebrated from the time of the Carolingian era.

Various Fathers of the Church testified to it, especially St. John Damascene and St. Germanus in the East. Pius XII states that although St. Thomas did not deal directly with the Assumption, he upheld this doctrine, as did St. Bonaventure and other theologians.

Concerning the world situation in which *Munificentissimus Deus* was promulgated, Europe and the world in 1950 were recovering from the devastation of two global wars. The diverse ideologies and political systems of the East and West built barriers of fear and hostility. Communists blamed the Christian churches for the world's problems, especially mass poverty. To achieve their goal of bread for every person, they believed it necessary to eradicate the churches and destroy the traditions of the nations, to plow under anything that had to do with *the old ways,* thus hoping to build a new and perfect society *in this world.* As a result,

---

1. Referenced in *LG* 59.

the Church in the East experienced severe persecution. At the same time, economic growth in the West after World War II slowly brought on its own form of materialism and secularization. People began to ask: what do we need from the churches when life can be so good, so satisfying, so prosperous? West and East feared one another, the so-called Iron Curtain was built. The West, secure in its *good life,* feared that their powerful foes in the East would wrest this prosperity from them.

In this atmosphere, Pius XII proclaimed 1950 as a Holy Year. The jubilee year reminded all people of their purpose on earth—that all are called to holiness, as individuals and as a society. This call included restoring the Christian social order. The Mystical Body of Christ was to realize its interrelationship with other people and act for the good of all. The proclamation of Mary's bodily Assumption into heaven should remind people of their final destiny. As the first and preeminent saint, Mary exemplified what it means to live in Christ and share his destiny.

The Teaching

As noted above Pope Pius XII begins *Munificentissimus Deus* by presenting the historical development of the teaching about Mary's Assumption. First he speaks of the state of Marian devotion in general: "Piety toward the Virgin Mother of God is flourishing and daily growing more fervent, and…almost everywhere on earth it is showing indications of a better and holier life" (n. 2). *Ineffabilis Deus,* the document on the Immaculate Conception, taught of Mary's privileges, but did not show her privileges in relation to the daily struggles of the Christian. It could seem that Mary had been above the common trials of life, but that she nevertheless could help us if we asked her. Pope Pius XII points out in *Munificentissimus Deus* that "the Virgin Mary, throughout the course of her earthly pilgrimage, led a life troubled by cares, hardships, and sorrows" (n. 14). She knows what suffering means. Her privileges are not meant to distance her from us.

Munificentissimus Deus states that besides Mary's sinlessness, God gave her yet another privilege: her sinless body, the dwelling place of Jesus Christ and divine life, would not undergo the corruption of the grave. Mary received "privileges which the most provident God has lavished upon this loving associate of our Redeemer, privileges which reach such an exalted plane that, except for her, nothing created by God other than the human nature of Jesus Christ has ever reached this level" (n. 14).

The solemn definition of the Assumption states:

> By the authority of our Lord Jesus Christ, of the Blessed Apostles Peter and Paul, and by our own authority, we pronounce, declare and define it to be a divinely revealed dogma: that the Immaculate Mother of God, the ever Virgin Mary, having completed the course of her earthly life, was assumed body and soul into heavenly glory.

In defining the dogma, Pope Pius XII based himself on the faith of the universal Church. On May 1, 1946, he had sent a letter to all the bishops of the world asking if they thought this dogma should be defined. 98.2% said yes, giving an overwhelming testimony to the faith of the Church.[2] Although Scripture does not explicitly testify to Mary's Assumption, the pope gives Scriptural references that are the basis for it.

The Question of Mary's Death

In defining the Assumption, the pope left open the question of Mary's death. He did not discuss whether Mary had died or not, but simply stated that she had "completed the course of her earthly life." The great majority of theologians hold that she did die, in order to be more fully conformed to the saving work of Christ. Her special gift of holiness exempted her from sin, but not from human suffering and death. On Calvary she united herself to the sufferings of Jesus. Some theologians think that because "Mary was associated at the foot of the cross with the sacrificial death of Christ, at the moment of her biological death she did not have to experience the sacrificial aspect of human death,"[3] having already done so. So her death can be seen as a joyous event, a transition to glory. Be that as it may, the Church has not ruled on how, when, or even precisely where Mary passed from this life to the next.

Today

After the dogma was proclaimed, the Christian world in the second half of the 20th century reacted to this teaching in diverse ways. Many Catholics could be described as *proud* of Mary, happy that she had attained this privilege. Other Christians said: this is going too far. *She* at-

---

2. Jacques Bur, *How to Understand the Virgin Mary* (New York: Continuum Publishing Company, 1996), 79.

3. Ibid., 77.

tained nothing. Some thought that the teaching removed Mary farther from the common lot of those struggling with life. Since one could not identify with her privileges, one could not identify with her.

In response, closer examination of the doctrine of Mary's Assumption underscores the importance and value of the human body, and kindles faith in our future resurrection. Vatican II presented the teaching's relevance to all Christians. In her Assumption, as in other aspects of her God-gifted personality, Mary is a figure of the Church as perfected through union with Christ. Mary is "the image and beginning of the Church as it is to be perfected in the world to come" (*LG* 68). As such, she is "a sign of sure hope and solace to the People of God during its sojourn on earth" (*LG* 68). She has a place in the ongoing work of salvation, which has as its goal "to gather up all things in him [Christ], things in heaven and things on earth" (Eph 1:10).

The *Catechism of the Catholic Church* teaches:

966 ...The Assumption of the Blessed Virgin is a singular participation in her Son's Resurrection and an anticipation of the resurrection of other Christians:

In giving birth you kept your virginity; in your Dormition you did not leave the world, O Mother of God, but were joined to the source of Life. You conceived the living God and, by your prayers, will deliver our souls from death.[4]

972 After speaking of the Church, her origin, mission, and destiny, we can find no better way to conclude than by looking to Mary. In her we contemplate what the Church already is in her mystery on her own "pilgrimage of faith," and what she will be in the homeland at the end of her journey. There, "in the glory of the Most Holy and Undivided Trinity," "in the communion of all the saints" (cf. Paul VI, *MC* 42, *SC* 103), the Church is awaited by the one she venerates as Mother of her Lord and as her own mother.

In the meantime the Mother of Jesus, in the glory which she possesses in body and soul in heaven, is the image and beginning of the Church as it is to be perfected in the world to come. Likewise she shines forth on earth, until the day of the Lord shall come, a sign of certain hope and comfort to the pilgrim People of God (*LG* 68; cf. 2 Pt 3:10).

---

4. Byzantine Liturgy, *Troparion,* Feast of the Dormition, August 15.

TOPICAL OUTLINE

1. Introduction: state of devotion to Mary (1–3)

2. Relation of the Immaculate Conception and the Assumption (4–6)

3. Preparation for the definition

    A. Petitions from the faithful (7–9)

    B. Consultation of the bishops (10–12)

4. Development of the doctrine (13)

    A. Constant belief of the faithful (14)

    B. Testimonies to the Church's belief in the Assumption: churches, images, etc. (15)

    C. Liturgical celebrations of the Assumption (16–19)

    D. The teachings of the Fathers on the Assumption (20–23)

    E. The teachings of theologians (24–37)

    F. Scripture as the ultimate foundation of the doctrine (38)

    G. Theological reasons for the teaching (39–40)

5. The definition of Mary's Assumption

    A. The appropriate moment has arrived (41)

    B. Hoped-for spiritual fruits of the definition (42–43)

    C. The definition itself (44)

6. Conclusion (45–48)

THE ASSUMPTION OF THE BLESSED VIRGIN MARY

Munificentissimus Deus

Promulgated by His Holiness Pope Pius XII
On November 1, 1950

1. The most bountiful God, who is almighty, the plan of whose Providence rests upon wisdom and love, tempers, in the secret purpose of his own mind, the sorrows of peoples and of individual men by means of joys that he interposes in their lives from time to time, in such a way that, under different conditions and in different ways, all things may work together unto good for those who love him (Rm 8:28).

2. Now, just like the present age, our pontificate is weighed down by ever so many cares, anxieties and troubles, by reason of very severe calamities that have taken place and by reason of the fact that many have strayed away from truth and virtue. Nevertheless, we are greatly consoled to see that, while the Catholic Faith is being professed publicly and vigorously, piety toward the Virgin Mother of God is flourishing and daily growing more fervent, and that almost everywhere on earth it is showing indications of a better and holier life. Thus, while the Blessed Virgin is fulfilling in the most affectionate manner her maternal duties on behalf of those redeemed by the blood of Christ, the minds and the hearts of her children are being vigorously aroused to a more assiduous consideration of her prerogatives.

3. Actually God, who from all eternity regards Mary with a most favorable and unique affection, has "when the fullness of time came" (Gal 4:4) put the plan of his providence into effect in such a way that all the privileges and prerogatives he had granted to her in his sovereign generosity were to shine forth in her in a kind of perfect harmony. And

although the Church has always recognized this supreme generosity and the perfect harmony of graces and has daily studied them more and more throughout the course of the centuries, still it is in our own age that the privilege of the bodily Assumption into heaven of Mary, the Virgin Mother of God, has certainly shone forth more clearly.

4. That privilege has shone forth in new radiance since our predecessor of immortal memory, Pius IX, solemnly proclaimed the dogma of the loving Mother of God's Immaculate Conception. These two privileges are most closely bound to one another. Christ overcame sin and death by his own death, and one who through Baptism has been born again in a supernatural way has conquered sin and death through the same Christ. Yet, according to the general rule, God does not will to grant to the just the full effect of the victory over death until the end of time has come. And so it is that the bodies of even the just are corrupted after death, and only on the last day will they be joined, each to its own glorious soul.

5. Now God has willed that the Blessed Virgin Mary should be exempted from this general rule. She, by an entirely unique privilege, completely overcame sin by her Immaculate Conception, and as a result she was not subject to the law of remaining in the corruption of the grave, and she did not have to wait until the end of time for the redemption of her body.

6. Thus, when it was solemnly proclaimed that Mary, the Virgin Mother of God, was from the very beginning free from the taint of original sin, the minds of the faithful were filled with a stronger hope that the day might soon come when the dogma of the Virgin Mary's bodily Assumption into heaven would also be defined by the Church's supreme teaching authority.

7. Actually it was seen that not only individual Catholics, but also those who could speak for nations or ecclesiastical provinces, and even a considerable number of the Fathers of the Vatican Council, urgently petitioned the Apostolic See to this effect.

8. During the course of time such postulations and petitions did not decrease but rather grew continually in number and in urgency. In this cause there were pious crusades of prayer. Many outstanding theologians eagerly and zealously carried out investigations on this subject, either privately or in public ecclesiastical institutions and in other schools where the sacred disciplines are taught. Marian Congresses, both national and international in scope, have been held in many parts of

the Catholic world. These studies and investigations have brought out into even clearer light the fact that the dogma of the Virgin Mary's Assumption into heaven is contained in the deposit of Christian faith entrusted to the Church. They have resulted in many more petitions, begging and urging the Apostolic See that this truth be solemnly defined.

9. In this pious striving, the faithful have been associated in a wonderful way with their own holy bishops, who have sent petitions of this kind, truly remarkable in number, to this See of the Blessed Peter. Consequently, when we were elevated to the throne of the supreme pontificate, petitions of this sort had already been addressed by the thousands from every part of the world and from every class of people, from our beloved sons the cardinals of the sacred college, from our venerable brethren, archbishops and bishops, from dioceses and from parishes.

10. Consequently, while we sent up earnest prayers to God that he might grant to our mind the light of the Holy Spirit, to enable us to make a decision on this most serious subject, we issued special orders in which we commanded that, by corporate effort, more advanced inquiries into this matter should be begun and that, in the meantime, all the petitions about the Assumption of the Blessed Virgin Mary into heaven which had been sent to this Apostolic See from the time of Pius IX, our predecessor of happy memory, down to our own days should be gathered together and carefully evaluated.[1]

11. And since we were dealing with a matter of such great moment and of such importance, we considered it opportune to ask all our venerable brethren in the episcopate directly and authoritatively, that each of them should make known to us his mind in a formal statement. Hence, on May 1, 1946, we gave them our letter *Deiparae Virginis Mariae,* a letter in which these words are contained: "Do you, venerable brethren, in your outstanding wisdom and prudence, judge that the bodily Assumption of the Blessed Virgin can be proposed and defined as a dogma of faith? Do you, with your clergy and people, desire it?"

12. But those whom "the Holy Spirit has placed as bishops to rule the Church of God" (Acts 20:28) gave an almost unanimous affirmative response to both these questions. This "outstanding agreement of the Catholic prelates and the faithful,"[2] affirming that the bodily Assump-

---

1. Cf. Hentrich-Von Moos, *Petitiones de Assumptione Corporea B. Virginis Mariae in Caelum Definienda ad S. Sedem Delatae,* 2 vols., Vatican Polyglot Press, 1942.

2. Bull *Ineffabilis Deus,* in the *Acta Pius IX,* pars 1, vol. 1, 615.

tion of God's Mother into heaven can be defined as a dogma of faith, since it shows us the concordant teaching of the Church's ordinary doctrinal authority and the concordant faith of the Christian people, which the same doctrinal authority sustains and directs, thus by itself and in an entirely certain and infallible way, manifests this privilege as a truth revealed by God and contained in that divine deposit which Christ has delivered to his Spouse to be guarded faithfully and to be taught infallibly.[3] Certainly this teaching authority of the Church, not by any merely human effort but under the protection of the Spirit of Truth (Jn 14:26), and therefore absolutely without error, carries out the commission entrusted to it, that of preserving the revealed truths pure and entire throughout every age, in such a way that it presents them undefiled, adding nothing to them and taking nothing away from them. For, as the Vatican Council teaches, "the Holy Spirit was not promised to the successors of Peter in such a way that, by his revelation, they might manifest new doctrine, but so that, by his assistance, they might guard as sacred and might faithfully propose the revelation delivered through the apostles, or the deposit of faith."[4] Thus, from the universal agreement of the Church's ordinary teaching authority we have a certain and firm proof, demonstrating that the Blessed Virgin Mary's bodily Assumption into heaven—which surely no faculty of the human mind could know by its own natural powers, as far as the heavenly glorification of the virginal body of the loving Mother of God is concerned—is a truth that has been revealed by God and consequently something that must be firmly and faithfully believed by all children of the Church. For as the Vatican Council asserts, "all those things are to be believed by divine and Catholic faith which are contained in the written Word of God or in Tradition, and which are proposed by the Church, either in solemn judgment or in its ordinary and universal teaching office, as divinely revealed truths which must be believed."[5]

13. Various testimonies, indications and signs of this common belief of the Church are evident from remote times down through the course of the centuries, and this same belief becomes more clearly manifest from day to day.

---

3. First Vatican Ecumenical Council, Constitution *Dei Filius,* c. 4.

4. First Vatican Ecumenical Council, Constitution *Pastor Aeternus,* c. 4.

5. Ibid., *Dei Filius,* c. 3.

14. Christ's faithful, through the teaching and the leadership of their pastors, have learned from the sacred books that the Virgin Mary, throughout the course of her earthly pilgrimage, led a life troubled by cares, hardships and sorrows, and that, moreover, what the holy old man Simeon had foretold actually came to pass, that is, that a terribly sharp sword pierced her heart as she stood under the cross of her divine Son, our Redeemer. In the same way, it was not difficult for them to admit that the great Mother of God, like her only-begotten Son, had actually passed from this life. But this in no way prevented them from believing and from professing openly that her sacred body had never been subject to the corruption of the tomb, and that the august tabernacle of the Divine Word had never been reduced to dust and ashes. Actually, enlightened by divine grace and moved by affection for her, God's Mother and our own dearest Mother, they have contemplated in an ever clearer light the wonderful harmony and order of those privileges which the most provident God has lavished upon this loving associate of our Redeemer, privileges which reach such an exalted plane that, except for her, nothing created by God other than the human nature of Jesus Christ has ever reached this level.

15. The innumerable temples which have been dedicated to the Virgin Mary assumed into heaven clearly attest this faith. So do those sacred images, exposed therein for the veneration of the faithful, which bring this unique triumph of the Blessed Virgin before the eyes of all men. Moreover, cities, dioceses and individual regions have been placed under the special patronage and guardianship of the Virgin Mother of God assumed into heaven. In the same way, religious institutes, with the approval of the Church, have been founded and have taken their name from this privilege. Nor can we pass over in silence the fact that in the rosary of Mary, the recitation of which this Apostolic See so urgently recommends, there is one mystery proposed for pious meditation which, as all know, deals with the Blessed Virgin's Assumption into heaven.

16. This belief of the sacred pastors and of Christ's faithful is universally manifested still more splendidly by the fact that, since ancient times, there have been both in the East and in the West solemn liturgical offices commemorating this privilege. The holy Fathers and Doctors of the Church have never failed to draw enlightenment from this fact since, as everyone knows, the sacred liturgy, "because it is the profession, subject to the supreme teaching authority within the Church, of heavenly

truths, can supply proofs and testimonies of no small value for deciding a particular point of Christian doctrine."[6]

17. In the liturgical books which deal with the Feast either of the Dormition or of the Assumption of the Blessed Virgin there are expressions that agree in testifying that, when the Virgin Mother of God passed from this earthly exile to heaven, what happened to her sacred body was, by the decree of divine Providence, in keeping with the dignity of the Mother of the Word incarnate, and with the other privileges she had been accorded. Thus, to cite an illustrious example, this is set forth in that sacramentary which Adrian I, our predecessor of immortal memory, sent to the Emperor Charlemagne. These words are found in this volume: "Venerable to us, O Lord, is the festivity of this day on which the holy Mother of God suffered temporal death, but still could not be kept down by the bonds of death, who has begotten your Son our Lord incarnate from herself."[7]

18. What is here indicated in that sobriety characteristic of the Roman liturgy is presented more clearly and completely in other ancient liturgical books. To take one as an example, the Gallican sacramentary designates this privilege of Mary's as "an ineffable mystery all the more worthy of praise as the Virgin's Assumption is something unique among men." And, in the Byzantine liturgy, not only is the Virgin Mary's bodily Assumption connected time and time again with the dignity of the Mother of God, but also with the other privileges, and in particular with the virginal motherhood granted her by a singular decree of God's Providence. "God, the King of the universe, has granted you favors that surpass nature. As he kept you a virgin in childbirth, thus he has kept your body incorrupt in the tomb and has glorified it by his divine act of transferring it from the tomb."[8]

19. The fact that the Apostolic See, which has inherited the function entrusted to the Prince of the Apostles, the function of confirming the brethren in the faith (Lk 22:32), has by its own authority, made the celebration of this feast ever more solemn, has certainly and effectively moved the attentive minds of the faithful to appreciate always more completely the magnitude of the mystery it commemorates. So it was

---

6. Encyclical Letter *Mediator Dei, AAS* 39, 541.

7. *Sacramentarium Gregorianum.*

8. *Menaei Totius Anni.*

that the Feast of the Assumption was elevated from the rank which it had occupied from the beginning among the other Marian feasts to be classed among the more solemn celebrations of the entire liturgical cycle. And when our predecessor St. Sergius I prescribed what is known as the litany, or the stational procession, to be held on four Marian feasts, he specified together the feasts of the Nativity, the Annunciation, the Purification and the Dormition of the Virgin Mary.[9] Again, St. Leo IV saw to it that the feast, which was already being celebrated under the title of the Assumption of the Blessed Mother of God, should be observed in even a more solemn way when he ordered a vigil to be held on the day before it and prescribed prayers to be recited after it until the octave day. When this had been done, he decided to take part himself in the celebration, in the midst of a great multitude of the faithful.[10] Moreover, the fact that a holy fast had been ordered from ancient times for the day prior to the feast is made very evident by what our predecessor St. Nicholas I testifies in treating of the principal fasts which "the Holy Roman Church has observed for a long time, and still observes."[11]

20. However, since the liturgy of the Church does not engender the Catholic faith, but rather springs from it, in such a way that the practices of the sacred worship proceed from the faith as the fruit comes from the tree, it follows that the holy Fathers and the great Doctors, in the homilies and sermons they gave the people on this feast day, did not draw their teaching from the feast itself as from a primary source, but rather they spoke of this doctrine as something already known and accepted by Christ's faithful. They presented it more clearly. They offered more profound explanations of its meaning and nature, bringing out into sharper light the fact that this feast shows, not only that the dead body of the Blessed Virgin Mary remained incorrupt, but that she gained a triumph out of death, her heavenly glorification after the example of her only-begotten Son, Jesus Christ—truths that the liturgical books had frequently touched upon concisely and briefly.

21. Thus St. John Damascene, an outstanding herald of this traditional truth, spoke out with powerful eloquence when he compared the bodily Assumption of the loving Mother of God with her other preroga-

---

9. *Liber Pontificalis.*
10. Ibid.
11. *Responsa Nicolai Papae I ad Consulta Bulgarorum.*

tives and privileges. "It was fitting that she, who had kept her virginity intact in childbirth, should keep her own body free from all corruption even after death. It was fitting that she, who had carried the Creator as a child at her breast, should dwell in the divine tabernacles. It was fitting that the spouse, whom the Father had taken to himself, should live in the divine mansions. It was fitting that she, who had seen her Son upon the cross and who had thereby received into her heart the sword of sorrow which she had escaped in the act of giving birth to him, should look upon him as he sits with the Father. It was fitting that God's Mother should possess what belongs to her Son, and that she should be honored by every creature as the Mother and as the handmaid of God."[12]

22. These words of St. John Damascene agree perfectly with what others have taught on this same subject. Statements no less clear and accurate are to be found in sermons delivered by Fathers of an earlier time or of the same period, particularly on the occasion of this feast. And so, to cite some other examples, St. Germanus of Constantinople considered the fact that the body of Mary, the virgin Mother of God, was incorrupt and had been taken up into heaven to be in keeping, not only with her divine motherhood, but also with the special holiness of her virginal body. "You are she who, as it is written, appears in beauty, and your virginal body is all holy, all chaste, entirely the dwelling place of God, so that it is henceforth completely exempt from dissolution into dust. Though still human, it is changed into the heavenly life of incorruptibility, truly living and glorious, undamaged and sharing in perfect life."[13] And another very ancient writer asserts: "As the most glorious Mother of Christ, our Savior and God and the giver of life and immortality, has been endowed with life by him, she has received an eternal incorruptibility of the body together with him, who has raised her up from the tomb and has taken her up to himself in a way known only to him."[14]

23. When this liturgical feast was being celebrated ever more widely and with ever increasing devotion and piety, the bishops of the Church and its preachers in continually greater numbers considered it their duty

---

12. St. John Damascene, *Encomium in Dormitionem Dei Genetricis Semperque Virginis Mariae, Homily* II, 14; cf. also ibid., 3.

13. St. Germanus of Constantinople, *In Sanctae Dei Genetricis Dormitionem, Sermo* I.

14. *Encomium in Dormitionem Sanctissimae Dominae Nostrate Deiparae Semperque Virginis Mariae,* attributed to St. Modestus of Jerusalem, n. 14.

openly and clearly to explain the mystery that the feast commemorates, and to explain how it is intimately connected with the other revealed truths.

24. Among the scholastic theologians there have not been lacking those who, wishing to inquire more profoundly into divinely revealed truths and desirous of showing the harmony that exists between what is termed the theological demonstration and the Catholic Faith, have always considered it worthy of note that this privilege of the Virgin Mary's Assumption is in wonderful accord with those divine truths given us in holy Scripture.

25. When they go on to explain this point, they adduce various proofs to throw light on this privilege of Mary. As the first element of these demonstrations, they insist upon the fact that, out of filial love for his mother, Jesus Christ has willed that she be assumed into heaven. They base the strength of their proofs on the incomparable dignity of her divine motherhood and of all those prerogatives which follow from it. These include her exalted holiness, entirely surpassing the sanctity of all men and of the angels, the intimate union of Mary with her Son, and the affection of preeminent love which the Son has for his most worthy Mother.

26. Often there are theologians and preachers who, following in the footsteps of the holy Fathers,[15] have been rather free in their use of events and expressions taken from Sacred Scripture to explain their belief in the Assumption. Thus, to mention only a few of the texts rather frequently cited in this fashion, some have employed the words of the psalmist: "Arise, O Lord, into your resting place: you and the ark, which you have sanctified" (Ps 131:8); and have looked upon the Ark of the Covenant, built of incorruptible wood and placed in the Lord's temple, as a type of the most pure body of the Virgin Mary, preserved and exempt from all the corruption of the tomb and raised up to such glory in heaven. Treating of this subject, they also describe her as the Queen entering triumphantly into the royal halls of heaven and sitting at the right hand of the divine Redeemer (Ps 44:10, 14 ff.) Likewise they mention the spouse of the Canticles "that goes up by the desert, as a pillar of smoke of aromatic spices, of myrrh and frankincense" to be crowned

---

15. Cf. St. John Damascene, *op. cit., Homily* II, 11; and also the *Encomium* attributed to St. Modestus.

(Sg 3:6; cf. also 4:8; 6:9). These are proposed as depicting that heavenly Queen and heavenly Spouse who has been lifted up to the courts of heaven with the divine Bridegroom.

27. Moreover, the scholastic Doctors have recognized the Assumption of the Virgin Mother of God as something signified, not only in various figures of the Old Testament, but also in that woman clothed with the sun whom John the Apostle contemplated on the Island of Patmos (Rv 12:1ff.). Similarly they have given special attention to these words of the New Testament: "Hail, full of grace, the Lord is with you, blessed are you among women" (Lk 1:28), since they saw, in the mystery of the Assumption, the fulfillment of that most perfect grace granted to the Blessed Virgin and the special blessing that countered the curse of Eve.

28. Thus, during the earliest period of scholastic theology, that most pious man, Amadeus, Bishop of Lausanne, held that the Virgin Mary's flesh had remained incorrupt—for it is wrong to believe that her body has seen corruption—because it was really united again to her soul and, together with it, crowned with great glory in the heavenly courts. "For she was full of grace and blessed among women. She alone merited to conceive the true God of true God, whom as a virgin, she brought forth, to whom as a virgin she gave milk, fondling him in her lap, and in all things she waited upon him with loving care."[16]

29. Among the holy writers who at that time employed statements and various images and analogies of Sacred Scripture to illustrate and to confirm the doctrine of the Assumption, which was piously believed, the Evangelical Doctor, St. Anthony of Padua, holds a special place. On the feast day of the Assumption, while explaining the prophet's words: "I will glorify the place of my feet" (Is 61:13), he stated it as certain that the divine Redeemer had bedecked with supreme glory his most beloved Mother from whom he had received human flesh. He asserts that "you have here a clear statement that the Blessed Virgin has been assumed in her body, where was the place of the Lord's feet. Hence it is that the holy Psalmist writes: 'Arise, O Lord, into your resting place: you and the ark which you have sanctified.'" And he asserts that, just as Jesus Christ has risen from the death over which he triumphed, and has ascended to the

---

16. Amadeus of Lausanne, *De Beatae Virginis Obitu, Assumptione in Caelum Exaltatione ad Filii Dexteram.*

right hand of the Father, so likewise the ark of his sanctification "has risen up, since on this day the Virgin Mother has been taken up to her heavenly dwelling."[17]

30. When, during the Middle Ages, scholastic theology was especially flourishing, St. Albert the Great who, to establish this teaching, had gathered together many proofs from Sacred Scripture, from the statements of older writers, and finally from the liturgy and from what is known as theological reasoning, concluded in this way: "From these proofs and authorities and from many others, it is manifest that the most Blessed Mother of God has been assumed above the choirs of angels. And this we believe in every way to be true."[18] And in a sermon which he delivered on the sacred day of the Blessed Virgin Mary's annunciation, explaining the words 'Hail, full of grace'—words used by the angel who addressed her—the Universal Doctor, comparing the Blessed Virgin with Eve, stated clearly and incisively that she was exempted from the fourfold curse that had been laid upon Eve.[19]

31. Following the footsteps of his distinguished teacher, the Angelic Doctor, despite the fact that he never dealt directly with this question, nevertheless, whenever he touched upon it, always held together with the Catholic Church, that Mary's body had been assumed into heaven along with her soul.[20]

32. Along with many others, the Seraphic Doctor held the same views. He considered it as entirely certain that, as God had preserved the most holy Virgin Mary from the violation of her virginal purity and integrity in conceiving and in childbirth, he would never have permitted her body to have been resolved into dust and ashes.[21] Explaining these words of Sacred Scripture: "Who is this that comes up from the desert, flowing with delights, leaning upon her beloved?" (Sg 8:5), and apply-

---

17. St. Anthony of Padua, *Sermones Dominicales et in Solemnitatibus, In Assumptione S. Mariae Virginis Sermo.*

18. St. Albert the Great, *Mariale,* q. 132.

19. St. Albert the Great, *Sermones de Sanctis, Sermo XV in Annuntiatione B. Mariae;* cf. also *Mariale,* q. 132.

20. St. Thomas Aquinas, *Summa Theol.,* Ill, q. 27, a. 1; q. 83, a. 5, *ad* 8; *Expositio Salutationis Angelicae; In Symb. Apostolorum Expositio,* a. 5; *In IV Sent.,* d. 12, q. 1, a. 3, sol. 3; d. 43, q. 1, a. 3, sol. 1, 2.

21. St. Bonaventure, *De Nativitate B. Mariae Virginis, Sermo* V.

ing them in a kind of accommodated sense to the Blessed Virgin, he reasons thus: "From this we can see that she is there bodily...her blessedness would not have been complete unless she were there as a person. The soul is not a person, but the soul, joined to the body, is a person. It is manifest that she is there in soul and in body. Otherwise she would not possess her complete beatitude."[22]

33. In the fifteenth century, during a later period of scholastic theology, St. Bernardine of Siena collected and diligently evaluated all that the medieval theologians had said and taught on this question. He was not content with setting down the principal considerations which these writers of an earlier day had already expressed, but he added others of his own. The likeness between God's Mother and her divine Son, in the way of the nobility and dignity of body and of soul—a likeness that forbids us to think of the heavenly Queen as being separated from the heavenly King—makes it entirely imperative that Mary "should be only where Christ is."[23] Moreover, it is reasonable and fitting that not only the soul and body of a man, but also the soul and body of a woman should have obtained heavenly glory. Finally, since the Church has never looked for the bodily relics of the Blessed Virgin nor proposed them for the veneration of the people, we have a proof on the order of a sensible experience.[24]

34. The above-mentioned teachings of the holy Fathers and of the Doctors have been in common use during more recent times. Gathering together the testimonies of the Christians of earlier days, St. Robert Bellarmine exclaimed: "And who, I ask, could believe that the ark of holiness, the dwelling place of the Word of God, the temple of the Holy Spirit, could be reduced to ruin? My soul is filled with horror at the thought that this virginal flesh which had begotten God, had brought him into the world, had nourished and carried him, could have been turned into ashes or given over to be food for worms."[25]

35. In like manner St. Francis de Sales, after asserting that it is wrong to doubt that Jesus Christ has himself observed, in the most per-

22. St. Bonaventure, *De Assumptione B. Mariae Virginis, Sermo* 1.

23. St. Bernardine of Siena, *In Assumptione B. Mariae Virginis, Sermo* 11.

24. Ibid.

25. St. Robert Bellarmine, *Conciones Habitae Lovanii,* 40, *De Assumption B. Mariae Virginis.*

fect way, the divine commandment by which children are ordered to honor their parents, asks this question: "What son would not bring his mother back to life and would not bring her into paradise after her death if he could?"[26] And St. Alphonsus writes that "Jesus did not wish to have the body of Mary corrupted after death, since it would have redounded to his own dishonor to have her virginal flesh, from which he himself had assumed flesh, reduced to dust."[27]

36. Once the mystery which is commemorated in this feast had been placed in its proper light, there were not lacking teachers who, instead of dealing with the theological reasonings that show why it is fitting and right to believe the bodily Assumption of the Blessed Virgin Mary into heaven, chose to focus their mind and attention on the faith of the Church itself, which is the Mystical Body of Christ without stain or wrinkle (Eph 5:27) and is called by the Apostle "the pillar and ground of truth" (1 Tm 3:15). Relying on this common faith, they considered the teaching opposed to the doctrine of our Lady's Assumption as temerarious, if not heretical. Thus, like not a few others, St. Peter Canisius, after he had declared that the very word "assumption" signifies the glorification, not only of the soul but also of the body, and that the Church has venerated and has solemnly celebrated this mystery of Mary's Assumption for many centuries, adds these words of warning: "This teaching has already been accepted for some centuries, it has been held as certain in the minds of pious people, and it has been taught to the entire Church in such a way that those who deny that Mary's body has been assumed into heaven are not to be listened to patiently, but are everywhere to be denounced as over-contentious or rash men, and as imbued with a spirit that is heretical rather than Catholic."[28]

37. At the same time the great Suarez was professing in the field of Mariology the norm that "keeping in mind the standards of propriety, and when there is no contradiction or repugnance on the part of Scripture, the mysteries of grace which God has wrought in the Virgin must be measured, not by the ordinary laws, but by the divine omnipotence."[29] Supported by the common faith of the entire Church on the

---

26. *Oeuvres de St. Francois De Sales,* sermon for the Feast of the Assumption.

27. St. Alphonsus Liguori, *The Glories of Mary,* Part 2, d. 1.

28. St. Peter Canisius, *De Maria Virgine.*

29. Suarez, *In Tertiam Partem D. Thomae,* q. 27, a. 2, disp. 3, sec. 5, n. 31.

subject of the mystery of the Assumption, he could conclude that this mystery was to be believed with the same firmness of assent as that given to the Immaculate Conception of the Blessed Virgin. Thus he already held that such truths could be defined.

38. All these proofs and considerations of the holy Fathers and the theologians are based upon the Sacred Writings as their ultimate foundation. These set the loving Mother of God as it were before our very eyes as most intimately joined to her divine Son and as always sharing his lot. Consequently it seems impossible to think of her, the one who conceived Christ, brought him forth, nursed him with her milk, held him in her arms, and clasped him to her breast, as being apart from him in body, even though not in soul, after this earthly life. Since our Redeemer is the Son of Mary, he could not do otherwise, as the perfect observer of God's law, than to honor, not only his eternal Father, but also his most beloved Mother. And, since it was within his power to grant her this great honor, to preserve her from the corruption of the tomb, we must believe that he really acted in this way.

39. We must remember especially that, since the second century, the Virgin Mary has been designated by the holy Fathers as the new Eve, who, although subject to the new Adam, is most intimately associated with him in that struggle against the infernal foe which, as foretold in the proto-evangelium (Gn 3:15), would finally result in that most complete victory over the sin and death which are always mentioned together in the writings of the Apostle of the Gentiles (Rm 5–6; 1 Cor 15:21–26, 54–57). Consequently, just as the glorious resurrection of Christ was an essential part and the final sign of this victory, so that struggle which was common to the Blessed Virgin and her divine Son should be brought to a close by the glorification of her virginal body, for the same Apostle says: "When this mortal thing hath put on immortality, then shall come to pass the saying that is written: Death is swallowed up in victory" (1 Cor 15:54).

40. Hence the revered Mother of God, from all eternity joined in a hidden way with Jesus Christ in one and the same decree of predestination,[30] immaculate in her conception, a most perfect virgin in her divine motherhood, the noble associate of the divine Redeemer who has won a

---

30. Bull *Ineffabilis Deus, loc. cit.,* 599.

complete triumph over sin and its consequences, finally obtained, as the supreme culmination of her privileges, that she should be preserved free from the corruption of the tomb and that, like her own Son, having overcome death, she might be taken up body and soul to the glory of heaven where, as Queen, she sits in splendor at the right hand of her Son, the immortal King of the Ages (1 Tm 1:17).

41. Since the universal Church, within which dwells the Spirit of Truth who infallibly directs it toward an ever more perfect knowledge of the revealed truths, has expressed its own belief many times over the course of the centuries, and since the bishops of the entire world are almost unanimously petitioning that the truth of the bodily Assumption of the Blessed Virgin Mary into heaven should be defined as a dogma of divine and Catholic faith—this truth which is based on the Sacred Writings, which is thoroughly rooted in the minds of the faithful, which has been approved in ecclesiastical worship from the most remote times, which is completely in harmony with the other revealed truths, and which has been expounded and explained magnificently in the work, the science and the wisdom of the theologians—we believe that the moment appointed in the plan of divine Providence for the solemn proclamation of this outstanding privilege of the Virgin Mary has already arrived.

42. We, who have placed our pontificate under the special patronage of the most holy Virgin, to whom we have had recourse so often in times of grave trouble, we who have consecrated the entire human race to her Immaculate Heart in public ceremonies, and who have time and time again experienced her powerful protection, are confident that this solemn proclamation and definition of the Assumption will contribute in no small way to the advantage of human society, since it redounds to the glory of the Most Blessed Trinity, to which the Blessed Mother of God is bound by such singular bonds. It is to be hoped that all the faithful will be stirred up to a stronger piety toward their heavenly Mother, and that the souls of all those who glory in the Christian name may be moved by the desire of sharing in the unity of Jesus Christ's Mystical Body and of increasing their love for her, who shows her motherly heart to all the members of this august body. And so we may hope that those who meditate upon the glorious example Mary offers us may be more and more convinced of the value of a human life entirely devoted to carrying out the heavenly Father's will and to bringing good to others. Thus, while the illusory teachings of materialism and the corruption of

morals that follows from these teachings threaten to extinguish the light of virtue and to ruin the lives of men by exciting discord among them, in this magnificent way all may see clearly to what a lofty goal our bodies and souls are destined. Finally it is our hope that belief in Mary's bodily Assumption into heaven will make our belief in our own resurrection stronger and render it more effective.

43. We rejoice greatly that this solemn event falls, according to the design of God's Providence, during this Holy Year, so that we are able, while the great Jubilee is being observed, to adorn the brow of God's Virgin Mother with this brilliant gem, and to leave a monument more enduring than bronze of our own most fervent love for the Mother of God.

44. For which reason, after we have poured forth prayers of supplication again and again to God, and have invoked the light of the Spirit of Truth, for the glory of Almighty God who has lavished his special affection upon the Virgin Mary, for the honor of her Son, the immortal King of the Ages and the Victor over sin and death, for the increase of the glory of that same august Mother, and for the joy and exultation of the entire Church, by the authority of our Lord Jesus Christ, of the Blessed Apostles Peter and Paul, and by our own authority, we pronounce, declare and define it to be a divinely revealed dogma: that the Immaculate Mother of God, the ever Virgin Mary, having completed the course of her earthly life, was assumed body and soul into heavenly glory.

45. Hence if anyone, which God forbid, should dare willfully to deny or to call into doubt that which we have defined, let him know that he has fallen away completely from the divine and Catholic Faith.

46. In order that this, our definition of the bodily Assumption of the Virgin Mary into heaven may be brought to the attention of the universal Church, we desire that this, our Apostolic Letter, should stand for perpetual remembrance, commanding that written copies of it, or even printed copies, signed by the hand of any public notary and bearing the seal of a person constituted in ecclesiastical dignity, should be accorded by all men the same reception they would give to this present letter, were it tendered or shown.

47. It is forbidden to any man to change this, our declaration, pronouncement and definition or, by rash attempt, to oppose and counter it. If any man should presume to make such an attempt, let him know that he will incur the wrath of Almighty God and of the Blessed Apostles Peter and Paul.

48. Given at Rome, at St. Peter's, in the year of the great Jubilee, 1950, on the first day of the month of November, on the Feast of All Saints, in the twelfth year of our pontificate.

I, Pius,
Bishop of the Catholic Church,
have signed, so defining.

DOGMATIC CONSTITUTION ON THE CHURCH

Lumen Gentium, Chapter VIII

Vatican II

INTRODUCTION[1]

At the time of its promulgation, chapter eight of *Lumen Gentium* was the most extensive magisterial teaching on the Blessed Virgin Mary in the history of the Roman Catholic Church.

Historical Perspectives

As already mentioned, the century preceding Vatican II was rich in Marian teachings. The popes defined two Marian dogmas and wrote many documents on devotion to Mary. Leo XIII published sixteen documents on the rosary alone.[2] In addition, approved apparitions of Mary played a part in developing new devotions and prayer forms. In the decades preceding Vatican II, Catholic children learned the stories of Mary's life,[3] of the Miraculous Medal (1830), Lourdes (1858), Knock (1879), Fatima (1917) and others.[4] The Church celebrated 1954 as a

---

1. *AAS* 57 (1965), 5–67. English source for the Vatican II documents: *The Sixteen Documents of Vatican II* (Boston: Pauline Books & Media, 1999), NCWC translation.

2. William Raymond Lawler, O.P., P. G., comp., *The Rosary of Mary: Translations of the Encyclicals and Apostolic Letters of Pope Leo XIII* (Paterson, NJ: St. Anthony Guild Press, 1944). Of these documents, twelve are encyclicals, three are apostolic letters, and one is an apostolic constitution. Eleven of these encyclicals are found in: Claudia Carlen, IHM, trans., *The Papal Encyclicals 1878–1903* (Wilmington, NC: McGrath Publishing Company, 1981).

3. A sampler of children's storybooks: Robert Bastin, *The Simple Story of the Blessed Virgin* (Our Lady of Grace Society); Sr. M. Jean Dorcy, *Mary, My Mother* and *Our Lady's Feasts* (New York: Sheed & Ward, 1945); F. R. Boschvogel, *Mary Is Our Mother* (New York: P. J. Kennedy and Sons, 1955); Sr. M. Paula, *The Virgin Mother* (New York: Benziger, 1934); Demetrius Manousos, *The Life of the Blessed Virgin* (St. Paul, MN: Catechetical Guild, 1951); Brother Ernest, *Your Mother and Mine* (Notre Dame, IN: Dujarie Press, 1954).

4. A sampler of books for primary children in the 1950's: Brother Robert, *Our Lady Comes to New Orleans* (Indiana: Dujarie Press, 1957); Brother Ernest, *Our Lady Comes to Fatima* and *Our Lady Comes to Lourdes* and *Our Lady Comes to Paris* (Indiana:

Marian Year, and on that October 11, Pope Pius XII published an encyclical establishing a new Feast of Mary's Queenship.[5]

Nevertheless, the document on Mary occasioned extensive formal debate at the Council.[6] Should Mary be treated in a separate document, or should she be included in the document on the Church? Wasn't she, as Cardinal Santos Rufini from Manila argued, "the first and the principal member of the Church," [but also] "somehow above the Church?"[7] Cardinal Francis König from Vienna saw Mary as a model of the Church, with "more of a ecclesio-typical, and 'sharing-oriented'"[8] emphasis. On the first vote on October 29, 1963, 1114 bishops voted for inclusion; 1074 wanted a separate document. The draft of the separate schema was half the size of the final version, so it was not a matter of a lesser treatment of Mary, but a greater. Cardinal Santos wanted the separate schema to be placed at the end of the document on the Church and include a new introduction that clearly showed Mary's relationship to and within the Church.[9] Or was a deeper question involved? Had over 400 years of post-Reformation argument about Mary cooled enthusiasm for her person, her role, her position—perhaps due to an interest in making the liturgy central? The interventions for or against inclusion indicate strong ecumenical sensitivities. The summary of the eighty-five written replies from the bishops often indicated concern for Mary's image as it appears to those outside the Catholic Church. The Japanese and Latin American bishops asked for a Mariology that would, in all things, see Christ as central and Mary's position in relation to him and to the Church—not isolated as a thing apart.[10]

The committee formed to write the revision consisted of both cardi-

Dujarie Press, 1951); Sr. Mary Jean, *Rosary Stories for Little Folk* (Milwaukee: Bruce, 1957); Sister M. Juliana of Maryknoll, *"Pray the Rosary"* (St. Paul, MN: Catechetical Guild, 1954).

5. *AAS* 46 (1954), 625–640. Later quoted in *Lumen Gentium* 59 and 67.

6. Frederick M. Jelly, O.P., "The Theological Context of and Introduction to Chapter 8 of *Lumen Gentium,"* *Marian Studies* 37 (1986): 43–73.

7. George H. Tavard, *The Thousand Faces of the Virgin Mary* (Collegeville, MN: The Liturgical Press, 1996), 203 (quoting the documents he kept from Vatican II; see his footnote 5, 217.

8. Jelly, 48.

9. Jelly, 55.

10. "Emendationes a patribus scripto exhibitae," *Acta Synodolia Sacrosancti Concilii Oecumenici Vaticani Secundi* 2:3 (1970): 300–337.

nals and *periti* with varying points of view.[11] After much discussion, the final vote on November 18, 1964, was 2096 for inclusion and twenty-three opposed.[12]

In reading the Vatican II documents today, we can hardly perceive the significance of this issue. We usually read the documents bound in one book; we know that they belong together. So what difference does it make whether Mary has a separate chapter at the end of one document, or begins a new document on the next page with an introduction that links her to the former document? The Vatican II documents were promulgated separately during the three years of the Council and gathered together only later. The time and the frame of reference for each document indicate the issues.

In regard to the vote, Fr. George H. Tavard says that "this slim margin of majority" fostered "a degree of bitterness."[13] But Fr. Frederick M. Jelly, O.P. doesn't find bitterness in the revisions and final consensus vote. His approach points out the advantages of the debate,[14] but he also notes that the news media had found a story that "seems to have played

---

11. Jelly, 60.

12. Tavard, 204.

13. Tavard, 203.

14. Jelly, 57–58. An example of one of the most influential interventions is given here. Cardinal König's debate listed the following reasons why the theological commission's majority opinion thought Mary should be included in the schema on the Church:

Theological: 1) The Church was the central theme of session two and of Vatican II; 2) a separate schema might give the "impression that Vatican II intended to define a new Marian dogma [but this was not] the mind of the Council"; 3) "the Blessed Virgin ought to be placed within the schema on the Church as the preeminent member of the People of God"; 4) Mary is the type of the Church—she conceived the one Mediator Jesus Christ, "not only bodily but also in her heart through loving faith and obedience;" 5) inclusion would mean a uniting of "ecclesio-typical Mariology [with] one that is Christo-typical."

Historical: 1) "Devotion to Mary...had arisen out of contemplation of the Church as mother...all titles [litanies] were originally predicated to the Church. Mary's privileges were portrayed within an ecclesiological perspective" [what applies to the Church applies to Mary]; 2) Paul VI prayed on October 11, 1963, showing the close relationship of Mary and the Church: "...her own mother and daughter and most elite sister, her incomparable model, her glory, her joy and her hope; 3) the theme of the Mariological Congress in Lourdes, 1958: "Mary and the Church."

Pastoral: "The devotional life of the faithful must be nourished on essentials, and so Catholics should be instructed in the right faith about the mystery of the Incarnation and Mary's role in it."

Ecumenical: "Such an approach would help make Mary as the venerable *Theotókos* more recognizable to the Eastern Church, and also assist [other] Christians in acknowledging the basis of Marian devotion in the testimony of Sacred Scripture and of ancient Tradition [emphasis on Scripture]."

no small part"[15] in making Mary a sign of division in post-Vatican II developments.

What effect did Vatican II have on Marian catechesis? Some thought that if Christ was truly central, or if the separated Churches were to be considered, perhaps Mary need not be discussed, or at least not stressed. Others wondered why the documents didn't mention certain things, including such devotions as the rosary. Did Vatican II teach anything *new* about Mary and Marian devotion, or was the Church to continue as before the Council? Each of these questions would ultimately be reflected in the so-called Marian question of the post-Vatican II period.

No matter what the diverse questions came to be, one factor remains outstanding: chapter eight of *Lumen Gentium* became the foundation for the majority of post-Vatican II magisterial documents that discussed the Blessed Virgin Mary, and it remains the normative magisterial document for the Catholic faithful. It is the basis of the Marian teachings in the *Catechism of the Catholic Church.* In addition, *Lumen Gentium* (chapter eight) cannot be isolated from the other Vatican II documents, nor is it the only Marian teaching in the documents. To see this context more fully, the next section discusses the Marian references in the conciliar documents according to their date of publication.

Lumen Gentium's place in Vatican II

The sequence of the conciliar documents indicates the immediate background for the development of Marian teachings at the Council.

Constitution on the Sacred Liturgy
(Sacrosanctum Concilium)
December 4, 1963

The first conciliar document approved at the end of the first session was the *Constitution on the Sacred Liturgy.* Between 1964 and 1974, Rome issued at least twenty-four further declarations or instructions in conjunction with this document. Not since Trent, 400 years earlier, had a council had such an impact on the universal Church. It caused immense adjustments in thinking, ritual and focus. The Council reaffirmed the centrality of the liturgy, especially the Eucharistic liturgy, as the focal

---

15. Jelly, 60.

point and gathering place of the People of God. The bishops wanted to draw everyone as close as possible to these sacred mysteries, and to Jesus Christ who established them and acts in them. Henceforth, all discussion would take place with a keen awareness of the changes involved (for example, use of the vernacular) and the goal to vivify and unite the Church in the liturgy.

The constitution contains one paragraph on Mary:

> In celebrating this annual cycle of Christ's mysteries, holy Church honors with especial love the Blessed Mary, Mother of God, who is joined by an inseparable bond to the saving work of her Son. In her the Church holds up and admires the most excellent fruit of the redemption and joyfully contemplates, as in a faultless image, that which she herself desires and hopes wholly to be (*SC* 103).

From the start, the Council affirmed its special love for Mary due to her role in salvation history and her inseparable link to Christ's work. Mary is admired and exalted because she is the first of the redeemed. This initial statement places Mary among us, as one of us. The Church looks at Mary as an example of what it means to be a redeemed person.[16]

Decree on the Means of Social Communication
(Inter Mirifica)
December 4, 1963

The second document, the *Decree on the Means of Social Communication,* promulgated on the same day as the *Constitution on the Sacred Liturgy,* highlights the Church's relationship to the world, especially the world of technology. Reflecting openness and initiative, it calls for Catholics to use the media to proclaim the Good News, with due discernment. This document makes a strong commitment to the Church *as a mother.*[17] Even though the Church is still somehow "out there" and "separate" from the world, at the same time social communication will help to

---

16. Though there is little evidence that the Marian paragraph in *The Constitution on the Sacred Liturgy* influenced *Lumen Gentium's* final draft, nevertheless article 103 on Mary is reflected in paragraphs 66 and 67 of *Lumen Gentium,* and article 103 appears in post-Vatican II documents. See also: U.S. Bishops, *Behold Your Mother* (Washington, DC: USCC Publication Office, 1973), 82, 81, 83, 84; *Marialis Cultus* Intro, 16, 22, 25, 32 which links Marian devotion to the liturgical worship of the Church; *Catechism of the Catholic Church,* 508, 971, 1172.

17. See the introduction to the document.

break down the separateness of the Church and the world. With these first two documents, the tone was set for the thinking of *Lumen Gentium.*

Decree on the Catholic Churches of the Eastern Rite *(Orientalium Ecclesiarum)* and Decree on Ecumenism *(Unitatis Redintegratio)* November 21, 1964

Along with *Lumen Gentium,* two documents treating ecumenical themes were promulgated on November 21, 1964, at the end of the second session: *Decree on the Catholic Churches of the Eastern Rite (Orientalium Ecclesiarum)* and *Decree on Ecumenism (Unitatis Redintegratio).* Discussion on Mary fairly well paralleled the discussion on ecumenism.[18] Both documents mention Mary.

The concluding article of *Orientalium Ecclesiarum* mentions Mary only in a formal way: in the struggle for unity, "all Christians, Eastern as well as Western, are earnestly asked to pray to God fervently and assiduously, nay, indeed daily, that with the aid of the most holy Mother of God, all may become one" (n. 30).

In *Unitatis Redintegratio,* the Marian text in article fifteen centers on the liturgy: "In this liturgical worship, the Christians of the East pay high tribute in beautiful hymns of praise to Mary ever Virgin, whom the ecumenical Council of Ephesus solemnly proclaimed to be the holy Mother of God, so that Christ might be acknowledged as being truly Son of God and Son of Man, according to the Scriptures." This article confirms the unity of the churches of the East and West in the two early Marian dogmas: Mary as the Mother of God *(Theotókos)* and ever Virgin.

The second mention of Mary, in article 20, articulates the difficulties: "We are aware indeed that there exist considerable divergences from the doctrine of the Catholic Church concerning Christ himself, the Word of God made flesh, the work of redemption and consequently, concerning the mystery and ministry of the Church, and the role of Mary in the plan of salvation." Having acknowledged Mary's role as one of the "considerable differences" dividing the churches, the bishops kept this in mind as they discussed Marian teaching at Vatican II.

---

18. "Emendationes," 2:3 (1970).

The Context of the Marian Articles in *Lumen Gentium*

Sketched briefly, the eight chapters of *Lumen Gentium* cover the following topics: the mystery of the Church, the People of God, the Church as hierarchical, the laity, the call to holiness, religious life, the pilgrim Church, and Mary in the mystery of Christ and in the mystery of the Church. *Lumen Gentium* first mentions Mary in chapter seven.

The chapter develops the theme of the Church's eschatological nature, putting it in the context of the communion of saints. This paves the way to seeing Mary in the same context: "The Church has always believed that the apostles and Christ's martyrs who had given the supreme witness of faith and charity by the shedding of their blood are closely joined with us in Christ, and she has always venerated them with special devotion, together with the Blessed Virgin Mary and the holy angels" (*LG* 50).

By placing the Church's Marian teaching at the concluding part of the document (chapter eight), the Council pointed to Mary as an image of the Church as it is and longs to be in its final state.[19]

The Teaching

The full title of the chapter, "The Blessed Virgin Mary, Mother of God, in the Mystery of Christ and the Church" is sometimes omitted in publication. Yet it has its significance. The Council participants had debated what to stress regarding Mary: the Christo-typical or the ecclesio-typical approach.[20] The bishops voted for the ecclesiotypical approach; nevertheless, chapter eight's title joined the two, for Christ and the Church belong together. Mary belongs fully to the mystery of Christ, but she also belongs fully to the Church.

The chapter consists of seventeen articles divided under five subtitles, beginning with an introduction. It introduces Mary as *the woman*

---

19. Charles W. Neumann, S.M., has outlined the content of chapter eight in *Marian Studies*. Source: "Appendix V: A Synopsis of the Chapters of *Lumen Gentium*," *Marian Studies* 37 (1986): 258. The content of chapter eight can be approached in many ways. The document can, for instance, be searched for themes. An extensive study of the themes from chapter eight and other post-Vatican II magisterial documents can be found on the Internet under Mary Page: www.udayton.edu/mary/resources/documents/themes.html

20. Jelly, 54; Tavard, 203.

(cf. Gal 4:4) of our creed from whom Christ became incarnate by the Holy Spirit. The document places Mary within the mystery of redemption. She deserves honor because she "received the Word of God in her heart and in her body and gave Life [Christ] to the world" (*LG* 53). She is honored in our liturgy, for she is a "preeminent and singular member of the Church" (*LG* 53). With painstaking care the Church teaches about her role and our duties toward her (*LG* 54).

The four remaining subtitles are:

- The Role of the Blessed Mother in the Economy of Salvation
- On the Blessed Virgin and the Church
- The Cult of the Blessed Virgin in the Church
- Mary, the Sign of Created Hope and Solace to the Wandering People of God

Lumen Gentium speaks of Mary as the "beloved daughter of the Father" (*LG* 53) and the "exalted Daughter of Zion" (*LG* 55), who plays an important role in the Father's plan of salvation. God prepared her for her task, adorning her "from the first instant of her conception with the radiance of an entirely unique holiness" (*LG* 56).

"The Virgin Mary…is acknowledged and honored as being truly the Mother of God and Mother of the Redeemer" (*LG* 53). A close bond links Mary with her son Jesus, a union which goes beyond that of motherhood and joins her to Jesus' saving work: "This union of the Mother with the Son in the work of salvation is made manifest from the time of Christ's virginal conception up to his death" (*LG* 57). Articles 57–59 discuss aspects of Mary's union with Jesus during his infancy and childhood, public life and after his resurrection. Mary freely and lovingly cooperated in the work of salvation and was "exalted by the Lord as Queen of the Universe, that she might be more fully conformed to her Son" (*LG* 59).

Because of her special gift of holiness, *Lumen Gentium* states that Mary was "fashioned by the Holy Spirit and formed as a new creature" (*LG* 56). Mary conceived the incarnate Word by the overshadowing of the Holy Spirit, whose temple she became. Awaiting Pentecost together with the apostles, Mary prayed for the outpouring of the gifts of the Spirit on the Church (cf. Acts 1:14).

The third section of chapter eight discusses the Blessed Virgin and the Church. Placing the discussion in the context of the unique mediation of Christ, it clearly states that Mary's maternal mediation "flows forth from the superabundance of the merits of Christ, rests on his mediation, depends entirely on it and draws all its power from it" (*LG* 60). Because of her unique role, Mary is "our mother in the order of grace" (*LG* 61). Through her intercession, Mary cares for the Church's members and sustains them on their journey.

Mary is a type of the Church: "For in the mystery of the Church, which is itself rightly called mother and virgin, the Blessed Virgin stands out in eminent and singular fashion as exemplar both of virgin and mother" (*LG* 63).

Mary is a model of virtues. In her, the Church has already reached the perfection of holiness that all its members are called to. Mary is a sign of eschatological hope for the pilgrim People of God.

As a daughter of Adam and member of the Chosen People, Mary was fully human. She was one of the lowly ones, the poor of Yahweh, who confidently looked to him for salvation and help. Mary's personality showed her humanness. She joyfully showed her newborn son to the shepherds and Magi; she felt compassion for the newlyweds of Cana; she pondered the Word of God in her heart. Mary had to search for God's will day by day. With Joseph she sought for the lost child Jesus with sorrow, and didn't understand what he said to them. She experienced human weakness and limitations, not knowing where God would lead her. Nevertheless she faithfully persevered.

Her haste to visit Elizabeth shows Mary's concern for others (cf. Lk 1:41–45). This social concern continues today, for she cares, by her maternal charity, for the brethren of her Son who still journey on earth.

Lumen Gentium (chapter eight) is biblical in its foundations and presents most scriptural passages that refer to Mary. The Council wanted Marian devotion to be solidly based. It should not be marked by an unreasoned acceptance of everything that comes along regarding devotion to Mary. "True devotion consists neither in sterile or transitory affection, nor in a certain vain credulity, but proceeds from true faith, by which we are led to know the excellence of the Mother of God, and we are moved to a filial love toward our mother and to the imitation of her virtues" (*LG* 67).

The Council recommends those forms of Marian piety that the magisterium has sanctioned through the centuries. Article sixty-six alludes to the *sub tuum praesidium,* the oldest Marian prayer known. The document doesn't specifically mention particular practices or devotions; however, it does state that previous magisterial decrees referring to sacred images be observed. The footnote here refers to the Second Council of Nicea, held in 787 to resolve the iconoclast controversy.

The document also urges theologians and preachers to take a balanced view toward Marian devotion, neither following exaggerated practices nor dismissing it. Mentioning Mary's place in liturgical celebrations, the Council urges that "the cult, especially the liturgical cult, of the Blessed Virgin be generously fostered" (*LG* 67).

Lumen Gentium also presents Mary as a model for evangelization. "The Church, in her apostolic work also, justly looks to her, who brought forth Christ, who was conceived of the Holy Spirit and born of the Virgin, that through the Church he may be born and may increase in the hearts of the faithful also" (*LG* 65). Mary's maternal love and example provide a model for those who carry out the Church's work of evangelization.

The document notes that after the Council of Ephesus, a remarkable growth occurred in the devotion of the faithful toward Mary. From then on, the Church's pastors often recommended her as a model for Christians.

Lumen Gentium also states that the Council did not intend to give a comprehensive doctrine on Mary, nor decide on those questions that theologians are still debating.

Lumen Gentium presents Mary as the lived and living Church. God's grace enriched this woman, one of God's people, and elevated her for Christ and for us. She journeyed with Christ from the moment of his conception to his death and beyond. Mary's role in God's plan of salvation is significant for Christ in his humanity, but also for Christ in his Church. Mary is always to be seen in the perspective of her relationship with Jesus Christ and the Church.

Marian Content in Other Vatican II Documents

The post-*Lumen Gentium* Vatican II texts that have references to Mary are listed below by date of publication.

Decree on the Adaptation and Renewal of Religious Life (*Perfectae Caritatis*) October 28, 1965

Perfectae Caritatis builds on *Lumen Gentium*. Its final article, by way of formal inclusion, points to Mary as model: "Let them beseech the Virgin Mary, the gentle Mother of God, 'whose life is a model for all,'[21] that their number may daily increase and their salutary work be more effective."

Decree on Priestly Training
(Optatam Totius)
October 28, 1965

Optatam Totius consists of twenty-two articles with seven subtitles. Article eight, devoted to spiritual training, recommends that seminarians: "...should love and venerate with a filial trust the most Blessed Virgin Mary, who was given as mother to the disciple by Christ Jesus as he was dying on the cross." The paragraph immediately following this recommendation advises students studying for the priesthood that "Those practices of piety that are commended by the long usage of the Church should be zealously cultivated, but care should be taken lest the spiritual formation consist in them alone or lest it develop only a religious affectation...." The close and purposeful proximity of these texts indicates that Marian devotion is encouraged and is to be based on Scripture.

Declaration on the Relation of the Church to
Non-Christian Religions
(Nostra Aetate)
October 28, 1965

Nostra Aetate consists of five articles calling for "greater care" in the Church's relation to non-Christian religions. "In her task of promoting unity and love among men, indeed among nations, she considers above all in this declaration what men have in common and what draws them to fellowship" (*NA* 1). In this context, the document finds a common basis with Muslims regarding Mary: "Though they do not acknowl-

---

21. St. Ambrose, *De Virginitate,* 1, II, c. II, n. 15.

Decree on the Apostolate of the Laity
(Apostolicam Actuositatem)
November 18, 1965

Apostolicam Actuositatem has thirty-three articles divided into six chapters. The Marian reference is found in article 4, which deals with the spirituality of lay people:

> The perfect example of this type of spiritual and apostolic life is the most Blessed Virgin Mary, queen of apostles, who while leading the life common to all here on earth, one filled with family concerns and labors, was always intimately united with her Son and in an entirely unique way cooperated in the work of the Savior. Having now been assumed into heaven, with her maternal charity she cares for these brothers of her Son who are still on their earthly pilgrimage and remain involved in dangers and difficulties until they are led into the happy fatherland (*LG* 62). All should devoutly venerate her and commend their life and apostolate to her maternal care.

Decree on the Ministry and Life of Priests
(Presbyterorum Ordinis)
December 7, 1965

Article eighteen of this document has a few words about Mary in the life of the priest:

> Nourished by spiritual reading, under the light of faith, they can more diligently seek signs of God's will and impulses of his grace in the various events of life, and so from day to day become more docile to the mission they have assumed in the Holy Spirit. They will always find a wonderful example of such docility in the Blessed Virgin Mary, who was led by the Holy Spirit to dedicate herself totally to the mystery of man's redemption (*LG* 65). Let priests love and venerate with filial devotion and veneration this mother of the eternal high priest, queen of apostles and protector of their own ministry.

Today

Just as Vatican II set down basic principles for other theological disciplines, it also did so for Marian teaching. As part of the *Dogmatic*

Constitution on the Church, chapter eight forms the foundation for future directions in Marian theology. It can be seen as the measuring rod for subsequent Marian teaching. Mary is and continues to be a model for all members of the Church. She lived a life like that of any other, and continues to assist us in heaven. We may entrust ourselves to her care.

In 1965, Pope Paul VI spoke about chapter eight:

> We feel, indeed, that the teaching on Mary and Marian devotion introduces us into the plan of salvation that Christ has established—in the sense that, as has been so well said, there is in Marian dogma a "symbolic summary of the Catholic doctrine on human cooperation in the redemption; in this way, it offers a kind of synthesis of the very dogma on the Church."[22]

22. Henri De Lubac, *Méditations sur l'Église,* 242, as quoted by Paul VI in *The Pope Speaks* 9–10 (1963–65): 103.

TOPICAL OUTLINE

The Blessed Virgin Mary, Mother of God, in the Mystery of Christ and the Church

1. Introduction: reverence for the Blessed Virgin (52–54)

2. The role of the Blessed Mother in the economy of salvation

    A. Testimony of Scripture (55)

    B. Mary's role in the Incarnation (56)

    C. Mary's union with Jesus in the work of salvation

        1. During Jesus' infancy and childhood (57)

        2. During Jesus' public life (58)

    D. Pentecost and the Assumption (59)

3. The Blessed Virgin and the Church

    A. The unique mediation of Christ (60)

    B. Mary is our mother in the order of grace (61)

    C. Mary's maternal intercession (62)

    D. Mary in the mystery of the Church (63)

    E. The Church as virgin and mother (64)

    F. Mary as a model of virtues (65)

4. Devotion to the Blessed Virgin

    A. Veneration of Mary (66)

    B. Balanced devotion (67)

5. Mary as a sign of hope

    A. Mary gives hope to and consoles the People of God on earth (68)

    B. Mary intercedes for the Church (69)

DOGMATIC CONSTITUTION ON THE CHURCH

Lumen Gentium, Chapter VIII

Promulgated by His Holiness Pope Paul VI
On November 21, 1964

THE BLESSED VIRGIN MARY, MOTHER OF GOD IN THE MYSTERY OF CHRIST AND THE CHURCH

I. Introduction

52. Wishing in his supreme goodness and wisdom to effect the redemption of the world, "when the fullness of time came, God sent his Son, born of a woman...that we might receive the adoption of sons" (Gal 4:4–5). "He for us men, and for our salvation, came down from heaven, and was incarnate by the Holy Spirit from the Virgin Mary."[1] This divine mystery of salvation is revealed to us and continued in the Church, which the Lord established as his body. Joined to Christ the head and in the unity of fellowship with all his saints, the faithful must in the first place reverence the memory "of the glorious ever Virgin Mary, Mother of our God and Lord Jesus Christ."[2]

53. The Virgin Mary, who at the message of the angel received the Word of God in her heart and in her body and gave Life to the world, is

---

1. Creed of the Roman Mass: Symbol of Constantinople: Mansi 3, 566; cf. Council of Ephesus, *ibid.* 4, 1130 (and *ibid.* 2, 665 and 4, 1071); Council of Chalcedon, *ibid.* 7, 111–116; Second Council of Constantinople, *ibid.* 9, 375–396.

2. Canon of the Roman Mass.

acknowledged and honored as being truly the Mother of God and Mother of the Redeemer. Redeemed by reason of the merits of her Son and united to him by a close and indissoluble tie, she is endowed with the high office and dignity of being the Mother of the Son of God, by which account she is also the beloved daughter of the Father and the temple of the Holy Spirit. Because of this gift of sublime grace she far surpasses all creatures, both in heaven and on earth. At the same time, however, because she belongs to the offspring of Adam she is one with all those who are to be saved. She is "the mother of the members of Christ...having cooperated by charity that faithful might be born in the Church, who are members of that head."[3] Wherefore she is hailed as a pre-eminent and singular member of the Church, and as its type and excellent exemplar in faith and charity. The Catholic Church, taught by the Holy Spirit, honors her with filial affection and piety as a most beloved mother.

54. Wherefore this holy synod, in expounding the doctrine on the Church, in which the divine Redeemer works salvation, intends to describe with diligence both the role of the Blessed Virgin in the mystery of the Incarnate Word and the Mystical Body, and the duties of redeemed mankind toward the Mother of God, who is mother of Christ and mother of men, particularly of the faithful. It does not, however, have it in mind to give a complete doctrine on Mary, nor does it wish to decide those questions which the work of theologians has not yet fully clarified. Those opinions, therefore, may be lawfully retained which are propounded in Catholic schools concerning her, who occupies a place in the Church which is the highest after Christ and yet very close to us.[4]

II. The Role of the Blessed Mother in the Economy of Salvation

55. The Sacred Scriptures of both the Old and the New Testament, as well as ancient Tradition, show the role of the Mother of the Savior in the economy of salvation in an ever clearer light and draw attention to it. The books of the Old Testament describe the history of salvation, by which the coming of Christ into the world was slowly prepared. These earliest documents, as they are read in the Church and are understood in the light of a further and full revelation, bring the figure of the woman,

---

3. St. Augustine, *De S. Virginitate* 6: *PL* 40, 399.
4. Cf. Paul VI, *Allocution to the Council* (Dec. 4, 1963): *AAS* 56 (1964), 37.

Mother of the Redeemer, into a gradually clearer light. When it is looked at in this way, she is already prophetically foreshadowed in the promise of victory over the serpent, which was given to our first parents after their fall into sin (cf. Gn 3:15). Likewise she is the Virgin who shall conceive and bear a son, whose name will be called Emmanuel (cf. Is 7:14; cf. Mi 5:2–3; Mt 1:22–23). She stands out among the poor and humble of the Lord, who confidently hope for and receive salvation from him. With her, the exalted Daughter of Sion, and after a long expectation of the promise, the times are fulfilled and the new economy established, when the Son of God took a human nature from her, that he might in the mysteries of his flesh free man from sin.

56. The Father of mercies willed that the Incarnation should be preceded by the acceptance of her who was predestined to be the mother of his Son, so that just as a woman contributed to death, so also a woman should contribute to life. That is true in outstanding fashion of the mother of Jesus, who gave to the world him who is Life itself and who renews all things, and who was enriched by God with the gifts which befit such a role. It is no wonder therefore that the usage prevailed among the Fathers whereby they called the mother of God entirely holy and free from all stain of sin, as though fashioned by the Holy Spirit and formed as a new creature.[5] Adorned from the first instant of her conception with the radiance of an entirely unique holiness, the Virgin of Nazareth is greeted, on God's command, by an angel messenger as "full of grace" (cf. Lk 1:28), and to the heavenly messenger she replies: "Behold the handmaid of the Lord, be it done unto me according to thy word" (Lk 1:38). Thus Mary, a daughter of Adam, consenting to the divine Word, became the mother of Jesus, the one and only Mediator. Embracing God's salvific will with a full heart and impeded by no sin, she devoted herself totally as a handmaid of the Lord to the person and work of her Son, under him and with him, by the grace of almighty God, serving the mystery of redemption. Rightly, therefore, the holy Fathers see her as used by God not merely in a passive way, but as freely cooperating in the work of human salvation through faith and obedience. For, as

---

5. Cf. St. Germanus of Constantinople, *Hom. in Annunt. Deiparae: PG* 98, 328 A; *In Dorm.* 2: col. 357; Anastasius of Antioch, *Serm. 2 de Annunt.,* 2: *PG* 89, 1377 AB; *Serm.* 3, 2: col. 1388 C; St. Andrew of Crete, *Can. in B. V. Nat.* 4: *PG* 97, 1321 B; *In B. V. Nat.,* 1: col. 812 A; *Hom. in Dorm.* 1: col. 1068 C; St. Sophronius, *Or. 2 in Annunt.,* 18: *PG* 87 (3), 3237 BD.

St. Irenaeus says, she "being obedient, became the cause of salvation for herself and for the whole human race."[6] Hence not a few of the early Fathers gladly assert in their preaching, "The knot of Eve's disobedience was untied by Mary's obedience; what the virgin Eve bound through her unbelief, the Virgin Mary loosened by her faith."[7] Comparing Mary with Eve, they call Mary "the Mother of the living,"[8] and still more often they say: "death through Eve, life through Mary."[9]

57. This union of the Mother with the Son in the work of salvation is made manifest from the time of Christ's virginal conception up to his death. It is shown first of all when Mary, arising in haste to go to visit Elizabeth, is greeted by her as blessed because of her belief in the promise of salvation and the precursor leaped with joy in the womb of his mother (cf. Lk 1:41–45). This union is manifest also at the birth of our Lord, who did not diminish his mother's virginal integrity but sanctified it[10] when the Mother of God joyfully showed her firstborn Son to the shepherds and Magi. When she presented him to the Lord in the temple, making the offering of the poor, she heard Simeon foretelling at the same time that her Son would be a sign of contradiction and that a sword would pierce the mother's soul, that out of many hearts thoughts might be revealed (cf. Lk 2:34–35). When the child Jesus was lost and they had sought him sorrowing, his parents found him in the temple, taken up with the things that were his Father's business, and they did not understand the word of their Son. His Mother indeed kept these things to be pondered over in her heart (cf. Lk 2:41–51).

58. In the public life of Jesus, Mary makes significant appearances. This is so even at the very beginning, when at the marriage feast of Cana, moved with pity, she brought about by her intercession the beginning of miracles of Jesus the Messiah (cf. Jn 2:1–11). In the course of her Son's preaching she received the words whereby, in extolling a king-

---

6. St. Irenaeus, *Against Heretics,* III, 22, 4: *PG* 7, 959 A; Harvey, 2, 123.

7. St. Irenaeus, *Against Heretics,* III, 22, 4: *PG* 7, 959 A; Harvey, 2, 124.

8. St. Epiphanius, *Haer.* 78, 18: *PG* 42, 728 CD; 729 AB.

9. St. Jerome, *Epist.* 22, 21: *PL* 22, 408; cf. St. Augustine, *Serm.* 51, 2, 3: *PL* 38, 335; *Serm.* 232, 2: col. 1108; St. Cyril of Jerusalem, *Catech.* 12, 15: *PG* 33, 741 AB; St. John Chrysostom, *In Ps.* 44, 7: *PG* 55, 193; St. John Damascene, *Hom. 2 in Dorm. B.M.V.,* 3: *PG* 96, 728.

10. Cf. Council of Lateran, (649 AD), can. 3: Mansi 10, 1151; St. Leo the Great, *Epist. ad Flav.: PL* 54, 759; Council of Chalcedon: Mansi 7, 462; St. Ambrose, *De Inst. Virg.: PL* 16, 320.

dom beyond the calculations and bonds of flesh and blood, he declared blessed (cf. Mk 3:35; par. Lk 11:27–28) those who heard and kept the Word of God, as she was faithfully doing (cf. Lk 2:19, 51). After this manner the Blessed Virgin advanced in her pilgrimage of faith, and faithfully persevered in her union with her Son unto the cross, where she stood, in keeping with the divine plan (cf. Jn 19:25), grieving exceedingly with her only-begotten Son, uniting herself with a maternal heart with his sacrifice, and lovingly consenting to the immolation of this victim which she herself had brought forth. Finally, she was given by the same Christ Jesus dying on the cross as a mother to his disciple with these words: "Woman, behold thy son" (cf. Jn 19:26–27).[11]

59. But since it has pleased God not to manifest solemnly the mystery of the salvation of the human race before he would pour forth the Spirit promised by Christ, we see the apostles before the day of Pentecost "persevering with one mind in prayer with the women and Mary, the Mother of Jesus, and with his brethren" (Acts 1:14), and Mary by her prayers imploring the gift of the Spirit, who had already overshadowed her in the annunciation. Finally, the Immaculate Virgin, preserved free from all guilt of original sin,[12] on the completion of her earthly sojourn was taken up body and soul into heavenly glory[13] and exalted by the Lord as queen of the universe, that she might be the more fully conformed to her Son, the Lord of lords (cf. Rv 19:16) and the conqueror of sin and death.[14]

III. On the Blessed Virgin and the Church

60. There is but one Mediator, as we know from the words of the Apostle, "for there is one God and one mediator of God and men, the man Christ Jesus, who gave himself a redemption for all" (1 Tm 2:5–6).

---

11. Cf. Pius XII, Encyclical Letter *Mystici Corporis* (June 29, 1943): *AAS* 35 (1943), 247–248.

12. Cf. Pius IX, Bull *Ineffabilis* (Dec. 8, 1854): Acts of Pius IX, I, I, 616; Denz. 1641 (2803).

13. Cf. Pius XII, Apostolic Constitution *Munificentissimus* (Nov. 1, 1950): *AAS* 42 (1950): Denz. 2333 (3903); cf. St. John Damascene, *Enc. in Dorm. Dei Genitricis,* Hom. 2 and 3: *PG* 96, 721–761, especially col. 728 B; St. Germanus of Constantinople, *In St. Dei Gen. Dorm., Serm.* 1: *PG* 98 (6), 340–348; *Serm.* 3: col. 361; St. Modestus of Jerusalem, *In Dorm. SS. Deiparae: PG* 86 (2), 3277–3312.

14. Cf. Pius XII, Encyclical Letter *Ad Coeli Reginam* (Oct. 11, 1954): *AAS* 46 (1954), 633–636; Denz. 3913ff.; cf. St. Andrew of Crete, *Hom. 3 in Dorm. SS. Deiparae: PG* 97, 1089–1109; St. John Damascene, *De Fide Orth.,* IV, 14: *PG* 94, 1153–1161.

The maternal duty of Mary toward men in no wise obscures or diminishes this unique mediation of Christ, but rather shows his power. For all the salvific influence of the Blessed Virgin on men originates, not from some inner necessity, but from the divine pleasure. It flows forth from the superabundance of the merits of Christ, rests on his mediation, depends entirely on it and draws all its power from it. In no way does it impede, but rather does it foster the immediate union of the faithful with Christ.

61. Predestined from eternity to be the Mother of God by that decree of divine Providence which determined the Incarnation of the Word, the Blessed Virgin was on this earth the virgin Mother of the Redeemer, and above all others and in a singular way the generous associate and humble handmaid of the Lord. She conceived, brought forth and nourished Christ. She presented him to the Father in the temple, and was united with him by compassion as he died on the cross. In this singular way she cooperated by her obedience, faith, hope and burning charity in the work of the Savior in giving back supernatural life to souls. Wherefore she is our mother in the order of grace.

62. This maternity of Mary in the order of grace began with the consent which she gave in faith at the annunciation and which she sustained without wavering beneath the cross, and lasts until the eternal fulfillment of all the elect. Taken up to heaven she did not lay aside this salvific duty, but by her constant intercession continued to bring us the gifts of eternal salvation.[15] By her maternal charity, she cares for the brethren of her Son, who still journey on earth surrounded by dangers and difficulties, until they are led into the happiness of their true home. Therefore the Blessed Virgin is invoked by the Church under the titles of Advocate, Auxiliatrix, Adjutrix and Mediatrix.[16] This, however, is to be so understood that it neither takes away from nor adds anything to the dignity and efficaciousness of Christ the one Mediator.[17]

For no creature could ever be counted as equal with the incarnate

---

15. Cf. Kleutgen, corrected text *De Mysterio Verbi Incarnati,* ch. IV: Mansi 53, 290; cf. St. Andrew of Crete, *In Nat. Mariae, Serm.* 4: *PG* 97, 865 A; St. Germanus of Constantinople, *In Annunt. Deiparae: PG* 98, 321 BC; *In Dorm. Deiparae,* III: col. 361 D; St. John Damascene, *In Dorm. B. V. Mariae,* Hom. 1, 8: *PG* 96, 712 BC–713 A.

16. Cf. Leo XIII, Encyclical Letter *Adiutricem Populi* (Sept. 5, 1895): *AAS* 15 (1895–96), 303; St. Pius X, Encyclical Letter *Ad Diem Illum* (Feb. 2, 1904): *Acta,* I, 154 Denz. 1978a (3370); Pius XI, Encyclical Letter *Miserentissimus* (May 8, 1928): *AAS* 20 (1928), 178; Pius XII, *Radio Message* (May 13, 1946): *AAS* 38 (1946), 266.

17. St. Ambrose, *Epist.* 63: *PL* 16, 1218.

Word and Redeemer. Just as the priesthood of Christ is shared in various ways both by the ministers and by the faithful, and as the one goodness of God is really communicated in different ways to his creatures, so also the unique mediation of the Redeemer does not exclude but rather gives rise to a manifold cooperation which is but a sharing in this one source.

The Church does not hesitate to profess this subordinate role of Mary. It knows it through unfailing experience of it and commends it to the hearts of the faithful, so that encouraged by this maternal help they may the more intimately adhere to the Mediator and Redeemer.

63. By reason of the gift and role of divine maternity, by which she is united with her Son, the Redeemer, and with his singular graces and functions, the Blessed Virgin is also intimately united with the Church. As St. Ambrose taught, the Mother of God is a type of the Church in the order of faith, charity and perfect union with Christ.[18] For in the mystery of the Church, which is itself rightly called mother and virgin, the Blessed Virgin stands out in eminent and singular fashion as exemplar both of virgin and mother.[19] By her belief and obedience, not knowing man but overshadowed by the Holy Spirit, as the new Eve she brought forth on earth the very Son of the Father, showing an undefiled faith, not in the word of the ancient serpent, but in that of God's messenger. The Son whom she brought forth is he whom God placed as the first-born among many brethren (Rm 8:29), namely the faithful, in whose birth and education she cooperates with a maternal love.

64. The Church indeed, contemplating her hidden sanctity, imitating her charity and faithfully fulfilling the Father's will, by receiving the Word of God in faith becomes herself a mother. By her preaching she brings forth to a new and immortal life the sons who are born to her in baptism, conceived of the Holy Spirit and born of God. She herself is a virgin, who keeps whole and entire the faith given to her by her spouse. Imitating the mother of her Lord, and by the power of the Holy Spirit, she keeps with virginal purity an entire faith, a firm hope and a sincere charity.[20]

---

18. St. Ambrose, *Expos. Lc.* II, 7: *PL* 15, 1555.

19. Cf. Pseudo-Peter Damian, *Serm.* 63: *PL* 144, 861 AB; Godfrey of St. Victor, *In Nat. B. M.,* Ms. Paris, Mazarine, 1002, fol. 109; Gerhoch of Reichersberg, *De Gloria et Honore Filii Hominis,* 10: *PL* 194, 1105 AB.

20. St. Ambrose, *loc. cit.* and *Expos. Lc.* X, 24–25: *PL* 15, 1810; St. Augustine, *In Io. Tr.* 13, 12: *PL* 35, 1499; cf. *Serm.* 191, 2, 3: *PL* 38, 1010, etc.; cf. also Ven. Bede, *In Lc. Expos.* I, ca 2: *PL* 92, 330; Isaac of Stella, *Serm.* 51: *PL* 194, 1863 A.

65. But while in the most holy Virgin the Church has already reached that perfection whereby she is without spot or wrinkle, the followers of Christ still strive to increase in holiness by conquering sin (cf. Eph 5:27). And so they turn their eyes to Mary, who shines forth to the whole community of the elect as the model of virtues. Piously meditating on her and contemplating her in the light of the Word made man, the Church with reverence enters more intimately into the great mystery of the Incarnation and becomes more and more like her spouse. For Mary, who since her entry into salvation history unites in herself and reechoes the greatest teachings of the faith as she is proclaimed and venerated, calls the faithful to her Son and his sacrifice and to the love of the Father. Seeking after the glory of Christ, the Church becomes more like her exalted type, and continually progresses in faith, hope and charity, seeking and doing the will of God in all things. Hence, the Church, in her apostolic work also, justly looks to her, who brought forth Christ, who was conceived of the Holy Spirit and born of the Virgin, that through the Church he may be born and may increase in the hearts of the faithful also. The Virgin in her own life lived an example of that maternal love, by which it behooves that all should be animated who cooperate in the apostolic mission of the Church for the regeneration of men.

IV. The Cult of the Blessed Virgin in the Church

66. Placed by the grace of God, as God's Mother, next to her Son and exalted above all angels and men, Mary intervened in the mysteries of Christ and is justly honored by a special cult in the Church. Clearly, from earliest times the Blessed Virgin is honored under the title of Mother of God, under whose protection the faithful took refuge in all their dangers and necessities.[21] Hence, after the Synod of Ephesus the cult of the People of God toward Mary wonderfully increased in veneration and love, in invocation and imitation, according to her own prophetic words: "All generations shall call me blessed, because he that is mighty hath done great things to me" (Lk 1:48). This cult, as it always existed, although it is altogether singular, differs essentially from the cult of adoration which is offered to the incarnate Word, as well to the Father and the Holy Spirit, and it is most favorable to it. The various

---

21. *Sub tuum praesidium.*

forms of piety toward the Mother of God, which the Church, within the limits of sound and orthodox doctrine, according to the conditions of time and place, and the nature and ingenuity of the faithful, has approved, bring it about that while the Mother is honored, the Son, through whom all things have their being (cf. Col 1:15–16) and in whom it has pleased the Father that all fullness should dwell (Col 1:19), is rightly known, loved and glorified, and that all his commands are observed.

67. This most holy synod deliberately teaches this Catholic doctrine and at the same time admonishes all the sons of the Church that the cult, especially the liturgical cult, of the Blessed Virgin be generously fostered, and the practices and exercises of piety, recommended by the magisterium of the Church toward her in the course of centuries, be made of great moment, and those decrees, which have been given in the early days regarding the cult of images of Christ, the Blessed Virgin and the saints, be religiously observed.[22] But it exhorts theologians and preachers of the divine Word to abstain zealously both from all gross exaggerations as well as from petty narrow-mindedness in considering the singular dignity of the Mother of God.[23] Following the study of Sacred Scripture, the holy Fathers, the doctors and liturgy of the Church, and under the guidance of the Church's magisterium, let them rightly illustrate the duties and privileges of the Blessed Virgin which always look to Christ, the source of all truth, sanctity and piety. Let them assiduously keep away from whatever, either by word or deed, could lead separated brethren or any other into error regarding the true doctrine of the Church. Let the faithful remember moreover that true devotion consists neither in sterile or transitory affection, nor in a certain vain credulity, but proceeds from true faith, by which we are led to know the excellence of the Mother of God, and we are moved to a filial love toward our mother and to the imitation of her virtues.

---

22. Second Council of Nicea (787): Mansi 13, 378–379; Denz. 302 (600–601); Council of Trent, Session 25: Mansi 33, 171–172.

23. Cf. Pius XII, *Radio Message* (Oct. 24, 1954): *AAS* 46 (1954), 679; Encyclical Letter *Ad Coeli Reginam* (Oct. 11, 1954): *AAS* 46 (1954), 637.

V. Mary the Sign of Created Hope and Solace to the Wandering People of God

68. In the interim, just as the Mother of Jesus, glorified in body and soul in heaven, is the image and beginning of the Church as it is to be perfected in the world to come, so too does she shine forth on earth, until the day of the Lord shall come (cf. 2 Pt 3:10), as a sign of sure hope and solace to the People of God during its sojourn on earth.

69. It gives great joy and comfort to this holy and general synod that even among the separated brethren there are some who give due honor to the Mother of our Lord and Savior, especially among the Orientals, who with devout mind and fervent impulse give honor to the Mother of God, ever Virgin.[24] The entire body of the faithful pours forth urgent supplications to the Mother of God and Mother of men, that she, who aided the beginnings of the Church by her prayers, may now, exalted as she is above all the angels and saints, intercede before her Son in the fellowship of all the saints, until all families of people, whether they are honored with the title of Christian or whether they still do not know the Savior, may be happily gathered together in peace and harmony into one People of God, for the glory of the most holy and undivided Trinity.

Each and all these items which are set forth in this dogmatic constitution have met with the approval of the Council fathers. And We by the apostolic power given Us by Christ, together with the venerable fathers in the Holy Spirit, approve, decree and establish it and command that what has thus been decided in the Council be promulgated for the glory of God.

Given in Rome at St. Peter's on November 21, 1964.

---

24. Cf. Pius XI, Encyclical Letter *Ecclesiam Dei* (Nov. 12, 1923): *AAS* 15 (1923) 581; Pius XII, Encyclical Letter *Fulgens Corona* (Sept. 8, 1953): *AAS* 45 (1953), 590–591.

THE MONTH OF MAY

Mense Maio

Encyclical Letter of Pope Paul VI
April 30, 1965

INTRODUCTION

Published five months after *Lumen Gentium, Mense Maio* calls the faithful to pray for peace in the world. The pastoral urgency of the struggle with communism prompted the letter.

Historical Perspectives

It is the first magisterial document after the Council to include the title "Mother of the Church." On November 21, 1964, the day *Lumen Gentium* was promulgated, Paul VI had officially given Mary this title. He proclaimed Mary as: "...most holy Mary Mother of the Church, that is of the whole Christian people, both faithful and pastors, who call her a most loving Mother.... We decree that henceforth the whole Christian people should, by this most sweet name, give still greater honor to the Mother of God and address prayers to her."[1]

In post-Vatican II catechesis, the title "Mother of the Church" has been given attention on a par with the Vatican II Marian references. The title appeared repeatedly in post-Vatican II Marian documents and in catechetical guidelines.

Mense Maio is a short document, and may at first appear to have only immediate pastoral significance. The text is not entirely devoted to Mary, but its Marian call to prayer is woven throughout. Although the document does not quote *Lumen Gentium,* it states that Mary had as-

---

1. *AAS* 56 (1964), 1015. See: George W. O'Shea, "Pope Paul VI and the 'Mother of the Church,'" *Marian Studies* 16 (1965): 21–28; Anthony T. Padovano, "Mary, Mother of the Church," *Marian Studies* 26 (1966): 27–45; Michael O'Carroll, C.S.Sp., "Mother of the Church," *Theotókos: A Theological Encyclopedia of the Blessed Virgin Mary* (Wilmington, Delaware: Michael Glazier, Inc., 1982), 251–252.

sisted the Council: "From the beginning of the Council she [Mary] has been unstinting in her loving help and will certainly not fail to continue her assistance to the final stage of the work" (*MM* 4).

The Teaching

The major theological, devotional and pastoral content reflects titles such as "Queen of Peace," in light of Pope Pius XII's encyclical, *Ad Caeli Reginam* (October 11, 1954), which established a feast in honor of Our Lady Queen of Heaven.[2] The encyclical also echoed the teaching of Pope Pius XII "to pilgrims at Fatima, May 13, 1946."[3]

The doctrinal aspects of *Mense Maio* consider the holiness of Mary (*MM* 10). "Every encounter with her can only result in an encounter with Christ himself.... We continually turn to Mary...to seek for the Christ she holds in her arms" (*MM* 2). "Mary most holy is his appointed steward and the generous bestower of the treasures of his mercy" (*MM* 10).

Intercession is a predominant theme. "The gifts of God's mercy come down to us" from Mary (*MM* 1); "our petitions find their way more easily to the compassionate heart of Our Blessed Lady" (*MM* 3). The pope urges the faithful to call on "the intercession and protection of the Virgin Mary, who is the Queen of Peace" (*MM* 9).

The wording of the document reflects pre-conciliar titles and devotion. Later documents take Christ's one mediation more into account than *Mense Maio* does. They more clearly show the relationship between Christ and Mary in the act of intercession. Nevertheless, Mary's humanness and our identification with her is reflected: [Mary] "knows the sufferings and troubles of life here below, the weariness of everyday work, the hardships and privations of poverty, the suffering of Calvary" (*MM* 10).

Whereas *Lumen Gentium* did not specify particular devotions, *Mense Maio* encourages the faithful to honor Mary in May, "a month which the piety of the faithful has specially dedicated to Our Blessed

---

2. *AAS* 46 (1954), 625–640. See also: O'Carroll, "Queen of Peace" and "Queenship, Mary's" in *Theotókos*, 301f.; Christopher O'Donnell, "The Queenship of Mary," in *At Worship with Mary* (Wilmington, DE: Michael Glazier, 1988), 148–157.

3. O'Carroll, 301.

Lady" (*MM* 1). It recommends prayer and veneration "in church and in the privacy of the home," (*MM* 1) and stresses the rosary (*MM* 11). *Mense Maio* asked the bishops to "make provision for special prayers in each diocese and every parish during...May, devoting...the feast of Our Lady Queen of Heaven to solemn public prayers" (*MM* 11).[4] The bishops are asked to teach that "to obtain God's light and blessings...we [are to] place our confidence in her...[the] Mother of the Church" (*MM* 7).

Today

Pope Paul VI's letter reaffirms pastoral methods used previous to Vatican II. The document acts as a bridge linking Marian devotion of the past and of the future.

---

4. Before the renewal of the liturgical calendar, the Feast of Our Lady Queen of Heaven was celebrated on May 31. In the revised calendar it is a memorial held on August 22.

TOPICAL OUTLINE

1. Introduction: Mary and the month of May (1)

2. Mary is the path that leads to Christ (2)

3. Appeal for prayers to Mary (3)

    A. For the Church and the ecumenical council (4)

    B. For peace in the world (5–9)

    C. Mary's intercession (10)

    D. Conclusion (11)

THE MONTH OF MAY

Mense Maio

Promulgated by His Holiness Pope Paul VI
On April 30, 1965

ENCYCLICAL LETTER ON THE OCCASION OF THE FIRST OF MAY

Venerable Brothers,

1. As the month of May draws near, a month which the piety of the faithful has specially dedicated to Our Blessed Lady, we are gladdened at the thought of the moving tribute of faith and love which Catholics in every part of the world will soon be paying to the Queen of Heaven. For this is the month during which Christians, both in church and in the privacy of the home, offer up to Mary from their hearts an especially fervent and loving homage of prayer and veneration. In this month, too, the gifts of God's mercy come down to us from her throne in greater abundance.

2. This pious practice, by which the Blessed Virgin is honored and the Christian people enriched with spiritual gifts, gladdens and consoles us. Mary remains ever the path that leads to Christ. Every encounter with her can only result in an encounter with Christ himself. For what other reason do we continually turn to Mary than to seek for the Christ she holds in her arms—to seek in her, through her and with her the Savior to whom men, in the perplexities and dangers of life here below,

must of necessity have recourse, and to whom they feel the ever recurring need of turning as to a haven of safety and an all-surpassing source of life?

3. It is precisely because the month of May is a powerful incentive to more fervent and trusting prayer, and because during it our petitions find their way more easily to the compassionate heart of Our Blessed Lady, that it has been a custom dear to our predecessors to choose this month, dedicated to Mary, for inviting the Christian people to offer up public prayers, whenever the needs of the Church demanded it, or whenever danger hovered menacingly over the world. This year, we too, venerable brothers, feel the need of sending out a similar appeal to the whole Catholic world. When we look at the present needs of the Church or at the state of peace in the world, we have compelling reasons for believing that the present hour is especially grave, that it makes a call for united prayer from the whole Christian people more than ever a matter of urgency.

4. The first reason for this appeal is suggested to us by this historic moment in the life of the Church, the period of the Ecumenical Council. This momentous event confronts the Church with the immense problem of how to renew herself in accordance with the needs of the times. On its outcome will depend for a long time to come the future of the Spouse of Christ and the destiny of innumerable souls. It is God's great time in the life of the Church and in world history. In this regard, although the amount of work happily brought to completion is great, heavy tasks still await you in the next session, which will be the final one. After that will follow the equally important period of implementing the Council's decisions, which likewise will demand the united effort of clergy and faithful for the effective and beneficial development of the seeds sown during the Council. To obtain God's light and blessings on this great volume of work ahead of us, we place our confidence in her whom we had the joy of proclaiming Mother of the Church in the last session. From the beginning of the Council she has been unstinting in her loving help and will certainly not fail to continue her assistance to the final stage of the work.

5. The other reason for our appeal comes from the international situation, which, as you are well aware, venerable brothers, is darker and more uncertain than ever, now that grave new threats are endangering the supreme benefit of world peace. Today, as if no lesson had been learned from the tragic experiences of the two conflicts which shed

blood on the first half of our century, we have the dreadful spectacle in certain parts of the world of antagonism on the increase between peoples, and see repeated the dangerous phenomenon of recourse to arms, instead of negotiation, to settle the disputes of the opposing parties. This means that populations of entire nations are subjected to unspeakable sufferings, caused by agitation, guerrilla warfare, acts of war, ever growing in extent and intensity, which could at any moment produce the spark for a terrible fresh conflict.

6. In view of these grave dangers to international life, and conscious of our duty as supreme Pastor, we judge it necessary to make known our anxieties and our fear that the disputes will become so embittered as to degenerate into a bloody war. We beg all who hold responsibility in public life not to remain deaf to the unanimous desire of mankind which wants peace. We ask that they do all in their power to preserve the peace that is threatened, and continue at all times to foster and encourage conversations and negotiations at all levels, that the dangerous resort to force with all its lamentable consequences, material, spiritual and moral, may be halted. Along the lines marked out by law, let efforts be made to single out for recognition every true and sincere yearning for justice and peace. Through this recognition let such yearnings find encouragement and fulfillment, and let confidence enrich every loyal act of good will so that the forces of order may prevail over those of disorder and ruin.

7. Unfortunately, in this painful situation we are forced to recognize with a heavy heart that all too often oblivion swallows up the respect due to the sacred and inviolable character of human life, and that recourse is had to methods and attitudes which stand in open revolt against the moral sensibilities and the customs of a civilized people. In this respect we cannot fail to raise our voice in defense of the dignity of man and of Christian civilization; we cannot fail to condemn acts of guerrilla warfare and of terrorism, the practice of holding hostages and of taking reprisals against unarmed civilians. These are crimes which not only reverse the development of the sense of what is fair and humane, but also embitter even more the hearts of those in conflict. These outrages can block the paths still open to mutual good will, or at least can render negotiations more difficult, which, if conducted with openness and fairness, could lead to a reasonable settlement.

8. These deep concerns of ours, as you well know, venerable brothers, are dictated not by any narrow interests, but solely by the desire to protect all who are suffering, and to promote the true welfare of all

peoples. We hope that awareness of personal responsibilities to God and to history will be powerful enough to impel governments to continue their generous efforts to safeguard peace, and to remove as far as possible those obstacles, real or imagined, which interfere with the achievement of secure and sincere agreement.

9. But peace, venerable brothers, is not merely of our own making; it is also, and particularly, a gift from God. Peace comes from heaven, and it will truly reign among men when we finally deserve to receive it from Almighty God who holds in his hands, not only the happiness and the destinies of peoples, but also their very hearts. Therefore, we shall do our utmost to obtain this incomparable blessing by prayer, praying, indeed, with constancy and watchfulness, as the Church has always prayed from her earliest days, and in a special way calling on the intercession and protection of the Virgin Mary, who is the Queen of Peace.

10. So, venerable brothers, let our prayers ascend to Mary in this month of hers, to implore her graces and favors with increased fervor and confidence. And if the grave faults of men weigh heavy in the scales of God's justice and provoke its just punishments, we also know that the Lord is "the Father of mercies and the God of all comfort" (2 Cor 1:3), and that Mary most holy is his appointed steward and the generous bestower of the treasures of his mercy. May she, who knows the sufferings and troubles of life here below, the weariness of everyday work, the hardships and privations of poverty, the sufferings of Calvary, bring help to the needs of the Church and the world, heed the appeals for peace rising to her from every part of the world, and enlighten those who rule the destinies of men. May she prevail on God, Lord of the winds and storms, to still also the tempests in men's conflicting hearts and "grant us peace in our time," true peace based on the solid lasting foundations of justice and love—of justice granted to the weakest as to the strongest, and love which prevents egoism from leading men astray, so that each one's rights may be safeguarded without forgetfulness or denial of the rights of others.

11. Inform the faithful in your charge, venerable brothers, in whatever way you judge best, of our wishes and exhortation, and make provision for special prayers in each diocese and every parish during this coming month of May, devoting in a special manner the Feast of Our Lady Queen of Heaven to solemn public prayers for the intentions we have mentioned. We would point out that we rely particularly on the prayers of the innocent and the suffering, for their voices more than any

others reach heaven and disarm God's justice. And since this is a fitting occasion, do not fail to lay careful stress on the saying of the rosary, the prayer so dear to Our Lady and so highly recommended by the Supreme Pontiffs. By this means the faithful can most pleasingly and most effectively carry out our Divine Master's command: "Ask and it shall be given you; seek and you shall find; knock and it shall be opened" (Mt 7:7).

With these thoughts and in the hope that our exhortation will be readily received in the souls of all, we grant to you from our heart, venerable brothers, and to all the faithful in your care, our apostolic blessing.

April 30, 1965

THE GREAT SIGN

Signum Magnum

Letter of Pope Paul VI
May 13, 1967

INTRODUCTION

The document addresses growing pastoral concerns regarding Marian devotion.

Historical Perspectives

Signum Magnum was presented during Paul VI's visit to Fatima to commemorate the 50th anniversary of the apparition.[1] The pope repeated the consecration of the world to the Immaculate Heart of Mary: "We have come as a lowly and trustful pilgrim to this blessed sanctuary. Here today we are celebrating the 50th anniversary of the apparitions at Fatima, and the 25th anniversary of the consecration of the world to the Immaculate Heart of Mary."[2]

Signum Magnum notes that Mary has been honored throughout history, establishes the basis for Marian devotion as well as its value for Christian unity, and clarifies that Marian devotion is consistent with liturgical reform.[3]

The document stresses Mary's privileges and her greatness, but also shows her humanness, inviting us to imitate her. Even though *Signum Magnum* builds on *Lumen Gentium,* its tone reflects more the privilege-centered Mariology prior to Vatican II than the Christ-centered and ecclesial-centered theology of the Council. The document accents Mary's responsibility toward the Church of which she is model, mother and great sign. Mary is not only a sign, but she has a hand in the education of the Christian.

---

1. O'Carroll, 326

2. Pope Paul VI, "Prayer Intentions at Fatima," *The Pope Speaks* 12 (1967): 193–96.

3. *Signum Magnum* was not published with article numbers; the numbers given are my numeration of paragraphs.

The Teaching

Two aspects are specifically treated: Mary as Mother and model, and our imitation of her.

After the Council, the theme of Mary's faith began to surface. She too met life's challenges as she grew in faith. The text speaks of imitating the virtues of Mary (*SM* Part II, based on *LG* 67). Mary is to be thanked, venerated, praised and loved; she is to be imitated in the example of goodness she bequeathed to us; imitating her "makes it more pleasant and easier" (*SM* II, 1) to imitate Christ. The document recommends Marian devotion, especially in the sections on Marian piety. The pope speaks of many ways to venerate Mary, such as religious ceremonies and liturgical services. *Lumen Gentium* 66–68 states that Mary deserves a special cult, but this cult will not interfere with the reform of the liturgy nor detract from the cult of adoration due to the Trinity. Contemplating "her maternal and compassionate heart"[4] Christians "draw from her a stimulus for trusting prayer, a spur to the practice of penance and to the holy fear of God" (*SM* II, 4). The document reflects the seriousness of the Fatima message, but does not expound it (*SM* II, 8).

Today

In *Signum Magnum* the bishops were exhorted to encourage the clergy and faithful entrusted to their care to develop their devotion to the Virgin Mother of God. All members of the Church were to be reminded of the close connection between Mary's spiritual motherhood (cf. *LG* 60–65) and the duties of all the redeemed toward her as Mother of the Church. These recommendations continue to be pastorally valid today.

The document encourages consecration to Mary's Immaculate Heart. Regarding catechesis, *Signum Magnum* calls for greater trust and devotion toward the Virgin Mother of God. Christians are to honor her and imitate her, for she is the great sign of the Church in the contemporary world, the great sign fully consecrated to Christ. She participates in his work of redemption by her close association with him and her cooperation with grace. Mary is also a sign of unity for the churches, and her intercession will help to bring about unity and salvation.

---

4. Pius XII, Radio address to people of Portugal during Fatima celebration (May 13, 1946): *AAS* 38 (1946), 264. A gold crown was placed on Mary's statue in the name of the Holy Father.

TOPICAL OUTLINE

1. Introduction: Mary as Mother of the Church

2. Part I: Mary as a model of the virtues

    A. Mary's intercession

    B. Her example

    C. Mary's life as an example of loving service

3. Part II: Imitation of Mary

    A. True devotion involves imitating Mary's virtues

    B. Marian devotion leads to Jesus Christ

    C. Mary as the New Eve

    D. Invitation to prayer and penance

    E. Christ gave us Mary as a model

    F. Marian devotion in the life of the Church

    G. Mary and ecumenism

    H. Consecration to Mary

THE GREAT SIGN

Signum Magnum

Promulgated by His Holiness Pope Paul VI
On May 13, 1967

To the Catholic Bishops of the World
Venerable brothers, health and apostolic blessings

Introduction

The great sign which the Apostle John saw in heaven, "a woman clothed with the sun" (cf. Rv 12:1), is interpreted by the sacred liturgy,[1] not without foundation, as referring to the most blessed Mary, the mother of all men by the grace of Christ the Redeemer.

The memory, venerable brothers, is still vivid in our mind of the great emotion we felt in proclaiming the august Mother of God as the spiritual Mother of the Church, that is to say, of all the faithful and of the sacred pastors, as the crowning of the third session of the Second Vatican Council, after having solemnly promulgated the *Dogmatic Constitution on the Church.*[2] Great also was the happiness of numerous Council Fathers, as well as of the faithful, who were present at the sacred rite in St. Peter's Basilica and of the entire Christian people scattered throughout the world.

---

1. Cf. Epistle of Mass for the Feast of the Apparition of Mary Immaculate, February 11.
2. Cf. *AAS* 57 (1965), 1–67.

The memory came spontaneously to many minds of the first grandiose triumph achieved by the humble "handmaid of the Lord" (cf. Lk 1:38) when the Fathers from East and West, gathered in an ecumenical council at Ephesus in the year 431, greeted Mary as *"Theotókos"*— *genitrix* of God. The Christian population of the illustrious city associated themselves with a jubilant impulse of faith with the exultance of the Fathers and accompanied them with torchlights to their dwelling.

Oh! with how much maternal satisfaction the Virgin Mary must have looked on the pastors and the faithful in that glorious hour of the history of the Church, recognizing in the hymns of praise, raised in honor principally of the Son and then in her own, the echo of the prophetic canticle which she herself, on the impulse of the Holy Spirit, had raised to the Most High:

> My soul magnifies the Lord,
> and my spirit rejoices in God my Savior,
> because he has regarded the lowliness of his handmaid;
> for behold, henceforth all generations shall call me blessed;
> because he who is mighty has done great things for me
> and holy is his name (Lk 1:46, 48–49).

On the occasion of the religious ceremonies which are taking place at this time in honor of the Virgin Mother of God in Fatima, Portugal, where she is venerated by countless numbers of the faithful for her motherly and compassionate heart,[3] we wish to call the attention of all sons of the Church once more to the indissoluble link between the spiritual motherhood of Mary, so amply illustrated in the (Council's) *Dogmatic Constitution on the Church*[4] and the duties of redeemed men toward her, the Mother of the Church.

Once it is acknowledged, by virtue of the numerous testimonies offered by the sacred texts and by the holy Fathers and remembered in the constitution mentioned above, that "Mary, the Mother of God and Mother of the Redeemer"[5] has been "united to him by a close and indissoluble tie"[6] and that she has a most singular role in "the mystery of the

---

3. *Radio Message* of Pius XII, May 13, 1946, given for the Christians of Portugal, *AAS* 38 (1946), 264.

4. Cf. chapter 8, paragraph 3, on the Blessed Virgin and the Church, *AAS* 57 (1965), 62–65.

5. Cf. ibid., 53, p. 58.

6. Cf. ibid.

Incarnate Word and of the Mystical Body,"[7] that is to say, in "the economy of salvation,"[8] it appears evident that the Virgin is "rightly honored by the Church with a special veneration,[9] particularly liturgical,"[10] not only as "the most holy Mother of God, who took part in the mysteries of Christ,"[11] but also "as the Mother of the Church."[12]

Nor is it to be feared that liturgical reform, if put into practice according to the formula "the law of faith must establish the law of prayer"[13] may be detrimental to the "wholly singular" veneration[14] due to the Virgin Mary for her prerogatives, first among these being the dignity of the Mother of God. Nor is it to be feared that the greater veneration, liturgical as well as private, given to her may obscure or diminish "the adoration which is offered to the Incarnate Word, as well as to the Father and to the Holy Spirit."[15]

Accordingly, without wishing to restate here, venerable brothers, the traditional doctrine of the Church regarding the function of the Mother of God on the plane of salvation and her relations with the Church, we believe that, if we dwell on the consideration of two truths which are very important for the renewal of Christian life, we would be doing something of great utility for the souls of the faithful.

---

7. Ibid., 54, p. 59.

8. Ibid., 55, p. 59.

9. Ibid., 66, p. 65.

10. *Allocution to the Council Fathers in the Vatican Basilica on the Feast of the Presentation,* third session of the Council, *AAS* 56 (1964), 1016.

11. Cf. Second Vatican Ecumenical Council, Dogmatic Constitution on the Church *Lumen Gentium,* 66: *AAS* 57 (1965), 65.

12. Cf. ibid., 67, p. 65.

13. Pius XII, Encyclical Letter *Mediator Dei: AAS* 39 (1947), 541.

14. Cf. Second Vatican Ecumenical Council, Dogmatic Constitution on the Church *Lumen Gentium,* 66: *AAS* 57 (1965), 65.

15. Ibid., 66, p. 65.

PART I

The first truth is this: Mary is the Mother of the Church not only because she is the Mother of Christ and his most intimate associate in "the new economy when the Son of God took a human nature from her, that he might in the mysteries of his flesh free man from sin,"[16] but also because "she shines forth to the whole community of the elect as a model of the virtues."[17] Indeed, just as no human mother can limit her task to the generation of a new man, but must extend it to the function of nourishing and educating her offspring, thus the Blessed Virgin Mary, after participating in the redeeming sacrifice of the Son, and in such an intimate way as to deserve to be proclaimed by him the Mother not only of his disciple John but—may we be allowed to affirm it—of mankind which he in some way represents,[18] now continues to fulfill from heaven her maternal function as the cooperator in the birth and development of divine life in the individual souls of redeemed men. This is a most consoling truth which, by the free consent of God the All-Wise, is an integrating part of the mystery of human salvation; therefore, it must be held as faith by all Christians.

But in what way does Mary cooperate in the growth of the members of the Mystical Body in the life of grace? First of all, by her unceasing prayers inspired by a most ardent charity. The Holy Virgin, in fact, though rejoicing in the union of the august Trinity, does not forget her Son's advancing, as she herself did in the "pilgrimage of the faith."[19]

---

16. Ibid., 55, p. 60.

17. Ibid., 65, p. 64, also n. 63.

18. Cf. ibid., 58, p. 61; Leo XIII, Encyclical Letter *Adiutricem Populi, Acts of Leo XIII,* 15 (1896), 302.

19. Second Vatican Ecumenical Council, Dogmatic Constitution on the Church *Lumen Gentium,* 58; *AAS* 57 (1967), 61.

Indeed, contemplating them in God and clearly seeing their necessities, in communion with Jesus Christ, "who continues forever and is therefore able at all times to intercede for them" (Heb 7:25), she makes herself their Advocate, Auxiliatrix, Adjutrix and Mediatrix.[20] Of this intercession of hers for the People of God with the Son, the Church has been persuaded, ever since the first centuries, as testified to by this most ancient antiphon which, with some slight difference, forms part of the liturgical prayer in the East as well as in the West: "We seek refuge under the protection of your mercies, O Mother of God; do not reject our supplication in need but save us from perdition, O you who alone are blessed."[21] Nor should anyone believe that the maternal intervention of Mary would prejudice the predominant and irreplaceable efficacy of Christ, our Savior. On the contrary, it draws its strength from the mediation of Christ, of which it is the luminous proof.[22]

But the cooperation of the Mother of the Church in the development of the divine life of the soul does not come to an end with the appeal to the Son. She exercises on redeemed men another influence: that of example, an influence which is indeed most important, according to the well-known axiom: *"Verba movent, exempla trahunt"* (words move, examples attract). In fact, just as the teachings of the parents become far more efficacious if they are strengthened by the example of a life conforming with the norms of human and Christian prudence, so the sweetness and the enchantment emanating from the sublime virtues of the immaculate Mother of God attract souls in an irresistible way to imitation of the divine model, Jesus Christ, of whom she was the most faithful image. Therefore the Council declared: "The Church, devotedly meditating on her and contemplating her in the light of the Word made man, enters more intimately into the supreme mystery of the Incarnation and becomes ever increasingly like her Spouse."[23]

---

20. Cf. Second Vatican Ecumenical Council, Dogmatic Constitution on the Church *Lumen Gentium,* 62: *AAS* 57 (1965), 61.

21. Cf. Dom F. Mercenier, *L'Antienne Mariale grecque la plus ancienne in Le Museon,* 52, 1939, pp. 229–233.

22. Cf. Second Vatican Ecumenical Council, Dogmatic Constitution on the Church *Lumen Gentium,* 62: *AAS* 57 (1965), 63.

23. Ibid., 65, p. 64.

Furthermore, it is well to bear in mind that Mary's eminent sanctity was not only a singular gift of divine liberality. It was also the fruit of the continuous and generous cooperation of her free will in the inner motions of the Holy Spirit. It is because of the perfect harmony between divine grace and the activity of her human nature that the Virgin rendered supreme glory to the Most Holy Trinity and became the illustrious ornament of the Church, which thus greets her in the sacred liturgy: "You are the glory of Jerusalem, the joy of Israel, the honor of our people."[24]

Let us then admire in the pages of the Gospel the testimonies of such sublime harmony. Mary, as soon as she was reassured by the voice of the Angel Gabriel that God had chosen her as the unblemished mother of his only-begotten Son, unhesitatingly gave her consent to a work which would have engaged all the energies of her fragile nature and declared: "Behold the handmaid of the Lord; be it done to me according to thy word" (Lk 1:38). From that moment, she consecrated all of herself to the service not only of the heavenly Father and of the Word Incarnate, who had become her Son, but also to all mankind, having clearly understood that Jesus, in addition to saving his people from the slavery of sin, would become the king of a messianic kingdom, universal and eternal (cf. Mt 1:21; Lk 1:33).

Therefore, the life of Joseph's pure spouse, who remained a virgin "during childbirth and after childbirth"—as the Catholic Church has always believed and professed,[25] and as was fitting for her who was raised to the incomparable dignity of divine motherhood[26]—was a life of such perfect union with the Son that she shared in his joys, sorrows and triumphs. And even after Christ had ascended to heaven she remained united to him by a most ardent love, while she faithfully fulfilled the new mission of spiritual Mother of the most beloved of the disciples and

---

24. Second Antiphon of lauds, Feast of the Immaculate Conception.

25. Cf. St. Leo, martyr, *Letter, Lectis dilectionis tuae to Flavianum, PL* 54, 759; idem., *Letter, Licet per nostros to Julian, Ep. Coensem:* 54; 803; St. Hormisdas, *Ep. Inter ea quae to Justinian, emperor, PL* 63, 407; Lateran Council, October 609, under Martin I, canon 3: Caspar, *ZKG,* 51, 1932, p. 88; Conc. Tolet. XVI, *Symbol,* article 22: J. Madoz, *El Simbolo del Concilio XVI de Toledo in Estudios Onienses,* ser. I, vol. 3, 1946; Second Vatican Ecumenical Council, Dogmatic Constitution on the Church *Lumen Gentium,* 52, 55, 57, 59, 63; *AAS* 57 (1965), 58–64.

26. Cf. St. Thomas, *Summa Theologica,* I, q. 25, a. 6, *ad* 4.

of the nascent Church. It can be asserted that the whole life of the humble handmaid of the Lord, from the moment when she was greeted by the angel, until her Assumption in body and soul to heavenly glory, was a life of loving service.

We, therefore, associating ourselves with the evangelists, with the Fathers and the Doctors of the Church recalled in the Dogmatic Constitution *Lumen Gentium* (Chap. 8), full of admiration, contemplate Mary, firm in her faith, ready in her obedience, simple in humility, exulting in praising the Lord, ardent in charity, strong and constant in the fulfillment of her mission to the point of sacrificing herself, in full communion of sentiments with her Son, who immolated himself on the cross to give men a new life.

Before such splendor of virtue, the first duty of all those who recognize in the Mother of Christ the model of the Church, is to unite themselves to her in giving thanks to the Most High for working great things in Mary for the benefit of all mankind. But this is not enough. It is also the duty of all the faithful to pay as tribute to the most faithful handmaid of the Lord, a veneration of praise, of gratitude and of love because, by a wise and mild divine provision, her free consent and her generous cooperation in the designs of God had, and still have, a great influence in the attainment of human salvation.[27] Therefore every Christian must make St. Anselm's prayer his own: "O glorious Lady, grant that through you we may deserve to ascend to Jesus, your Son, who through you deigned to descend among us."[28]

---

27. Cf. Second Vatican Ecumenical Council, Dogmatic Constitution on the Church *Lumen Gentium,* 56; *AAS* 57 (1965), 60.

28. *Orat.* 54, *PL* 158, 961.

PART II: DEVOUT IMITATION
OF THE VIRTUES OF THE MOST HOLY MARY

1. True Devotion to the Most Holy Mary
Reflects Her Virtues

Neither the grace of the divine Redeemer, nor the powerful intercession of his Mother and our spiritual Mother, nor yet her sublime sanctity, could lead us to the port of salvation if we did not respond to them by our persevering will to honor Jesus Christ and the Holy Virgin with our devout imitation of their sublime virtue.

It is therefore the duty of all Christians to imitate in a reverent spirit the examples of goodness left to them by their heavenly Mother. This, venerable brothers, is the other truth to which we are pleased to call to your attention and to the attention of the faithful entrusted to your pastoral care, that they may second with docility the exhortation of the Fathers of the Second Vatican Council: "Let the faithful remember that true devotion consists neither in fruitless and passing emotion, nor in a certain vain credulity. Rather, it proceeds from true faith, by which we are led to know the excellence of the Mother of God, and are moved to a filial love toward our Mother and to the imitation of her virtues."[29]

Imitation of Jesus Christ is undoubtedly the regal way to be followed to attain sanctity and reproduce in ourselves, according to our forces, the absolute perfection of the heavenly Father. But while the Catholic Church has always proclaimed a truth so sacrosanct, it has also affirmed that imitation of the Virgin Mary, far from distracting souls from the faithful following of Christ, makes it more pleasant and easier for them. For, since she had always done the will of God, she was the

---

29. Second Vatican Ecumenical Council, Dogmatic Constitution on the Church *Lumen Gentium,* 67; *AAS* 57 (1965), 66; cf. St. Thomas, *Summa Theologica,* II–II, q. 81, a. 1, *ad* 1; III, q. 25, aa. 1, 5.

first to deserve the praise which Christ addressed to his disciples: "Whoever does the will of my Father in heaven is my brother and sister and mother" (Mt 12:50).

2. "Through Mary to Jesus"

The general norm "Through Mary to Jesus" is therefore valid also for the imitation of Christ. Nevertheless, let our faith not be perturbed, as if the intervention of a creature in every way similar to us, except as regards sin, offended our personal dignity and prevented the intimacy and immediacy of our relationships of adoration and friendship with the Son of God. Let us rather recognize the "goodness and the love of God the Savior" (cf. Ti 3:4) who, condescending to our misery, so remote from his infinite sanctity, wished to make it easier for us to imitate it by giving us as a model the human person of his Mother. She, in fact, among human beings, offers the most shining example and the closest to us, of that perfect obedience whereby we lovingly and readily conform with the will of the eternal Father. Christ himself, as we well know, made this full closeness to the approval of the Father, the supreme ideal of his human behavior, declaring: "I do always the things that are pleasing to him" (Jn 8:29).

3. Mary, the New Eve, the Dawn of the New Testament.

If we then contemplate the Virgin of Nazareth in the halo of her prerogative and of her virtues, we will see her shine before our eyes as the "New Eve,"[30] the exalted Daughter of Zion, the summit of the Old Testament and the dawn of the New, in which "the fullness of time" (Gal 4:4) was realized, which was preordained by God for the mission in the world of his only-begotten Son. In truth, the Virgin Mary, more than all the patriarchs and prophets, more than the "just" and "pious" Simeon, awaited and implored "the consolation of Israel...the Christ of the Lord" (Lk 2:25–26) and then greeted his advent with the hymn of "Magnificat" when he descended into her most chaste womb to take on our flesh.

---

30. Cf. St. Irenaeus, *Adv. Haer.*, III, 22, 4: *PG* 959; St. Epiphanius, *Haer.* 78, 18: *PG* 42, 728–729; St. John Damascene, *First Homily on the Birth of Mary: PG* 96, 671ff.; Second Vatican Ecumenical Council, Dogmatic Constitution on the Church *Lumen Gentium,* 56; *AAS* 57 (1965), 60–61.

It is in Mary, therefore, that the Church of Christ indicates the example of the worthiest way of receiving in our spirits the Word of God, in accordance with the luminous sentence of St. Augustine: "Mary was therefore more blessed in receiving the faith in Christ than in conceiving the flesh of Christ. Accordingly, maternal consanguinity would not have benefited Mary if she had not felt more fortunate in having Christ in her heart than in her womb."[31] And it is still in her that Christians can admire the example of how to fulfill, with humility and at the same time with magnanimity, the mission which God entrusts to each one in this world, in relation to his own salvation and that of his fellow beings.

"Therefore, I beg you, be imitators of me as I am of Christ" (1 Cor 4:16). These words, and with greater reason than the Apostle Paul to the Christians of Corinth, can be addressed by the Mother of the Church to the multitudes of the faithful, who, in a symphony of faith and love with the generations of past centuries, acclaim her as blessed (cf. Lk 1:48). It is an invitation which it is a duty to heed docilely.

4. Marian Message of Invitation to Prayer, Penance and the Fear of God

And then a message of supreme utility seems today to reach the faithful from her who is the Immaculate, the holy, the cooperator with the Son in the work of restoration of supernatural life in souls.[32] In fact, in devoutly contemplating Mary they draw from her a stimulus for trusting prayer, a spur to the practice of penance and to the holy fear of God. Likewise, it is in this Marian elevation that they more often hear echoing the words with which Jesus Christ announced the advent of the kingdom of heaven: "Repent and believe in the Gospel" (Mk 1:15; cf. Mt 3:2; 4:17); and his severe admonition: "Unless you repent you will all perish in the same manner" (Lk 13:5).

Therefore, impelled by love and by the wish to placate God for the offenses against his sanctity and his justice and, at the same time, moved by trust in his infinite mercy, we must bear the sufferings of the spirit and of the body that we may expiate our sins and those of our fellow

---

31. *Sermon* 215, 1: *PL* 38, 1074.

32. Cf. Second Vatican Ecumenical Council, Dogmatic Constitution on the Church *Lumen Gentium,* 61; *AAS* 57 (1965), 63.

beings, and so avoid the twofold penalty of "harm" and of "sense," that is to say, the loss of God—the supreme good—and eternal fire.[33]

5. Christ Himself Indicates the Mother as the Model of the Church

What must stimulate the faithful even more to follow the examples of the most holy Virgin is the fact that Jesus himself, by giving her to us as our Mother, has tacitly indicated her as the model to be followed. It is, in fact, a natural thing that the children should have the same sentiments of their mothers and should reflect their merits and virtues. Therefore, as each one of us can repeat with St. Paul: "The Son of God loved me and gave himself up for me" (Gal 2:20; cf. Eph 5:2), so in all trust he can believe that the divine Savior has left to him also, in spiritual heritage, his Mother, with all the treasures of grace and virtues with which he had endowed her, that she may pour them over us through the influence of her powerful intercession and our willing imitation. This is why St. Bernard rightly affirms: "Coming to her the Holy Spirit filled her with grace for herself; when the same Spirit pervaded her again she became superabundant and redounding in grace for us also."[34]

6. The History of the Church Is Always Illumined by the Edifying Presence of Mary

From what we have been illustrating in the light of the holy Gospel and of Catholic tradition, it appears evident that the spiritual motherhood of Mary transcends space and time and belongs to the universal history of the Church, since she has always been present in the Church with her maternal assistance. Likewise the meaning of the affirmation appears clear, which is so often repeated: our era may well be called the Marian era. In fact, if it is true that, by an exalted grace of the Lord, the providential role of the most holy Mary in the history of salvation has been more deeply understood by the vast strata of the Christian people, this, however, should not lead us to believe that in past ages we had no

---

33. Cf. Mt 25:41; Second Vatican Ecumenical Council, Dogmatic Constitution on the Church *Lumen Gentium,* 48: *AAS* 57 (1965), 54.

34. Second homily *Super Missus est,* 2: *PL* 183, 64.

intuition whatever of this truth or that future ones will ignore it. In truth, all periods of the Church's history have benefited and will benefit from the maternal presence of the Mother of God, because she will remain always indissolubly joined to the mystery of the Mystical Body, of whose Head it was written: "Jesus Christ is the same, yesterday and to-day, yes, and forever" (Heb 13:8).

7. The Mother of the Church, Banner of Unity, Stimulus for Perfect Brotherhood among All Christians

Venerable brothers, the persuasion that the thought of the Church regarding the veneration of praise, gratitude and love due to the most Blessed Virgin is in full accord with the doctrine of the holy Gospel, as it was more precisely understood and explained by the tradition of the East as well as of the West, stirs in our spirit the hope that this pastoral exhortation of ours for an ever more fervid and more fruitful Marian piety will be received with generous acceptance not only by the faithful entrusted to your care, but also by those who, while not enjoying full communion with the Catholic Church, nevertheless, together with us, admire and venerate the handmaid of the Lord, the Virgin Mary, Mother of the Son of God.

May the Immaculate Heart of Mary shine before the eyes of all Christians as the model of perfect love toward God and toward our fellow beings; may it lead them toward the holy sacraments by virtue of which souls are cleansed from the stains of sin and are preserved from it. May it also stimulate them to make reparation for the innumerable offenses against the Divine Majesty. Lastly, may it shine like a banner of unity and a spur to perfect the bonds of brotherhood among all Christians in the bosom of the one Church of Jesus Christ, which "taught by the Holy Spirit, honors her with filial affection and piety as a most beloved mother."[35]

---

35. Second Vatican Ecumenical Council, Dogmatic Constitution on the Church *Lumen Gentium,* 53: *AAS* 53, 57 (1965), 59.

8. Invitation to Renew Personal Consecration to the Immaculate Heart of Mary

Since the 25th anniversary is recalled this year of the solemn conse-cration of the Church and of mankind to Mary, the Mother of God, and to her Immaculate Heart, by our predecessor of venerated memory, Pius XII, on October 31, 1942, on the occasion of the broadcast message to the Portuguese nation[36]—a consecration which we ourself have renewed on November 21, 1964[37]—we exhort all the sons of the Church to renew personally their consecration to the Immaculate Heart of the Mother of the Church and to bring alive this most noble act of veneration through a life ever more consonant with the divine will[38] and in a spirit of filial service and of devout imitation of their heavenly Queen.

Lastly, venerable brothers, we express the trust that, thanks to your encouragement, the clergy and the Christian people entrusted to your pastoral ministry will respond in a generous spirit to this exhortation of ours, so as to demonstrate toward the Virgin Mother of God a more ar-dent piety and a firmer confidence. Meanwhile while we are comforted by the certainty that the glorious Queen of Heaven and our most sweet Mother will never cease to assist all and each one of her sons and will never withdraw from the entire Church of Christ her heavenly patron-age, to you yourselves and to your faithful, as a pledge of divine favors and as a sign of our benevolence, we wholeheartedly impart the apos-tolic blessing.

Given in Rome, at St. Peter's, on the 13th day of the month of May in the year 1967, the fourth of our pontificate.

Paul VI

---

36. Cf. *Discourses and Radio Messages of Pius XII,* vol. 4, 260–262; cf. *AAS* 34, 1942, 345–346.
37. Cf. *AAS* 56 (1964), p. 1017.
38. Cf. Oration for Feast of the Immaculate Heart of Mary, August 22.

FOR THE RIGHT ORDERING AND DEVELOPMENT OF DEVOTION TO THE BLESSED VIRGIN MARY

Marialis Cultus

Apostolic Exhortation of Pope Paul VI
February 2, 1974

INTRODUCTION

On February 2, 1974, the feast of the Presentation, Pope Paul VI published a Marian document for the "right ordering and development of devotion to the Blessed Virgin Mary." The Church at the time needed this "exhortation" concerning the mounting Marian crisis in the universal Church.

Historical Perspectives

The document was prepared from 1970 to 1974, during the time after the Council when Marian devotion seemed to decline. Paul VI wrote to his fellow bishops and insisted in strong language that the bishops urge the People of God to take notice of this important aspect of our tradition. According to authors like Thomas A. Thompson, S.M., of the International Marian Research Institute in Dayton, Ohio, *Marialis Cultus* gave necessary guidelines for contemporary Marian liturgical and devotional reform.[1]

Thompson states, "The document is not about the Blessed Virgin Mary, but about Marian devotion and the Virgin's Mary's role in the Church's worship."[2] *Marialis Cultus* was highly influenced by the *Constitution on the Sacred Liturgy*.[3] The second major influence was *Lumen Gentium*. Article 103 of the liturgy document states:

> In celebrating this annual cycle of Christ's mysteries, holy Church honors with especial love the Blessed Mary, Mother of God, who is

---

1. Thomas A. Thompson, SM, "The Virgin Mary in the Liturgy: 1963–1988," *Marian Studies* 40 (1989): 81.

2. Thompson, 82.

3. Thompson, 77.

joined by an inseparable bond to the saving work of her Son. In her the Church holds up and admires the most excellent fruit of the redemption and joyfully contemplates, as in a faultless image, that which she herself desires and hopes wholly to be.

The article emphasizes the Church's special love for Mary, and the inseparable bond linking Mary to her son's saving work.[4] These themes occur repeatedly in *Marialis Cultus*.

Johann G. Roten, S.M., director of the International Marian Research Institute, writes that *Lumen Gentium* and *Marialis Cultus* have differing points of departure. Roten states, "The Council's theology of Mary is based primarily on the biblical narrative of her relation to Christ and his Church, whereas *Marialis Cultus* uses more personalist language to rekindle and deepen the memory of Mary."[5]

Thompson synthesizes a number of studies on *Marialis Cultus* in his article.[6] He states: *"Marialis Cultus* was a response to 'the Marian crisis' and the questions of many who wondered whether Marian devotion could be integrated into the orientations of Vatican II."[7] Roten states that, "in their finality *Lumen Gentium* and *Marialis Cultus* are significantly the same: they both attempt to retrieve the living memory of Mary." *Lumen Gentium* concentrates on knowing the *memoria; Marialis Cultus* "concentrates on the *memoria* itself, that is, on how it can be reached in and through her."[8]

Although the document focuses on liturgy and devotion, some statements in the document apply to catechesis, such as this one in the introduction:

> In our time, the changes that have occurred in social behavior, people's sensibilities, manners of expression in art and letters and in the forms of social communication have also influenced the manifestations of re-

---

4. Thompson, 78.

5. John G. Roten, S.M., "Memory and Mission: A Theological Reflection on Mary in the Paschal Mysteries," *Marian Studies* 42 (1991): 86.

6. Thompson, p. 82, footnotes: René Laurentin, "Bulletin sur la Vierge Marie," *Revue des sciences philosophiques et théologiques* 2 (1976): 324–25. *Estudios Marianos* 43 (1978) and *Marianum* 39 (1977). Dom Billet, "L'exhortation apostolique," 550–558. Charles W. Neumann, S. M. *Marialis Cultus: Mini-Course* (Leesburg, VA: The Catholic Home Study Institute, 1987–88).

7. Thompson, 82.

8. Roten, 86.

ligious sentiment.... In many places people are seeking new ways of expressing the unchangeable relationship of creatures with their Creator, of children with their Father.

The Teaching

The document's introduction situates the initial Vatican II reforms in a positive light: "We contemplate with joy and gratitude the work so far accomplished and the first positive results of the liturgical renewal, destined as they are to increase as this renewal comes to be understood in its basic purpose and correctly applied." At the same time, the pope speaks of his "vigilant solicitude" to see that the renewal continues in an orderly way "in spirit and truth (cf. Jn 4:24)."

Marialis Cultus has three major divisions:

1) Marian devotion and the liturgical renewal, 2) the renewal of Marian devotion, including biblical, liturgical, ecumenical and anthropological guidelines for its development and 3) observations on two devotions that bridge the past and are valid for the future, the Angelus and the rosary.

Part one discusses the Blessed Virgin in the revised Roman liturgy. Its first section lists the new elements in Vatican II's liturgical reform, which increased the number of Marian texts in the liturgy. The second section of part one presents the Blessed Virgin as the model of the Church in divine worship, "namely, Mary as a model of the spiritual attitude with which the Church celebrates and lives the divine mysteries" (*MC* 16). Mary is "the attentive Virgin," "the Virgin in prayer," the believing and obeying "Virgin-Mother," and "the Virgin presenting offerings" (cf. *MC* 17–23).

Part two is titled "The Renewal of Devotion to Mary." The principles and guidelines set down in these paragraphs affect the catechetical process. Section one treats the Trinitarian, Christological and ecclesial aspects of devotion to Mary. Section two gives four guidelines for devotion to Mary: the biblical, liturgical, ecumenical and anthropological elements which are to be considered when teaching Marian doctrine.

A third part is titled "Observations on Two Exercises of Piety: The Angelus and the Rosary" (*MC* 40–55). Fourteen articles discuss the rosary as a gospel prayer. The conclusion of the document treats the "Theological and Pastoral Value of Devotion to the Blessed Virgin" (*MC* 56–57).

Today

In evaluating Marian teachings and Marian devotions, the norms and guidelines of *Marialis Cultus* become key elements which must be taken into account. In 1997, twenty-three years after *Marialis Cultus,* these norms were incorporated into the magisterium's catechetical directives concerning Marian catechesis and popular devotion:

> 196. Multiple forms of devotion to the Mother of God have developed in different circumstances of time and place, in response to popular sensibilities and cultural differences. Certain forms of Marian devotion however, because of long usage, require a renewed catechesis to restore to them elements that have become lost or obscured. By such catechesis the perennial value of Marian devotion can be emphasized, doctrinal elements gleaned from theological reflection and the Church's Magisterium assimilated. Catechesis on the Blessed Virgin Mary should always express clearly the intrinsic Trinitarian, Christological and ecclesiological aspects of Mariology. In revising or drawing up materials for use in Marian piety account should be taken of biblical, liturgical, ecumenical and anthropological orientations.[9]

Mary is always to be seen in relationship. She is fully centered on the triune God, on her divine Son, but also the community of the Church. Studies about her and devotion to her must be rooted in the Word. She worshipped God; she gathered in prayer with the peoples of many tongues at Pentecost; she was fully human—and that is why the Church celebrates her with such joy.

---

9. Congregation for the Clergy, *General Directory for Catechesis* (Washington, DC: United States Catholic Conference, 1998), p. 185.

TOPICAL OUTLINE

1. Introduction: The Blessed Virgin and Christian worship

2. Part I: Devotion to Mary in the liturgy

    A. The Blessed Virgin in the revised Roman liturgy (1)

        1. Restoration of the liturgical calendar and Marian feasts (2–9)

        2. Marian themes and texts in the revised missal (10–11)

        3. Revision of the lectionary (12)

        4. Revision of the Liturgy of the Hours (13)

        5. Veneration of Mary and the revised liturgy (14–15)

    B. Mary as the model of the Church in divine worship (16)

        1. Mary as the attentive Virgin (17)

        2. Mary as the Virgin in prayer (18)

        3. Mary as the Virgin Mother (19)

        4. Mary as the Virgin presenting offerings (20)

        5. Mary as a teacher of the spiritual life (21)

        6. Mary and the Church's devotion (22–23)

3. Part II: The renewal of devotion to Mary

    A. Various aspects of devotion to the Blessed Virgin Mary (24)

        1. Trinitarian and Christological aspects (25)

        2. Mary and the Holy Spirit (26–27)

        3. Ecclesial aspects (28)

B. Guidelines for Marian devotion (29)

   1. Biblical guidelines (30)

   2. Liturgical guidelines (31)

   3. Ecumenical guidelines (32–33)

   4. Anthropological guidelines (34)

   5. Response to certain difficulties regarding Marian devotion (35–37)

   6. Authentic Marian devotion (38–39)

4. Observations on the Angelus and the rosary (40)

   A. The Angelus (41)

   B. The rosary (42–55)

5. Conclusion: Theological and pastoral value of Marian devotion (56–58)

FOR THE RIGHT ORDERING AND DEVELOPMENT OF DEVOTION TO THE BLESSED VIRGIN MARY

Marialis Cultus

Promulgated by His Holiness Pope Paul VI
On February 2, 1974

*To All Bishops in Peace and Communion
with the Apostolic See*

INTRODUCTION

Division of the Treatise Occasion and Purpose of the Document

Venerable Brothers: Health and the Apostolic Blessing

From the moment when we were called to the See of Peter, we have constantly striven to enhance devotion to the Blessed Virgin Mary, not only with the intention of interpreting the sentiments of the Church and our own personal inclination, but also because, as is well known, this devotion forms a very noble part of the whole sphere of that sacred worship in which there intermingle the highest expressions of wisdom and of religion,[1] and which is therefore the primary task of the People of God.

Precisely with a view to this task, we have always favored and encouraged the great work of liturgical reform promoted by the Second

---

1. Cf. Lactantius, *Divinae Institutiones* IV, 3, 6–10: *CSEL* 19, 279.

Vatican Ecumenical Council, and it has certainly come about, not without a particular design of divine Providence, that the first conciliar document which together with the venerable Fathers we approved and signed *in Spiritu Sancto* was the Constitution *Sacrosanctum Concilium.* The purpose of this document was precisely to restore and enhance the liturgy and to make more fruitful the participation of the faithful in the sacred mysteries.[2] From that time onward, many acts of our pontificate have been directed toward the improvement of divine worship, as is demonstrated by the fact that we have promulgated in these recent years numerous books of the Roman Rite, restored according to the principles and norms of the same Council. For this we profoundly thank the Lord, the giver of all good things, and we are grateful to the episcopal conferences and individual bishops who in various ways have collaborated with us in the preparation of these books.

We contemplate with joy and gratitude the work so far accomplished and the first positive results of the liturgical renewal, destined as they are to increase as this renewal comes to be understood in its basic purposes and correctly applied. At the same time we do not cease with vigilant solicitude to concern ourself with whatever can give orderly fulfillment to the renewal of the worship with which the Church in spirit and truth (cf. Jn 4:24) adores the Father and the Son and the Holy Spirit, "venerates with special love Mary the most holy Mother of God"[3] and honors with religious devotion the memory of the martyrs and the other saints.

The development, desired by us, of devotion to the Blessed Virgin Mary is an indication of the Church's genuine piety. This devotion fits— as we have indicated above—into the only worship that is rightly called "Christian," because it takes its origin and effectiveness from Christ, finds its complete expression in Christ, and leads through Christ in the Spirit to the Father. In the sphere of worship this devotion necessarily reflects God's redemptive plan, in which a special form of veneration is appropriate to the singular place which Mary occupies in that plan.[4] In-

---

2. Cf. Second Vatican Ecumenical Council, Constitution on the Sacred Liturgy *Sacrosanctum Concilium,* 1–3, 11, 21, 48, *AAS* 56 (1964), 97–98, 102–103, 105–106, 113.

3. Second Vatican Ecumenical Council, Constitution on the Sacred Liturgy *Sacrosanctum Concilium,* 103: *AAS* 56 (1964), 125.

4. Cf. Second Vatican Ecumenical Council, Dogmatic Constitution on the Church *Lumen Gentium,* 66: *AAS* 57 (1965), 65.

deed every authentic development of Christian worship is necessarily followed by a fitting increase of veneration for the Mother of the Lord. Moreover, the history of piety shows how "the various forms of devotion toward the Mother of God that the Church has approved within the limits of wholesome and orthodox doctrine"[5] have developed in harmonious subordination to the worship of Christ, and have gravitated toward this worship as to their natural and necessary point of reference. The same is happening in our own time. The Church's reflection today on the mystery of Christ and on her own nature has led her to find at the root of the former and as a culmination of the latter the same figure of a woman: the Virgin Mary, the Mother of Christ and the Mother of the Church. And the increased knowledge of Mary's mission has become joyful veneration of her and adoring respect for the wise plan of God, who has placed within his family (the Church), as in every home, the figure of a woman, who in a hidden manner and in a spirit of service watches over that family "and carefully looks after it until the glorious day of the Lord."[6]

In our time, the changes that have occurred in social behavior, people's sensibilities, manners of expression in art and letters and in the forms of social communication have also influenced the manifestations of religious sentiment. Certain practices of piety that not long ago seemed suitable for expressing the religious sentiment of individuals and of Christian communities seem today inadequate or unsuitable because they are linked with social and cultural patterns of the past. On the other hand in many places people are seeking new ways of expressing the unchangeable relationship of creatures with their Creator, of children with their Father. In some people this may cause temporary confusion. But anyone who, with trust in God, reflects upon these phenomena discovers that many tendencies of modern piety (for example, the interiorization of religious sentiment) are meant to play their part in the development of Christian piety in general and devotion to the Blessed Virgin in particular. Thus our own time, faithfully attentive to tradition and to the progress of theology and the sciences, will make its contribution of praise to her whom, according to her own prophetic words, all generations will call blessed (cf. Lk 1:48).

---

5. Ibid.
6. Votive Mass of the Blessed Virgin Mary, Mother of the Church, Preface.

We therefore judge it in keeping with our apostolic service, venerable brothers, to deal, in a sort of dialogue, with a number of themes connected with the place that the Blessed Virgin occupies in the Church's worship. These themes have already been partly touched upon by the Second Vatican Council[7] and also by ourself,[8] but it is useful to return to them in order to remove doubts, and especially to help the development of that devotion to the Blessed Virgin which in the Church is motivated by the Word of God and practiced in the Spirit of Christ.

We therefore wish to dwell upon a number of questions concerning the relationship between the sacred liturgy and devotion to the Blessed Virgin (I), to offer considerations and directives suitable for favoring the development of that devotion (II), and finally to put forward a number of reflections intended to encourage the restoration, in a dynamic and more informed manner, of the recitation of the rosary, the practice of which was so strongly recommended by our predecessors and is so widely diffused among the Christian people (III).

---

7. Cf. Second Vatican Ecumenical Council, Dogmatic Constitution on the Church *Lumen Gentium,* 66–67: *AAS* 57 (1965), 65–66. Constitution on the Sacred Liturgy *Sacrosanctum Concilium,* 103: *AAS* 56 (1964), 125.

8. Apostolic Exhortation *Signum Magnum: AAS* 59 (1967), 465–475.

PART ONE: DEVOTION TO THE
BLESSED VIRGIN MARY IN THE LITURGY

1. As we prepare to discuss the place which the Blessed Virgin Mary occupies in Christian worship, we must first turn our attention to the sacred liturgy. In addition to its rich doctrinal content, the liturgy has an incomparable pastoral effectiveness and a recognized exemplary conduct for the other forms of worship. We would have liked to take into consideration the various liturgies of the East and the West, but for the purpose of this document we shall dwell almost exclusively on the books of the Roman Rite. In fact, in accordance with the practical norms issued by the Second Vatican Council,[9] it is this rite alone which has been the object of profound renewal. This is true also in regard to expressions of veneration for Mary. This rite therefore deserves to be carefully considered and evaluated.

Section One: The Blessed Virgin in the Revised Roman Liturgy

2. The reform of the Roman liturgy presupposed a careful restoration of its general calendar. This calendar is arranged in such a way as to give fitting prominence to the celebration on appropriate days of the work of salvation. It distributes throughout the year the whole mystery of Christ, from the Incarnation to the expectation of his return in glory,[10] and thus makes it possible in a more organic and closely-knit fashion to include the commemoration of Christ's Mother in the annual cycle of the mysteries of her Son.

---

9. Cf. Second Vatican Ecumenical Council, Constitution on the Sacred Liturgy *Sacrosanctum Concilium,* 3: *AAS* 56 (1964), 98.

10. Cf. Second Vatican Ecumenical Council, Constitution on the Sacred Liturgy *Sacrosanctum Concilium,* 102: *AAS* 56 (1964), 125.

3. For example, during Advent there are many liturgical references to Mary besides the solemnity of December 8, which is a joint celebration of the Immaculate Conception of Mary, of the basic preparation (cf. Is 11:1, 10) for the coming of the Savior and of the happy beginning of the Church without spot or wrinkle.[11] Such liturgical references are found especially on the days from December 17 to 24, and more particularly on the Sunday before Christmas, which recalls the ancient prophecies concerning the Virgin Mother and the Messiah[12] and includes readings from the Gospel concerning the imminent birth of Christ and his precursor.[13]

4. In this way the faithful, living in the liturgy the spirit of Advent, by thinking about the inexpressible love with which the Virgin Mother awaited her Son,[14] are invited to take her as a model and to prepare themselves to meet the Savior who is to come. They must be "vigilant in prayer and joyful in...praise."[15] We would also remark that the Advent liturgy, by linking the awaiting of the Messiah and the awaiting of the glorious return of Christ with the admirable commemoration of his Mother, presents a happy balance in worship. This balance can be taken as a norm for preventing any tendency (as has happened at times in certain forms of popular piety) to separate devotion to the Blessed Virgin from its necessary point of reference—Christ. It also ensures that this season, as liturgy experts have noted, should be considered as a time particularly suited to devotion to the Mother of the Lord. This is an orientation that we confirm and which we hope to see accepted and followed everywhere.

---

11. Cf. *Roman Missal,* restored by decree of the Second Vatican Ecumenical Council, promulgated by authority of Pope Paul VI, typical edition, December 8, 1970, Preface.

12. *Roman Missal,* restored by decree of the Second Vatican Ecumenical Council, promulgated by authority of Pope Paul VI. *Ordo Lectionum Missae,* typical edition, 1969, 8, First Reading (Year A: Is 7:10–14: "Behold a virgin shall conceive"; Year B: 2 Sam 7:1–15; 8b–11, 16: "The throne of David shall be established forever before the face of the Lord"; Year C: Mic 5:2a [Heb 1–4a]: "Out of you will be born for me the one who is to rule over Israel").

13. Ibid., 8, Gospel (Year A: Mt 1:18–24: "Jesus is born of Mary who was espoused to Joseph, the son of David"; Year B: Lk 1:26–38: "You are to conceive and bear a son"; Year C: Lk 1:39–45: "Why should I be honored with a visit from the Mother of my Lord?").

14. Cf. *Roman Missal,* Advent Preface, II.

15. *Roman Missal,* ibid.

5. The Christmas season is a prolonged commemoration of the divine, virginal and salvific motherhood of her whose "inviolate virginity brought the Savior into the world."[16] In fact, on the Solemnity of the Birth of Christ the Church both adores the Savior and venerates his glorious Mother. On the Epiphany, when she celebrates the universal call to salvation, the Church contemplates the Blessed Virgin, the true Seat of Wisdom and true Mother of the King, who presents to the Wise Men, for their adoration, the Redeemer of all peoples (cf. Mt 2:11). On the Feast of the Holy Family of Jesus, Mary and Joseph (the Sunday within the octave of Christmas), the Church meditates with profound reverence upon the holy life led in the house at Nazareth by Jesus, the Son of God and Son of Man, Mary his Mother, and Joseph the just man (cf. Mt 1:19).

In the revised ordering of the Christmas period it seems to us that the attention of all should be directed toward the restored Solemnity of Mary the holy Mother of God. This celebration, placed on January 1 in conformity with the ancient indication of the liturgy of the city of Rome, is meant to commemorate the part played by Mary in this mystery of salvation. It is meant also to exalt the singular dignity which this mystery brings to the "holy Mother...through whom we were found worthy to receive the Author of Life."[17] It is likewise a fitting occasion for renewing adoration of the newborn Prince of Peace, for listening once more to the glad tidings of the angels (cf. Lk 2:14), and for imploring from God, through the Queen of Peace, the supreme gift of peace. It is for this reason that, in the happy concurrence of the Octave of Christmas and the first day of the year, we have instituted the World Day of Peace, an occasion that is gaining increasing support and already bringing forth fruits of peace in the hearts of many.

6. To the two solemnities already mentioned (the Immaculate Conception and the Divine Motherhood) should be added the ancient and venerable celebrations of March 25 and August 15.

For the Solemnity of the Incarnation of the Word, in the Roman calendar the ancient title—the Annunciation of the Lord—has been deliberately restored, but the feast was and is a joint one of Christ and of the Blessed Virgin: of the Word, who becomes Son of Mary (Mk 6:3), and

---

16. *Roman Missal,* Eucharistic Prayer I, *Communicantes* for Christmas and its octave.
17. *Roman Missal,* January 1, Entrance antiphon and Collect.

of the Virgin, who becomes Mother of God. With regard to Christ, the East and the West, in the inexhaustible riches of their liturgies, celebrate this solemnity as the commemoration of the salvific *fiat* of the incarnate Word, who, entering the world, said: "God, here I am! I am coming to obey your will" (cf. Heb 10:7; Ps 39:8–9). They commemorate it as the beginning of the redemption and of the indissoluble and wedded union of the divine nature with human nature in the one Person of the Word. With regard to Mary, these liturgies celebrate it as a feast of the New Eve, the obedient and faithful virgin, who with her generous *fiat* (cf. Lk 1:38) became, through the working of the Spirit, the Mother of God, but also the true Mother of the living, and, by receiving into her womb the one Mediator (cf. 1 Tm 2:5), became the true Ark of the Covenant and true Temple of God. These liturgies celebrate it as a culminating moment in the salvific dialogue between God and man, and as a commemoration of the Blessed Virgin's free consent and cooperation in the plan of redemption.

The solemnity of August 15 celebrates the glorious Assumption of Mary into heaven. It is a feast of her destiny of fullness and blessedness, of the glorification of her immaculate soul and of her virginal body, of her perfect configuration to the risen Christ; a feast that sets before the eyes of the Church and of all mankind the image and the consoling proof of the fulfillment of their final hope, namely, that this full glorification is the destiny of all those whom Christ has made his brothers, having "flesh and blood in common with them" (Heb 2:14; cf. Gal 4:4). The Solemnity of the Assumption is prolonged in the celebration of the Queenship of the Blessed Virgin Mary, which occurs seven days later. On this occasion we contemplate her who, seated beside the King of Ages, shines forth as Queen and intercedes as Mother.[18] These four solemnities, therefore, mark with the highest liturgical rank the main dogmatic truths concerning the handmaid of the Lord.

7. After the solemnities just mentioned, particular consideration must be given to those celebrations that commemorate salvific events in which the Blessed Virgin was closely associated with her Son. Such are the feasts of the Nativity of Our Lady (September 8), "the hope of the entire world and the dawn of salvation";[19] and the Visitation (May 31),

---

18. Cf. *Roman Missal,* August 22, Collect.
19. *Roman Missal,* September 8, Prayer after Communion.

in which the liturgy recalls the "Blessed Virgin Mary carrying her Son within her,"[20] and visiting Elizabeth to offer charitable assistance and to proclaim the mercy of God the Savior.[21] Then there is the commemoration of Our Lady of Sorrows (September 15), a fitting occasion for reliving a decisive moment in the history of salvation and for venerating, together with the Son "lifted up on the cross, his suffering Mother."[22]

The feast of February 2, which has been given back its ancient name, the Presentation of the Lord, should also be considered as a joint commemoration of the Son and of the Mother, if we are fully to appreciate its rich content. It is the celebration of a mystery of salvation accomplished by Christ, a mystery with which the Blessed Virgin was intimately associated as the Mother of the Suffering Servant of Yahweh, as the one who performs a mission belonging to ancient Israel, and as the model for the new People of God, which is ever being tested in its faith and hope by suffering and persecution (cf. Lk 2:21–35).

8. The restored Roman calendar gives particular prominence to the celebrations listed above, but it also includes other kinds of commemorations connected with local devotions and which have acquired a wider popularity and interest (e.g., February 11, Our Lady of Lourdes; August 5, the Dedication of the Basilica of St. Mary Major). Then there are others, originally celebrated by particular religious families but which today, by reason of the popularity they have gained, can truly be considered ecclesial (e.g., July 16, Our Lady of Mount Carmel; October 7, Our Lady of the Rosary). There are still others which, apart from their apocryphal content, present lofty and exemplary values and carry on venerable traditions having their origin especially in the East (e.g., the Immaculate Heart of the Blessed Virgin, celebrated on the Saturday following the second Sunday after Pentecost).

9. Nor must one forget that the general Roman calendar does not include all celebrations in honor of the Blessed Virgin. Rather, it is for individual calendars to include, with fidelity to liturgical norms but with sincere endorsement, the Marian feasts proper to the different local Churches. Lastly, it should be noted that frequent commemorations of the Blessed Virgin are possible through the use of the Saturday Masses

---

20. *Roman Missal,* May 31, Collect.

21. Cf. ibid., Collect and Prayer over the gifts.

22. Cf. *Roman Missal,* September 15, Collect.

of our Lady. This is an ancient and simple commemoration, and one that is made very adaptable and varied by the flexibility of the modern calendar and the number of formulas provided by the missal.

10. In this Apostolic Exhortation we do not intend to examine the whole content of the new Roman Missal. But by reason of the work of evaluation that we have undertaken to carry out in regard to the revised books of the Roman Rite,[23] we would like to mention some of the aspects and themes of the missal. In the first place, we are pleased to note how the Eucharistic Prayers of the missal, in admirable harmony with the Eastern liturgies,[24] contain a significant commemoration of the Blessed Virgin. For example, the ancient Roman Canon commemorates the Mother of the Lord in terms full of doctrine and devotional inspiration: "In union with the whole Church we honor Mary, the ever Virgin Mother of Jesus Christ our Lord and God." In a similar way the recent Eucharistic Prayer III expresses with intense supplication the desire of those praying to share with the Mother the inheritance of sons: "May he make us an everlasting gift to you [the Father] and enable us to share in the inheritance of your saints, with Mary, the Virgin Mother of God." This daily commemoration, by reason of its place at the heart of the divine sacrifice, should be considered a particularly expressive form of the veneration that the Church pays to the "Blessed of the Most High" (cf. Lk 1:28).

11. As we examine the texts of the revised missal, we see how the great Marian themes of the Roman prayer book have been accepted in perfect doctrinal continuity with the past. Thus, for example, we have the themes of Mary's Immaculate Conception and fullness of grace, the divine motherhood, the unblemished and fruitful virginity, the temple of the Holy Spirit, Mary's cooperation in the work of her Son, her exemplary sanctity, merciful intercession, assumption into heaven, maternal queenship and many other themes. We also see how other themes, in a certain sense new ones, have been introduced in equally perfect harmony with the theological developments of the present day. Thus, for example, we have the theme of Mary and the Church, which has been

---

23. Cf. 1, p. 15.

24. From among the many anaphoras, cf. the following which are held in special honor by the Eastern rites: *Anaphora Marci Evangelistae: Prex Eucharistica,* ed. A. Hänggi-I, Pahl, Fribourg, Editions Universitaires, 1968, 107; *Anaphora Iacobi fratris Domini graeca,* ibid., 257; *Anaphora Ioannis Chrysostomi,* ibid., 229.

inserted into the texts of the missal in a variety of aspects, a variety that matches the many and varied relations that exist between the Mother of Christ and the Church. For example, in the celebration of the Immaculate Conception, the texts recognize the beginning of the Church, the spotless Bride of Christ.[25] In the Assumption they recognize the beginning that has already been made and the image of what, for the whole Church, must still come to pass.[26] In the mystery of Mary's motherhood they confess that she is the Mother of the Head and of the members—the holy Mother of God and therefore the provident Mother of the Church.[27]

When the liturgy turns its gaze either to the primitive Church or to the Church of our own day it always finds Mary. In the primitive Church she is seen praying with the apostles;[28] in our own day she is actively present, and the Church desires to live the mystery of Christ with her: "Grant that your Church, which with Mary shared Christ's passion, may be worthy to share also in his resurrection."[29] She is also seen represented as a voice of praise in unison with which the Church wishes to give glory to God: "...with her [Mary] may we always praise you."[30] And since the liturgy is worship that requires a way of living consistent with it, it asks that devotion to the Blessed Virgin should become a concrete and deeply-felt love for the Church, as is wonderfully expressed in the prayer after Communion in the Mass of September 15: "...that as we recall the sufferings shared by the Blessed Virgin Mary, we may with the Church fulfill in ourselves what is lacking in the sufferings of Christ."

12. The lectionary is one of the books of the Roman Rite that has greatly benefited from the post-conciliar reform, by reason both of its added texts and of the intrinsic value of these texts, which contain the ever-living and efficacious Word of God (cf. Heb 4:12). This rich collection of biblical texts has made it possible to arrange the whole history of salvation in an orderly three-year cycle and to set forth more completely the mystery of Christ. The logical consequence has been that the

---

25. Cf. *Roman Missal,* December 8, Preface.

26. Cf. *Roman Missal,* August 15, Preface.

27. Cf. *Roman Missal,* January 1, Prayer after Communion.

28. Cf. *Roman Missal,* Common of the Blessed Virgin Mary, 6, Paschaltide, Collect.

29. *Roman Missal,* September 15, Collect.

30. *Roman Missal,* May 31, Collect. On the same lines is the Preface of the Blessed Virgin Mary, 1: "We do well...in celebrating the memory of the Virgin Mary...to glorify your love for us in the words of her song of thanksgiving."

lectionary contains a larger number of Old and New Testament readings concerning the Blessed Virgin. This numerical increase has not, however, been based on random choice: only those readings have been accepted which in different ways and degrees can be considered Marian, either from the evidence of their content or from the results of careful exegesis, supported by the teachings of the Magisterium or by solid tradition. It is also right to observe that these readings occur not only on feasts of the Blessed Virgin but are read on many other occasions, for example on certain Sundays during the liturgical year,[31] in the celebration of rites that deeply concern the Christian's sacramental life and the choices confronting him,[32] as also in the joyful or sad experiences of his life on earth.[33]

13. The Liturgy of the Hours, the revised book of the Office, also contains outstanding examples of devotion to the Mother of the Lord. These are to be found in the hymns—which include several masterpieces of universal literature, such as Dante's sublime prayer to the Blessed Virgin[34]—and in the antiphons that complete the daily Office. To these lyrical invocations there has been added the well known prayer *Sub tuum praesidium,* venerable for its antiquity and admirable for its content. Other examples occur in the prayers of intercession at Lauds and Vespers, prayers which frequently express trusting recourse to the Mother of Mercy. Finally there are selections from the vast treasury of writings on our Lady composed by authors of the first Christian centuries, of the Middle Ages and of modern times.

---

31. Cf. Lectionary, Third Sunday of Advent (Year C: Zeph 3:14–18a); Fourth Sunday of Advent (cf. footnote 12 above); Sunday within the octave of Christmas (Year A: Mt 2:13–15; Year B: Lk 2:22–40; Year C: Lk 2:41–52); Second Sunday after Christmas (Jn 1:1–18); Seventh Sunday after Easter (Year A: Acts 1:12–14); Second Sunday of the Year C: Jn 1:1–12); Tenth Sunday of the Year (Year B: Gn 3:9–15); Fourteenth Sunday of the Year (Year B: Mk 6:16).

32. Cf. Lectionary, the catechumenate and baptism of adults: the Lord's Prayer (Second Reading, 2, Gal 4:47); Christian initiation outside the Easter Vigil (Gospel, 7, Jn 1:1–5; 9–16; 16–18); Nuptial Mass (Gospel, 7, Jn 2:1–11); consecration of virgins and religious profession (First Reading, 7, Is 61:9–11; Gospel, 6, Mk 3:31–35; Lk 1:26–38 [cf. *Ordo Consecrationis Virginum,* 130; *Ordo Professionis Religiosae, pars alter,* 145]).

33. Cf. Lectionary, For refugees and exiles (Gospel, 1, Mt 2:13–15; 19–23); In thanksgiving (First Reading, 4, Zeph 3:14–15).

34. Cf. *The Divine Comedy, Paradiso* 33, 1–9; cf. Liturgy of the Hours, remembrance of Our Lady on Saturdays, Office of Readings Hymn.

14. The commemoration of the Blessed Virgin occurs often in the missal, the lectionary and the Liturgy of the Hours—the hinges of the liturgical prayer of the Roman Rite. In the other revised liturgical books also, expressions of love and suppliant veneration addressed to the *Theotókos* are not lacking. Thus the Church invokes her, the Mother of Grace, before immersing candidates in the saving waters of baptism;[35] the Church invokes her intercession for mothers who, full of gratitude for the gift of motherhood, come to church to express their joy;[36] the Church holds her up as a model to those who follow Christ by embracing the religious life[37] or who receive the consecration of virgins.[38] For these people the Church asks Mary's motherly assistance.[39] The Church prays fervently to Mary on behalf of her children who have come to the hour of their death.[40] The Church asks Mary's intercession for those who have closed their eyes to the light of this world and appeared before Christ, the eternal Light;[41] and the Church, through Mary's prayers, invokes comfort upon those who in sorrow mourn with faith the departure of their loved ones.[42]

15. The examination of the revised liturgical books leads us to the comforting observation that the post-conciliar renewal has, as was previously desired by the liturgical movement, properly considered the Blessed Virgin in the mystery of Christ, and, in harmony with tradition, has recognized the singular place that belongs to her in Christian worship as the holy Mother of God and the worthy associate of the Redeemer.

It could not have been otherwise. If one studies the history of Christian worship, in fact, one notes that both in the East and in the West the highest and purest expressions of devotion to the Blessed Virgin have sprung from the liturgy or have been incorporated into it.

---

35. *Ordo Baptismi Parvulorum*, 48: *Ordo Initiationis Christiana Adultorum*, 214.

36. Cf. *Rituale Romanum*, Tit. VII, cap. III, *De Benedictione Mulieris Post Partum*.

37. Cf. *Ordo Professionis Religiosae, pars prior,* 57 and 67.

38. Cf. *Ordo Consecrationis Virginum*, 16.

39. Cf. *Ordo Professionis Religiosae, pars prior*, 62 and 142; *pars altera,* 67 and 158; *Ordo Consecrationis Virginum*, 18 and 20.

40. Cf. *Ordo Unctionis Infirmorum Eorumque Pastoralis Curae*, 143, 146, 147, 150.

41. Cf. *Roman Missal,* Masses for the Dead, For dead brothers and sisters, relations and benefactors, Collect.

42. Cf. *Ordo Exsequiarum*, 226.

We wish to emphasize the fact that the veneration which the universal Church today accords to Blessed Mary is a derivation from and an extension and unceasing increase of the devotion that the Church of every age has paid to her, with careful attention to truth and with an ever watchful nobility of expression. From perennial tradition kept alive by reason of the uninterrupted presence of the Spirit and continual attention to the Word, the Church of our time draws motives, arguments and incentives for the veneration that she pays to the Blessed Virgin. And the liturgy, which receives approval and strength from the Magisterium, is a most lofty expression and an evident proof of this living tradition.

Section Two: The Blessed Virgin as the Model of the Church in Divine Worship

16. In accordance with some of the guidelines of the Council's teaching on Mary and the Church, we now wish to examine more closely a particular aspect of the relationship between Mary and the liturgy—namely, Mary as a model of the spiritual attitude with which the Church celebrates and lives the divine mysteries. That the Blessed Virgin is an exemplar in this field derives from the fact that she is recognized as a most excellent exemplar of the Church in the order of faith, charity and perfect union with Christ,[43] that is, of that interior disposition with which the Church, the beloved spouse, closely associated with her Lord, invokes Christ and through him worships the eternal Father.[44]

17. Mary is *the attentive Virgin*, who receives the Word of God with faith, that faith which in her case was the gateway and path to divine motherhood, for, as St. Augustine realized, "Blessed Mary by believing conceived him [Jesus] whom believing she brought forth."[45] In fact, when she received from the angel the answer to her doubt (cf. Lk 1:34–37), "full of faith, and conceiving Christ in her mind before conceiving him in her womb, she said, 'I am the handmaid of the Lord, let what you have said be done to me'"[46] (Lk 1:38). It was faith that was for her the

---

43. Cf. Second Vatican Ecumenical Council, Dogmatic Constitution on the Church *Lumen Gentium,* 63: *AAS* 57 (1965), 64.

44. Cf. Second Vatican Ecumenical Council, Constitution on the Sacred Liturgy *Sacrosanctum Concilium,* 7: *AAS* 56 (1964), 100–101.

45. *Sermo* 215, 4: *PL* 38, 1074.

46. Ibid.

cause of blessedness and certainty in the fulfillment of the promise: "Blessed is she who believed that the promise made her by the Lord would be fulfilled" (Lk 1:45). Similarly, it was faith with which she, who played a part in the Incarnation and was a unique witness to it, thinking back on the events of the infancy of Christ, meditated upon these events in her heart (cf. Lk 2:19, 51). The Church also acts in this way, especially in the liturgy, when with faith she listens, accepts, proclaims and venerates the Word of God, distributes it to the faithful as the bread of life,[47] and in the light of that word examines the signs of the times and interprets and lives the events of history.

18. Mary is also *the Virgin in prayer.* She appears as such in the visit to the mother of the precursor, when she pours out her soul in expressions glorifying God, and expressions of humility, faith and hope. This prayer is the Magnificat (cf. Lk 1:46–55), Mary's prayer par excellence, the song of the messianic times in which there mingles the joy of the ancient and the new Israel. As St. Irenaeus seems to suggest, it is in Mary's canticle that there was heard once more the rejoicing of Abraham who foresaw the Messiah (cf. Jn 8:56),[48] and there rang out in prophetic anticipation the voice of the Church: "In her exultation Mary prophetically declared in the name of the Church: 'My soul proclaims the glory of the Lord....'"[49] And in fact Mary's hymn has spread far and wide and has become the prayer of the whole Church in all ages.

At Cana, Mary appears once more as the Virgin in prayer: when she tactfully told her Son of a temporal need she also obtained an effect of grace, namely, that Jesus, in working the first of his "signs," confirmed his disciples' faith in him (cf. Jn 2:1–12).

Likewise, the last description of Mary's life presents her as praying. The apostles "joined in continuous prayer, together with several women, including Mary the mother of Jesus, and with his brothers" (Acts 1:14). We have here the prayerful presence of Mary in the early Church and in the Church throughout all ages, for, having been assumed into heaven, she has not abandoned her mission of intercession

---

47. Cf. Second Vatican Ecumenical Council, Dogmatic Constitution on Divine Revelation *Dei Verbum,* 21: *AAS* 58 (1966), 827–828.

48. Cf. *Adversus Haereses,* IV, 7, 1: *PG* 7, 1, 990–991: *SCh.* 100, t, II, 454–458.

49. Cf. *Adversus Haereses,* III, 10, 2: *PG* 7, 1, 873: *SCh.* 34, 164.

and salvation.[50] The title "Virgin in Prayer" also fits the Church, which day by day presents to the Father the needs of her children, "praises the Lord unceasingly and intercedes for the salvation of the world."[51]

19. Mary is also *the Virgin-Mother*—she who "believing and obeying...brought forth on earth the Father's Son. This she did, not knowing man but overshadowed by the Holy Spirit."[52] This was a miraculous motherhood, set up by God as the type and exemplar of the fruitfulness of the Virgin-Church, which "becomes herself a mother.... For by her preaching and by Baptism she brings forth to a new and immortal life children who are conceived by the power of the Holy Spirit and born of God."[53] The ancient Fathers rightly taught that the Church prolongs in the sacrament of Baptism the virginal motherhood of Mary. Among such references we like to recall that of our illustrious predecessor, St. Leo the Great, who in a Christmas homily says: "The origin which [Christ] took in the womb of the Virgin he has given to the baptismal font: he has given to water what he had given to his Mother—the power of the Most High and the overshadowing of the Holy Spirit (cf. Lk 1:35), which was responsible for Mary's bringing forth the Savior, has the same effect, so that water may regenerate the believer."[54] If we wished to go to liturgical sources, we could quote the beautiful *Illatio* of the Mozarabic liturgy: "The former [Mary] carried Life in her womb; the latter [the Church] bears Life in the waters of Baptism. In Mary's members Christ was formed; in the waters of the Church Christ is put on."[55]

20. Mary is, finally, *the Virgin presenting offerings*. In the episode of the Presentation of Jesus in the Temple (cf. Lk 2:22–35), the Church, guided by the Spirit, has detected, over and above the fulfillment of the laws regarding the offering of the firstborn (cf. Ex 13:11–16) and the

---

50. Cf. Second Vatican Ecumenical Council, Dogmatic Constitution on the Church *Lumen Gentium*, 62: *AAS* 57 (1965), 63.

51. Second Vatican Ecumenical Council, Constitution on the Sacred Liturgy *Sacrosanctum Concilium*, 83: *AAS* 56 (1964), 121.

52. Second Vatican Ecumenical Council, Dogmatic Constitution on the Church *Lumen Gentium*, 63: *AAS* 57 (1965), 64.

53. Ibid., 64: *AAS* 57 (1965), 64.

54. *Tractatus 25 (In Nativitate Domini)*, 5: *CCL* 138, 123; *SCh.* 22, 132; cf. also *Tractatus 29 (In Nativitate Domini)*, 1: *CCL* ibid., 147; *SCh.* ibid., 178; *Tractatus 63 (De Passione Domini)*, 6: *CCL* ibid. 386: *SCh.* 74, 82.

55. M. Ferotin, *Le Liber Mozarabicus Sacramentorum*, col. 56.

purification of the mother (cf. Lv 12:6–8), a mystery of salvation related to the history of salvation. That is, she has noted the continuity of the fundamental offering that the incarnate Word made to the Father when he entered the world (cf. Heb 15:5–7). The Church has seen the universal nature of salvation proclaimed, for Simeon, greeting in the Child the light to enlighten the peoples and the glory of the people Israel (cf. Lk 2:32), recognized in him the Messiah, the Savior of all. The Church has understood the prophetic reference to the passion of Christ: the fact that Simeon's words, which linked in one prophecy the Son as "the sign of contradiction" (Lk 2:34) and the Mother, whose soul would be pierced by a sword (cf. Lk 2:35), came true on Calvary. It is a mystery of salvation, therefore, that in its various aspects orients the episode of the Presentation in the Temple to the salvific event of the cross. But the Church herself, in particular from the Middle Ages onward, has detected in the heart of the Virgin taking her Son to Jerusalem to present him to the Lord (cf. Lk 2:22) a desire to make an offering, a desire that exceeds the ordinary meaning of the rite. A witness to this intuition is found in the loving prayer of St. Bernard: "Offer your Son, holy Virgin, and present to the Lord the blessed fruit of your womb. Offer for the reconciliation of us all the holy Victim which is pleasing to God."[56]

This union of the Mother and the Son in the work of redemption[57] reaches its climax on Calvary, where Christ "offered himself as the perfect sacrifice to God" (Heb 9:14) and where Mary stood by the cross (cf. Jn 19:25), "suffering grievously with her only-begotten Son. There she united herself with a maternal heart to his sacrifice, and lovingly consented to the immolation of this victim which she herself had brought forth"[58] and also was offering to the eternal Father.[59] To perpetuate down the centuries the sacrifice of the cross, the divine Savior instituted the Eucharistic Sacrifice, the memorial of his death and resurrection, and entrusted it to his spouse the Church,[60] which, especially on Sundays, calls the faithful together to cel-

---

56. *In Purificatione B. Mariae., Sermo III,* 2: *PL* 183, 370; *Sancti Bernardi Opera,* ed. J. Leclercq-H. Rochais, vol. IV, Rome, 1966, 342.

57. Cf. Second Vatican Ecumenical Council, Dogmatic Constitution on the Church *Lumen Gentium,* 57: *AAS* 57 (1965), 61.

58. Ibid., 58: *AAS* 57 (1965), 61.

59. Cf. Pius XII, Encyclical Letter *Mystici Corporis: AAS* 35 (1943), 247.

60. Cf. Second Vatican Ecumenical Council, Constitution on the Sacred Liturgy *Sacrosanctum Concilium,* 47: *AAS* 56 (1964), 113.

ebrate the Passover of the Lord until he comes again.[61] This the Church does in union with the saints in heaven and in particular with the Blessed Virgin,[62] whose burning charity and unshakable faith she imitates.

21. Mary is not only an example for the whole Church in the exercise of divine worship but is also, clearly, a teacher of the spiritual life for individual Christians. The faithful at a very early date began to look to Mary and to imitate her in making their lives an act of worship of God, and making their worship a commitment of their lives. As early as the fourth century, St. Ambrose, speaking to the people, expressed the hope that each of them would have the spirit of Mary in order to glorify God: "May the heart of Mary be in each Christian to proclaim the greatness of the Lord; may her spirit be in everyone to exult in God."[63] But Mary is above all the example of that worship that consists in making one's life an offering to God. This is an ancient and ever new doctrine that each individual can hear again by heeding the Church's teaching, but also by heeding the very voice of the Virgin as she, anticipating in herself the wonderful petition of the Lord's Prayer— "Your will be done" (Mt 6:10)—replied to God's messenger: "I am the handmaid of the Lord. Let what you have said be done to me" (Lk 1:38). And Mary's "yes" is for all Christians a lesson and example of obedience to the will of the father, which is the way and means of one's own sanctification.

22. It is also important to note how the Church expresses in various effective attitudes of devotion the many relationships that bind her to Mary: in profound veneration, when she reflects on the singular dignity of the Virgin who, through the action of the Holy Spirit has become Mother of the incarnate Word; in burning love, when she considers the spiritual motherhood of Mary toward all members of the Mystical Body; in trusting invocation, when she experiences the intercession of her advocate and helper;[64] in loving service, when she sees in the humble

---

61. Ibid., 102, 106: *AAS* 56 (1964), 125, 126.

62. "Deign to remember all who have been pleasing to you throughout the ages: the holy fathers, the patriarchs, prophets, apostles...and the holy and glorious Mother of God and all the saints...may they remember our misery and poverty, and together with us may they offer you this great and unbloody sacrifice": *Anaphora Iacobi fratris Domini syriaca: Prex Eucharistica,* ed. A. Hänggi-I. Pahl, Fribourg, Editions Universitaires, 1968, 274.

63. *Expositio Evangelii secundum Lucam,* 11, 26: *CSEL* 32, IV, 55: *SCh.* 45, 83–84.

64. Cf. Second Vatican Ecumenical Council, Dogmatic Constitution on the Church *Lumen Gentium,* 62: *AAS* 57 (1965), 63.

handmaid of the Lord the Queen of Mercy and the Mother of Grace; in zealous imitation, when she contemplates the holiness and virtues of Mary who is "full of grace" (Lk 1:28); in profound wonder, when she sees in her, "as in a faultless model, that which she herself wholly desires and hopes to be";[65] in attentive study, when she recognizes in the associate of the Redeemer, who already shares fully in the fruits of the Paschal Mystery, the prophetic fulfillment of her own future, until the day on which, when she has been purified of every spot and wrinkle (cf. Eph 5:27), she will become like a bride arrayed for the bridegroom, Jesus Christ (cf. Rv 21:2).

23. Therefore, venerable brothers, as we consider the piety that the liturgical tradition of the universal Church and the renewed Roman Rite expresses toward the holy Mother of God, and as we remember that the liturgy through its preeminent value as worship constitutes the golden norm for Christian piety, and finally as we observe how the Church, when she celebrates the sacred mysteries, assumes an attitude of faith and love similar to that of the Virgin, we realize the rightness of the exhortation that the Second Vatican Council addresses to all the children of the Church, namely "that the cult, especially the liturgical cult, of the Blessed Virgin be generously fostered."[66] This is an exhortation that we would like to see accepted everywhere without reservation and put into zealous practice.

---

65. Cf. Second Vatican Ecumenical Council, Constitution on the Sacred Liturgy *Sacrosanctum Concilium,* 103: *AAS* 56 (1964), 125.

66. Cf. Second Vatican Ecumenical Council, Dogmatic Constitution on the Church *Lumen Gentium,* 67: *AAS* 57 (1965), 65–66.

PART TWO: THE RENEWAL
OF DEVOTION TO MARY

24. The Second Vatican Council also exhorts us to promote other forms of piety side by side with liturgical worship, especially those recommended by the Magisterium.[67] However, as is well known, the piety of the faithful and their veneration of the Mother of God has taken on many forms according to circumstances of time and place, the different sensibilities of peoples and their different cultural traditions. Hence it is that the forms in which this devotion is expressed, being subject to the ravages of time, show the need for a renewal that will permit them to substitute elements that are transient, to emphasize the elements that are ever new, and to incorporate the doctrinal data obtained from theological reflection and the proposals of the Church's Magisterium. This shows the need for episcopal conferences, local churches, religious families and communities of the faithful to promote a genuine creative activity and at the same time to proceed to a careful revision of expressions and exercises of piety directed toward the Blessed Virgin. We would like this revision to be respectful of wholesome tradition and open to the legitimate requests of the people of our time. It seems fitting therefore, venerable brothers, to put forward some principles for action in this field.

Section One: Trinitarian, Christological and Ecclesial Aspects of Devotion to the Blessed Virgin

25. In the first place it is supremely fitting that exercises of piety directed toward the Virgin Mary should clearly express the Trinitarian and Christological note that is intrinsic and essential to them. Christian worship in fact is of itself worship offered to the Father and to the Son

---

67. Cf. Ibid.

and to the Holy Spirit, or, as the liturgy puts it, to the Father through Christ in the Spirit. From this point of view worship is rightly extended, though in a substantially different way, first and foremost and in a special manner, to the Mother of the Lord and then to the saints, in whom the Church proclaims the Paschal Mystery, for they have suffered with Christ and have been glorified with him.[68] In the Virgin Mary everything is relative to Christ and dependent upon him. It was with a view to Christ that God the Father from all eternity chose her to be the all-holy Mother and adorned her with gifts of the Spirit granted to no one else. Certainly genuine Christian piety has never failed to highlight the indissoluble link and essential relationship of the Virgin to the divine Savior.[69] Yet it seems to us particularly in conformity with the spiritual orientation of our time, which is dominated and absorbed by the "question of Christ,"[70] that in the expressions of devotion to the Virgin the Christological aspect should have particular prominence. It likewise seems to us fitting that these expressions of devotion should reflect God's plan, which laid down "with one single decree the origin of Mary and the Incarnation of the divine Wisdom."[71] This will without doubt contribute to making piety toward the Mother of Jesus more solid, and to making it an effective instrument for attaining to full "knowledge of the Son of God, until we become the perfect man, fully mature with the fullness of Christ himself" (Eph 4:13). It will also contribute to increasing the worship due to Christ himself, since, according to the perennial mind of the Church authoritatively repeated in our own day,[72] "what is given to the handmaid is referred to the Lord; thus what is given to the Mother redounds to the Son...and thus what is given as humble tribute to the Queen becomes honor rendered to the King."[73]

---

68. Cf. Second Vatican Ecumenical Council, Constitution on the Sacred Liturgy *Sacrosanctum Concilium,* 104: *AAS* 56 (1964), 125–126.

69. Cf. Second Vatican Ecumenical Council, Dogmatic Constitution on the Church *Lumen Gentium,* 66: *AAS* 57 (1965), 65.

70. Cf. Paul IV, Talk of April 24, 1970, in the Church of Our Lady of Bonaria in Cagliari: *AAS* 62 (1970), 300.

71. Pius IX, Apostolic Letter *Ineffabilis Deus;* Pius IX, *Pontificis Maximi Acta,* l, 1, Rome, 1854, 599. Cf. also V. Sardi, *La solenne definizione del dogma dell'Immacolato concepimento di Maria Santissima, Atti e documenti,* Rome, 1904–1905, vol. II, 302.

72. Cf. Second Vatican Ecumenical Council, Dogmatic Constitution on the Church *Lumen Gentium,* 66: *AAS* 57 (1965), 65.

73. St. Ildephonsus, *De Virginitate Perpetua Sanctae Mariae,* chapter XII: *PL* 96, 108.

26. It seems to us useful to add to this mention of the Christological orientation of devotion to the Blessed Virgin a reminder of the fittingness of giving prominence in this devotion to one of the essential facts of the faith: the Person and work of the Holy Spirit. Theological reflection and the liturgy have in fact noted how the sanctifying intervention of the Spirit in the Virgin of Nazareth was a culminating moment of the Spirit's action in the history of salvation. Thus, for example, some Fathers and writers of the Church attributed to the work of the Spirit the original holiness of Mary, who was as it were "fashioned by the Holy Spirit into a kind of new substance and new creature."[74] Reflecting on the Gospel texts— "The Holy Spirit will come upon you and the power of the Most High will cover you with his shadow" (Lk 1:35) and "[Mary] was found to be with child through the Holy Spirit.... She has conceived what is in her by the Holy Spirit" (Mt 1:18, 20)—they saw in the Spirit's intervention an action that consecrated and made fruitful Mary's virginity[75] and transformed her into the "Abode of the King" or "Bridal Chamber of the Word,"[76] the "Temple" or "Tabernacle of the Lord,"[77] the "Ark of the Covenant" or "the Ark of Holiness,"[78] titles rich

---

74. Cf. Second Vatican Ecumenical Council, Dogmatic Constitution on the Church *Lumen Gentium,* 56: *AAS* 57 (1965), 60, and the authors mentioned in note 176 of the document.

75. Cf. St. Ambrose, *De Spiritu Sancto,* II, 37–38: *CSEL* 79, 100–101; Cassian, *De Incarnatione Domini,* II, chapter 2: *CSEL* 17, 247–249; St. Bede, *Homily,* 1, 3: *CCL* 122, 18, 20.

76. Cf. St. Ambrose, *De Institutione Virginis,* chapter 12, 79: *PL* 16 (ed. 1880), 339; *Epistula* 30, 3 and *Epistula* 42, 7: ibid., 1107, 1175; *Expositio Evangelii Secundum Lucam,* 10, 132. *SCh.* 52, 200; St. Proclus of Constantinople, *Oratio* 1, 1 and *Oratio* 5, 3: *PG* 65, 681 and 720; St. Basil of Seleucia, *Oratio* 39, 3: *PG* 85, 433; St. Andrew of Crete, *Oratio* 4: *PG* 97, 868; St. Germanus of Constantinople, *Oratio* 3, 15: *PG* 98, 305.

77. Cf. St. Jerome, *Adversus Iovinianum,* I, 33: *PL* 23, 267; St. Ambrose, *Epistula* 63, 33: *PL* 16 (ed. 1880), 1249; *De Institutione Virginis,* chapter 17, 105: ibid., 346; *De Spiritu Sancto,* III, 79–80: *CSEL* 79, 182–183; Sedulius, Hymn *"A solis ortus cardine,"* verses 13–14: *CSEL* 10, 164; *Akathistos Hymn,* Str 23; ed. I. B. Pitra, *Analecta Sacra,* I, 261; St. Proclus of Constantinople, *Oratio* 1, 3: *PG* 65, 648; *Oratio* 2, 6: ibid., 700; St. Basil of Seleucia, *Oratio* 4, *In Nativitatem B. Mariae: PG* 97, 868; St. John Damascene, *Oratio* 4, 10: *PG* 96, 677.

78. Cf. Severus of Antioch, *Homily* 57: *PG* 8, 357–358; Hesychius of Jerusalem, *Homilia de Sancta Maria Deipara: PG* 93, 1464; Chrysippus of Jerusalem, *Oratio in Sanctam Mariam Deiparam,* 2: *PG* 19, 338: St. Andrew of Crete, *Oratio* 5: *PG* 97, 896; St. John Damascene, *Oratio* 6, 6: *PG* 96, 972.

in biblical echoes. Examining more deeply still the mystery of the Incarnation, they saw in the mysterious relationship between the Spirit and Mary an aspect redolent of marriage, poetically portrayed by Prudentius: "The unwed Virgin espoused the Spirit,"[79] and they called her the "Temple of the Holy Spirit,"[80] an expression that emphasizes the sacred character of the Virgin, now the permanent dwelling of the Spirit of God. Delving deeply into the doctrine of the Paraclete, they saw that from him as from a spring there flowed forth the fullness of grace (cf. Lk 1:28) and the abundance of gifts that adorned her. Thus they attributed to the Spirit the faith, hope and charity that animated the Virgin's heart, the strength that sustained her acceptance of the will of God, and the vigor that upheld her in her suffering at the foot of the cross.[81] In Mary's prophetic canticle (cf. Lk 1:46–55) they saw a special working of the Spirit who had spoken through the mouths of the prophets.[82] Considering, finally, the presence of the Mother of Jesus in the upper room, where the Spirit came down upon the infant Church (cf. Acts 1:12–14; 2:1–4), they enriched with new developments the ancient theme of Mary and the Church.[83] Above all they had recourse to the Virgin's intercession in order to obtain from the Spirit the capacity for engendering Christ in their own soul, as is attested to by St. Ildephonsus in a prayer

---

79. *Liber Apotheosis,* verses 571–572: *CCL* 126, 97.

80. Cf. St. Isidore, *De Ortu et Obitu Patrum,* chapter 67, 3: *PL* 83, 148; St. Ildephonsus, *De Virginitate Perpetua Sanctae Mariae,* chapter 10: *PL* 96, 95; St. Bernard, *In Assumptione B. Virginis Mariae: Sermo* 4, 4: *PL* 183, 428: *In Nativitate B. Virginis Mariae:* ibid. 442; St. Peter Damien, *Carmina Sacra et Preces, II, Oratio ad Deum Filium: PL* 145, 921; *Antiphonalium Officii,* ed. R. J. Hesbert, Rome, 1970, vol. 4, 6314, 80.

81. Cf. Paulus Diaconus, *Homily I, In Assumptione B. Mariae Virginis: PL* 95, 1567: *De Assumptione Sanctae Mariae Virginis:* Paschasius Radbertus, trib., 31, 42, 57, 83: ed. A. Ripberger, in "Spicilegium Friburgense," 9, 1962, 72, 76, 84, 96–97; Eadmer of Canterbury, *De Excellentia Virginis Mariae,* chapters 4–5: *PL* 159, 562–567; St. Bernard, *In Laudibus Virginis Matris, Homilia* 4, 3: *Sancti Bernardi Opera,* ed. J. Leclercq-H. Rochais, 4, Rome, 1966, 49–50.

82. Cf. Origen, *In Lucam Homilia* 7, 3: *PG* 13, 1817: *SCh.* 87, 156; St. Cyril of Alexandria, *Commentarius in Aggaeum Prophetam,* chapter 19: *PG* 71, 1060; St. Ambrose, *De Fide,* 4, 9, 113–114: *CSEL* 78, 197–198: *Expositio Evangelii Secundum Lucam,* I; 23, 27–28: *CSEL* 32, IV, 53–54 and 55–56; Severianus Gabalensis, Antipater of Bostra, *Homilia in Sanctissimae Deiparae Annuntiationem,* 16: *PG* 85, 1785.

83. Cf. Eadmer of Canterbury, *De Excellentia Virginis Mariae,* chapter 7: *PG* 159, 571; St. Amadeus of Lausanne, *De Maria Virginea Matre, Homily* 7: *PL* 188, 1337: *SCh.* 72, 184.

of supplication, amazing in its doctrine and prayerful power: "I beg you, holy Virgin, that I may have Jesus from the Holy Spirit, by whom you brought Jesus forth. May my soul receive Jesus through the Holy Spirit by whom your flesh conceived Jesus.... May I love Jesus in the Holy Spirit, in whom you adore Jesus as Lord and gaze upon him as your Son."[84]

27. It is sometimes said that many spiritual writings today do not sufficiently reflect the whole doctrine concerning the Holy Spirit. It is the task of specialists to verify and weigh the truth of this assertion, but it is our task to exhort everyone, especially those in the pastoral ministry and also theologians, to meditate more deeply on the working of the Holy Spirit in the history of salvation, and to ensure that Christian spiritual writings give due prominence to his life-giving action. Such a study will bring out in particular the hidden relationship between the Spirit of God and the Virgin of Nazareth, and show the influence they exert on the Church. From a more profound meditation on the truths of the faith will flow a more vital piety.

28. It is also necessary that exercises of piety with which the faithful honor the Mother of the Lord should clearly show the place she occupies in the Church: "the highest place and the closest to us after Christ."[85] The liturgical buildings of Byzantine rite, both in the architectural structure itself and in the use of images, show clearly Mary's place in the Church. On the central door of the iconostasis there is a representation of the annunciation, and in the apse an image of the glorious *Theotókos*. In this way one perceives how through the assent of the humble handmaid of the Lord mankind begins its return to God, and sees in the glory of the all-holy Virgin the goal toward which it is journeying. The symbolism by which a church building demonstrates Mary's place in the mystery of the Church is full of significance, and gives grounds for hoping that the different forms of devotion to the Blessed Virgin may everywhere be open to ecclesial perspectives.

The faithful will be able to appreciate more easily Mary's mission in the mystery of the Church and her preeminent place in the communion of saints if attention is drawn to the Second Vatican Council's references

---

84. *De Virginitate Perpetua Sanctae Mariae,* chapter 12: *PL* 96, 106.

85. Second Vatican Ecumenical Council, Dogmatic Constitution on the Church *Lumen Gentium,* 54: *AAS* 57 (1965), 59. Cf. Paul VI, *Allocution to the Council Fathers,* December 4, 1963: *AAS* 56 (1964), 37.

to the fundamental concepts of the nature of the Church as the Family of God, the People of God, the Kingdom of God and the Mystical Body of Christ.[86] This will also bring the faithful to a deeper realization of the brotherhood which unites all of them as sons and daughters of the Virgin Mary, "who with a mother's love has cooperated in their rebirth and spiritual formation,"[87] and as sons and daughters of the Church, since "we are born from the Church's womb; we are nurtured by the Church's milk; we are given life by the Church's Spirit."[88] They will also realize that both the Church and Mary collaborate to give birth to the Mystical Body of Christ since "both of them are the Mother of Christ, but neither brings forth the whole [body] independently of the other."[89] Similarly the faithful will appreciate more clearly that the action of the Church in the world can be likened to an extension of Mary's concern. The active love she showed at Nazareth, in the house of Elizabeth, at Cana and on Golgotha—all salvific episodes having vast ecclesial importance—finds its extension in the Church's maternal concern that all men should come to knowledge of the truth (cf. 1 Tm 2:4), in the Church's concern for people in lowly circumstances and for the poor and weak, and in her constant commitment to peace and social harmony, as well as in her untiring efforts to ensure that all men will share in the salvation which was merited for them by Christ's death. Thus love for the Church will become love for Mary, and vice versa, since the one cannot exist without the other, as St. Chromatius of Aquileia observed with keen discernment: "The Church was united...in the upper room with Mary the Mother of Jesus and with his brethren. The Church therefore cannot be referred to as such unless it includes Mary the Mother of our Lord, together with his brethren."[90] In conclusion, therefore, we repeat that devotion to the Blessed Virgin must explicitly show its intrinsic and ecclesiological content: thus it will be enabled to revise its forms and texts in a fitting way.

---

86. Second Vatican Ecumenical Council, Dogmatic Constitution on the Church *Lumen Gentium,* 6, 7–8, 9–11: *AAS* 57 (1965), 8–9, 9–12, 12–21.

87. Ibid., 63: *AAS* 57 (1965), 64.

88. St Cyprian, *De Catholicae Ecclesiae Unitate,* 5: *CSEL* 3, 214.

89. Isaac de Stella, *Sermo 51, In Assumptione B. Mariae: PL* 194, 1863.

90. *Sermo* 30, I: *SCh.* 164, 134.

Section Two: Four Guidelines for Devotion to the Blessed Virgin: Biblical, Liturgical, Ecumenical and Anthropological

29. The above considerations spring from an examination of the Virgin Mary's relationship with God—the Father and the Son and the Holy Spirit—and with the Church. Following the path traced by conciliar teaching,[91] we wish to add some further guidelines from Scripture, liturgy, ecumenism and anthropology. These are to be borne in mind in any revision of exercises of piety or in the creation of new ones, in order to emphasize and accentuate the bond which unites us to Mary, who is the Mother of Christ and our Mother in the communion of saints.

30. Today it is recognized as a general need of Christian piety that every form of worship should have a biblical imprint. The progress made in biblical studies, the increasing dissemination of the Sacred Scriptures, and above all the example of tradition and the interior action of the Holy Spirit are tending to cause the modern Christian to use the Bible ever increasingly as the basic prayer book, and to draw from it genuine inspiration and unsurpassable examples. Devotion to the Blessed Virgin cannot be exempt from this general orientation of Christian piety;[92] indeed it should draw inspiration in a special way from this orientation in order to gain new vigor and sure help. In its wonderful presentation of God's plan for man's salvation, the Bible is replete with the mystery of the Savior, and from Genesis to the Book of Revelation, also contains clear references to Mary, who was the Mother and associate of the Savior. We would not, however, wish this biblical imprint to be merely a diligent use of texts and symbols skillfully selected from the Sacred Scriptures. More than this is necessary. What is needed is that texts of prayers and chants should draw their inspiration and their wording from the Bible, and above all that devotion to the Virgin should be imbued with the great themes of the Christian message. This will ensure that, as they venerate the Seat of Wisdom, the faithful in their turn will be enlightened by the divine word, and be inspired to live their lives in accordance with the precepts of incarnate Wisdom.

---

91. Cf. Second Vatican Ecumenical Council, Dogmatic Constitution on the Church *Lumen Gentium,* 66–69: *AAS* 57 (1965), 65–67.

92. Cf. Second Vatican Ecumenical Council, Dogmatic Constitution on Divine Revelation *Dei Verbum,* 25: *AAS* 58 (1966), 829–830.

31. We have already spoken of the veneration which the Church gives to the Mother of God in the celebration of the sacred liturgy. However, speaking of the other forms of devotion and of the criteria on which they should be based, we wish to recall the norm laid down in the Constitution *Sacrosanctum Concilium.* This document, while wholeheartedly approving of the practices of piety of the Christian people, goes on to say: "...it is necessary, however, that such devotions with consideration for the liturgical seasons should be so arranged as to be in harmony with the sacred liturgy. They should somehow derive their inspiration from it, and because of its preeminence they should orient the Christian people toward it."[93] Although this is a wise and clear rule, its application is not an easy matter, especially in regard to Marian devotions, which are so varied in their formal expressions. What is needed on the part of the leaders of the local communities is effort, pastoral sensitivity and perseverance, while the faithful on their part must show a willingness to accept guidelines and ideas drawn from the true nature of Christian worship; this sometimes makes it necessary to change longstanding customs wherein the real nature of this Christian worship has become somewhat obscured.

In this context we wish to mention two attitudes which in pastoral practice could nullify the norm of the Second Vatican Council. In the first place there are certain persons concerned with the care of souls who scorn *a priori,* devotions of piety which in their correct forms have been recommended by the Magisterium, who leave them aside and in this way create a vacuum which they do not fill. They forget that the Council has said that devotions of piety should harmonize with the liturgy, not be suppressed. Secondly, there are those who, without wholesome liturgical and pastoral criteria, mix practices of piety and liturgical acts in hybrid celebrations. It sometimes happens that novenas or similar practices of piety are inserted into the very celebration of the Eucharistic Sacrifice. This creates the danger that the Lord's Memorial Rite, instead of being the culmination of the meeting of the Christian community, becomes the occasion, as it were, for devotional practices. For those who act in this way we wish to recall the rule laid down by the Council pre-

---

93. *Op. cit.,* 13: *AAS* 56 (1964), 103.

scribing that exercises of piety should be harmonized with the liturgy, not merged into it. Wise pastoral action should, on the one hand, point out and emphasize the proper nature of the liturgical acts, while on the other hand it should enhance the value of practices of piety in order to adapt them to the needs of individual communities in the Church and to make them valuable aids to the liturgy.

32. Because of its ecclesial character, devotion to the Blessed Virgin reflects the preoccupations of the Church herself. Among these especially in our day is her anxiety for the re-establishment of Christian unity. In this way devotion to the Mother of the Lord is in accord with the deep desires and aims of the ecumenical movement, that is, it acquires an ecumenical aspect. This is so for a number of reasons.

In the first place, in venerating with particular love the glorious *Theotókos* and in acclaiming her as the "Hope of Christians,"[94] Catholics unite themselves with their brethren of the Orthodox Churches, in which devotion to the Blessed Virgin finds its expression in a beautiful lyricism and in solid doctrine. Catholics are also united with Anglicans, whose classical theologians have already drawn attention to the sound scriptural basis for devotion to the Mother of our Lord, while those of the present day increasingly underline the importance of Mary's place in the Christian life. Praising God with the very words of the Virgin (cf. Lk 1:46–55), they are united, too, with their brethren in the Churches of the Reform, where love for the Sacred Scriptures flourishes.

For Catholics, devotion to the Mother of Christ and Mother of Christians is also a natural and frequent opportunity for seeking her intercession with her Son in order to obtain the union of all the baptized within a single People of God.[95] Yet again, the ecumenical aspect of Marian devotion is shown in the Catholic Church's desire that, without in any way detracting from the unique character of this devotion,[96] every care should be taken to avoid any exaggeration which could mislead

---

94. Cf. *Officum Magni Canonis Paracletici, Magnum Orologion*, Athens, 1963, 558: *passim* in liturgical canons and prayers: cf. Sophronius Eustradiadou, *Theotokarion,* Chennevières-su Marne, 1931, 9, 19.

95. Cf. Second Vatican Ecumenical Council, Dogmatic Constitution on the Church *Lumen Gentium,* 69: *AAS* 57 (1965), 66–67.

96. Cf. ibid., 66: *AAS* 57 (1965), 65; Constitution on the Sacred Liturgy *Sacrosanctum Concilium,* 103: *AAS* 56 (1964), 125.

other Christian brethren about the true doctrine of the Catholic Church.[97] Similarly, the Church desires that any manifestation of cult which is opposed to correct Catholic practice should be eliminated.

Finally, since it is natural that in true devotion to the Blessed Virgin "the Son should be duly known, loved and glorified...when the Mother is honored,"[98] such devotion is an approach to Christ, the source and center of ecclesiastical communion, in which all who openly confess that he is God and Lord, Savior and sole Mediator (cf. 1 Tm 2:5) are called to be one, with one another, with Christ and with the Father in the unity of the Holy Spirit.[99]

33. We realize that there exist important differences between the thought of many of our brethren in other Churches and ecclesial communities and the Catholic doctrine on "Mary's role in the work of salvation."[100] In consequence there are likewise differences of opinion on the devotion which should be shown to her. Nevertheless, since it is the same power of the Most High which overshadowed the Virgin of Nazareth (cf. Lk 1:35) and which today is at work within the ecumenical movement and making it fruitful, we wish to express our confidence that devotion to the humble handmaid of the Lord, in whom the Almighty has done great things (cf. Lk 1:49), will become, even if only slowly, not an obstacle but a path and a rallying point for the union of all who believe in Christ. We are glad to see that, in fact, a better understanding of Mary's place in the mystery of Christ and of the Church on the part also of our separated brethren is smoothing the path to union. Just as at Cana the Blessed Virgin's intervention resulted in Christ's performing his first miracle (cf. Jn 2:1–12), so today her intercession can help to bring to realization the time when the disciples of Christ will again find full communion in faith. This hope of ours is strengthened by a remark of our predecessor Leo XIII, who wrote that the cause of Christian unity "properly pertains to the role of Mary's spiritual motherhood. For Mary did

---

97. Second Vatican Ecumenical Council, Dogmatic Constitution on the Church *Lumen Gentium,* 67: *AAS* 57 (1965), 65–66.

98. Ibid, 66: *AAS* 57 (1965), 65.

99. Cf. Paul VI, *Address in the Vatican Basilica to the Fathers of the Council,* November 21, 1964: *AAS* 56 (1964), 1017.

100. Second Vatican Ecumenical Council, Decree on Ecumenism *Unitatis Redintegratio,* 20: *AAS* 57 (1965), 105.

not and cannot engender those who belong to Christ, except in one faith and one love: for 'Is Christ divided?' (1 Cor 1:13) We must all live together the life of Christ, so that in one and the same body 'we may bear fruit for God'"[101] (Rm 7:4).

34. Devotion to the Blessed Virgin must also pay close attention to certain findings of the human sciences. This will help to eliminate one of the causes of the difficulties experienced in devotion to the Mother of the Lord, namely, the discrepancy existing between some aspects of this devotion and modern anthropological discoveries, and the profound changes which have occurred in the psycho-sociological field in which modern man lives and works. The picture of the Blessed Virgin presented in a certain type of devotional literature cannot easily be reconciled with today's lifestyle, especially the way women live today. In the home, woman's equality and coresponsibility with man in the running of the family are being justly recognized by laws and the evolution of customs. In the sphere of politics, women have in many countries gained a position in public life equal to that of men. In the social field, women are at work in a whole range of different employments, getting further away every day from the restricted surroundings of the home. In the cultural field, new possibilities are opening up for women in scientific research and intellectual activities.

In consequence of these phenomena, some people are becoming disenchanted with devotion to the Blessed Virgin and finding it difficult to take as an example Mary of Nazareth because the horizons of her life, so they say, seem rather restricted in comparison with the vast spheres of activity open to mankind today. In this regard we exhort theologians, those responsible for the local Christian communities and the faithful themselves to examine these difficulties with due care. At the same time we wish to take the opportunity of offering our own contribution to their solution by making a few observations.

35. First, the Virgin Mary has always been proposed to the faithful by the Church as an example to be imitated, not precisely in the type of life she led, and much less for the socio-cultural background in which she lived and which today scarcely exists anywhere. She is held up as an

---

101. Encyclical Letter *Adiutricem Populi: AAS* 28 (1895–1896), 135.

example to the faithful rather for the way in which, in her own particular life, she fully and responsibly accepted the will of God (cf. Lk 1:38), because she heard the Word of God and acted on it, and because charity and a spirit of service were the driving force of her actions. She is worthy of imitation because she was the first and the most perfect of Christ's disciples. All of this has a permanent and universal exemplary value.

36. Secondly, we would like to point out that the difficulties alluded to above are closely related to certain aspects of the image of Mary found in popular writings. They are not connected with the Gospel image of Mary, nor with the doctrinal data which have been made explicit through a slow and conscientious process of drawing from revelation. It should be considered quite normal for succeeding generations of Christians in differing socio-cultural contexts to have expressed their sentiments about the Mother of Jesus in a way and manner which reflected their own age. In contemplating Mary and her mission these different generations of Christians, looking on her as the New Woman and perfect Christian, found in her as a virgin, wife and mother the outstanding type of womanhood and the preeminent exemplar of life lived in accordance with the Gospels and summing up the most characteristic situations in the life of a woman. When the Church considers the long history of Marian devotion, she rejoices at the continuity of the element of cult which it shows, but she does not bind herself to any particular expression of an individual cultural epoch or to the particular anthropological ideas underlying such expressions. The Church understands that certain outward religious expressions, while perfectly valid in themselves, may be less suitable to men and women of different ages and cultures.

37. Finally, we wish to point out that our own time, no less than former times, is called upon to verify its knowledge of reality with the Word of God, and, keeping to the matter at present under consideration, to compare its anthropological ideas and the problems springing therefrom with the figure of the Virgin Mary as presented by the Gospel. The reading of the divine Scriptures, carried out under the guidance of the Holy Spirit, and with the discoveries of the human sciences and the different situations in the world today being taken into account, will help us to see how Mary can be considered a mirror of the expectations of the men and women of our time. Thus, the modern woman, anxious to participate with decision-making power in the affairs of the community, will contemplate with intimate joy Mary who, taken into dialogue with

God, gives her active and responsible consent,[102] not to the solution of a contingent problem, but to that "event of world importance," as the Incarnation of the Word has been rightly called.[103] The modern woman will appreciate that Mary's choice of the state of virginity, which in God's plan prepared her for the mystery of the Incarnation, was not a rejection of any of the values of the married state but a courageous choice which she made in order to consecrate herself totally to the love of God. The modern woman will note with pleasant surprise that Mary of Nazareth, while completely devoted to the will of God, was far from being a timidly submissive woman or one whose piety was repellent to others; on the contrary, she was a woman who did not hesitate to proclaim that God vindicates the humble and the oppressed, and removes the powerful people of this world from their privileged positions (cf. Lk 1:51–53). The modern woman will recognize in Mary, who "stands out among the poor and humble of the Lord,"[104] a woman of strength, who experienced poverty and suffering, flight and exile (cf. Mt 2:13–23). These are situations that cannot escape the attention of those who wish to support, with the Gospel spirit, the liberating energies of man and of society. And Mary will appear not as a Mother exclusively concerned with her own divine Son, but rather as a woman whose action helped to strengthen the apostolic community's faith in Christ (cf. Jn 2:1–12), and whose maternal role was extended and became universal on Calvary.[105] These are but examples, but examples which show clearly that the figure of the Blessed Virgin does not disillusion any of the profound expectations of the men and women of our time but offers them the perfect model of the disciple of the Lord: the disciple who builds up the earthly and temporal city while being a diligent pilgrim toward the heavenly and eternal city; the disciple who works for that justice which sets free the oppressed, and for that charity which assists the needy; but above all, the disciple who is the active witness of that love which builds up Christ in people's hearts.

---

102. Second Vatican Ecumenical Council, Dogmatic Constitution on the Church *Lumen Gentium,* 56: *AAS* 57 (1965), 60.

103. Cf. St. Peter Chrysologus, *Sermo* 143: *PL* 52, 583.

104. Second Vatican Ecumenical Council, Dogmatic Constitution on the Church *Lumen Gentium,* 55: *AAS* 57 (1965), 59–60.

105. Cf. Paul VI Apostolic Constitution *Signum Magnum,* 1: *AAS* 59 (1967), 467–468: *Roman Missal,* September 15, Prayer over the gifts.

38. Having offered these directives, which are intended to favor the harmonious development of devotion to the Mother of the Lord, we consider it opportune to draw attention to certain attitudes of piety which are incorrect. The Second Vatican Council has already authoritatively denounced both the exaggeration of content and form which even falsifies doctrine, and likewise the small-mindedness which obscures the figure and mission of Mary. The Council has also denounced certain devotional deviations, such as vain credulity, which substitutes reliance on merely external practices for serious commitment. Another deviation is sterile and ephemeral sentimentality, so alien to the spirit of the Gospel that demands persevering and practical action.[106] We reaffirm the Council's reprobation of such attitudes and practices. They are not in harmony with the Catholic Faith and therefore they must have no place in Catholic worship. Careful defense against these errors and deviations will render devotion to the Blessed Virgin more vigorous and more authentic. It will make this devotion solidly based, with the consequence that study of the sources of revelation and attention to the documents of the Magisterium will prevail over the exaggerated search for novelties or extraordinary phenomena. It will ensure that this devotion is objective in its historical setting, and for this reason everything that is ob-viously legendary or false must be eliminated. It will ensure that this devotion matches its doctrinal content—hence the necessity of avoiding a one-sided presentation of the figure of Mary, which by overstressing one element compromises the overall picture given by the Gospel. It will make this devotion clear in its motivation; hence every unworthy self-interest is to be carefully banned from the area of what is sacred.

39. Finally, insofar as it may be necessary we would like to repeat that the ultimate purpose of devotion to the Blessed Virgin is to glorify God and to lead Christians to commit themselves to a life which is in absolute conformity with his will. When the children of the Church unite their voices with the voice of the unknown woman in the Gospel and glorify the Mother of Jesus by saying to him: "Blessed is the womb that bore you and the breasts that you sucked" (Lk 11:27), they will be led to ponder the Divine Master's serious reply: "Blessed rather are those who hear the

---

106. Second Vatican Ecumenical Council Dogmatic Constitution on the Church *Lumen Gentium,* 67: *AAS* 57 (1965), 65–66.

Word of God and keep it!" (Lk 11:28). While it is true that this reply is in itself lively praise of Mary, as various Fathers of the Church interpreted it[107] and the Second Vatican Council has confirmed,[108] it is also an admonition to us to live our lives in accordance with God's commandments. It is also an echo of other words of the Savior: "Not everyone who says to me 'Lord, Lord,' will enter the kingdom of heaven, but he who does the will of my Father who is in heaven" (Mt 7:21); and again: "You are my friends if you do what I command you " (Jn 15:14).

---

107. St. Augustine, *In Iohannis Evangelium, Tractatus* 10, 3: *CCL* 36, 101–102; *Epistula* 243, *Ad Laetum,* 9: *CSEL* 57, 575–576; St. Bede, *In Lucae Evangelium Expositio,* 4, 11, 28: *CCL* 120, 237: *Homily* I, 4: *CCL* 122, 26–27.

108. Second Vatican Ecumenical Council, Dogmatic Constitution on the Church *Lumen Gentium,* 58: *AAS* 57 (1965), 61.

PART THREE: OBSERVATIONS
ON TWO EXERCISES OF PIETY:
THE ANGELUS AND THE ROSARY

40. We have indicated a number of principles which can help to give fresh vigor to devotion to the Mother of the Lord. It is now up to episcopal conferences, to those in charge of local communities and to the various religious congregations prudently to revise practices and exercises of piety in honor of the Blessed Virgin, and to encourage the creative impulse of those who through genuine religious inspiration or pastoral sensitivity wish to establish new forms of piety. For different reasons we nevertheless feel it is opportune to consider here two practices which are widespread in the West, and with which this Apostolic See has concerned itself on various occasions: the Angelus and the rosary.

The Angelus

41. What we have to say about the Angelus is meant to be only a simple but earnest exhortation to continue its traditional recitation wherever and whenever possible. The Angelus does not need to be revised, because of its simple structure, its biblical character, its historical origin which links it to the prayer for peace and safety, and its quasi-liturgical rhythm which sanctifies different moments during the day, and because it reminds us of the Paschal Mystery, in which, recalling the Incarnation of the Son of God, we pray that we may be led "through his passion and cross to the glory of his resurrection."[109] These factors ensure that the Angelus, despite the passing of centuries, retains an unaltered value and

---

109. *Roman Missal,* Fourth Sunday of Advent, Collect. Similarly the Collect of March 25, which may be used in place of the previous one in the recitation of the Angelus.

an intact freshness. It is true that certain customs traditionally linked with the recitation of the Angelus have disappeared or can continue only with difficulty in modern life. But these are marginal elements. The value of contemplation on the mystery of the Incarnation of the Word, of the greeting to the Virgin, and of recourse to her merciful intercession remains unchanged. And despite the changed conditions of the times, for the majority of people there remain unaltered the characteristic periods of the day—morning, noon and evening—which mark the periods of their activity and constitute an invitation to pause in prayer.

The Rosary

42. We wish now, venerable brothers, to dwell for a moment on the renewal of the pious practice which has been called "the compendium of the entire Gospel:"[110] the rosary. To this our predecessors have devoted close attention and care. On many occasions they have recommended its frequent recitation, encouraged its diffusion, explained its nature, recognized its suitability for fostering contemplative prayer—prayer of both praise and petition—and recalled its intrinsic effectiveness for promoting Christian life and apostolic commitment.

We, too, from the first general audience of our pontificate on July 13, 1963, have shown our great esteem for the pious practice of the rosary.[111] Since that time we have underlined its value on many different occasions, some ordinary, some grave. Thus, at a moment of anguish and uncertainty, we published the Letter *Christi Matri* (September 15, 1966), in order to obtain prayers to Our Lady of the Rosary and to implore from God the supreme benefit of peace.[112] We renewed this appeal in our Apostolic Exhortation *Recurrens Mensis* October (October 7, 1969), in which we also commemorated the fourth centenary of the Apostolic Letter *Consueverunt Romani Pontifices* of our predecessor St. Pius V, who in that document explained and in a certain sense established the traditional form of the rosary.[113]

---

110. Pius XII, Letter to the Archbishop of Manila *Philippinas Insulas: AAS* 38 (1946), 419.

111. *Discourse to the Participants in the III Dominican International Rosary Congress: Insegnamenti di Paolo VI,* 1, (1963), 463–464.

112. In *AAS* 58 (1966), 745–749.

113. In *AAS* 61 (1969), 649–654.

43. Our assiduous and affectionate interest in the rosary has led us to follow very attentively the numerous meetings which in recent years have been devoted to the pastoral role of the rosary in the modern world, meetings arranged by associations and individuals profoundly attached to the rosary and attended by bishops, priests, religious and lay people of proven experience and recognized ecclesial awareness. Among these people special mention should be made of the sons of St. Dominic, by tradition the guardians and promoters of this very salutary practice. Parallel with such meetings has been the research work of historians, work aimed not at defining in a sort of archaeological fashion the primitive form of the rosary but at uncovering the original inspiration and driving force behind it and its essential structure. The fundamental characteristics of the rosary, its essential elements and their mutual relationship have all emerged more clearly from these congresses and from the research carried out.

44. Thus, for instance, the Gospel inspiration of the rosary has appeared more clearly: the rosary draws from the Gospel the presentation of the mysteries and its main formulas. As it moves from the angel's joyful greeting and the Virgin's pious assent, the rosary takes its inspiration from the Gospel to suggest the attitude with which the faithful should recite it. In the harmonious succession of Hail Mary's, the rosary puts before us once more a fundamental mystery of the Gospel—the Incarnation of the Word, contemplated at the decisive moment of the annunciation to Mary. The rosary is thus a Gospel prayer, as pastors and scholars like to define it, more today perhaps than in the past.

45. It has also been more easily seen how the orderly and gradual unfolding of the rosary reflects the very way in which the Word of God, mercifully entering into human affairs, brought about the redemption. The rosary considers in harmonious succession the principal salvific events accomplished in Christ, from his virginal conception and the mysteries of his childhood to the culminating moments of the Passover—the blessed passion and the glorious resurrection—and to the effects of this on the infant Church on the day of Pentecost, and on the Virgin Mary when at the end of her earthly life she was assumed body and soul into her heavenly home. It has also been observed that the division of the mysteries of the rosary into three parts not only adheres strictly to the chronological order of the facts but above all reflects the plan of the original proclamation of the faith and sets forth once more the mystery of Christ in the very way in which it is seen by St. Paul in

the celebrated "hymn" of the Letter to the Philippians—*kenosis,* death and exaltation (cf. 2:6–11).

46. As a Gospel prayer, centered on the mystery of the redemptive Incarnation, the rosary is therefore a prayer with a clearly Christological orientation. Its most characteristic element, in fact, the litany-like succession of Hail Mary's, becomes in itself an unceasing praise of Christ, who is the ultimate object both of the angel's announcement and of the greeting of the mother of John the Baptist: "Blessed is the fruit of your womb" (Lk 1:42). We would go further and say that the succession of Hail Mary's constitutes the warp on which is woven the contemplation of the mysteries. The Jesus that each Hail Mary recalls is the same Jesus whom the succession of the mysteries proposes to us—now as the Son of God, now as the Son of the Virgin—at his birth in a stable at Bethlehem, at his presentation by his Mother in the Temple, as a youth full of zeal for his Father's affairs, as the Redeemer in agony in the garden, scourged and crowned with thorns, carrying the cross and dying on Calvary, risen from the dead and ascended to the glory of the Father to send forth the gift of the Spirit. As is well known, at one time there was a custom, still preserved in certain places, of adding to the name of Jesus in each Hail Mary reference to the mystery being contemplated. And this was done precisely in order to help contemplation and to make the mind and the voice act in unison.

47. There has also been felt with greater urgency the need to point out once more the importance of a further essential element in the rosary, in addition to the value of the elements of praise and petition, namely the element of contemplation. Without this the rosary is a body without a soul, and its recitation is in danger of becoming a mechanical repetition of formulas and of going counter to the warning of Christ: "And in praying do not heap up empty phrases as the Gentiles do, for they think that they will be heard for their many words" (Mt 6:7). By its nature the recitation of the rosary calls for a quiet rhythm and a lingering pace, helping the individual to meditate on the mysteries of the Lord's life as seen through the eyes of she who was closest to the Lord. In this way the unfathomable riches of these mysteries are unfolded.

48. Finally, as a result of modern reflection, the relationships between the liturgy and the rosary have been more clearly understood. On the one hand it has been emphasized that the rosary is, as it were, a branch sprung from the ancient trunk of the Christian liturgy, the Psalter of the Blessed Virgin, whereby the humble were associated in the

Church's hymn of praise and universal intercession. On the other hand it has been noted that this development occurred at a time—the last period of the Middle Ages—when the liturgical spirit was in decline and the faithful were turning from the liturgy toward a devotion to Christ's humanity and to the Blessed Virgin Mary, a devotion favoring a certain external sentiment of piety. Not many years ago some people began to express the desire to see the rosary included among the rites of the liturgy, while other people, anxious to avoid repetition of former pastoral mistakes, unjustifiably disregarded the rosary. Today the problem can easily be solved in light of the principles of the Constitution *Sacrosanctum Concilium*. Liturgical celebrations and the pious practice of the rosary must be neither set in opposition to one another nor considered as being identical.[114] The more an expression of prayer preserves its own true nature and individual characteristics, the more fruitful it becomes. Once the preeminent value of liturgical rites has been reaffirmed, it will not be difficult to appreciate the fact that the rosary is a practice of piety which easily harmonizes with the liturgy. In fact, like the liturgy, it is of a community nature, draws its inspiration from Sacred Scripture and is oriented toward the mystery of Christ. The commemoration in the liturgy and the contemplative remembrance proper to the rosary, although existing on essentially different planes of reality, have as their object the same salvific events wrought by Christ. The former presents anew, under the veil of signs and operative in a hidden way, the great mysteries of our redemption. The latter, by means of devout contemplation, recalls these same mysteries to the mind of the person praying, and stimulates the will to draw from them the norms of living. Once this substantial difference has been established, it is not difficult to understand that the rosary is an exercise of piety that draws its motivating force from the liturgy and leads naturally back to it, if practiced in conformity with its original inspiration. It does not, however, become part of the liturgy. In fact, meditation on the mysteries of the rosary, by familiarizing the hearts and minds of the faithful with the mysteries of Christ, can be an excellent preparation for the celebration of those same mysteries in the liturgical action and can also become a continuing echo thereof. However, it is a mistake to recite the rosary during the celebration of the liturgy, though unfortunately this practice still persists here and there.

---

114. Cf. 13: *AAS* 56 (1964), 103.

49. The rosary of the Blessed Virgin Mary, according to the tradition accepted by our predecessor St. Pius V and authoritatively taught by him, consists of various elements disposed in an organic fashion:

a) Contemplation in communion with Mary, of a series of *mysteries of salvation,* wisely distributed into three cycles. These mysteries express the joy of the messianic times, the salvific suffering of Christ, and the glory of the risen Lord which fills the Church. This contemplation by its very nature encourages practical reflection and provides stimulating norms for living.

b) The Lord's Prayer, or Our Father, which by reason of its immense value is at the basis of Christian prayer and ennobles that prayer in its various expressions.

c) The litany-like succession of the Hail Mary, which is made up of the angel's greeting to the Virgin (cf. Lk 1:28), and of Elizabeth's greeting (cf. Lk 1:42), followed by the ecclesial supplication, Holy Mary. The continued series of Hail Mary's is the special characteristic of the rosary, and their number, in the full and typical number of one hundred and fifty, presents a certain analogy with the Psalter and is an element that goes back to the very origin of the exercise of piety. But this number, divided, according to a well-tried custom, into decades attached to the individual mysteries, is distributed in the three cycles already mentioned, thus giving rise to the rosary of fifty Hail Mary's as we know it. This latter has entered into use as the normal measure of the pious exercise and as such has been adopted by popular piety and approved by papal authority, which also enriched it with numerous indulgences.

d) The doxology Glory be to the Father which, in conformity with an orientation common to Christian piety, concludes the prayer with the glorifying of God who is one and three, from whom, through whom and in whom all things have their being (cf. Rm 11:36).

50. These are the elements of the rosary. Each has its own particular character which, wisely understood and appreciated, should be reflected in the recitation in order that the rosary may express all its richness and variety. Thus the recitation will be grave and suppliant during the Lord's Prayer, lyrical and full of praise during the tranquil succession of Hail Mary's, contemplative in the recollected meditation on the mysteries, and full of adoration during the doxology. This applies to all the ways in which the rosary is usually recited: privately, in intimate recollection with the Lord; in community, in the family or in groups of the faithful gathered

together to ensure the special presence of the Lord (cf. Mt 18:20); or publicly, in assemblies to which the ecclesial community is invited.

51. In recent times certain exercises of piety have been created which take their inspiration from the rosary. Among such exercises we wish to draw attention to and recommend those which insert into the ordinary celebration of the Word of God some elements of the rosary, such as meditation on the mysteries and litany-like repetition of the angel's greeting to Mary. In this way these elements gain in importance, since they are found in the context of Bible readings, illustrated with a homily, accompanied by silent pauses and emphasized with song. We are happy to know that such practices have helped to promote a more complete understanding of the spiritual riches of the rosary itself, and have served to restore esteem for its recitation among youth associations and movements.

52. We now desire, as a continuation of the thought of our predecessors, to recommend strongly the recitation of the family rosary. The Second Vatican Council has pointed out how the family, the primary and vital cell of society, "shows itself to be the domestic sanctuary of the Church through the mutual affection of its members and the common prayer they offer to God."[115] The Christian family is thus seen to be a domestic Church[116] if its members, each according to his proper place and tasks, all together promote justice, practice works of mercy, devote themselves to helping their brethren, take part in the apostolate of the wider local community and play their part in its liturgical worship.[117] This will be all the more true if together they offer up prayers to God. If this element of common prayer were missing, the family would lack its very character as a domestic Church. Thus there must logically follow a concrete effort to reinstate communal prayer in family life if there is to be a restoration of the theological concept of the family as the domestic Church.

---

115. Decree on the Apostolate of the Laity *Apostolicam Actuositatem,* 11: *AAS* 58 (1966), 848.

116. Second Vatican Ecumenical Council, Dogmatic Constitution on the Church *Lumen Gentium,* 11: *AAS* 57 (1965), 16.

117. Cf. Second Vatican Ecumenical Council, Decree on the Apostolate of the Laity *Apostolicam Actuositatem,* 11: *AAS* 58 (1966), 848

53. In accordance with the directives of the Council, the *Institutio Generalis de Liturgia Horarum* rightly numbers the family among the groups in which the Divine Office can suitably be celebrated in community: "It is fitting...that the family, as a domestic sanctuary of the Church, should not only offer prayers to God in common, but also, according to circumstances, should recite parts of the Liturgy of the Hours, in order to be more intimately linked with the Church."[118] No avenue should be left unexplored to ensure that this clear and practical recommendation finds within Christian families growing and joyful acceptance.

54. But there is no doubt that, after the celebration of the Liturgy of the Hours, the high point which family prayer can reach, the rosary should be considered as one of the best and most efficacious prayers in common that the Christian family is invited to recite. We like to think, and sincerely hope, that when the family gathering becomes a time of prayer, the rosary is a frequent and favored manner of praying. We are well aware that the changed conditions of life today do not make family gatherings easy, and that even when such a gathering is possible many circumstances make it difficult to turn it into an occasion of prayer. There is no doubt of the difficulty. But it is characteristic of the Christian in his manner of life not to give in to circumstances but to overcome them, not to succumb but to make an effort. Families which want to live in full measure the vocation and spirituality proper to the Christian family must therefore devote all their energies to overcoming the pressures that hinder family gatherings and prayer in common.

55. In concluding these observations, which give proof of the concern and esteem which the Apostolic See has for the rosary of the Blessed Virgin, we desire at the same time to recommend that this very worthy devotion should not be propagated in a way that is too one-sided or exclusive. The rosary is an excellent prayer, but the faithful should feel serenely free in its regard. They should be drawn to its calm recitation by its intrinsic appeal.

---

118. *Op. cit.,* 27.

CONCLUSION

Theological and Pastoral Value of Devotion to the Blessed Virgin

56. Venerable brothers, as we come to the end of this Apostolic Exhortation we wish to sum up and emphasize the theological value of devotion to the Blessed Virgin, and to recall briefly its pastoral effectiveness for renewing the Christian way of life.

The Church's devotion to the Blessed Virgin is an intrinsic element of Christian worship. The honor which the Church has always and everywhere shown to the Mother of the Lord, from the blessing with which Elizabeth greeted Mary (cf. Lk 1:42–45), right up to the expressions of praise and petition used today, is a very strong witness to the Church's norm of prayer and an invitation to become more deeply conscious of her norm of faith. And the converse is likewise true. The Church's norm of faith requires that her norm of prayer should everywhere blossom forth with regard to the Mother of Christ. Such devotion to the Blessed Virgin is firmly rooted in the revealed word and has solid dogmatic foundations. It is based on the singular dignity of Mary, "Mother of the Son of God, and therefore beloved daughter of the Father and Temple of the Holy Spirit—Mary, who, because of this extraordinary grace, is far greater than any other creature on earth or in heaven."[119] This devotion takes into account the part she played at decisive moments in the history of the salvation which her Son accomplished, and her holiness, already full at her Immaculate Conception, yet increasing all the time as she obeyed the will of the Father and accepted the path of suffering (cf. Lk 2:34–35, 41–52; Jn 19:25–27), growing constantly in faith,

---

119. Second Vatican Ecumenical Council, Dogmatic Constitution on the Church *Lumen Gentium,* 53: *AAS* 57 (1965), 58–59.

hope and charity. Devotion to Mary recalls too her mission and the special position she holds within the People of God, of which she is the preeminent member, a shining example and the loving Mother; it recalls her unceasing and efficacious intercession which, although she is assumed into heaven, draws her close to those who ask her help, including those who do not realize that they are her children. It recalls Mary's glory which ennobles the whole of mankind, as the outstanding phrase of Dante recalls: "You have so ennobled human nature that its very Creator did not disdain to share in it."[120] Mary, in fact, is one of our race, a true daughter of Eve—though free of that mother's sin—and truly our sister, who as a poor and humble woman fully shared our lot.

We would add further that devotion to the Blessed Virgin finds its ultimate justification in the unfathomable and free will of God who, being eternal and divine charity (cf. 1 Jn 4:7–8, 16), accomplishes all things according to a loving design. He loved her and did great things for her (cf. Lk 1:49). He loved her for his own sake, and he loved her for our sake, too; he gave her to himself and he gave her also to us.

57. Christ is the only way to the Father (cf. Jn 14:4–11), and the ultimate example to whom the disciple must conform his own conduct (cf. Jn 13:15), to the extent of sharing Christ's sentiments (cf. Phil 2:5), living his life and possessing his Spirit (cf. Gal 2:20; Rm 8:10–11). The Church has always taught this, and nothing in pastoral activity should obscure this doctrine. But the Church, taught by the Holy Spirit and benefiting from centuries of experience, recognizes that devotion to the Blessed Virgin, subordinated to worship of the divine Savior and in connection with it, also has a great pastoral effectiveness and constitutes a force for renewing Christian living. It is easy to see the reason for this effectiveness. Mary's many-sided mission to the People of God is a supernatural reality which operates and bears fruit within the body of the Church. One finds cause for joy in considering the different aspects of this mission, and seeing how each of these aspects with its individual effectiveness is directed toward the same end, namely, producing in the children the spiritual characteristics of the first-born Son. The Virgin's maternal intercession, her exemplary holiness and the divine grace which is in her become for the human race a reason for divine hope.

---

120. *The Divine Comedy,* Paradiso 33, 4–6.

The Blessed Virgin's role as Mother leads the People of God to turn with filial confidence to her, who is ever ready to listen with a mother's affection and efficacious assistance.[121] Thus the People of God have learned to call on her as the Consoler of the afflicted, the Health of the sick, and the Refuge of sinners, that they may find comfort in tribulation, relief in sickness and liberating strength in guilt. For she, who is free from sin, leads her children to combat sin with energy and resoluteness.[122] This liberation from sin and evil (cf. Mt 6:13)—it must be repeated—is the necessary premise for any renewal of Christian living.

The Blessed Virgin's exemplary holiness encourages the faithful to "raise their eyes to Mary who shines forth before the whole community of the elect as a model of the virtues."[123] It is a question of solid, evangelical virtues: faith and the docile acceptance of the Word of God (cf. Lk 1:26–38, 1:45, 11:27–28; Jn 2:5), generous obedience (cf. Lk 1:38), genuine humility (cf. Lk 1:48), solicitous charity (cf. Lk 1:39–56), profound wisdom (cf. Lk 1:29, 34; 2:19, 33:51), worship of God manifested in alacrity in the fulfillment of religious duties (cf. Lk 2:21–41), in gratitude for gifts received (cf. Lk 1:46–49), in her offering in the Temple (cf. Lk 2:22–24) and in her prayer in the midst of the apostolic community (cf. Acts 1:12–14), her fortitude in exile (cf. Mt 2:13–23) and in suffering (cf. Lk 2:34–35, 49; Jn 19:25), her poverty reflecting dignity and trust in God (cf. Lk 1:48, 2:24), her attentive care for her Son—from his humble birth to the ignominy of the cross (cf. Lk 2:1–7; Jn 19:25–27), her delicate forethought (cf. Jn 2:1–11), her virginal purity (cf. Mt 1:18–25; Lk 1:26–38), her strong and chaste married love. These virtues of the Mother will also adorn her children who steadfastly study her example in order to reflect it in their own lives. And this progress in virtue will appear as the consequence and the already mature fruit of that pastoral zeal which springs from devotion to the Blessed Virgin.

Devotion to the Mother of the Lord becomes for the faithful an opportunity for growing in divine grace, and this is the ultimate aim of all pastoral activity. For it is impossible to honor her, who is "full of grace" (Lk 1:28), without thereby honoring in oneself the state of grace, which

---

121. Cf. Second Vatican Ecumenical Council, Dogmatic Constitution on the Church *Lumen Gentium,* 60–63: *AAS* 57 (1965), 62–64.

122. Cf. ibid., 65: *AAS* 57 (1965), 64–65.

123. Ibid., 65: *AAS* 57 (1965), 64.

is friendship with God, communion with him and the indwelling of the Holy Spirit. It is this divine grace which takes possession of the whole man and conforms him to the image of the Son of God (cf. Rm 8:29; Col 1:18). The Catholic Church, endowed with centuries of experience, recognizes in devotion to the Blessed Virgin a powerful aid for man as he strives for fulfillment. Mary, the New Woman, stands at the side of Christ, the New Man, within whose mystery the mystery of man[124] alone finds true light; she is given to us as a pledge and guarantee that God's plan in Christ for the salvation of the whole man has already achieved realization in a creature: in her. Contemplated in the episodes of the Gospels and in the reality which she already possesses in the City of God, the Blessed Virgin Mary offers a calm vision and a reassuring word to modern man, torn as he often is between anguish and hope, defeated by the sense of his own limitations and assailed by limitless aspirations, troubled in his mind and divided in his heart, uncertain before the riddle of death, oppressed by loneliness while yearning for fellowship, a prey to boredom and disgust. She shows forth the victory of hope over anguish, of fellowship over solitude, of peace over anxiety, of joy and beauty over boredom and disgust, of eternal visions over earthly ones, of life over death.

Let the very words that she spoke to the servants at the marriage feast of Cana, "Do whatever he tells you" (Jn 2:5), be a seal on our Exhortation and a further reason in favor of the pastoral value of devotion to the Blessed Virgin as a means of leading men to Christ. Those words, which at first sight were limited to the desire to remedy an embarrassment at the feast, are seen in the context of St. John's Gospel to reecho the words used by the people of Israel to give approval to the covenant at Sinai (cf. Ex 19:8, 24:3, 7; Dt 5:27) and to renew their commitments (cf. Jos 24:24; Ezra 10:12; Neh 5:12). And they are words which harmonize wonderfully with those spoken by the Father at the theophany on Mount Tabor: "Listen to him" (Mt 17:5).

---

124. Cf. Second Vatican Ecumenical Council, Pastoral Constitution on the Church in the Modern World *Gaudium et Spes,* 22: *AAS* 58 (1966), 1042–1044.

EPILOGUE

58. Venerable brothers, we have dealt at length with an integral element of Christian worship: devotion to the Mother of the Lord. This has been called for by the nature of the subject, one which in these recent years has been the object of study and revision and at times the cause of some perplexity. We are consoled to think that the work done by this Apostolic See and by yourselves in order to carry out the norms of the Council—particularly the liturgical reform—is a stepping stone to an ever more lively and adoring worship of God, the Father and the Son and the Holy Spirit, and to an increase of the Christian life of the faithful. We are filled with confidence when we note that the renewed Roman liturgy, also taken as a whole, is a splendid illustration of the Church's devotion to the Blessed Virgin. We are upheld by the hope that the directives issued in order to render this devotion ever more pure and vigorous will be applied with sincerity. We rejoice that the Lord has given us the opportunity of putting forward some points for reflection in order to renew and confirm esteem for the practice of the rosary. Comfort, confidence, hope and joy are the sentiments which we wish to transform into fervent praise and thanksgiving to the Lord as we unite our voice with that of the Blessed Virgin in accordance with the prayer of the Roman liturgy.[125]

Dear brothers, while we express the hope that, thanks to your generous commitment, there will be among the clergy and among the people entrusted to your care a salutary increase of devotion to Mary with un-

---

125. Cf. *Roman Missal,* May 31, Collect.

doubted profit for the Church and for society, we cordially impart our special apostolic blessing to yourselves and to all the faithful people to whom you devote your pastoral zeal.

Given in Rome, at St. Peter's, on the second day of February, the Feast of the Presentation of the Lord, in the year 1974, the eleventh of our pontificate.

Paul VI

ON CHRISTIAN JOY

Gaudete in Domino

Apostolic Exhortation of Pope Paul VI
May 9, 1975

INTRODUCTION

Historical Perspectives

Pope Paul VI issued this document during the Holy Year of 1975. In his typical fashion, he clearly states the concerns and problems of the time, but focuses on the remedy provided by the Holy Spirit. Instead of emphasizing difficulties, the pope points out the sources of joy in the Christian life. Christian joy flows from the gifts of the indwelling Holy Spirit. To live in grace is to find joy. The document states:

> Unfortunately, in our century which is so threatened by the illusion of false happiness, we do not lack opportunities of noting the psychic inability of man to accept "the gifts of the Spirit of God, for they are folly to him, and he is not able to understand them because they are spiritually discerned" (1 Cor 2:14).

The Teaching

For the Christian, profound spiritual discernment is possible only in the Holy Spirit. Mary is a masterpiece of this discernment, and she can sing, "My soul rejoices in God my Savior" (cf. Lk 1:46–48). The pope states:

> The attainment of such an outlook is not just a matter of psychology. It is also a fruit of the Holy Spirit. This Spirit, who dwells fully in the person of Jesus, made him during his earthly life so alert to the joys of daily life, so tactful and persuasive for putting sinners back on the road to a new youth of heart and mind! It is this same Spirit who animated the Blessed Virgin and each of the saints.

In chapter four of the document, "Joy in the Hearts of the Saints," the pope presents Mary as the primary model of Christian joy. She knows joy because she recognizes the great things God has done, and rejoices over them in her heart. Great sufferings came into her life, yet these opened her to the joy of the resurrection.

Mary knows the beatitude promised by the outpouring of the Spirit: "With Christ, she sums up in herself all joys; she lives the perfect joy promised to the Church: *Mater plena sanctae laetitiae.* And it is with good reason that her children on earth, turning to her, who is the mother of hope and of grace, invoke her as the cause of their joy: *causa nostrae laetitiae.*"

Today

The *Catechism of the Catholic Church* continues the above theme and teaches us to pray "in communion with the holy Mother of God" in paragraphs 2673–2679. Here we find honored the varied ways that the Christian people rejoice in the Lord with Mary and turn to her "because she now knows the humanity which, in her, the Son of God espoused" (*CCC* 2675). Here, too, we find the explanation of the Hail Mary (or Rejoice, Mary).

ON CHRISTIAN JOY

Gaudete in Domino

Promulgated by His Holiness Pope Paul VI
On May 9, 1975

III. Joy according to the New Testament

No one is excluded from the joy brought by the Lord. The great joy announced by the angel on Christmas night is truly for all the people (cf. Lk 2:10), both for the people of Israel then anxiously awaiting a Savior, and for the numberless people made up of all those who, in time to come, would receive its message and strive to live by it. The Blessed Virgin Mary was the first to have received its announcement, from the Angel Gabriel, and her Magnificat was already the exultant hymn of all the humble. Whenever we say the rosary, the joyful mysteries thus place us once more before the inexpressible event which is the center and summit of history: the coming on earth of Emmanuel, God with us. John the Baptist, whose mission is to point Him out to the expectation of Israel, had himself leapt for joy, in His presence, in the womb of his mother (cf. Lk 1:44). When Jesus begins His ministry, John "rejoices greatly at the bridegroom's voice..."(Jn 3:29).

IV. Joy in the hearts of the saints

Dear brothers and sons and daughters, such is the joyful hope drawn from the very sources of God's Word. For twenty centuries, this source of joy has not ceased to spring up in the Church, and especially in the hearts of the saints. We must now recall some echoes of this spiritual

181

experience; according to the diversity of charisms and particular vocations, it illustrates the mystery of Christian joy.

In the first rank is the Virgin Mary, full of grace, the Mother of the
Savior. She, accepting the announcement from on high, the Servant of
the Lord, Spouse of the Spirit and Mother of the Eternal Son, manifests
her joy before her cousin Elizabeth who celebrates her faith: "My soul
magnifies the Lord, and my spirit rejoices in God my Savior...henceforth
all generations will call me blessed" (Lk 1:46–48). She has grasped, better than all other creatures, that God accomplishes wonderful things: his
name is holy; he shows his mercy; he raises up the humble; he is faithful
to his promises. Not that the apparent course of her life in any way de-
parts from the ordinary, but she meditates on the least signs of God, pondering them in her heart. Not that she is in any way spared sufferings:
she stands, the Mother of Sorrows, at the foot of the cross, associated in
an eminent way with the sacrifice of the innocent Servant. But she is
also open in an unlimited degree to the joy of the resurrection, and she is
also taken up, body and soul, into the glory of heaven. The first of the
redeemed, immaculate from the moment of her conception, the incomparable dwelling place of the Spirit, the pure abode of the Redeemer of
mankind, she is at the same time the beloved Daughter of God and, in
Christ, the Mother of all. She is the perfect model of the Church both on
earth and in glory. What a marvelous echo the prophetic words about the
new Jerusalem find in her wonderful existence as the Virgin of Israel: "I
will greatly rejoice in the Lord, my soul shall exult in my God, for he
has clothed me with the garment of salvation; he has covered me with
the robe of righteousness, as a bridegroom decks himself with a garland
and as a bride adorns herself with her jewels" (Is 61:10). With Christ,
she sums up in herself all joys; she lives the perfect joy promised to the
Church: *Mater plena sanctae laetitiae.* And it is with good reason that
her children on earth, turning to her, who is the mother of hope and of
grace, invoke her as the cause of their joy: *Causa nostrae laetitiae.*

THE REDEEMER OF MAN

Redemptor Hominis

Encyclical Letter of Pope John Paul II
March 4, 1979

INTRODUCTION

Pope John Paul II was elected on October 16, 1978. From the beginning of his papacy, his devotion to the Blessed Virgin Mary was evident. In accepting his election he said: "So I present myself to you all to confess our common faith, our hope, our confidence in the Mother of Christ and of the Church, and also to start anew on this road of history and of the Church, with the help of God and with the help of men."[1]

Historical Perspectives

From the start, John Paul II often referred to Mary. In his first encyclical, *Redeemer of Man,* he set a direction for future documents. The pope indicates that he is following the lead of *Lumen Gentium,* with its profound teaching about Mary. The thought of the Council has been essential for him. In his teaching he constantly returns to its themes. He then speaks of Mary as the Mother of the Church, using the title Paul VI proclaimed. Mary, giving birth to the Church, is a pattern for our daily lives and actions.

The Teaching

Pope John Paul II sketches the theme of Mary's role in the mystery of the redemption, which he will later fully develop in *Redemptoris Mater.* Mary brings us into this mystery, because God has brought her into it in an exceptional way. The "mystery of the Mother" consists in Mary's unique role: "The special characteristic of the motherly love that the Mother of God inserts in the mystery of the redemption and the life

---

1. *Talks of John Paul II* (Boston: St. Paul Editions, 1979), 49.

of the Church finds expression in its exceptional closeness to man and all that happens to him." Through her maternal love, Mary brings the Father's love close to us: "The Father's eternal love...comes close to each of us through this Mother and thus takes on tokens that are of more easy understanding and access by each person."

Today

In this first encyclical of Pope John Paul II, and later in his pastoral visits to the nations, he often indicates his own *exceptional closeness* to the Mother of God. *This Mother* leads him deeply to Christ and to the Father's eternal love. He is convinced that "the mother"—Mary, the Mother, and all Christians who accept the role of bringing Christ to birth—has an essential role in the redemption of the world.

THE REDEEMER OF MAN

Redemptor Hominis

Promulgated by His Holiness John Paul II
On March 4, 1979

THE MOTHER IN WHOM WE TRUST

22. When, therefore, at the beginning of the new pontificate I turn my thoughts and my heart to the Redeemer of man, I thereby wish to enter and penetrate into the deepest rhythm of the Church's life. Indeed, if the Church lives her life, she does so because she draws it from Christ, and he always wishes but one thing, namely that we should have life and have it abundantly (cf. Jn 10:10). This fullness of life in him is at the same time for man. Therefore the Church, uniting herself with all the riches of the mystery of the redemption, becomes the Church of living people, living because given life from within by the working of "the Spirit of truth" (Jn 16:13) and visited by the love that the Holy Spirit has poured into our hearts (cf. Rm 5:5). The aim of any service in the Church, whether the service is apostolic, pastoral, priestly or episcopal, is to keep up this dynamic link between the mystery of the redemption and every man.

If we are aware of this task, then we seem to understand better what it means to say that the Church is a mother[1] and also what it means to

---

1. Cf. Second Vatican Ecumenical Council, Dogmatic Constitution on the Church *Lumen Gentium,* 63–64: *AAS* 57 (1965), 64.

say that the Church always, and particularly at our time, has need of a mother. We owe a debt of special gratitude to the Fathers of the Second Vatican Council, who expressed this truth in the Constitution *Lumen Gentium* with the rich Mariological doctrine contained in it.[2] Since Paul VI, inspired by that teaching, proclaimed the Mother of Christ "Mother of the Church,"[3] and that title has become known far and wide, may it be permitted to his unworthy successor to turn to Mary as Mother of the Church at the close of these reflections which it was opportune to make at the beginning of his papal service. Mary is Mother of the Church because, on account of the eternal Father's ineffable choice[4] and due to the Spirit of Love's special action,[5] she gave human life to the Son of God, "for whom and by whom all things exist" (Heb 2:10), and from whom the whole of the People of God receives the grace and dignity of election. Her Son explicitly extended his Mother's maternity in a way that could easily be understood by every soul and every heart by designating, when he was raised on the cross, his beloved disciple as her son (cf. Jn 19:26). The Holy Spirit inspired her to remain in the upper room after our Lord's ascension, recollected in prayer and expectation, together with the apostles, until the day of Pentecost, when the Church was to be born in visible form, coming forth from darkness (cf. Acts 1:14; 2). Later, all the generations of disciples, of those who confess and love Christ, like the Apostle John, spiritually took this Mother to their own homes (cf. Jn 19:27), and she was thus included in the history of salvation and in the Church's mission from the very beginning, that is from the moment of the annunciation. Accordingly, we who form today's generation of disciples of Christ all wish to unite ourselves with her in a special way. We do so with all our attachment to our ancient tradition and also with full respect and love for the members of all the Christian communities.

We do so at the urging of the deep need of faith, hope and charity. For if we feel a special need, in this difficult and responsible phase of the history of the Church and of mankind, to turn to Christ, who is Lord of the Church and Lord of man's history on account of the mystery of the redemption, we believe that nobody else can bring us as Mary can

---

2. Cf. Ibid., 52–69: *AAS* 57 (1965), 58–67.

3. Paul VI, *Closing Address* at the Third Session of the Second Vatican Ecumenical Council (November 21, 1964): *AAS* 56 (1964), 1015.

4. Cf. Second Vatican Ecumenical Council, Dogmatic Constitution on the Church *Lumen Gentium,* 56: *AAS* 57 (1965), 60.

5. Ibid.

into the divine and human dimension of this mystery. Nobody has been brought into it by God himself as Mary has. It is in this that the exceptional character of the grace of the divine motherhood consists. Not only is the dignity of this motherhood unique and unrepeatable in the history of the human race, but Mary's participation, due to this maternity, in God's plan for man's salvation through the mystery of the redemption is also unique in profundity and range of action.

We can say that the mystery of the redemption took shape beneath the heart of the Virgin of Nazareth when she pronounced her *fiat*. From then on, under the special influence of the Holy Spirit, this heart, the heart of both a virgin and a mother, has always followed the work of her Son and has gone out to all those whom Christ has embraced and continues to embrace with inexhaustible love. For that reason her heart must also have the inexhaustibility of a mother. The special characteristic of the motherly love that the Mother of God inserts in the mystery of the redemption and the life of the Church finds expression in its exceptional closeness to man and all that happens to him. It is in this that the mystery of the Mother consists. The Church, which looks to her with altogether special love and hope, wishes to make this mystery her own in an ever deeper manner. For in this the Church also recognizes the way for her daily life, which is each person.

The Father's eternal love, which has been manifested in the history of mankind through the Son whom the Father gave, "that whoever believes in him should not perish but have eternal life" (Jn 3:16), comes close to each of us through this Mother and thus takes on tokens that are of more easy understanding and access by each person. Consequently, Mary must be on all the ways for the Church's daily life. Through her maternal presence, the Church acquires certainty that she is truly living the life of her Master and Lord and that she is living the mystery of the redemption in all its life-giving profundity and fullness. Likewise the Church, which has struck root in many varied fields of the life of the whole of present-day humanity, also acquires the certainty and, one could say, the experience of being close to man, to each person, of being each person's Church, the Church of the People of God.

Faced with these tasks that appear along the ways for the Church, those ways that Pope Paul VI clearly indicated in the first encyclical of his pontificate, and aware of the absolute necessity of all these ways and also of the difficulties thronging them, we feel all the more our need for a profound link with Christ. We hear within us, as a resounding echo, the words that he spoke: "Apart from me you can do nothing" (Jn 15:5). We feel not only the need but even a categorical imperative for great, intense and growing prayer by all the Church. Only prayer can prevent all these great succeeding tasks and difficulties from becoming a source of crisis and make them instead the occasion and, as it were, the foundation for ever more mature achievements on the People of God's march toward the Promised Land in this stage of history approaching the end of the second millennium. Accordingly, as I end this meditation with a warm and humble call to prayer, I wish the Church to devote herself to this prayer, together with Mary the Mother of Jesus (cf. Acts 1:14), as the apostles and disciples of the Lord did in the upper room in Jerusalem after his ascension (cf. Acts 1:13). Above all, I implore Mary, the heavenly Mother of the Church, to be so good as to devote herself to this prayer of humanity's new advent, together with us who make up the Church, that is to say the Mystical Body of her only Son. I hope that through this prayer we shall be able to receive the Holy Spirit coming upon us (cf. Acts 1:8) and thus become Christ's witnesses "to the end of the earth" (cf. Acts 1:8), like those who went forth from the upper room in Jerusalem on the day of Pentecost.

ON CATECHESIS IN OUR TIME

Catechesi Tradendae

Apostolic Exhortation of
Pope John Paul II
October 16, 1979

INTRODUCTION

Historical Perspectives

In 1977, the synod of bishops met in Rome to discuss the theme of catechesis. This synod was a follow-up to the synod on evangelization that had taken place three years earlier. The ensuing document on evangelization, *Evangelii Nuntiandi,* which gave Mary the title "Star of Evangelization," had sparked new interest in the spread of the Christian message. In a sense, the two synods were like twins in the ministry of the Word. Evangelization is the beginning stage, the first proclamation leading hearers to embrace the faith; catechesis is the deepening, the instruction in doctrine once the faith decision has been made.

The bishops of the synod defined catechesis as "every ecclesial activity which seeks to bring about growth in faith."[1] A major topic discussed during the synod was adult catechesis—both the rite of initiation and ongoing instruction.[2] Catechesis for the young and for adults go together. Especially for adults, spiritual formation assists catechesis and is often its starting point. The first school of catechesis is the family, which is assisted by schools and programs for religious instruction.

In regard to Marian catechesis, Cardinal Carberry of St. Louis presented an American contribution at the synod. He spoke on "The Role of the Blessed Virgin Mary in Catechetics." From this talk Pope John

---

1. Joseph L. Bernardin, "Introduction," in *Synod of Bishops–1977: Message to the People of God and Interventions of the U. S. Delegates* (Washington, USCC: 1978), 2.

2. The intent of the synod was to discuss catechesis of the young; however, adult catechesis was an urgent current topic for the synod bishops. In 1972 the Vatican had published norms for RCIA *(Rite of Christian Initiation of Adults)* parish programs as we know them today. See: Bernard Marthaler, "The Modern Catechetical Movement in Roman Catholicism: Issues and Personalities," *Sourcebook*, 285–286.

Paul II culled the phrases: Mary is a "compendium of catechetics," "a living catechism."[3]

The document on catechesis wasn't completed until October 1979. Although the teachings in the *General Catechetical Directory* were to remain the norm for catechesis, *Catechesi Tradendae* did make some significant contributions, not least in its teachings about the Blessed Virgin Mary.[4]

The Teaching

Here, perhaps for the first time since Vatican II, Mary is extensively recognized as a disciple who followed Jesus, even during his public life.

The Marian content is found in articles 30 and 47, and in the conclusion, article 73, which is significant for its anthropological approach to Mary. Article 30 deals with integrity of catechetical content and notes that Mary's role in God's plan of salvation should be included among the essential teachings. In article 47, the pope states that certain ecclesial events which offer occasions for catechizing, such as pilgrimages or conventions, could be centered on a Marian theme. Finally, article 73 presents Mary as the teacher of Jesus, who was in turn taught by him. Mary was Jesus' first disciple not only in time, but in the depth of her understanding.

Today

Mary's faith in Jesus Christ, which led her to become his committed and faithful disciple, remains for every Christian an example of one who points the way.

"Jesus, the only mediator, is the way of our prayer; Mary, his mother and ours, is wholly transparent to him: she 'shows the way' (*hodigitria*), and is herself 'the Sign' of the way…" (*CCC* 2674).

---

3. John Joseph Cardinal Carberry, "The Role of the Blessed Mother in Catechetics, in *Synod of Bishops–1977: Message to the People of God and Interventions of the U. S. Delegates* (Washington, USCC: 1978), 23.

4. In 1997, the Congregation for the Clergy published a new directory, *General Directory for Catechesis*. This normative document draws on the guidelines of *Marialis Cultus* for incorporation in Marian teachings. See the concluding paragraph in the introduction to *Marialis Cultus* above.

ON CATECHESIS IN OUR TIME

Catechesi Tradendae

Promulgated by His Holiness John Paul II
On October 16, 1979

INTEGRITY OF CONTENT

30. With regard to the content of catechesis, three important points deserve special attention today.

The first point concerns the integrity of the content. In order that the sacrificial offering of his or her faith (cf. Phil 2:17) should be perfect, the person who becomes a disciple of Christ has the right to receive "the word of faith" (Rm 10:8) not in mutilated, falsified or diminished form but whole and entire, in all its rigor and vigor. Unfaithfulness on some point to the integrity of the message means a dangerous weakening of catechesis and putting at risk the results that Christ and the ecclesial community have a right to expect from it. It is certainly not by chance that the final command of Jesus in Matthew's Gospel bears the mark of a certain entireness: "All authority...has been given to me...make disciples of all nations...teaching them to observe all.... I am with you always." This is why, when a person first becomes aware of "the surpassing worth of knowing Christ Jesus" (Phil 3:8), whom he has encountered by faith, and has the perhaps unconscious desire to know him more extensively and better, "hearing about him and being taught in him, as the truth is in Jesus" (cf. Eph 4:20–21), there is no valid pretext for refusing him any part whatever of that knowledge. What kind of catechesis would it be that failed to give their full place to man's creation and sin; to God's plan of redemption and its long, loving preparation and realization; to the incarnation of the Son of God; to Mary, the Immaculate One, the Mother of God, ever Virgin, raised body and soul to the glory of heaven, and to her role in the mystery of salvation; to the mystery of lawlessness at work in our lives (cf. 2 Thes 2:7) and the power of God freeing us from it; to the need for penance and asceticism; to the sacramental and liturgical actions; to the reality of the Eucharistic Presence; to participation in divine life here and hereafter, and so on? Thus, no true catechist can lawfully, on his own initiative, make a selection of what he considers important in the deposit of faith as opposed to what he considers unimportant, so as to teach the one and reject the other.

Utilization of Various Places, Occasions and Gatherings

47. I am also thinking of various occasions of special value which are exactly suitable for catechesis: for example, diocesan, regional, or national pilgrimages, which gain from being centered on some judiciously chosen theme based on the life of Christ, of the Blessed Virgin or of the saints.

Mary, Mother and Model of the Disciple

73. May the Virgin of Pentecost obtain this for us through her intercession. By a unique vocation, she saw her Son Jesus "increase in wisdom and in stature, and in favor" (cf. Lk 2:52). As he sat on her lap and later as he listened to her throughout the hidden life at Nazareth, this Son, who was "the only Son from the Father," "full of grace and truth," was formed by her in human knowledge of the Scriptures and of the history of God's plan for his people, and in adoration of the Father.[1] She in turn was the first of his disciples. She was the first in time, because even when she found her adolescent Son in the temple she received from him lessons that she kept in her heart (cf. Lk 2:51). She was the first disciple above all else because no one has been "taught by God" (cf. Jn 6:45) to such depth. She was "both mother and disciple," as St. Augustine

---

1. Cf. Jn 1:14; Heb 10:5; *Summa Theol.,* III, a. 12, a. 2; a. 3, *ad* 3.

said of her, venturing to add that her discipleship was more important for her than her motherhood.[2] There are good grounds for the statement made in the synod hall that Mary is "a living catechism" and "the mother and model of catechists."

May the presence of the Holy Spirit, through the prayers of Mary, grant the Church unprecedented enthusiasm in the catechetical work that is essential for her. Thus will she effectively carry out, at this moment of grace, her inalienable and universal mission, the mission given her by her Teacher: "Go therefore and make disciples of all nations" (Mt 28:19).

---

2. Cf. Sermo 25, 7: *PL* 46, 937–938.

ON THE MERCY OF GOD

Dives in Misericordia

Encyclical Letter of Pope John Paul II
November 30, 1980

INTRODUCTION

Historical Perspectives

The Mercy of God, Pope John Paul II's second encyclical, focuses on the merciful love of God the Father as revealed in Jesus Christ. Jesus is the Incarnation of divine mercy. He revealed the Father's love and mercy throughout his life, but especially in his passion and death.

The Teaching

The brief Marian section in this document is found in chapter five, which focuses on the Paschal Mystery. The pope presents Mary as the Mother of Mercy. In her Magnificat, she praises God's mercy: "His mercy is…from generation to generation" (Lk 1:50). John Paul offers three reasons why Mary is Mother of Mercy: 1) she obtained mercy abundantly, 2) she shared in revealing divine mercy, and 3) she continues to exercise a mission of mercy.

John Paul states that "Mary is also the one who obtained mercy in a particular and exceptional way, as no other person has" (*DM* 9). At first, this statement might sound strange, for Mary never sinned. Why did she need mercy? God preserved her from sin, right from the moment of her conception. This exceptional grace was a gift of God's mercy to her. God not only preserved Mary from original sin, but gifted her with an exceptional holiness. He did this to prepare her for her special mission of being the Mother of God. At the annunciation, God invited Mary to this mission and she freely responded with an act of faith. Because of her "yes," the Incarnation took place, and through it, God's mercy was shown to the world.

This leads to the pope's next point that Mary shared in revealing God's mercy. She shared in it because through her, Jesus Christ came into the world to reveal divine mercy. This revelation took place especially through the events of Jesus' passion and death. As Mary stood by the cross on Calvary, "she made possible with the sacrifice of her heart her own sharing in revealing God's mercy." The cross shows us the infinite depths of divine love and mercy. Mary offered her sufferings in union with Christ's, sharing in his mission.

Today

Because of this sharing in Christ's life and cross, Mary "was called in a special way to bring close to people that love which he [Christ] had come to reveal." Mary was present in prayer with the apostles in the upper room as they awaited the coming of the Holy Spirit. She was present at the heart of the Church as it began its mission, and she continues that mission from her place in heaven. Her spiritual motherhood obtains gifts of grace for the Church's members through all times. With all the graciousness of her maternal love, she draws us close to the merciful heart of the Father.

ON THE MERCY OF GOD

Dives in Misericordia

Promulgated by His Holiness Pope John Paul II
On November 30, 1980

MOTHER OF MERCY

9. These words of the Church at Easter reecho in the fullness of their prophetic content the words that Mary uttered during her visit to Elizabeth, the wife of Zechariah: "His mercy is...from generation to generation" (Lk 1:50). At the very moment of the Incarnation, these words open up a new perspective of salvation history. After the resurrection of Christ, this perspective is new on both the historical and the eschatological level. From that time onwards there is a succession of new generations of individuals in the immense human family, in ever-increasing dimensions; there is also a succession of new generations of the People of God, marked with the sign of the cross and of the resurrection and "sealed" (cf. 2 Cor 1:21–22) with the sign of the Paschal Mystery of Christ, the absolute revelation of the mercy that Mary proclaimed on the threshold of her kinswoman's house: "His mercy is...from generation to generation" (Lk 1:50).

Mary is also the one who obtained mercy in a particular and exceptional way, as no other person has. At the same time, still in an exceptional way, she made possible with the sacrifice of her heart her own sharing in revealing God's mercy. This sacrifice is intimately linked with the cross of her Son, at the foot of which she was to stand on Calvary. Her sacrifice is a unique sharing in the revelation of mercy, that is, a sharing in the absolute fidelity of God to his own love, to the covenant that he willed from eternity and that he entered into in time with man, with the people, with humanity; it is a sharing in that revelation that was definitively fulfilled through the cross. *No one has experienced, to the same degree as the Mother of the crucified One,* the mystery of the cross, the overwhelming encounter of divine transcendent justice with love: that "kiss" given by mercy to justice (cf. Ps 85 [84]:11). No one has received into his heart, as much as Mary did, that mystery, that truly divine dimension of the redemption effected on Calvary by means of the death of the Son, together with the sacrifice of her maternal heart, together with her definitive *fiat.*

Mary, then, is the one who *has the deepest knowledge of the mystery of God's mercy.* She knows its price; she knows how great it is. In this sense, we call her the *Mother of Mercy:* Our Lady of Mercy, or Mother of Divine Mercy; in each one of these titles there is a deep theological meaning, for they express the special preparation of her soul, of her whole personality, so that she was able to perceive, through the complex events, first of Israel, then of every individual and of the whole of humanity, that mercy of which "from generation to generation" (Lk 1:50) people become sharers according to the eternal design of the Most Holy Trinity.

The above titles which we attribute to the Mother of God speak of her principally, however, as the Mother of the crucified and risen One; as *the One who, having obtained mercy in an exceptional way,* in an equally exceptional way *"merits" that mercy* throughout her earthly life and, particularly, at the foot of the cross of her Son; and finally as the one who, through her hidden and at the same time incomparable sharing in the messianic mission of her Son, was called in a special way to bring close to people that love which he had come to reveal: the love that finds its most concrete expression vis-a-vis the suffering, the poor, those deprived of their own freedom, the blind, the oppressed and sinners, just as Christ spoke of them in the words of the prophecy of Isaiah, first in the synagogue at Nazareth (cf. Lk 4:18) and then in response to the question of the messengers of John the Baptist (cf. Lk 7:22).

It was precisely this "merciful" love, which is manifested above all in contact with moral and physical evil, that the heart of her who was the Mother of the crucified and risen One shared in singularly and exceptionally—that Mary shared in. In her and through her, this love continues to be revealed in the history of the Church and of humanity. This revelation is especially fruitful because in the Mother of God it is based upon the unique tact of her maternal heart, on her particular sensitivity, on her particular fitness to reach all those *who most easily accept the merciful love of a mother.* This is one of the great life-giving mysteries of Christianity, a mystery intimately connected with the mystery of the Incarnation.

"The motherhood of Mary in the order of grace," as the Second Vatican Council explains, "lasts without interruption from the consent which she faithfully gave at the annunciation and which she sustained without hesitation under the cross, until the eternal fulfillment of all the elect. In fact, being assumed into heaven she has not laid aside this office of salvation, but by her manifold intercession she continues to obtain for us the graces of eternal salvation. By her maternal charity, she takes care of the brethren of her Son who still journey on earth surrounded by dangers and difficulties, until they are led into their blessed home."[1]

---

1. Dogmatic Constitution on the Church *Lumen Gentium,* 62: AAS 57 (1965), p. 63.

FOR THE 1600ᵀᴴ ANNIVERSARY OF THE FIRST COUNCIL OF CONSTANTINOPLE AND THE 1550ᵀᴴ ANNIVERSARY OF THE COUNCIL OF EPHESUS

Letter of Pope John Paul II

March 25, 1981

INTRODUCTION

Historical Perspectives

This document commemorates the Church's early ecumenical councils and recalls the Creed, the common foundation of the churches of East and West. A concern for ecumenism often surfaces in the works of John Paul II. His Slavic background has given him a close proximity to the Eastern Churches. Taking every opportunity to foster unity, the pope has often stated that the Church must breathe with two lungs—East and West.

As the Holy Father states, "...the teaching of the First Council of Constantinople is still *the expression of the one common faith* of the Church, of the whole of Christianity. As we confess this faith—as we do every time that we recite the creed...we wish to emphasize the things which unite us...".

The Teaching

Regarding the Council of Ephesus, the document states that this council was Christological in its orientation, defining the truth of the two natures in Jesus Christ, the divine and the human. The council wanted to correct the false teaching of the bishop Nestorius, who denied the unity of Christ's person, and consequently also denied that Mary is the Mother of God. The council defined its teaching about Mary as the Mother of God in order to safeguard the truth about Jesus Christ. The document explains the Christian belief in the Incarnation of Jesus Christ by the Holy Spirit and the cooperation of the Blessed Virgin Mary.

Today

Besides this doctrinal purpose, the Holy Father also presents Mary as our guide for the new millennium. He writes: "And it is wonderful that, just as Mary awaited with faith the coming of the Lord, so also in this last part of the second millennium she should be present to illuminate our faith as we await this 'advent.'"

TOPICAL OUTLINE

1. The Council of Constantinople (1–2)

    A. The occasion of the letter

    B. The Holy Spirit and the creed

2. The Council of Ephesus (3–5)

    A. Its Christological and soteriological significance

    B. Its Marian significance

    C. The Holy Spirit

    D. Ecumenical hopes

3. Ecclesiological context of the anniversaries (6–8)

    A. The Church today and the Second Vatican Council

    B. Mary's role in the Incarnation

4. Plans for the commemoration of the anniversaries (9–11)

5. Conclusion (12)

FOR THE 1600th ANNIVERSARY OF THE FIRST COUNCIL OF CONSTANTINOPLE AND THE 1550th ANNIVERSARY OF THE COUNCIL OF EPHESUS

Promulgated by His Holiness Pope John Paul II
On March 25, 1981

LETTER OF HIS HOLINESS JOHN PAUL II
TO THE BISHOPS OF THE CATHOLIC CHURCH

My dear brothers in the episcopate,

I

1. I am impelled to write you this letter—which is both a theological reflection and a pastoral invitation coming from the depths of my heart—first of all, by the sixteenth centenary of the First Council of Constantinople, which was held in the year 381. As I pointed out at the beginning of the new year in St. Peter's Basilica, "after the Council of Nicaea this was the second ecumenical council of the Church.... To it we owe the *Credo* that is constantly recited in the liturgy. A particular heritage of that Council is the doctrine on the Holy Spirit, thus proclaimed in the Latin Liturgy: *Credo in Spiritum Sanctum, Dominum et Vivificantem...qui cum Patre et Filio simul adoratur et conglorificatur, qui locutus est per prophetas.*"[1]

---

1. *L'Osservatore Romano,* January 2–3, 1981.

These words repeated in the creed by so many generations of Christians will have a particular significance both of doctrine and religious sentiment for us this year and will remind us of the profound bonds that link the Church of today—as we look toward the coming of the third millennium of her life, a life so wonderfully rich and tested, continually sharing in the cross and resurrection of Christ, in the power of the Holy Spirit—with the Church of the fourth century, in the one continuity of her first beginnings, and in fidelity to the teaching of the Gospel and the preaching of the apostles.

What has just been said suffices to enable us to understand how the teaching of the First Council of Constantinople is still *the expression of the one common faith* of the Church, of the whole of Christianity. As we confess this faith—as we do every time that we recite the creed—and as we revive it in the forthcoming centenary commemoration, we wish to emphasize the things which unite us with all our brothers, notwithstanding the divisions that have occurred in the course of the centuries. As we do this, 1600 years after the First Council of Constantinople, we give thanks to God for the *truth of the Lord,* which thanks to the teaching of that Council, enlightens the paths of our faith, and the paths of life by virtue of that faith. In this anniversary we not only call to mind a formula of faith that has been in force for sixteen centuries in the Church; at the same time we make ever more present to our spirit, in reflection, in prayer, in the contribution of spirituality and theology, that personal divine power which gives life, that hypostatic Gift—*Dominum et vivificantem*—that third Person of the most Holy Trinity who in this faith is shared in by each individual soul and by the whole Church. The Holy Spirit continues to vivify the Church and to guide her along the paths to holiness and love. As St. Ambrose pointed out so well in his work *De Spiritu Sancto,* "although he is inaccessible by nature, yet he can be received by us, thanks to his goodness; he fills everything with his power, but only the just share in him; he is simple in his substance, rich in power, present in all, shares that which is his in order to give it to each one, and is wholly present in every place."[2]

2. The memory of the Council of Constantinople, which was the second ecumenical council of the Church, makes us, the Christians of the

---

2. St. Ambrose, *De Spiritu Sancto,* I, V, 72; ed. O. Faller; *CSEL* 79, Vindobonae 1964, 45.

period toward the end of the second millennium, aware of how lively was the need, in the first centuries of the first millennium, among the growing community of believers, to understand and to proclaim *correctly,* in the confession of the Church, the inscrutable mystery of God in his absolute transcendence: Father, Son and Holy Spirit. This and other key principles of truth and of Christian life first attracted the attention of the faithful; and with regard to these principles there arose numerous interpretations, some of them divergent ones, which made necessary the voice of the Church, her solemn witness given in virtue of the promise made by Christ in the upper room: "The Counselor, the Holy Spirit, whom the Father will send in my name...will bring to your remembrance all that I have said to you" (Jn 14:26); he, the Spirit of truth, "will guide you into all the truth" (Jn 16:13).

Therefore, in the present year, 1981, we ought to give thanks to the Holy Spirit in a special way because, in the midst of the many fluctuations of human thought, he has enabled the Church to express her faith, in the manners of expression peculiar to the age, in complete harmony with "all the truth."

"I believe in the Holy Spirit, the Lord, the giver of life, who proceeds from the Father. With the Father and the Son he is worshiped and glorified. He has spoken through the Prophets": these are the words of the Creed of the First Council of Constantinople in 381,[3] that elucidated the mystery of the Holy Spirit and his origin from the Father, thus affirming the unity and equality in divinity of the Holy Spirit with the Father and the Son.

---

3. Thus quoted for the first time in the *Acts of the Council of Chalcedon,* act. II: ed. E. Schwartz, *Acta Conciliorum Oecumenicorum, II Concilium Universale Chalcedonense,* Berolini et Lipsiae 1917–32, I, 2, p. 80; cf. also *Conciliorum Oecumenicorum Decreta,* Bologna 1973, 24.

II

3. As I recall the sixteenth centenary of the First Council of Constantinople, I cannot pass over in silence yet another significant occasion that concerns 1981: this year, in fact, there also occurs the 1550th anniversary of the Council of Ephesus, which was held in 431. This anniversary is, as it were, overshadowed by the preceding council, but it too has a particular importance for our faith, and is supremely worthy of being remembered.

In that same creed, in fact, we recite, in the midst of the liturgical community as it prepares to relive the divine mysteries, the words: *et incarnatus est de Spiritu Sancto ex Maria Virgine, et homo factus est:* by the power of the Holy Spirit he became incarnate from the Virgin Mary, and was made man. The Council of Ephesus thus had *a value that was above all Christological,* for it defined the two natures in Jesus Christ, the divine and the human, in order to state exactly the authentic doctrine of the Church already expressed by the Council of Nicaea in 325, but which had been imperiled by the spread of certain formulas used in the Nestorian teaching. In close connection with these affirmations, the Council of Ephesus *also had a soteriological significance,* for it illustrated the fact that—as the well known axiom has it—"what is not assumed is not saved." But just as closely linked with the value of these dogmatic truths was also the truth concerning the Blessed Virgin, called to the unique and unrepeatable dignity of being the Mother of God, the *Theotókos,* as was so clearly shown principally by the Letter of St. Cyril to Nestorius[4] and by the splendid *Formula Unionis* of 433.[5] It was a

---

4. *Acta Conciliorum Oecumenicorum, I Concilium Universale Ephesinum:* ed. E. Schwartz, I, 1, pp. 25–28, 223–242; cf. also *Conciliorum Oecumenicorum Decreta,* Bologna 1973, pp. 40–44; 50–61.

5. *Acta Conciliorum Oecumenicorum,* I, I, 4, pp. 8 ff. (A); cf. also *Conciliorum Oecumenicorum Decreta,* pp. 69 ff.

whole hymn raised by those ancient Fathers to the Incarnation of the only-begotten Son of God, in the full truth of the two natures in the one person; it was a hymn to the work of salvation, accomplished in the world through the working of the Holy Spirit; and all of this could not fail to redound to the honor of the Mother of God, the first cooperator with the power of the Almighty, which overshadowed her at the moment of the annunciation in the luminous coming of the Holy Spirit (cf. Lk 1:35). And this is how our brothers and sisters of Ephesus understood it, when, on the evening of June 22, the first day of the Council, celebrated in the Cathedral of the "Mother of God," they acclaimed the Virgin Mary with this title and carried the Fathers in triumph at the end of that first session.

It therefore seems to me very opportune that this ancient Council too, the third in the history of the Church, should be remembered by us in its rich theological and ecclesial context. The most Blessed Virgin is she who, by the overshadowing of the power of the Trinity, was the creature most closely associated with the work of salvation. The Incarnation of the Word took place beneath her heart, by the power of the Holy Spirit. In her there dawned the new humanity which with Christ was presented in the world in order to bring to completion the original plan of the covenant with God, broken by the disobedience of the first man. *Et incarnatus est de Spiritu Sancto ex Maria Virgine.*

4. These two anniversaries, though for different reasons and with differing historical relevance, redound to the honor of the Holy Spirit. All was accomplished *by the power of the Holy Spirit.* One can see how profoundly these two great commemorations, to which it is proper to make reference in this year of the Lord 1981, are linked to one another in the teaching and in the profession of faith of the Church, of the faith of all Christians: faith in the Most Holy Trinity; faith in the Father, from whom all gifts come (cf. Jas 1:17); faith in Christ, the Redeemer of man; faith in the Holy Spirit. And, in this light, veneration of the Blessed Virgin, who "by thus consenting to the divine utterance...became the Mother of Jesus. Embracing God's saving will with a full heart and impeded by no sin, she devoted herself totally as a handmaid of the Lord to the person and work of her Son" and "the holy Fathers see her as used by God not merely in a passive way, but as cooperating in the work of human salvation through free faith and obedience."[6] And it is wonderful

---

6. Second Vatican Ecumenical Council, Dogmatic Constitution on the Church *Lumen Gentium,* 56.

that, just as Mary awaited with faith the coming of the Lord, so also in this last part of the second millennium she should be present to illuminate our faith as we await this "advent."

All this is for us a *source* of immense *joy,* a source of *gratitude* for the light of this faith, whereby we share in the inscrutable mysteries of God, making them the living content of our souls, expanding thereby the horizons of the understanding of our spiritual dignity and of our individual destinies. And so, these great anniversaries, too, cannot remain for us merely a memory of the distant past. They must take on fresh life in the faith of the Church; they must reecho anew in her spirituality; indeed they must find an external manifestation of their ever living relevance for the entire community of believers.

5. I write these things in the first place to you, my dear and venerable *brothers in the episcopal service.* I address myself at the same time to my *brother priests,* your closest collaborators in your pastoral care *in virtute Spiritus Sancti.* I address the brothers and sisters of all *the religious families* of men and women, in the midst of which there should be a particularly lively witness of the Spirit of Christ and likewise a particular love for the mission of Mary, who consented to be the handmaid of the Lord (cf. Lk 1:38). I finally address myself to *all* my brothers and sisters *of the laity* of the Church, who, in professing their faith together with all the other members of the ecclesial community, have so often and for so many generations rendered ever living the memory of the great councils. I am convinced that they will accept with gratitude the evocation of these dates and anniversaries, especially when together we realize how relevant are, at the same time, the mysteries to which the two councils gave authoritative expression as long ago as the first half of the first millennium of the history of the Church.

I also venture to hope that the commemoration of the Councils of Constantinople and Ephesus, which were expressions of the faith taught and professed by the undivided Church, will make us grow in mutual understanding with our beloved brothers in the East and in the West, with whom we are still not united by full ecclesial communion, but together with whom we seek in prayer, with humility and with trust, the paths to unity in truth. What indeed can more effectively hasten the journey toward that unity than the memory and, at the same time the reliving, of that which for so many centuries has been the content of the faith professed in common, indeed which has not ceased to be so, even after the sad divisions which have occurred in the course of the centuries?

III

6. It is therefore my aim that these events should be lived within *the whole of their ecclesiological context.* We should not merely commemorate these great anniversaries as things that happened in the past; we must give them life in our own times and establish a deep link between them and the life and role *of the Church of our period,* as that life and role have been given expression throughout the message of *the Council* of our period, the Second Vatican Council. How deeply rooted in that teaching are the truths defined in the two councils that we are commemorating! To how great an extent those truths have permeated the Second Vatican Council's central doctrine on the Church! How substantial and constitutive they are for that doctrine! And likewise how intensely these fundamental and central truths of our faith live, so to speak, a new life and shine with a new light throughout the teaching of the Second Vatican Council!

While the chief task of our generation, and perhaps also of future generations in the Church, will be to carry out and make part of life the teaching and guidance of this great Council, the anniversaries this year of the First Council of Constantinople and the Council of Ephesus give us an opportunity for performing this task in the living context of the truth that lasts throughout the ages to eternity.

7. When the Son had accomplished the work that the Father gave him to do on earth (cf. Jn 17:4), the Holy Spirit was sent on the day of Pentecost, in order that he might continually sanctify the Church, and that through Christ those who believe might thus have access in one Spirit to the Father (cf. Eph 2:18). He is the Spirit of life, a spring of water welling up to eternal life (cf. Jn 4:14; 7:38–39); through him the Father gives life to people who are dead because of sin, until the day when, in Christ, he raises to life their mortal bodies (cf. Rm 8:10–11). The Spirit dwells in the Church and in the hearts of the faithful, as in a

temple (cf. 1 Cor 3:16; 6:19). In them he prays and bears witness to their adoption as children (cf. Gal 4:6; Rm 8:15–18, 26). He guides the Church into all the truth (cf. Jn 16:13), unifies her in communion and ministry, provides her with varied hierarchic and charismatic gifts, through which he directs her, and adorns her with his fruits (cf. Eph 4:11–12; 1 Cor 12:4; Gal 5:22). He rejuvenates the Church by the power of the Gospel, continually renews her and leads her to perfect union with her Bridegroom. For the Spirit and the Bride say to the Lord Jesus: 'Come' (cf. Rv 22:17). Thus the universal Church is seen to be 'a people brought into unity from the unity of the Father, the Son and the Holy Spirit.'[7] This is certainly the richest and most synthetic text, although not a unique one, indicating how *the truth about the Holy Spirit,* to which expression was given so authoritatively 1600 years ago by the First Council of Constantinople, lives with new life and shines with new splendor throughout the teaching of the Second Vatican Council.

The whole *work of renewal of the Church,* so providentially set forth and initiated by the Second Vatican Council—a renewal that must be both an updating and a consolidation of what is eternal and constitutive of the Church's mission—can be carried out only *in the Holy Spirit,* that is to say, with the aid of his light and his power. This is important, so important, for the whole of the universal Church and also for each particular Church in its communion with all the other particular Churches. This is important also for the ecumenical process within Christianity and for the Church's path in the modern world, which must extend in the direction of justice and peace. This is important also for activity in favor of priestly or religious vocations, as well as for the apostolate of the laity, as the fruit of a new maturity in their faith.

8. The two phrases in the Nicene-Constantinopolitan Creed, *"Et incarnatus est de Spiritu Sancto"* and *"Credo in Spiritum Sanctum, Dominum et Vivificantem,"* remind us that the greatest work of the Holy Spirit, one to which all the others unceasingly refer as a source from which they draw, is that of *the Incarnation of the Eternal Word* by the power of the Spirit from the Virgin Mary.

---

7. Second Vatican Ecumenical Council, Dogmatic Constitution on the Church *Lumen Gentium,* 4.

Christ, the Redeemer of man and the world, is the center of history: "Jesus Christ is the same yesterday and today and forever" (Heb 13:8). Our thoughts and our hearts are turned to him in view of the approaching end of the second millennium separating us from his first coming into the world, but for that very reason they turn *to the Holy Spirit,* through whose power his human conception took place, and to *the Virgin Mary,* by whom he was conceived and from whom he was born. The anniversaries of the two great councils this year direct our thoughts and hearts in a special way to the Holy Spirit and to Mary, the Mother of God. While we recall the joy and exultation that the profession of faith in the divine motherhood of the Virgin Mary *(Theotókos)* aroused 1550 years ago at Ephesus, we understand that that profession of faith also glorified *the particular work of the Holy Spirit,* the work composed of both the human conception and birth of the Son of God by the power of the Holy Spirit and, again by the power of the Holy Spirit, the holy motherhood of the Virgin Mary. This motherhood is not only the source and foundation of all her exceptional holiness and her very special participation in the whole plan of salvation; it also establishes a permanent maternal link with the Church, as a result of the fact that she was chosen by the Holy Trinity as the Mother of Christ, who is "the Head of the body, the Church" (Col 1:18). This link was revealed especially beneath the cross, where she, "enduring with her only-begotten Son the intensity of his suffering, associated herself with his sacrifice in her mother's heart.... She was given by the same Christ Jesus dying on the cross as a Mother to his disciple, with these words: 'Woman, behold your son!'"[8]

The Second Vatican Council summarizes in felicitous words Mary's unbreakable relationship with Christ and with the Church: "Since it had pleased God not to manifest solemnly the mystery of the salvation of the human race before he would pour forth the Spirit promised by Christ, we see the apostles before the day of Pentecost 'with one accord devoting themselves to prayer, together with the women and Mary the mother of Jesus, and with his brethren' (cf. Acts 1:14), and we also see Mary by her prayers imploring the gift of the Spirit, who

---

8. Second Vatican Ecumenical Council, Dogmatic Constitution on the Church *Lumen Gentium,* 58.

had already overshadowed her in the annunciation."[9] With these words the Council text links the two moments in which Mary's motherhood is most closely united with the work of the Holy Spirit: firstly, the moment of the Incarnation, and secondly, that of the birth of the Church in the upper room in Jerusalem.

9. Second Vatican Ecumenical Council, Dogmatic Constitution on the Church *Lumen Gentium,* 59.

IV

9. Accordingly, all these great and important motives and the coincidence of such meaningful circumstances are reasons for giving particular emphasis throughout the Church this year, which is the jubilee of two events, to the solemnity of Pentecost.

I therefore invite all the episcopal conferences of the Catholic Church and the patriarchates and metropolitan provinces of the Eastern Catholic Churches to send the representatives they wish to Rome for that day, in order that we may together renew the inheritance that we have received from the Pentecost upper room in the power of the Holy Spirit. He it is who showed the Church, at the moment of her birth, the way that leads to all nations, all peoples and tongues, and to the heart of every individual.

Finding ourselves gathered in collegial unity, as inheritors of the apostolic solicitude for all the churches (cf. 2 Cor 11:28), we shall draw from the abundant source of the same Spirit, who guides the Church's mission on the paths of present day humanity, at the close of the second millennium after the Word became incarnate by the power of the Holy Spirit in the womb of the Virgin Mary.

10. First, on the morning of the solemnity we shall come together in the *Basilica of St. Peter in the Vatican* to sing with all our hearts our belief in *Spiritum Sanctum, Dominum et vivificantem...qui locutus est per prophetas.... Et unam sanctam catholicam et apostolicam Ecclesiam.* We are prompted to do this by the 1600th anniversary of the First Council of Constantinople. Like the apostles in the upper room and the Fathers of that Council, we shall be brought together by the one who "rejuvenates the Church by the power of the Gospel" and "constantly renews her."[10]

---

10. Cf. Second Vatican Ecumenical Council, Dogmatic Constitution on the Church *Lumen Gentium,* 4.

Thus this year's solemnity of Pentecost will be a sublime and grateful profession of the faith in the Holy Spirit, the Lord, the Giver of Life, that we owe in a particular way to that Council. It will also be a humble and ardent prayer that the Holy Spirit will help us "renew the face of the earth"—among other ways by means of the Church's work of renewal in accordance with the thought of the Second Vatican Council. It will be a prayer that this work may be carried out maturely and in a regular way in all the Churches and Christian communities, and that the work may, first and foremost, be carried out within people's souls, since no true renewal is possible without continual conversion to God. We shall ask the Spirit of Truth that we may, *on the path of this renewal,* remain *perfectly faithful to what the Spirit says* to us at the present time in the teaching of the Second Vatican Council, not abandoning this way at the prompting of a certain regard for the spirit of the world. We shall also ask him who is *fons vivus, ignis, caritas* (living water, fire and love) to permeate us and the whole Church, and also the human family, with the love that "hopes all things, endures all things" and "never ends" (1 Cor 13:7–8).

There is no doubt that at the present stage of the history of the Church and of humanity a special need is felt to go deeper into and give new life to the truth about the Holy Spirit. The commemoration at Pentecost of the sixteenth centenary of the First Council of Constantinople will give us an occasion for doing this. May the Holy Spirit accept our manifestation of faith. In the liturgical function of the solemnity of Pentecost may he accept us as we humbly open our hearts to him, the Consoler, in whom the gift of unity is revealed and brought to realization.

11. In the second part of the celebration, we shall gather in the late afternoon of the same day in *the Basilica of Saint Mary Major.* There the morning part will be completed by the thoughts presented by the 1550th anniversary of the Council of Ephesus. We shall also be prompted to do this because by a singular coincidence Pentecost will this year fall on June 7, as it did in 431, when on that solemn day, on which the council sessions, later postponed to June 22, were to begin, the first groups of bishops began to arrive in Ephesus.

These thoughts will also be reflected on in the light of the Second Vatican Council, with special attention to the marvelous eighth chapter of the Constitution *Lumen Gentium.* Just as the Council of Ephesus' Christological and soteriological teaching made it possible to confirm the truth about the divine motherhood of Mary, the *Theotókos,* so too the

Second Vatican Council enables us to recall that, when the Church was born by the power of the Holy Spirit in the upper room in Jerusalem, she began to look to Mary as the example for her own spiritual motherhood and, therefore, as her archetype. On that day the one whom Paul VI called *Mother of the Church* irradiated the power of her intercession over the *Church as Mother* and protected the apostolic zeal by which the Church still lives, generating for God the believers of all times and all geographical areas.

Accordingly, the afternoon liturgy of the solemnity of Pentecost will gather us in the chief Marian Basilica of Rome, in order thus to recall in a special way that in the upper room at Jerusalem the apostles "with one accord devoted themselves to prayer, together with...Mary the mother of Jesus..." (Acts 1:14), in preparation for the coming of the Holy Spirit. We, too, likewise wish on that important day to devote ourselves with one accord to prayer, together with her who, as Mother of God, is, in the words of the Second Vatican Council's *Dogmatic Constitution on the Church,* "a type of the Church in the order of faith, charity and perfect union with Christ."[11] Thus, devoting ourselves to prayer, together with her, and full of trust in her, we shall entrust to the power of the Holy Spirit the Church and her mission among all the nations of the world of today and tomorrow. For we have within us the heritage of those who were commanded by the risen Christ to go into all the world and preach the Gospel to all creation (cf. Mk 16:15).

On the day of Pentecost, gathered in prayer, together with Mary the Mother of Jesus, they became convinced that they could *carry out this command* with the power of the Holy Spirit that had come upon them, as the Lord had foretold (cf. Acts 1:8). On the same day we, their heirs, shall join together in the same act of faith and prayer.

---

11. Second Vatican Ecumenical Council, Dogmatic Constitution on the Church *Lumen Gentium,* 63.

V

12. Dear brothers,

I know that on Holy Thursday you renew within the community of the presbyterium of your dioceses the memorial of the Last Supper, during which, by the words of Christ and the power of the Holy Spirit, the bread and wine become the Body and Blood of our Savior, that is to say, the Eucharist of our redemption.

On that day, or also on other suitable occasions, speak to all the People of God about these important anniversaries and events, in order that in every local church and every community of the Church they may similarly be recalled and lived as they deserve, in the manner that will be decided by the individual bishops in accordance with the indications of the respective episcopal conferences or of the patriarchates or metropolitan provinces of the Eastern Churches.

Looking forward eagerly to the celebrations that I have announced, I gladly impart my special apostolic blessing to all of you, venerable and dear brothers in the episcopate, and together with you to your ecclesial communities.

Given in Rome, at St. Peter's on March 25, 1981, the Solemnity of the Annunciation of the Lord, the third year of my pontificate.

John Paul II

MOTHER OF THE REDEEMER

Redemptoris Mater

Encyclical Letter of Pope John Paul II
March 25, 1987

INTRODUCTION

Historical Perspectives

Redemptoris Mater was published for the Marian Year that Pope John Paul II proclaimed in 1987–88. In article forty-eight, he declared that the purpose of this year was:

> ...to promote a new and more careful reading of what the Council said about the Blessed Virgin Mary, Mother of God, in the mystery of Christ and of the Church.... We speak not only of *the doctrine of faith* but also of *the life of faith,*[1] and thus of authentic "Marian spirituality," seen in the light of tradition, and especially the spirituality to which the Council exhorts us (*LG* 66–67).

For John Paul II, doctrine and the life of faith are meant to be integrated—Christian spirituality centers on this. Sacred Scripture presents us with an example of this in the Blessed Virgin Mary. Whereas *Marialis Cultus* exhorted the faithful to correct devotion—that is, correct liturgical celebration and public expression of devotion based on doctrinal criteria—*Redemptoris Mater* aimed at formation of life based on doctrine.

Redemptoris Mater is related to the pope's previous encyclicals which discuss the theme of redemption in a Trinitarian focus: *Redemptor Hominis,* which treats Jesus Christ the Redeemer; *On the Mercy of God,* on God the Father; and *Dominum et Vivificantem,* on the Holy Spirit. The Marian encyclical has a strong Christological focus, and further develops the theme of redemption discussed in the other encyclicals, especially *Redemptor Hominis.*

---

1. Unless otherwise indicated, the italics are in the original document in this and the following documents.

Clearly, *Lumen Gentium* provides the foundation for *Redemptoris Mater*. In a later document, *Mulieris Dignitatem*, the pope specifically states that *Redemptoris Mater* "develops and updates" chapter eight of *Lumen Gentium* (*MD* 2).

The Teaching

Redemptoris Mater is divided into three major sections: Mary in the mystery of Christ, the Mother of God at the center of the pilgrim Church, and maternal mediation. The document announces and explains the Marian Year, and the text treats of pastoral concerns arising from women's issues.

Redemptoris Mater gives its own statement of intention. The encyclical is to be:

1) a *reflection* on the role of Mary in the mystery of Christ and on her active and exemplary presence in the life of the Church. The mission of Mary brings us to reflect on "the love of the Father, the mission of the Son, the gift of the Spirit, the role of the woman from whom the Redeemer was born, and our own divine filiation, in the mystery of the 'fullness of time'" (n. 1);

2) a *jubilee* in celebration of the birth of Mary, in remote preparation for the great Jubilee of the year 2000. Since the beginning of his pontificate, John Paul II has focused on leading the Church into the new millennium.

Grace, Discipleship and Faith

Redemptoris Mater gives a rich and extensive teaching about grace. *Full of grace* is Mary's name *(kécharitômenê)*. It signifies Mary's election, her sharing in supernatural life; it is like a seed of holiness. It signifies that she: *"is eternally loved in this 'beloved Son'"* (*RM* 8). It signifies her rich supernatural gifts, the singularity and uniqueness of her place in the mystery of Christ. Even though Mary:

> ...is placed *at the very center of that enmity,* that struggle which accompanies the history of humanity on earth and the history of salvation itself...she who belongs to the "weak and poor of the Lord" bears in herself, like no other member of the human race, that "glory of grace" which the Father "has bestowed on us in his beloved Son," and this *grace determines the extraordinary greatness and beauty* of her whole being (*RM* 11).

This grace bore tremendous fruit in Mary, the handmaid of the Lord. She fully joined herself to Christ and cooperated with him. Just as she was united with Christ in the *"first coming,* so through her continued collaboration with him she will also be united with him in expectation of the second" (*RM* 41). Mary consented to her motherhood, which "is above all *a result of her total self-giving to God in virginity.* Mary accepted her election as Mother of the Son of God, guided by spousal love, the love which totally 'consecrates' a human being to God. By virtue of this love, Mary wished to be always and in all things 'given to God'" (*RM* 39). Expanding the vocation of Mary as handmaid, the pope states: "The words 'Behold, I am the handmaid of the Lord' express the fact that from the outset she accepted and understood her own motherhood as a total *gift of self,* a gift of her person to the service of the saving plans of the Most High" (*RM* 39).

This self-gift enabled her to fully live as Christ's disciple. In a sense she became the first disciple, the first to follow Christ. As his disciple, she served the one who came to serve (cf. Mt 20:28; *RM* 20, 41). Mary was the first disciple because she was the first in faith.

The pope gives an extended treatment of Mary's faith. She "bears within herself the radical 'newness' of faith: *the beginning of the New Covenant"* (*RM* 17). But, *Redemptoris Mater* continues, this faith also experiences the dark night: *"Through this faith Mary is perfectly united with Christ in his self-emptying....* At the foot of the cross Mary shares through faith in the shocking mystery of this self-emptying. This is perhaps the deepest *'kenosis' of faith* in human history" (*RM* 18). The key to Mary's religious experience and her blessedness is her faith.

The document goes on to speak in detail about the meeting in the upper room where "Mary's journey meets the Church's journey of faith" (*RM* 26). This sequence of thought is new to the post-Vatican II documents. Mary was not one of those Jesus had called to go out "to the whole world to teach all nations" (cf. Mt 28:19). But she was in the upper room in prayer, present with the apostles preparing to be sent. The Church looked at her as the first believer:

> It is precisely Mary's faith which marks the beginning of the new and eternal Covenant of God with man in Jesus Christ; this heroic *faith* of hers *"precedes"* the apostolic *witness* of the Church, and ever remains in the Church's heart, hidden like a special heritage of God's revelation. All those who from generation to generation accept the apostolic witness of the Church share in that mysterious inheritance, and *in a sense share in Mary's faith* (*RM* 27).

At the beginning of the document, John Paul II writes: "I wish to consider primarily that 'pilgrimage of faith' in which 'the Blessed Virgin advanced,' faithfully preserving her union with Christ (*LG* 52). In this way the *'twofold bond'* which unites the Mother of God *with Christ and with the Church* takes on historical significance" (*RM* 5). The pope goes on to add: "Nor is it just a question of the Virgin Mother's life story, of her personal journey of faith and 'the better part' which is hers in the mystery of salvation; it is also a question of the history of the whole People of God, *of all those who take part* in the same *'pilgrimage of faith'"* (*RM* 5).

Mary and the Church

The Blessed Virgin is the first to live the pilgrimage of faith; the Church follows her pilgrimage and venerates her as a model of faith. The document quotes *Lumen Gentium* and interchanges the word "model" with "figure": "She is present in the midst of the pilgrim Church from generation to generation through faith and as the model of the hope which does not disappoint (cf. Rm 5:5)" (*RM* 42).

The doctrine of the Church's motherhood finds its model in Mary's motherhood: "She recognizes the maternal dimension of her vocation, which is essentially bound to her sacramental nature, in 'contemplating Mary's mysterious sanctity, imitating her charity and faithfully fulfilling the Father's will'" (*LG* 64). The Church is more than a symbol of union with God, it is a sign and instrument:

> If the Church is the sign and instrument of intimate union with God, she is so by reason of her motherhood, because, receiving life from the Spirit, she "generates" sons and daughters of the human race to a new life in Christ. For, just as *Mary is at the service of the mystery of the Incarnation,* so *the Church* is always *at the service of the mystery of adoption to sonship* through grace (*RM* 43).

The committed, consecrated element of Mary's virginity is also a model for the Church:

> Likewise, following the example of Mary, the Church remains the virgin faithful to her spouse: "The Church herself is a virgin who keeps whole and pure the fidelity she has pledged to her Spouse" (*LG* 64)....
> Precisely such virginity, after the example of the Virgin of Nazareth, is the source of a special spiritual fruitfulness: *it is the source of motherhood in the Holy Spirit* (*RM* 43).

Mary's Presence in the Church

The pope stresses that Mary *is present* in the Church's mission, and through her presence she aids the Church's work of spreading the kingdom (cf. *RM* 28). The document lists some ways Mary is present:

—in the faith and piety of individual believers;

—through the traditions of Christian families or "domestic churches," of parish and missionary communities, and of religious institutes and dioceses;

—through the great Marian shrines (cf. *RM* 28).

In all this, the Holy Spirit continues to work through Mary. Her "saving influence is sustained by the Holy Spirit, who, just as he overshadowed the Virgin Mary when he began in her the divine motherhood, in a similar way constantly sustains her solicitude for the brothers and sisters of her Son" (*RM* 38).

One cannot think of the Incarnation nor the birth of the Church without Mary, but she depends on the action of the Holy Spirit. Mary is the person who links the Incarnation of the Word and the birth of the Church. Both at Nazareth and in the upper room at Jerusalem, Mary's "presence indicates the path of 'birth from the Holy Spirit.' Thus she who is present in the mystery of Christ as Mother becomes—by the will of the Son and the power of the Holy Spirit—present in the mystery of the Church" (*RM* 24).

Motherhood and Mediation

Part three of *Redemptoris Mater* discusses Mary's maternal mediation. First, the pope stresses that Mary's mediation is completely subordinate to that of Christ. It does not rival his, but flows from Jesus' saving work and draws all its power from him. In distinguishing between Christ's mediation and Mary's, the pope remarks that Mary participates in it in a unique way: "Mary *entered, in a way all her own, into the one mediation* 'between God and men' *which is the mediation of the man Christ Jesus"* (*RM* 39).

John Paul also stresses that Mary's mediation is "intimately linked with her motherhood" (*RM* 38). Her mediation flows from her spiritual motherhood. *Redemptoris Mater* links the two and explains them, indicating how the Church's members are to imitate this spiritual motherhood. The pope equates mediation with intercession and a mother's action. Referring to the events at Cana, the document states: *"The Mother* of Christ presents herself as the *spokeswoman of her Son's will,* pointing out those things which must be done so that the salvific power of the messiah may be manifested" (*RM* 21).

The pope defines mediation, stating: "Mary places herself between her Son and mankind in the reality of their wants, needs and sufferings. *She puts herself 'in the middle,'* that is to say *she acts as a mediatrix not as an outsider, but in her position as mother....* And 'this *maternity of Mary in the order of grace*...will last without interruption until the eternal fulfillment of all the elect' (*LG* 62)" (*RM* 21).

Besides linking Mary's mediation with her motherhood, the pope links her motherhood with her virginity. He says that Mary's "consent to motherhood is above all *a result of her total self-giving to God in virginity"* (*RM* 39). This self-gift opened Mary to fully cooperate with the Father's plan.

Redemptoris Mater points out that Mary does more than provide a model; she actively cooperates in the work of the Church: *"with maternal love she cooperates in the birth and development'* (cf. *LG* 63) of the sons and daughters of Mother Church" (*RM* 44). God prepared her for this task in the Church, so that she could become for all people their "mother in the order of grace" (*RM* 39).

John Paul places the discussion of Mary's mediation in the context of the communion of saints. Meditating on her Assumption, the pope sees in Mary the eschatological icon of the Church. Already in glory, she is a sign to us of the life to come. But she still cares deeply about those on the way, and intercedes for us until we reach fulfillment in heaven (cf. *RM* 41).

Mary and Ecumenism

A section in part two of the encyclical discusses Mary and ecumenism. The pope first mentions dialogues taking place between the Catholic Church and the Churches and ecclesial communities of the West. Though there is still a good deal of divergence, the pope finds signs of hope in the more profound studies of Mary that are taking place.

John Paul then turns his attention to the Eastern and the Orthodox Churches. He specifically mentions the Greek Fathers, the Byzantine tradition, the Coptic and the Ethiopian heritages. The pope asks: "Why should we not all together look to her as *our common Mother,* who prays for the unity of God's family and who 'precedes' us all at the head of the long line of witnesses of faith in the one Lord, the Son of God, who was conceived in her virginal womb by the power of the Holy Spirit?" (*RM* 30). In terms of devotion, John Paul II makes a personal request: "I also recall the icon of the Virgin of the Cenacle, praying with the apostles as they awaited the Holy Spirit: could she not become the sign of hope for all those who, in fraternal dialogue, wish to deepen their obedience of faith?" (*RM* 33).

Mary and Woman

The anthropological dimension of *Redemptoris Mater* is seen throughout. In discussing motherhood, the pope's emphasis on the human person stands out: "Of the essence of motherhood is the fact that it concerns the person. Motherhood always establishes a *unique and unrepeatable relationship* between two people: *between mother and child* and *between child and mother"* (*RM* 45).

Motherhood is a gift and Mary's motherhood is Christ's personal gift to every individual: "Thus, throughout her life, the Church maintains with the Mother of God a link which embraces, in the saving mystery, the past, the present and the future, and venerates her as the spiritual mother of humanity and the advocate of grace" (*RM* 47).

The person of Mary is a historical reality, but "a presence so discreet as to pass almost unnoticed by the eyes of her contemporaries" (*RM* 3). The document calls her part of "a great historical process, comparable 'to a journey'" (*RM* 6). What happened to Mary at the annunciation took place at Nazareth, "within the concrete circumstances of the history of Israel, the people which first received God's promises" (*RM* 8). Mary's Jewishness and the locations of events are also noted in *Redemptoris Mater.*

In the document, Mary is a woman who belongs to the "weak and poor of the Lord" (*RM* 11). But her creatureliness is defined within the context of her motherhood, albeit, her virginal, chosen and privileged motherhood. It is not that Mary is elevated above other women, as much as all women are elevated in Mary: "The figure of Mary of Nazareth sheds light *on womanhood as such* by the very fact that God, in the sublime event of the Incarnation of his Son, entrusted himself to the ministry, the free and active ministry, of a woman" (*RM* 46).

Although the subject of feminism often occasions controversy,[2] *Redemptoris Mater* indicates the pope's high regard for women and presents their dignity as secured in Mary.

Today

Throughout the document, the pastoral and catechetical aspects of Marian doctrine are applied to our lives. Mary's life and being teaches us how to live out Christ's teachings as she did, through a deep inner openness, that is, through faith, creating in our own hearts an "interior space" consecrated to the Lord in his Church and world (cf. *RM* 28).

The language and tone of *Redemptoris Mater* is a like a friendly invitation to taste the glory and beauty of the Christian life. The pope speaks of one compelling duty, to safeguard carefully the importance of "the poor" and of "the option in favor of the poor" in the word of the living God (cf. *RM* 37).

The encyclical's positive tone, descriptive, close-to-life biblical images, and application to every person's journey of faith makes *Redemptoris Mater* an effective teaching tool. Its doctrinal content is interwoven with liturgical expressions, an anthropological perspective, ecumenical thought, and especially biblical elements. Although Scripture plays a large part in the pope's writings, in *Redemptoris Mater* this aspect stands out. It is like a biblical meditation on Mary. The text builds on trinitarian, Christological and ecclesial foundations. Over and above this, many forms of piety, as well as an appreciation of liturgical art, give variety and diversity to the treatment of Marian pastoral and catechetical themes.

---

2. For a discussion on this topic, see: Joyce A. Little, "*Redemptoris Mater:* The Significance of Mary for Women," *Marian Studies* 39 (1988): 136–158 and Charles W. Neumann, S.M., "Observations on the Paper by Dr. Little," (ibid.): 159–162.

TOPICAL OUTLINE

1. Introduction: Mary's place in the plan of salvation

   A. Mary's pilgrimage of faith (1–2)

   B. The Jubilee of the year 2000 (3)

   C. Marian teaching of Vatican II (4–5)

   D. Mary as the eschatological fulfillment of the Church (6)

2. Part I: Mary in the mystery of Christ

   A. Full of grace

      1. Mary's place in the Father's plan of salvation (7)

      2. Meaning of Mary's name as "full of grace" (8)

      3. Mary's election as the Mother of the Son of God (9)

      4. Mary's Immaculate Conception (10)

      5. The proto-evangelium (11)

   B. Blessed is she who believed

      1. Mary's visit to Elizabeth and its meaning (12)

      2. Mary's response of faith at the annunciation and beyond (13–15)

      3. Simeon's words to Mary: a second annunciation (16)

      4. Mary's faith during the hidden life at Nazareth (17)

      5. The deepest kenosis of faith: Calvary (18)

      6. The blessing of faith and the biblical "beginning": Eve-Mary (19)

C. Behold your mother

    1. The spiritual dimension of motherhood (20)

    2. The significance of Cana and Mary's mediation (21)

    3. Vatican II's teaching on Mary's mediation (22)

    4. The significance of Calvary and Mary's motherhood (23)

    5. Mary's maternal presence in the Church (24)

3. Part II: The Mother of God at the center of the pilgrim Church

A. The Church, the People of God present in all nations

    1. The Church as the pilgrim people of God (25)

    2. Mary and the Church's journey of faith (26–27)

    3. Mary's presence in the Church's mission (28)

B. The Church's journey and the unity of all Christians

    1. Ecumenism and the Churches and ecclesial communities of the West (29–30)

    2. The ancient Churches of the East (31–32)

    3. Icons of Mary and traditions of East and West (33–34)

C. The Magnificat of the pilgrim Church

    1. The Church lives Mary's Magnificat (35)

    2. The Magnificat as Mary's response of faith (36)

    3. Love for the poor (37)

4. Part III: Maternal mediation

A. Mary, the handmaid of the Lord

    1. The unique mediation of Christ and Mary's maternal sharing in it (38)

    2. The relation of Mary's virginity and her motherhood (39)

    3. Mary's mediation as a unique association with the work of Christ (39)

    4. The universal dimension of Mary's maternal mediation (40)

    5. The Assumption and the eschatological nature of Mary's mediation (41)

B. Mary in the life of the Church and of every Christian

    1. Mary as a figure of the Church (42)

    2. The Church as virgin and mother (43)

    3. Mary's motherhood in the order of grace (44)

    4. The Marian dimension of discipleship (45)

    5. Mary and the vocation of woman (46)

    6. Mary as Mother of the Church (47)

C. The meaning of the Marian Year

    1. Marian spirituality and devotion in the light of Vatican II (48)

    2. Mary precedes the Church's journey of faith (49)

    3. Hoped-for unity with the Eastern Churches (50)

5. Conclusion

A. The wonder of Mary's divine motherhood (51)

B. Mary and the transformation of humanity (52)

MOTHER OF THE REDEEMER

Redemptoris Mater

Promulgated by His Holiness Pope John Paul II
On March 25, 1987

ON THE BLESSED VIRGIN MARY
IN THE LIFE OF THE PILGRIM CHURCH

Venerable Brothers and dear Sons and Daughters,
Health and the Apostolic Blessing!

Introduction

1. The Mother of the Redeemer has a precise place in the plan of salvation, for "when the time had fully come, God sent forth his Son, born of woman, born under the law, to redeem those who were under the law, so that we might receive adoption as sons. And because you are sons, God has sent the Spirit of his Son into our hearts, crying, 'Abba! Father!'" (Gal 4:4–6).

With these words of the Apostle Paul, which the Second Vatican Council takes up at the beginning of its treatment of the Blessed Virgin Mary,[1] I too wish to begin my reflection on the role of Mary in the mystery of Christ and on her active and exemplary presence in the life of the

---

1. Cf. Second Vatican Ecumenical Council, Dogmatic Constitution on the Church *Lumen Gentium,* 52 and the whole of Chapter VIII, entitled "The Role of the Blessed Virgin Mary, Mother of God, in the Mystery of Christ and the Church."

Church. For they are words which celebrate together the love of the Father, the mission of the Son, the gift of the Spirit, the role of the woman from whom the Redeemer was born, and our own divine filiation, in the mystery of the "fullness of time."[2]

This "fullness" indicates the moment fixed from all eternity when the Father sent his Son "that whoever believes in him should not perish but have eternal life" (Jn 3:16). It denotes the blessed moment when the Word that "was with God...became flesh and dwelt among us" (Jn 1:1, 14), and made himself our brother. It marks the moment when the Holy Spirit, who had already infused the fullness of grace into Mary of Nazareth, formed in her virginal womb the human nature of Christ. This "fullness" marks the moment when, with the entrance of the eternal into time, time itself is redeemed, and being filled with the mystery of Christ becomes definitively "salvation time." Finally, this "fullness" designates the hidden beginning of the Church's journey. In the liturgy the Church salutes Mary of Nazareth as the Church's own beginning,[3] for in the event of the Immaculate Conception the Church sees projected, and anticipated in her most noble member, the saving grace of Easter. And above all, in the Incarnation she encounters Christ and Mary indissolubly joined: he who is the Church's Lord and Head and she who, uttering the first *fiat* of the New Covenant, prefigures the Church's condition as spouse and mother.

2. Strengthened by the presence of Christ (cf. Mt 28:20), the Church journeys through time toward the consummation of the ages and goes to meet the Lord who comes. But on this journey—and I wish to make this

---

2. The expression "fullness of time" *(pléroma tou chrónou)* is parallel with similar expressions of Judaism, both Biblical (cf. Gn 29:21; 1 Sam 7:12; Tob 14:5) and extra-Biblical, and especially of the New Testament (cf. Mk 1:15; Lk 21:24; Jn 7:8; Eph 1:10). From the point of view of form, it means not only the conclusion of a chronological process but also and especially the coming to maturity or completion of a particularly important period, one directed toward the fulfillment of an expectation, a coming to completion which thus takes on an eschatological dimension. According to Gal 4:4 and its context, it is the coming of the Son of God that reveals that time has, so to speak, reached its limit. That is to say, the period marked by the promise made to Abraham and by the Law mediated by Moses has now reached its climax, in the sense that Christ fulfills the divine promise and supersedes the old Law.

3. Cf. *Roman Missal,* Preface of December 8, Immaculate Conception of the Blessed Virgin Mary; St. Ambrose, *De Institutione Virginis,* XV, 93–94: *PL* 16, 342; Second Vatican Ecumenical Council, Dogmatic Constitution on the Church *Lumen Gentium,* 68.

point straightaway—she proceeds along the path already trodden by the Virgin Mary, who *"advanced in her pilgrimage of faith, and loyally persevered in her union with her Son unto the cross."*[4]

I take these very rich and evocative words from the Constitution *Lumen Gentium,* which in its concluding part offers a clear summary of the Church's doctrine on the Mother of Christ, whom she venerates as her beloved Mother and as her model in faith, hope and charity.

Shortly after the Council, my great predecessor Paul VI decided to speak further of the Blessed Virgin. In the Encyclical Epistle *Christi Matri* and subsequently in the Apostolic Exhortations *Signum Magnum and Marialis Cultus,*[5] he expounded the foundations and criteria of the special veneration which the Mother of Christ receives in the Church, as well as the various forms of Marian devotion—liturgical, popular and private—which respond to the spirit of faith.

3. The circumstance which now moves me to take up this subject once more *is the prospect of the year 2000,* now drawing near, in which the bimillennial jubilee of the birth of Jesus Christ at the same time directs our gaze toward his Mother. In recent years, various opinions have been voiced suggesting that it would be fitting to precede that anniversary by a similar jubilee in celebration of the birth of Mary.

In fact, even though it is not possible to establish an exact *chronological point* for identifying the date of Mary's birth, the Church has constantly been aware that *Mary appeared* on the horizon of *salvation history before Christ.*[6] It is a fact that when "the fullness of time" was definitively drawing near—the saving advent of Emmanuel—he who was from eternity destined to be his Mother already existed on earth. The fact that she "preceded" the coming of Christ is reflected every year *in the liturgy of Advent.* Therefore, if to that ancient historical expectation of the Savior we compare these years which are bringing us closer to the end of the second millennium after Christ and to the beginning of

---

4. Second Vatican Ecumenical Council, Dogmatic Constitution on the Church *Lumen Gentium,* 58.

5. Pope Paul VI, Encyclical Epistle *Christi Matri* (September 15, 1966): *AAS* 58 (1966), 745–749; Apostolic Exhortation *Signum Magnum* (May 13,1967): *AAS* 59 (1967), 465–475; Apostolic Exhortation *Marialis Cultus* (February 2, 1974): *AAS* 66 (1974), 113–168.

6. The Old Testament foretold in many different ways the mystery of Mary: cf. St. John Damascene, *Hom. in Dormitionem* 1, 8–9: *SCh.* 80, 103–107.

the third, it becomes fully comprehensible that in this present period we wish to turn in a special way to her, the one who in the "night" of the Advent expectation began to shine like a true "Morning Star" *(Stella Matutina)*. For just as this star, together with the "dawn," precedes the rising of the sun, so Mary from the time of her Immaculate Conception preceded the coming of the Savior, the rising of the "Sun of Justice" in the history of the human race.[7]

Her presence in the midst of Israel—a presence so discreet as to pass almost unnoticed by the eyes of her contemporaries—shone very clearly before the Eternal One, who had associated this hidden "Daughter of Zion" (cf. Zeph 3:14; 2:10) with the plan of salvation embracing the whole history of humanity. With good reason, then, at the end of this millennium, we Christians, who know that the providential plan of the Most Holy Trinity is *the central reality of revelation and of faith,* feel the need to emphasize the unique presence of the Mother of Christ in history, especially during these last years leading up to the year 2000.

4. The Second Vatican Council prepares us for this by presenting in its teaching *the Mother of God in the mystery of Christ and of the Church.* If it is true, as the Council itself proclaims,[8] that "only in the mystery of the incarnate Word does the mystery of man take on light," then this principle must be applied in a very particular way to that exceptional "daughter of the human race," that extraordinary "woman" who became the Mother of Christ. *Only in the mystery of Christ is her mystery fully made clear.* Thus has the Church sought to interpret it from the very beginning: the mystery of the Incarnation has enabled her to penetrate and to make ever clearer the mystery of the Mother of the incarnate Word. The Council of Ephesus (431) was of decisive importance in clarifying this, for during that Council, to the great joy of Christians, the truth of the divine motherhood of Mary was solemnly confirmed as a truth of the Church's faith. Mary *is the Mother of God (Theotókos),* since by the power of the Holy Spirit she conceived in her virginal womb and brought into the world Jesus Christ, the Son of God, who is

---

7. Cf. *Insegnamenti di Giovanni Paolo II,* VI/2 (1983), 225f.; Pope Pius IX, Apostolic Letter *Ineffabilis Deus* (December 8, 1854): *Pius IX P. M. Acta, pars* I, 597–599.

8. Cf. Pastoral Constitution on the Church in the Modern World *Gaudium et Spes,* 22.

of one being with the Father.[9] "The Son of God...born of the Virgin Mary...has truly been made one of us,"[10] has been made man. Thus, through the mystery of Christ, on the horizon of the Church's faith there shines in its fullness the mystery of his Mother. In turn, the dogma of the divine motherhood of Mary was for the Council of Ephesus and is for the Church like a seal upon the dogma of the Incarnation, in which the Word truly assumes human nature into the unity of his person, without canceling out that nature.

5. The Second Vatican Council, by presenting Mary in the mystery of Christ, also finds the path to a deeper understanding of the mystery of the Church. Mary, as the Mother of Christ, *is in a particular way united with the Church,* "which the Lord established as his own body."[11] It is significant that the conciliar text places this truth about the Church as the Body of Christ (according to the teaching of the Pauline Letters) in close proximity to the truth that the Son of God "through the power of the Holy Spirit was born of the Virgin Mary." The reality of the Incarnation finds a sort of extension *in the mystery of the Church—the Body of Christ.* And one cannot think of the reality of the Incarnation without referring to Mary, the Mother of the incarnate Word.

In these reflections, however, I wish to consider primarily that "pilgrimage of faith" in which "the Blessed Virgin advanced," faithfully preserving her union with Christ.[12] In this way the *"twofold bond"* which unites the Mother of God *with Christ and with the Church* takes on historical significance. Nor is it just a question of the Virgin Mother's life story, of her personal journey of faith and "the better part" which is hers in the mystery of salvation; it is also a question of the history of the whole People of God, *of all those who take part* in the same *"pilgrimage of faith."*

---

9. Ecumenical Council of Ephesus, in *Conciliorum Oecumenicorum Decreta,* Bologna 1973, 41–44, 59–61: *DS* 250–264; cf. Ecumenical Council of Chalcedon, *op.cit.* 84–87: *DS* 300–303.

10. Second Vatican Ecumenical Council, Pastoral Constitution on the Church in the Modern World *Gaudium et Spes,* 22.

11. Dogmatic Constitution on the Church *Lumen Gentium,* 52.

12. Cf. ibid., 58.

The Council expresses this when it states in another passage that Mary "has gone before," becoming "a model of the Church in the matter of faith, charity and perfect union with Christ."[13] This *"going before" as a figure or model* is in reference to the intimate mystery of the Church, as she actuates and accomplishes her own saving mission by uniting in herself—as Mary did—the qualities *of mother and virgin.* She is a virgin who "keeps whole and pure the fidelity she has pledged to her Spouse" and "becomes herself a mother," for "she brings forth to a new and immortal life children who are conceived of the Holy Spirit and born of God."[14]

6. All this is accomplished in a great historical process, comparable "to a journey." *The pilgrimage of faith indicates the interior history,* that is, the story of souls. But it is also the story of all human beings, subject here on earth to transitoriness, and part of the historical dimension. In the following reflections we wish to concentrate first of all on the present, which in itself is not yet history, but which nevertheless is constantly forming it, also in the sense of the history of salvation. Here there opens up a broad prospect, within which the *Blessed Virgin Mary continues to "go before" the People of God.* Her exceptional pilgrimage of faith represents a constant point of reference for the Church, for individuals and for communities, for peoples and nations and, in a sense, for all humanity. It is indeed difficult to encompass and measure its range.

The Council emphasizes that *the Mother of God is already the eschatological fulfillment of the Church:* "In the most holy Virgin the Church has already reached that perfection whereby she exists without spot or wrinkle (cf. Eph 5:27)"; and at the same time the Council says that "the followers of Christ still strive to increase in holiness by conquering sin, and so *they raise their eyes to Mary,* who shines forth to the whole community of the elect as a model of the virtues."[15] The pilgrimage of faith no longer belongs to the Mother of the Son of God: glorified at the side of her Son in heaven, Mary has already crossed the threshold between faith and that vision which is "face to face" (1 Cor 13:12). At the same time, however, in this eschatological fulfillment, Mary does

---

13. Ibid., 63, cf. St. Ambrose, *Expos. Evang. sec. Lucam,* II, 7: *CSEL* 32/4, 45; *De Institutione Virginis,* XIV, 88–89: *PL* 16, 341.

14. Cf. Dogmatic Constitution on the Church *Lumen Gentium,* 64.

15. Ibid., 65.

not cease to be the "Star of the Sea" *(Maris Stella)*[16] for all those who are still on the journey of faith. If they lift their eyes to her from their earthly existence, they do so because "the Son whom she brought forth is he whom God placed as the first-born among many brethren (Rm 8:29),"[17] and also because "in the birth and development" of these brothers and sisters "she cooperates with a maternal love."[18]

---

16. "Take away this star of the sun which illuminates the world: where does the day go? Take away Mary, this star of the sea, of the great and boundless sea: what is left but a vast obscurity and the shadow of death and deepest darkness?": St. Bernard, *In Navitate Beatae Mariae Sermo, De Aquaeductu,* 6: *Sancti Bernardi Opera,* V, 1968, 279; cf. *In laudibus Virginis Matris Homilia* II, 17: *ed. cit.,* IV, 1966, 34f.

17. Dogmatic Constitution on the Church *Lumen Gentium,* 63.

18. Ibid., 63.

PART I: MARY IN THE MYSTERY OF CHRIST

1. Full of Grace

7. "Blessed be the God and Father of our Lord Jesus Christ, who has blessed us in Christ with every spiritual blessing in the heavenly places" (Eph 1:3). These words of the *Letter to the Ephesians* reveal the eternal design of God the Father, his plan of man's salvation in Christ. It is a universal plan, which concerns all men and women created in the image and likeness of God (cf. Gn 1:26). Just as all are included in the creative work of God "in the beginning," so all are eternally included in the divine plan of salvation, which is to be completely revealed, in the "fullness of time," with the final coming of Christ. In fact, the God who is the "Father of our Lord Jesus Christ"—these are the next words of the same *letter—"chose us* in him *before the foundation of the world,* that we should be holy and blameless before him. He destined us in love to be his sons through Jesus Christ, according to the purpose of his will, to the praise of his glorious grace, which he freely bestowed on us in *the Beloved.* In him we have redemption through his blood, the forgiveness of our trespasses, according to the riches of his grace" (Eph 1:4–7).

The divine plan of salvation—which was fully revealed to us with the coming of Christ—is eternal. And according to the teaching contained in the *Letter* just quoted and in other Pauline Letters (cf. Col 1:12–14; Rm 3:24; Gal 3:13; 2 Cor 5:18–29), it is also *eternally linked to Christ.* It includes everyone, but it reserves a special place for the *"woman"* who is the Mother of him to whom the Father has entrusted the work of salvation.[19] As the Second Vatican Council says, "she is al-

---

19. Concerning the predestination of Mary, cf. St. John Damascene, *Hom. in Nativitatem,* 7, 10: *SCh.* 80, 65; 73; *Hom. in Dormitionem* 1, 3: *SCh.* 80, 85: "For it is

ready prophetically foreshadowed in that promise made to our first parents after their fall into sin"—according to the Book of *Genesis* (cf. 3:15). "Likewise she is the Virgin who is to conceive and bear a son, whose name will be called Emmanuel"—according to the words of Isaiah (cf. 7:14).[20] In this way the Old Testament prepares that "fullness of time" when God "sent forth his Son, born of woman...so that we might receive adoption as sons." The coming into the world of the Son of God is an event recorded in the first chapters of the Gospels according to Luke and Matthew.

8. *Mary* is definitively *introduced into the mystery of Christ through* this event: *the annunciation* by the angel. This takes place at Nazareth, within the concrete circumstances of the history of Israel, the people which first received God's promises. The divine messenger says to the Virgin: "Hail, full of grace, the Lord is with you" (Lk 1:28). Mary "was greatly troubled at the saying, and considered in her mind what sort of greeting this might be" (Lk 1:29): what could those extraordinary words mean, and in particular the expression "full of grace" *(kécharitôménê)*.[21]

If we wish to meditate together with Mary on these words, and especially on the expression "full of grace," we can find a significant echo in the very passage from the *Letter to the Ephesians* quoted above. And if after the announcement of the heavenly messenger the Virgin of Nazareth is also called "blessed among women" (cf. Lk 1:42), it is because of that blessing with which "God the Father" has filled us "in the

---

she, who, chosen from the ancient generations, by virtue of the predestination and benevolence of the God and Father who generated you (the Word of God) outside time without coming out of himself or suffering change, it is she who gave you birth, nourished of her flesh, in the last time...."

20. Dogmatic Constitution on the Church *Lumen Gentium,* 55.

21. In Patristic tradition there is a wide and varied interpretation of this expression: cf. Origen, *In Lucam homiliae,* VI, 7: *SCh.* 87, 148; Severianus of Gabala, *In mundi creationem, Oratio* VI, 10: *PG* 56, 497f.; St. John Chrysostom (Pseudo), *In Annuntiationem Deiparae et contra Arium impium, PG* 62, 765f.; Basil of Seleucia, *Oratio* 39, *In Sanctissimae Deiparae Annuntiationem,* 5: *PG* 85, 441–46; Antipater of Bosra, *Hom. II, In Sanctissimae Deiparae Annuntiationem,* 3–11: *PG* 85, 1777–1783; St. Sophronius of Jerusalem, *Oratio 11, In Sanctissimae Deiparae Annuntiationem,* 17–19: *PG* 87/3, 3235–3240; St. John Damascene *Hom. in Dormitionem,* 1, 70: *SCh.* 80, 96–101; St. Jerome, *Epistola* 65, 9: *PL* 22, 628, St. Ambrose, *Expos. Evang. sec. Lucam,* II, 9: *CSEL* 32/4, 45f.; St. Augustine, *Sermo* 291, 4–6: *PL* 38, 131 8f.; *Enchiridion,* 36, 11: *PL* 40, 250; St. Peter Chrysologus, *Sermo* 142: *PL* 52, 579f.; *Sermo* 143: *PL* 52, 583; St. Fulgentius of Ruspe, *Epistola* 17, VI, 12: *PL* 65, 458; St. Bernard, *In laudibus Virginis Matris, Homilia* III, 2–3: *Sancti Bernardi Opera,* IV, 1966, 36–38.

heavenly places, in Christ." It is a *spiritual blessing* which is meant for all people and which bears in itself fullness and universality ("every blessing"). It flows from that love which, in the Holy Spirit, unites the consubstantial Son to the Father. At the same time, it is a blessing poured out through Jesus Christ upon human history until the end: upon all people. This blessing, however, refers *to Mary in a special and exceptional degree:* for she was greeted by Elizabeth as "blessed among women."

The double greeting is due to the fact that in the soul of this "Daughter of Zion" there is manifested, in a sense, all the "glory of grace," that grace which "the Father...has given us in his beloved Son." For the messenger greets Mary as "full of grace"; he calls her thus as if it were her real name. He does not call her by her proper earthly name: Miryam (Mary), but *by this new name: "full of grace."* What does this name mean? Why does the archangel address the Virgin of Nazareth in this way?

In the language of the Bible "grace" means a special gift, which according to the New Testament has its source precisely in the Trinitarian life of God himself, God who is love (cf. 1 Jn 4:8). The fruit of this love is *"the election"* of which the *Letter to the Ephesians* speaks. On the part of God, this election is the eternal desire to save man through a sharing in his own life (cf. 2 Pt 1:4) in Christ: it is salvation through a sharing in supernatural life. The effect of this eternal gift, of this grace of man's election by God, is like a *seed of holiness,* or a spring which rises in the soul as a gift from God himself, who through grace gives life and holiness to those who are chosen. In this way there is fulfilled, that is to say there comes about, that "blessing" of man "with every spiritual blessing," that "being his adopted sons and daughters...in Christ," in him who is eternally the "beloved Son" of the Father.

When we read that the messenger addresses Mary as "full of grace," the Gospel context, which mingles revelations and ancient promises, enables us to understand that among all the "spiritual blessings in Christ" this is a special "blessing." In the mystery of Christ she is *present* even "before the creation of the world," as the one whom the Father "has chosen" *as Mother* of his Son in the Incarnation. And, what is more, together with the Father, the Son has chosen her, entrusting her eternally to the Spirit of holiness. In an entirely special and exceptional way Mary is united to Christ, and similarly she *is eternally loved in this "beloved Son,"* this Son who is of one being with the Father, in whom is concentrated all the "glory of grace." At the same time, she is and remains perfectly open to this "gift from above" (cf. Jas 1:17). As the Council teaches, Mary "stands out among the poor and humble of the Lord, who confidently await and receive salvation from him."[22]

9. If the greeting and the name "full of grace" say all this, in the context of the angel's announcement they refer first of all *to the election of Mary as Mother of the Son of God.* But at the same time the "fullness of grace" indicates all the supernatural munificence from which Mary benefits by being chosen and destined to be the Mother of Christ. If this election is fundamental for the accomplishment of God's salvific designs for humanity, and if the eternal choice in Christ and the vocation to the dignity of adopted children is the destiny of everyone, then the election of Mary is wholly exceptional and unique. Hence also the singularity and uniqueness of her place in the mystery of Christ.

The divine messenger says to her: "Do not be afraid, Mary, for you have found favor with God. And behold, you will conceive in your womb and bear a son, and you shall call his name Jesus. He will be great, and will be called the Son of the Most High" (Lk 1:30–32). And when the Virgin, disturbed by that extraordinary greeting, asks: "How shall this be, since I have no husband?" she receives from the angel the confirmation and explanation of the preceding words. Gabriel says to her*: "The Holy Spirit will come upon you,* and the power of the Most High will overshadow you; therefore the child to be born will be called holy, the Son of God" (Lk 1:35).

The annunciation, therefore, is the revelation of the mystery of the Incarnation at the very beginning of its fulfillment on earth. God's salvific giving of himself and his life, in some way to all creation but directly to man, reaches *one of its high points in the mystery of the Incarnation.* This is indeed a high point among all the gifts of grace conferred in the history of man and of the universe: Mary is "full of grace," because it is precisely in her that the Incarnation of the Word, the hypostatic union of the Son of God with human nature, is accomplished and fulfilled. As the Council says, Mary is "the Mother of the Son of God. As a result she is also the favorite daughter of the Father and the temple of the Holy Spirit. Because of this gift of sublime grace, she far surpasses all other creatures, both in heaven and on earth."[23]

---

22. Dogmatic Constitution on the Church *Lumen Gentium,* 55.
23. Ibid., 53.

10. The *Letter to the Ephesians,* speaking of the "glory of grace" that "God, the Father...has bestowed on us in his beloved Son," adds: "In him we have redemption through his blood" (Eph 1:7). According to the belief formulated in solemn documents of the Church, this "glory of grace" is manifested in the Mother of God through the fact that she has been "redeemed in a more sublime manner."[24] By virtue of the richness of the grace of the beloved Son, by reason of the redemptive merits of him who willed to become her Son, Mary was *preserved from the inheritance of original sin.*[25] In this way, from the first moment of her conception—which is to say of her existence—she belonged to Christ, sharing in the salvific and sanctifying grace and in that love which has its beginning in the "Beloved," the Son of the Eternal Father, who through the Incarnation became her own Son. Consequently, through the power of the Holy Spirit, in the order of grace, which is a participation in the divine nature, *Mary receives life from him to whom she herself,* in the order of earthly generation, *gave life* as a mother. The liturgy does not hesitate to call her "mother of her Creator"[26] and to hail her with the words which Dante Alighieri places on the lips of St. Bernard: "daughter of your Son."[27] And since Mary receives this "new life" with a fullness corresponding to the Son's love for the Mother, and thus corresponding to the dignity of the divine motherhood, the angel at the annunciation calls her "full of grace."

11. In the salvific design of the Most Holy Trinity, the mystery of the Incarnation constitutes the superabundant *fulfillment of the promise* made by God to man *after original sin,* after that first sin whose effects oppress the whole earthly history of man (cf. Gn 3:15). And so, there comes into the world a Son, "the seed of the woman" who will crush the evil of sin in its very origins: "he will crush the head of the serpent." As

---

24. Cf. Pope Pius IX, Apostolic Letter *Ineffabilis Deus* (December 8, 1854): *Pius IX P. M. Acta, pars* I, 616; Second Vatican Ecumenical Council, Dogmatic Constitution on the Church *Lumen Gentium,* 53.

25. Cf. St. Germanus of Constantinople, *In Annuntiationem SS. Deiparae Hom.: PG* 98, 327 f.; St. Andrew of Crete, *Canon in B. Mariae Natalem,* 4. *PG* 97, 1321 f., *In Nativitatem B. Mariae,* I: *PG* 97, 811–812; *Hom. in Dormitionem S. Mariae* I: *PG* 97, 1067 f.

26. *Liturgy of the Hours* of August 15, Assumption of the Blessed Virgin Mary, Hymn at First and Second Vespers; St. Peter Damian, *Carmina et Preces,* 47: *PL* 145, 934.

27. *Divina Commedia, Paradiso,* XXXIII, 1; cf. *Liturgy of the Hours,* Memorial of the Blessed Virgin Mary on Saturday, Hymn II in the Office of Readings.

we see from the words of the Proto-gospel, the victory of the woman's Son will not take place without a hard struggle, a struggle that is to extend through the whole of human history. The "enmity," foretold at the beginning, is confirmed in the Apocalypse (the book of the final events of the Church and the world), in which there recurs the sign of the "woman," this time "clothed with the sun" (Rv 12:1).

Mary, Mother of the incarnate Word, is placed *at the very center of that enmity,* that struggle which accompanies the history of humanity on earth and the history of salvation itself. In this central place, she who belongs to the "weak and poor of the Lord" bears in herself, like no other member of the human race, that "glory of grace" which the Father "has bestowed on us in his beloved Son," and this *grace determines the extraordinary greatness and beauty* of her whole being. Mary thus remains before God, and also before the whole of humanity, as the unchangeable and inviolable sign of God's election, spoken of in Paul's letter: "in Christ...he chose us...before the foundation of the world...he destined us...to be his sons" (Eph 1:4, 5). This election is more powerful than any experience of evil and sin, than all that "enmity" which marks the history of man. In this history Mary remains a sign of sure hope.

2. Blessed is she who believed

12. Immediately after the narration of the annunciation, the Evangelist Luke guides us in the footsteps of the Virgin of Nazareth toward "a city of Judah" (Lk 1:39). According to scholars this city would be the modern Ain Karim, situated in the mountains, not far from Jerusalem. Mary arrived there "in haste," *to visit Elizabeth* her kinswoman. The reason for her visit is also to be found in the fact that at the annunciation Gabriel had made special mention of Elizabeth, who in her old age had conceived a son by her husband Zechariah, through the power of God: "Your kinswoman Elizabeth in her old age has also conceived a Son; and this is the sixth month with her who was called barren. *For with God nothing will be impossible"* (Lk 1:36–37). The divine messenger had spoken of what had been accomplished in Elizabeth in order to answer Mary's question. "How shall this be, since I have no husband?" (Lk 1:34). It is to come to pass precisely through the "power of the Most High," just as it happened in the case of Elizabeth, and even more so.

Moved by charity, therefore, Mary goes to the house of her kinswoman. When Mary enters, Elizabeth replies to her greeting and feels the child leap in her womb, and being "filled with the Holy Spirit" she *greets Mary* with a loud cry: "Blessed are you among women, and blessed is the fruit of your womb!" (cf. Lk 1:40–42). Elizabeth's exclamation or acclamation was subsequently to become part of the *Hail Mary,* as a continuation of the angel's greeting, thus becoming one of the Church's most frequently used prayers. But still more significant are the words of Elizabeth in the question which follows: "And why is this granted me, that the mother of my Lord should come to me?" (Lk 1:43). Elizabeth bears witness to Mary: she recognizes and proclaims that before her stands the Mother of the Lord, the Mother of the messiah. The son whom Elizabeth is carrying in her womb also shares in this witness: "The babe in my womb leaped for joy" (Lk 1:44). This child is the future John the Baptist, who at the Jordan will point out Jesus as the messiah.

While every word of Elizabeth's greeting is filled with meaning, her final words would seem to have *fundamental importance:* "And blessed is she who believed that there would be a fulfillment of what was spoken to her from the Lord" (Lk 1:45).[28] These words can be linked with the little "full of grace" of the angel's greeting. Both of these texts reveal an essential Mariological content, namely the truth about Mary, who has become really present in the mystery of Christ precisely because she "has believed." The *fullness of grace* announced by the angel means the gift of God himself. *Mary's faith,* proclaimed by Elizabeth at the visitation, indicates *how* the Virgin of Nazareth *responded to this gift.*

13. As the Council teaches, "'The obedience of faith' (Rm 16:26; cf. Rm 1:5; 2 Cor 10:5–6) must be given to God who reveals, an obedience by which man entrusts his whole self freely to God."[29] This description of faith found perfect realization in Mary. The "decisive" moment was the annunciation, and the very words of Elizabeth: "And blessed is she who believed" refer primarily to that very moment.[30]

---

28. Cf. St. Augustine, *De Sancta Virginitate,* III, 3: *PL* 40, 398; *Sermo* 25, 7: *PL* 46,

29. Dogmatic Constitution on Divine Revelation *Dei Verbum,* 5

30. This is a classic theme, already expounded by St. Irenaeus: "And, as by the action of the disobedient virgin, man was afflicted and, being cast down, died, so also by the action of the Virgin who obeyed the Word of God, man being regenerated received, through life, life.... For it was meet and just...that Eve should be "recapitulated" in Mary, so that the Virgin, becoming the advocate of the virgin, should dissolve and destroy the virginal disobedience by means of virginal obedience": *Expositio Doctrinae Apostolicae,* 33: *SCh.* 62, 83–86; cf. also *Adversus Haereses,* V, 19, 1: 5. Ch. 153, 248–250.

Indeed, at the annunciation Mary entrusted herself to God completely, with the "full submission of intellect and will," manifesting "the obedience of faith" to him who spoke to her through his messenger.[31] She responded, therefore, *with all her human and feminine "I,"* and this response of faith included both perfect cooperation with "the grace of God that precedes and assists" and perfect openness to the action of the Holy Spirit, who "constantly brings faith to completion by his gifts."[32]

The word of the living God, announced to Mary by the angel, referred to her: "And behold, you will conceive in your womb and bear a son" (Lk 1:31). By accepting this announcement, Mary was to become the "Mother of the Lord," and the divine mystery of the Incarnation was to be accomplished in her. "The Father of mercies willed that the consent of the predestined Mother should precede the Incarnation."[33] And Mary gives this consent, after she has heard everything the messenger has to say. She says: "Behold, I am the handmaid of the Lord; let it be to me according to your word" (Lk 1:38). This *fiat* of Mary—"let it be to me"—was decisive, on the human level, for the accomplishment of the divine mystery. There is a complete harmony with the words of the Son, who, according to the *Letter to the Hebrews,* says to the Father as he comes into the world: "Sacrifices and offering you have not desired, but *a body you have prepared for me....* Lo, I have come to do your will, O God" (Heb 10:5–7). The mystery of the Incarnation was accomplished when Mary uttered her *fiat:* "Let it be to me according to your word," which made possible, as far as it depended upon her in the divine plan, the granting of her Son's desire.

Mary uttered this *fiat in faith.* In faith she entrusted herself to God without reserve and "devoted herself totally as the handmaid of the Lord to the person and work of her Son."[34] And as the Fathers of the Church teach—she conceived this Son in her mind before she conceived him in her womb: precisely in faith![35] Rightly, therefore, does Elizabeth praise

---

31. Second Vatican Ecumenical Council, Dogmatic Constitution on Divine Revelation *Dei Verbum,* 5.

32. Ibid., 5, cf. Dogmatic Constitution on the Church *Lumen Gentium,* 56.

33. Second Vatican Ecumenical Council, Dogmatic Constitution on the Church *Lumen Gentium,* 56.

34. Ibid., 56.

35. Cf. ibid., 53; St. Augustine, *De Sancta Virginitate,* III, 3: *PL* 40, 398; *Sermo* 215, 4; *PL* 38, 1074; *Sermo* 196, I: *PL* 38, 1019; *De peccatorum meritis et remissione,* I, 29, 57:

Mary: "And blessed is she who believed *that there would be a fulfill-ment* of what was spoken to her from the Lord." These words have already been fulfilled: Mary of Nazareth presents herself at the thresh-old of Elizabeth and Zechariah's house as the Mother of the Son of God. This is Elizabeth's joyful discovery: "The mother of my Lord comes to me"!

14. Mary's faith can also be *compared to that of Abraham,* whom St. Paul calls "our father in faith" (cf. Rm 4:12). In the salvific economy of God's revelation, Abraham's faith constitutes the beginning of the Old Covenant; Mary's faith at the annunciation inaugurates the New Cov-enant. Just as Abraham *"in hope believed against hope,* that he should become the father of many nations" (cf. Rm 4:18), so Mary, at the an-nunciation, having professed her virginity ("How shall this be, since I have no husband?") *believed* that through the power of the Most High, by the power of the Holy Spirit, she would become the Mother of God's Son in accordance with the angel's revelation: "The child to be born will be called holy, the Son of God" (Lk 1:35).

However, Elizabeth's words "And blessed is she who believed" do not apply only to that particular moment of the annunciation. Certainly the annunciation is the culminating moment of Mary's faith in her awaiting of Christ, but it is also the point of departure from which her whole "journey toward God" begins, her whole pilgrimage of faith. And on this road, in an eminent and truly heroic manner—indeed with an ever greater heroism of faith—the "obedience" which she professes to the word of divine revelation will be fulfilled. Mary's "obedience of faith" during the whole of her pilgrimage will show surprising simi-larities to the faith of Abraham. Just like the patriarch of the People of God, so too Mary, during the pilgrimage of her filial and maternal *fiat,* "in hope believed against hope." Especially during certain stages of this journey the blessing granted to her "who believed" will be re-vealed with particular vividness. To believe means "to abandon one-self" to the truth of the word of the living God, knowing and humbly recognizing "how unsearchable are his judgments and how *inscrutable his ways"* (Rm 11:33). Mary, who by the eternal will of the Most High stands, one may say, at the very center of those "inscrutable ways" and

PL 44, 142; Sermo 25, 7: *PL* 46, 937–938; St. Leo the Great, *Tractatus* 21, *De Natale Domini,* I: *CCL* 138, 86.

"unsearchable judgments" of God, conforms herself to them in the dim light of faith, accepting fully and with a ready heart everything that is decreed in the divine plan.

15. When at the annunciation Mary hears of the Son whose Mother she is to become and to whom "she will give the name Jesus" (Savior), she also learns that "the Lord God will give to him the throne of his father David," and that "he will reign over the house of Jacob forever and of his kingdom there will be no end" (Lk 1:32–33). The hope of the whole of Israel was directed toward this. The promised messiah is to be "great," and the heavenly messenger also announces that *"he will be great"*—great both by bearing the name of *Son of the Most High* and by the fact that he is to assume the *inheritance of David.* He is therefore to be a king; he is to reign "over the house of Jacob." Mary had grown up in the midst of these expectations of her people: could she guess, at the moment of the annunciation, the vital significance of the angel's words? And how is one to understand that "kingdom" which "will have no end"?

Although through faith she may have perceived in that instant she was the mother of the "messiah King," nevertheless she replied: *"Behold, I am the handmaid of the Lord; let it be to me according to your word"* (Lk 1:38). From the first moment Mary professed above all the "obedience of faith," abandoning herself to the meaning which was given to the words of the annunciation by him from whom they proceeded: God himself.

16. Later, a little further along this way of the "obedience of faith," Mary hears *other words:* those uttered by *Simeon* in the Temple of Jerusalem. It was now forty days after the birth of Jesus when, in accordance with the precepts of the Law of Moses, Mary and Joseph "brought him up to Jerusalem to present him to the Lord" (Lk 2:22). The birth had taken place in conditions of extreme poverty. We know from Luke that when, on the occasion of the census ordered by the Roman authorities, Mary went with Joseph to Bethlehem, having found "no place in the inn," *she gave birth to her Son in a stable* and "laid him in a manger" (cf. Lk 2:7).

A just and God-fearing man called Simeon appears at this beginning of Mary's "journey" of faith. His words, suggested by the Holy Spirit (cf. Lk 2:25–27), confirm the truth of the annunciation. For we read that he took up in his arms the child to whom—in accordance with the angel's command—the name Jesus was given (cf. Lk 2:21). Simeon's words match the meaning of this name, which is Savior: "God is salvation." Turning to the Lord, he says: "For my eyes have seen your *salvation* which you have prepared *in the presence of all peoples,* a light for revelation to the Gentiles, and for glory to your people Israel" (Lk 2:30–32). At the same time, however, Simeon addresses Mary with the following words: "Behold, this child is set for the fall and rising of many in Israel, and for a *sign that is spoken against,* that thoughts out of many hearts may be revealed"; and he adds with direct reference to her: "and a sword will pierce through your own soul also" (cf. Lk 2:34–35). Simeon's words cast new light on the announcement which Mary had heard from the angel: Jesus is the Savior, he is "a *light* for revelation" to mankind. Is not this what was manifested in a way on Christmas night, when the *shepherds* came to the stable (cf. Lk 2:8–20)? Is not this what was to be manifested even more clearly in the coming of the *Magi from the East* (cf. Mt 2:1–12)? But at the same time, at the very beginning of his life, the Son of Mary, and his Mother with him, will experience in themselves the truth of those other words of Simeon: "a sign that is spoken against" (Lk 2:34). Simeon's words seem like a *second annunciation to Mary,* for they tell her of the actual historical situation in which the Son is to accomplish his mission, namely, in misunderstanding and sorrow. While this announcement on the one hand confirms her faith in the accomplishment of the divine promises of salvation, on the other hand it also reveals to her that she will have to live her obedience of faith in suffering, at the side of the suffering Savior, and that her motherhood will be mysterious and sorrowful. Thus, after the visit of the Magi who came from the East, after their homage ("they fell down and worshipped him") and after they had offered gifts (cf. Mt 2:11), Mary together with the child *has to flee into Egypt* in the protective care of Joseph, for "Herod is about to search for the child, to destroy him" (cf. Mt 2:13). And until the death of Herod they will have to remain in Egypt (cf. Mt 2:15).

17. When the Holy Family returns to Nazareth after Herod's death, there begins the long *period of the hidden life.* She "who believed that there would be a fulfillment of what was spoken to her from the Lord" (Lk 1:45) lives the reality of these words day by day. And daily at her side is the Son to whom *"she gave the name Jesus";* therefore, in contact with him she certainly uses this name, a fact which would have surprised no one, since the name had long been in use in Israel. Nevertheless, Mary knows that he who bears the name *Jesus has been called by the angel "the Son of the Most High"* (cf. Lk 1:32). Mary knows she has

conceived and given birth to him "without having a husband," by the power of the Holy Spirit, by the power of the Most High who overshadowed her (cf. Lk 1:35), just as at the time of Moses and the patriarchs the cloud covered the presence of God (cf. Ex 24:16; 40:34–35; 1 Kgs 8:10–12). Therefore Mary knows that the Son to whom she gave birth in a virginal manner is precisely that "Holy One," the Son of God, of whom the angel spoke to her.

During the years of Jesus' hidden life in the house at Nazareth, *Mary's life* too is *"hidden with Christ in God"* (cf. Col 3:3) *through faith.* For faith is contact with the mystery of God. Every day Mary is in constant contact with the ineffable mystery of God made man, a mystery that surpasses everything revealed in the Old Covenant. From the moment of the annunciation, the mind of the Virgin Mother has been initiated into the radical "newness" of God's self-revelation and has been made aware of the mystery. She is the first of those "little ones" of whom Jesus will say one day: "Father...you have hidden these things from the wise and understanding and revealed them to babes" (Mt 11:25). For "no one knows the Son except the Father" (Mt 11:27). If this is the case, how can Mary "know the Son"? Of course she does not know him as the Father does, and yet she is *the first of those to whom the Father "has chosen to reveal him"* (cf. Mt 11:26–27; 1 Cor 2:11). If though, from the moment of the annunciation, the Son—whom only the Father knows completely, as the one who begets him in the eternal "today" (cf. Ps 2:7) was revealed to Mary, she, his Mother, is in contact with the truth about her Son only in faith and through faith! She is therefore blessed, because "she has believed," and continues to *believe day after day* amidst all the trials and the adversities of Jesus' infancy and then during the years of the hidden life at Nazareth, where he "was obedient to them" (Lk 2:51). He was obedient both to Mary and also to Joseph, since Joseph took the place of his father in people's eyes; for this reason, the Son of Mary was regarded by the people as "the carpenter's son" (Mt 13:55).

The Mother of *that Son,* therefore, mindful of what has been told her at the annunciation and in subsequent events, bears within herself the radical "newness" of faith: *the beginning of the New Covenant.* This is the beginning of the Gospel, the joyful Good News. However, it is not difficult to see in that beginning *a particular heaviness of heart,* linked with a sort of "night of faith"—to use the words of St. John of the cross—a kind of "veil" through which one has to draw near to the Invisible One and to live in intimacy with the mystery.[36] And this is the way that Mary, for many years, *lived in intimacy with the mystery of her Son,* and went forward in her "pilgrimage of faith," while Jesus "increased in wisdom...and in favor with God and man" (Lk 2:52). God's predilection for him was manifested ever more clearly to people's eyes. The first human creature thus permitted to discover Christ was Mary, who lived with Joseph in the same house at Nazareth.

However, when he had been found in the Temple, and his Mother asked him, "Son, why have you treated us so?" *the twelve-year-old Jesus* answered: "Did you not know that I must be in my Father's house?" And the evangelist adds: *"And they* [Joseph and Mary] *did not understand* the saying which he spoke to them" (Lk 2:48–50). Jesus was aware that "no one knows the Son except the Father" (cf. Mt 11:27); thus even his Mother, to whom had been revealed most completely the mystery of his divine sonship, lived in intimacy with this mystery only through faith! Living side by side with her Son under the same roof, and faithfully persevering "in her union with her Son," she *"advanced in her pilgrimage of faith,"* as the Council emphasizes.[37] And so it was during Christ's public life too (cf. Mk 3:21–35) that day by day there was fulfilled in her the blessing uttered by Elizabeth at the visitation: "Blessed is she who believed."

18. This blessing reaches its full meaning *when Mary stands beneath the cross* of her Son (cf. Jn 19:25). The Council says that this happened "not without a divine plan": by "suffering deeply with her only-begotten Son and joining herself with her maternal spirit to his sacrifice, lovingly consenting to the immolation of the victim to whom she had given birth"; in this way Mary "faithfully preserved her union with her Son even to the cross."[38] It is a union through faith—the same faith with which she had received the angel's revelation at the annunciation. At that moment she had also heard the words: "He will be great...and *the Lord God* will give to him the throne of his father David, and he will reign over the house of Jacob forever; and of his kingdom there will be no end" (Lk 1:32–33).

---

36. *Ascent of Mount Carmel,* 1, II, Ch. 3, 4–6.
37. Cf. Dogmatic Constitution on the Church *Lumen Gentium,* 58.
38. Ibid., 58.

And now, standing at the foot of the cross, Mary is the witness, humanly speaking, of the complete *negation of these words*. On that wood of the cross her Son hangs in agony as one condemned. "He was despised and rejected by men; a man of sorrows...he was despised, and we esteemed him not": as one destroyed (cf. Is 53:3–5). How great, how heroic then is the *obedience of faith* shown by Mary in the face of God's "unsearchable judgments"! How completely she "abandons herself to God" without reserve, offering the full assent of the intellect and the will"[39] to him whose "ways are inscrutable" (cf. Rm 11:33)! And how powerful too is the action of grace in her soul, how all-pervading is the influence of the Holy Spirit and of his light and power!

Through this faith Mary is perfectly united with Christ in his self-emptying. For "Christ Jesus, who, though he was in the form of God, did not count equality with God a thing to be grasped, but emptied himself, taking the form of a servant, being born in the likeness of men": precisely on Golgotha "humbled himself and became obedient unto death, even death on a cross" (cf. Phil 2:5–8). At the foot of the cross Mary shares through faith in the shocking mystery of this self-emptying. This is perhaps the deepest *"kenosis" of faith* in human history. Through faith the Mother shares in the death of her Son, in his redeeming death; but in contrast with the faith of the disciples who fled, hers was far more enlightened. On Golgotha, Jesus through the cross definitively confirmed that he was the "sign of contradiction" foretold by Simeon. At the same time, there were also fulfilled on Golgotha the words which Simeon had addressed to Mary: "and a sword will pierce through your own soul also."[40]

19. Yes, truly "blessed is she who believed"! These words, spoken by Elizabeth after the annunciation, here at the foot of the cross seem to reecho with supreme eloquence, and the power contained within them becomes something penetrating. From the cross, that is to say from the very heart of the mystery of redemption, there radiates and spreads out the prospect of that blessing of faith. It goes right back to "the begin-

---

39. Cf. Second Vatican Ecumenical Council, Dogmatic Constitution on Divine Revelation *Dei Verbum,* 5.

40. Concerning Mary's participation or "compassion" in the death of Christ, cf. St. Bernard, *In Dominica Infra Octavam Assumptionis Sermo,* 14: *Sancti Bernardi Opera,* V, 1968, 273.

ning," and as a sharing in the sacrifice of Christ—the new Adam—it becomes in a certain sense *the counterpoise to the disobedience and disbelief* embodied in the sin of our first parents. Thus teach the Fathers of the Church and especially St. Irenaeus, quoted by the Constitution *Lumen Gentium:* "The knot of Eve's disobedience was untied by Mary's obedience; what the virgin Eve bound through her unbelief, the Virgin Mary *loosened by her faith.* "[41] In the light of this comparison with Eve, the Fathers of the Church—as the Council also says—call Mary the "mother of the living" and often speak of "death through Eve, life through Mary."[42]

In the expression "Blessed is she who believed," we can therefore rightly find *a kind of "key"* which unlocks for us the innermost reality of Mary, whom the angel hailed as "full of grace." If as "full of grace" she has been eternally present in *the mystery of Christ,* through faith she became a sharer in that mystery in every extension of her earthly journey. She "advanced in her pilgrimage of faith" and at the same time, in a discreet yet direct and effective way, she made present to humanity the mystery of Christ. And she still continues to do so. Through the mystery of Christ, she too is present within mankind. Thus through the mystery of the Son the mystery of the Mother is also made clear.

3. Behold your mother

20. The Gospel of Luke records the moment when "a woman in the crowd raised her voice" and said to Jesus: *"Blessed is the womb that bore you, and the breasts that you sucked!"* (Lk 11:27). These words were an expression of praise of Mary as Jesus' mother according to the flesh. Probably the Mother of Jesus was not personally known to this woman; in fact, when Jesus began his messianic activity Mary did not accompany him but continued to remain at Nazareth. One could say that the words of that unknown woman in a way brought Mary out of her hiddenness.

Through these words, there flashed out in the midst of the crowd, at least for an instant, the gospel of Jesus' infancy. This is the gospel in which Mary is present as the mother who conceives Jesus in her womb,

---

41. St. Irenaeus, *Adversus Haereses,* III, 22, 4: *SCh.* 211, 438–444; cf. Dogmatic Constitution on the Church *Lumen Gentium,* 56, note 6.

42. Cf. Dogmatic Constitution on the Church *Lumen Gentium,* 56, and the Fathers quoted there in notes 8 and 9.

gives him birth and nurses him: the nursing mother referred to by the woman in the crowd. *Thanks to this motherhood, Jesus,* the Son of the Most High (cf. Lk 1:32), is a true *son of man.* He is "flesh," like every other man: he is "the Word (who) became flesh" (cf. Jn 1:14). He is of the flesh and blood of Mary![43]

But to the blessing uttered by that woman upon her, who was his mother according to the flesh, Jesus replies in a significant way: "Blessed rather are *those who hear the Word of God and keep it"* (Lk 11:28). He wishes to divert attention from motherhood understood only as a fleshly bond, in order to direct it toward those mysterious bonds of the spirit which develop from hearing and keeping God's word.

This same shift into the sphere of spiritual values is seen even more clearly in another response of Jesus reported by all the synoptics. When Jesus is told that "his mother and brothers are standing outside and wish to see him," he replies: *"My mother and my brothers are those who hear the word of God and do it"* (cf. Lk 8:20–21). This he said "looking around on those who sat about him," as we read in Mark (3:34) or, according to Matthew (12:49), "stretching out his hand toward his disciples."

These statements seem to *fit in with the reply which the twelve-year-old Jesus* gave to Mary and Joseph when he was found after three days in the Temple at Jerusalem.

Now, when Jesus left Nazareth and began his public life throughout Palestine, *he was completely and exclusively "concerned with his Father's business"* (cf. Lk 2:49). He announced the kingdom: the "kingdom of God" and "his Father's business," which add a new dimension and meaning to everything human, and therefore to every human bond, insofar as these things relate to the goals and tasks assigned to every human being. Within this new dimension, also a bond such as that of "brotherhood" means something different from "brotherhood according to the flesh" deriving from a common origin from the same set of parents. *"Motherhood,"* too, *in the dimension of the kingdom of God and in the radius of the fatherhood of God himself, takes on another meaning.* In the words reported by Luke, Jesus teaches precisely this new meaning of motherhood.

---

43. "Christ is truth, Christ is flesh: Christ truth in the mind of Mary, Christ flesh in the womb of Mary": St. Augustine, *Sermo 25 (Sermones inediti),* 7: *PL* 46, 938.

Is Jesus thereby distancing himself from his mother according to the flesh? Does he perhaps wish to leave her in the hidden obscurity which she herself has chosen? If this seems to be the case from the tone of those words, one must nevertheless note that the new and different motherhood which Jesus speaks of to his disciples refers precisely to Mary in a very special way. Is not Mary *the first of "those who hear the Word of God and do it"?* And therefore does not the blessing uttered by Jesus in response to the woman in the crowd refer primarily to her? Without any doubt, Mary is worthy of blessing by the very fact that she became the mother of Jesus according to the flesh ("Blessed is the womb that bore you, and the breasts that you sucked"), but also and especially because already at the annunciation she accepted the Word of God, because she believed it, *because she was obedient to God,* and because she "kept" the word and "pondered it in her heart" (cf. Lk 1:38, 45; 2:19, 51) and by means of her whole life accomplished it. Thus we can say that the blessing proclaimed by Jesus is not in opposition, despite appearances, to the blessing uttered by the unknown woman, but rather coincides with that blessing in the person of this Virgin Mother, who called herself only "the handmaid of the Lord" (Lk 1:38). If it is true that "all generations will call her blessed" (cf. Lk 1:48), then it can be said that the unnamed woman was the first to confirm unwittingly that prophetic phrase of Mary's Magnificat and to begin the Magnificat of the ages.

If *through faith* Mary became the bearer of the Son given to her by the Father through the power of the Holy Spirit, while preserving her virginity intact, in that same faith she *discovered and accepted the other dimension of motherhood* revealed by Jesus during his messianic mission. One can say that this dimension of motherhood belonged to Mary from the beginning, that is to say from the moment of the conception and birth of her Son. From that time she was "the one who believed." But as the messianic mission of her Son grew clearer to her eyes and spirit, she herself as a mother became ever more open *to that new dimension of motherhood* which was to constitute her "part" beside her Son. Had she not said from the very beginning: "Behold, I am the handmaid of the Lord; let it be to me according to your word" (Lk 1:38)? Through faith Mary continued to hear and to ponder that word, in which there became ever clearer, in a way "which surpasses knowledge" (Eph 3:19), the self-revelation of the living God. Thus *in a sense* Mary as Mother became *the first "disciple" of her Son,* the first to whom he seemed to say: "Follow me," even before he addressed this call to the apostles or to anyone else (cf. Jn 1:43).

21. From this point of view, particularly eloquent is the passage in the *Gospel of John* which presents Mary at the wedding feast of Cana. She appears there as the Mother of Jesus at the beginning of his public life: "There was a *marriage at Cana in Galilee,* and the mother of Jesus was there; Jesus also was invited to the marriage, with his disciples" (Jn 2:1–2). From the text it appears that Jesus and his disciples were invited together with Mary, as if by reason of her presence at the celebration; the Son seems to have been invited because of his mother. We are familiar with the sequence of events which resulted from that invitation, that "beginning of the signs" wrought by Jesus—the water changed into wine—which prompts the evangelist to say that Jesus "manifested his glory, and his disciples believed in him" (Jn 2:11).

Mary is present at Cana in Galilee as the *Mother of Jesus,* and in a significant way she *contributes* to that "beginning of the signs" which reveal the messianic power of her Son. We read: "When the wine gave out, the mother of Jesus said to him, 'They have no wine.' And Jesus said to her, 'O woman, what have you to do with me? My hour has not yet come'" (Jn 2:3–4). In John's Gospel that "hour" means the time appointed by the Father when the Son accomplishes his task and is to be glorified (cf. Jn 7:30; 8:20; 12:23, 27; 13:1; 17:1; 19:27). Even though Jesus' reply to his mother sounds like a refusal (especially if we consider the blunt statement "My hour has not yet come" rather than the question), Mary nevertheless turns to the servants and says to them: "Do whatever he tells you" (Jn 2:5). Then Jesus orders the servants to fill the stone jars with water, and the water becomes wine, better than the wine which has previously been served to the wedding guests.

What deep understanding existed between Jesus and his mother? How can we probe the mystery of their intimate spiritual union? But the fact speaks for itself. It is certain that that event already quite clearly outlines *the new dimension,* the new meaning *of Mary's motherhood.* Her motherhood has a significance which is not exclusively contained in the words of Jesus and in the various episodes reported by the synoptics (Lk 11:27–28; Lk 8:19–21; Mt 12:46–50; Mk 3:31–35). In these texts Jesus means above all to contrast the motherhood resulting from the fact of birth with what this "motherhood" (and also "brotherhood") is to be in the dimension of the kingdom of God, in the salvific radius of God's fatherhood. In John's text, on the other hand, the description of the Cana event outlines what is actually manifested as a new kind of motherhood according to the spirit and not just according to the flesh, that is to say *Mary's solicitude for human beings,* her coming to them in the wide variety of their wants and needs. At Cana in Galilee there is shown only one concrete aspect of human need, apparently a small one of little importance ("They have no wine"). But it has a symbolic value: this coming to the aid of human needs means, at the same time, bringing those needs within the radius of Christ's messianic mission and salvific power. Thus there is a mediation: Mary places herself between her Son and mankind in the reality of their wants, needs and sufferings. *She puts herself "in the middle,"* that is to say *she acts as a mediatrix not as an outsider, but in her position as mother.* She knows that as such she can point out to her Son the needs of mankind, and in fact, she "has the right" to do so. Her mediation is thus in the nature of intercession: Mary "intercedes" for mankind. And that is not all. As a mother she also *wishes the messianic power of her Son to be manifested,* that salvific power of his which is meant to help man in his misfortunes, to free him from the evil which in various forms and degrees weighs heavily upon his life, precisely as the Prophet Isaiah had foretold about the messiah in the famous passage which Jesus quoted before his fellow townsfolk in Nazareth: "To preach good news to the poor...to proclaim release to the captives and recovering of sight to the blind..." (cf. Lk 4:18).

Another essential element of Mary's maternal task is found in her words to the servants: "Do whatever he tells you." *The Mother* of Christ presents herself as the *spokeswoman of her Son's will,* pointing out those things which must be done so that the salvific power of the messiah may be manifested. At Cana, thanks to the intercession of Mary and the obedience of the servants, Jesus begins "his hour." At Cana Mary appears as *believing in Jesus.* Her faith evokes his first "sign" and helps to kindle the faith of the disciples.

22. We can therefore say that in this passage of John's Gospel we find as it were a first manifestation of the truth concerning Mary's maternal care. This truth has also found expression *in the teaching of the Second Vatican Council.* It is important to note how the Council illustrates Mary's maternal role as it relates to the mediation of Christ. Thus we read: "Mary's maternal function toward mankind in no way obscures or diminishes the unique mediation of Christ, but rather shows its efficacy," because "there is one mediator between God and men, the man

Christ Jesus" (1 Tm 2:5). This maternal role of Mary flows, according to God's good pleasure, "from the superabundance of the merits of Christ; it is founded on his mediation, absolutely depends on it, and draws all its efficacy from it."[44] It is precisely in this sense that the episode at Cana in Galilee offers us *a sort of first announcement of Mary's mediation,* wholly oriented toward Christ and tending to the revelation of his salvific power.

From the *text of John* it is evident that it is a mediation which is maternal. As the Council proclaims, Mary became "a mother to us in the order of grace." This motherhood in the order of grace flows from her divine motherhood. Because she was, by the design of divine Providence, the mother who nourished the divine Redeemer, Mary became "an associate of unique nobility, and the Lord's humble handmaid," who "cooperated by her obedience, faith, hope and burning charity in the Savior's work of restoring supernatural life to souls."[45] And "this *maternity of Mary in the order of grace...*will last without interruption until the eternal fulfillment of all the elect."[46]

23. If John's description of the event at Cana presents Mary's caring motherhood at the beginning of Christ's messianic activity, another passage from the same Gospel confirms this motherhood in the salvific economy of grace at its crowning moment, namely when Christ's sacrifice on the cross, his Paschal Mystery, is accomplished. John's description is concise: *"Standing by the cross of Jesus* were his mother, and his mother's sister, Mary the wife of Clopas, and Mary Magdalene. When Jesus saw his mother, and the disciple whom he loved standing near, he said to his mother: 'Woman, behold your son!' Then he said to the disciple, 'Behold, your mother!' And from that hour the disciple took her to his own home" (Jn 19:25–27).

Undoubtedly, we find here an expression of the Son's particular solicitude for his Mother, whom he is leaving in such great sorrow. And yet the "testament of Christ's cross" says more. Jesus highlights a new relationship between Mother and Son, the whole truth and reality of which he solemnly confirms. One can say that if Mary's motherhood of the human race had already been outlined, now it is clearly stated and

---

44. Dogmatic Constitution on the Church *Lumen Gentium,* 60.
45. Ibid., 61.
46. Ibid., 62.

established. It *emerges* from the definitive accomplishment *of the Redeemer's Paschal Mystery.* The Mother of Christ, who stands at the very center of this mystery—a mystery which embraces each individual and all humanity—is given as mother to every single individual and all mankind. The man at the foot of the cross is John, "the disciple whom he loved."[47] But it is not he alone. Following tradition, the Council does not hesitate to call Mary *"the Mother of Christ and mother of mankind":* since she "belongs to the offspring of Adam she is one with all human beings.... Indeed she is 'clearly the mother of the members of Christ...since she cooperated out of love so that there might be born in the Church the faithful.'"[48]

And so this "new motherhood of Mary," generated by faith, is *the fruit of the "new" love* which came to definitive maturity in her at the foot of the cross, through her sharing in the redemptive love of her Son.

24. Thus we find ourselves at the very center of the fulfillment of the promise contained in the Proto-gospel: the "seed of the woman...will crush the head of the serpent" (cf. Gn 3:15). By his redemptive death Jesus Christ conquers the evil of sin and death at its very roots. It is significant that, as he speaks to his mother from the cross, he calls her "woman" and says to her: "Woman, behold your son!" Moreover, he had addressed her by the same term at Cana too (cf. Jn 2:4). How can one doubt that especially now, on Golgotha, this expression goes to the very heart of the mystery of Mary, and indicates the unique *place* which she occupies *in the whole economy of salvation?* As the Council teaches, in Mary "the exalted Daughter of Zion, and after a long expectation of the promise, the times were at length fulfilled and the new dispensation established. All this occurred when the Son of God took a human nature from her, that he might in the mysteries of his flesh free man from sin."[49]

The words uttered by Jesus from the cross signify that *the motherhood* of her who bore Christ finds a "new" continuation *in the Church*

---

47. There is a well known passage of Origen on the presence of Mary and John on Calvary: "The Gospels are the first fruits of all Scripture and the Gospel of John is the first of the Gospels: no one can grasp its meaning without having leaned his head on Jesus' breast and having received from Jesus, Mary as Mother": *Comm. in Ioan.,* I, 6: *PG* 14, 31; cf. St. Ambrose, *Expos. Evang. sec. Lucam,* X, 129–131: *CSEL* 32/4, 504f.

48. Dogmatic Constitution on the Church *Lumen Gentium,* 54 and 53; the latter text quotes St. Augustine, *De Sancta Virginitate,* VI, 6: *PL* 40, 399.

49. Dogmatic Constitution on the Church *Lumen Gentium,* 55.

and through the Church, symbolized and represented by John. In this way, she who as the one "full of grace" was brought into the mystery of Christ in order to be his Mother and thus *the Holy Mother of God,* through the Church remains in that mystery as *"the woman"* spoken of by the Book of Genesis (3:15) at the beginning and by the *Apocalypse* (12:1) at the end of the history of salvation. In accordance with the eternal plan of Providence, Mary's divine motherhood is to be poured out upon the Church, as indicated by statements of Tradition, according to which Mary's "motherhood" of the Church is the reflection and extension of her motherhood of the Son of God.[50]

According to the Council the very moment of the Church's birth and full manifestation to the world enables us to glimpse this continuity of Mary's motherhood: "Since it pleased God not to manifest solemnly the mystery of the salvation of the human race until he poured forth the Spirit promised by Christ, we see the *apostles* before the day of Pentecost 'continuing with one mind *in prayer* with the women and *Mary the mother of Jesus,* and with his brethren' (Acts 1:14). We see Mary prayerfully imploring the gift of the Spirit, who had already overshadowed her in the annunciation."[51]

And so, in the redemptive economy of grace, brought about through the action of the Holy Spirit, there is a unique correspondence between the moment of the Incarnation of the Word and the moment of the birth of the Church. The person who links these two moments is Mary: *Mary at Nazareth* and *Mary in the upper room at Jerusalem.* In both cases her discreet yet essential presence indicates the path of "birth from the Holy Spirit." Thus she who is present in the mystery of Christ as Mother becomes—by the will of the Son and the power of the Holy Spirit—present in the mystery of the Church. In the Church too she continues to be *a maternal presence,* as is shown by the words spoken from the cross: "Woman, behold your son!" "Behold, your mother."

---

50. Cf. St. Leo the Great, *Tractatus 26, De Natale Domini,* 2: *CCL* 138, 126.
51. Dogmatic Constitution on the Church *Lumen Gentium,* 59.

PART II:THE MOTHER OF GOD
AT THE CENTER OF THE PILGRIM CHURCH

1. The Church, the People of God present in all the nations of the earth

25. "The Church 'like a pilgrim in a foreign land, presses forward amid the persecutions of the world and the consolations of God,'[52] announcing the cross and death of the Lord until he comes (cf. 1 Cor 11:26)."[53] "Israel according to the flesh, which wandered as an exile in the desert, was already called the Church of God (cf. 2 Esd 13:1; Num 20:4; Dt 23:1ff.). Likewise the new Israel...is also called the Church of Christ (cf. Mt 16:18). For he has bought it for himself with his blood (Acts 20:28), has filled it with his Spirit, and provided it with those means which befit it as a visible and social unity. *God has gathered together as one all those who in faith look upon Jesus* as the author of salvation and the source of unity and peace, and has established them as Church, that for each and all she may be the visible sacrament of this saving unity."[54]

The Second Vatican Council speaks of the pilgrim Church, establishing an analogy with the Israel of the Old Covenant journeying through the desert. The journey also has an *external character,* visible in the time and space in which it historically takes place. For the Church "is destined to extend to all regions of the earth and so to enter into the history of mankind," but at the same time "she transcends all limits of time and of space."[55] And yet the essential *character* of her pilgrimage is

---

52. St. Augustine, *De Civitate Dei,* XVIII, 51: *CCL* 48, 650.

53. Second Vatican Ecumenical Council, Dogmatic Constitution on the Church *Lumen Gentium,* 8.

54. Ibid., 9.

55. Ibid., 9.

interior: it is a question of a *pilgrimage through faith,* by "the power of the risen Lord,"[56] a pilgrimage in the Holy Spirit, given to the Church as the invisible Comforter *(parákletos)* (cf. Jn 14:26; 15:26; 16:7): "Moving forward through trial and tribulation, the Church is strengthened by the power of God's grace promised to her by the Lord, so that...moved by the Holy Spirit, she may never cease to renew herself, until through the cross she arrives at the light which knows no setting."[57]

It is precisely *in this ecclesial journey or pilgrimage* through space and time, and even more through the history of souls, that *Mary is present,* as the one who is "blessed because she believed," as the one who advanced on the pilgrimage of faith, sharing unlike any other creature in the mystery of Christ. The Council further says that "Mary figured profoundly in the history of salvation and in a certain way unites and mirrors within herself the central truths of the faith."[58] Among all believers she is *like a "mirror"* in which are reflected in the most profound and limpid way "the mighty works of God" (Acts 2:11).

26. Built by Christ upon the apostles, the Church became fully aware of these mighty works of God *on the day of Pentecost,* when those gathered together in the upper room "were all filled with the Holy Spirit and began to speak in other tongues, as the Spirit gave them utterance" (Acts 2:4). From that moment there also *begins* that journey of faith, *the Church's pilgrimage* through the history of individuals and peoples. We know that at the beginning of this journey Mary is present. We see her in the midst of the apostles in the upper room, "prayerfully imploring the gift of the Spirit."[59]

In a sense her journey of faith is longer. The Holy Spirit had already come down upon her, and she became his faithful spouse *at the annunciation,* welcoming the Word of the true God, offering "the full submission of intellect and will...and freely assenting to the truth revealed by him," indeed abandoning herself totally to God through "the obedience of faith,"[60] whereby she replied to the angel: "Behold, I am the handmaid of

---

56. Ibid., 8.
57. Ibid., 9.
58. Ibid., 65.
59. Ibid., 59.
60. Cf. Second Vatican Ecumenical Council, Dogmatic Constitution on Divine Revelation *Dei Verbum,* 5.

the Lord; let it be to me according to your word." The journey of faith made by Mary, whom we see praying in the upper room, is thus longer than that of the others gathered there: Mary "goes before them," "leads the way" for them.[61] *The moment of Pentecost* in Jerusalem had been prepared for by the *moment of the annunciation* in Nazareth, as well as by the cross. In the upper room Mary's journey meets the Church's journey of faith. In what way?

Among those who devoted themselves to prayer in the upper room, preparing to go "into the whole world" after receiving the Spirit, some *had been called by Jesus* gradually from the beginning of his mission in Israel. Eleven of them *had been made apostles,* and to them Jesus had passed on the mission which he himself had received from the Father. "As the Father has sent me, even so I send you" (Jn 20:21), he had said to the apostles after the resurrection. And forty days later, before returning to the Father, he had added: "when the Holy Spirit has come upon you...*you shall be my witnesses*...to the end of the earth" (cf. Acts 1:8). This mission of the apostles began the moment they left the upper room in Jerusalem. The Church is born and then grows through the testimony that Peter and the apostles bear to the crucified and risen Christ (cf. Acts 2:31–34; 3:15–18; 4:10–12; 5:30–32).

Mary did not directly receive this apostolic mission. She was not among those whom Jesus sent "to the whole world to teach all nations" (cf. Mt 28:19) when he conferred this mission on them. But she was in the upper room, where the apostles were preparing to take up this mission with the coming of the Spirit of Truth; she was present with them. In their midst Mary was "devoted to prayer" as the "mother of Jesus" (cf. Acts 1:13–14), of the crucified and risen Christ. And that first group of those who in faith looked "upon Jesus as the author of salvation,"[62] knew that Jesus was the Son of Mary, and that she was his Mother, and that as such she was from the moment of his conception and birth a unique witness to *the mystery of Jesus,* that mystery which before their eyes had been disclosed and confirmed in the cross and resurrection. Thus, from the very first moment, the Church "looked at" Mary through Jesus, just as she "looked at" Jesus through Mary. For the Church of that

---

61. Cf. Second Vatican Ecumenical Council, Dogmatic Constitution on the Church *Lumen Gentium,* 63.

62. Cf. ibid., 9.

time and of every time Mary is a singular witness to the years of Jesus' infancy and hidden life at Nazareth, when she "kept all these things, pondering them in her heart" (Lk 2:19; cf. Lk 2:51).

But above all, in the Church of that time and of every time Mary was and is the one who is "blessed because she believed"; *she was the first to believe.* From the moment of the annunciation and conception, from the moment of his birth in the stable at Bethlehem, Mary followed Jesus step by step in her maternal pilgrimage of faith. She followed him during the years of his hidden life at Nazareth; she followed him also during the time after he left home, when he began "to do and to teach" (cf. Acts 1:1) in the midst of Israel. Above all she followed him in the tragic experience of Golgotha. Now, while Mary was with the apostles in the upper room in Jerusalem at the dawn of the Church, *her faith, born from the words of the annunciation, found confirmation.* The angel had said to her then: "You will conceive in your womb and bear a son, and you shall call his name Jesus. He will be great...and he will reign over the house of Jacob forever; and of his kingdom there will be no end." The recent events on Calvary had shrouded that promise in darkness, yet not even beneath the cross did Mary's faith fail. She had still remained the one who, like Abraham, "in hope believed against hope" (Rm 4:18). But it was only after the resurrection that hope had shown its true face and *the promise had begun to be transformed into reality.* For Jesus, before returning to the Father, had said to the apostles: "Go therefore and make disciples of all nations...Lo, I am with you always, to the close of the age" (cf. Mt 28:19–20). Thus had spoken the One who by his resurrection had revealed himself as the conqueror of death, as the One who possessed the kingdom of which, as the angel said, "there will be no end."

27. Now, at the first dawn of the Church, at the beginning of the long journey through faith which began at Pentecost in Jerusalem, Mary was with all those who were the seed of the "new Israel." She was present among them as an exceptional witness to the mystery of Christ. And the Church was assiduous in prayer together with her, and at the same time *"contemplated her in the light of the Word made man."* It was always to be so. For when the Church "enters more intimately into the supreme mystery of the Incarnation," she thinks of the Mother of Christ with profound reverence and devotion.[63] Mary belongs indissolubly to the mys-

---

63. Cf. ibid., 65.

tery of Christ, and she belongs also to the mystery of the Church from the beginning, from the day of the Church's birth. At the basis of what the Church has been from the beginning, and of what she must continually become from generation to generation, in the midst of all the nations of the earth, we find the one "who believed that there would be a fulfillment of what was spoken to her from the Lord" (Lk 1:45). It is precisely Mary's faith which marks the beginning of the new and eternal Covenant of God with man in Jesus Christ; this heroic *faith* of hers *"precedes"* the apostolic witness of the Church, and ever remains in the Church's heart, hidden like a special heritage of God's revelation. All those who from generation to generation accept the apostolic witness of the Church share in that mysterious inheritance, and *in a sense share in Mary's faith.*

Elizabeth's words "Blessed is she who believed" continue to accompany the Virgin also at Pentecost; they accompany her from age to age, wherever knowledge of Christ's salvific mystery spreads, through the Church's apostolic witness and service. Thus is fulfilled the prophecy of the Magnificat: *"All generations will call me blessed; for he who is mighty has done great things for me, and holy is his name"* (Lk 1:48–49). For knowledge of the mystery of Christ leads us to bless his Mother, in the form of special veneration for the *Theotókos.* But this veneration always includes a blessing of her faith, for the Virgin of Nazareth became blessed above all through this faith, in accordance with Elizabeth's words. Those who from generation to generation among the different peoples and nations of the earth accept with faith the mystery of Christ, the incarnate Word and Redeemer of the world, not only turn with veneration to Mary and confidently have recourse to her as his Mother, but also *seek in her faith support for their own.* And it is precisely this lively sharing in Mary's faith that determines her special place in the Church's pilgrimage as the new People of God throughout the earth.

28. As the Council says, "Mary figured profoundly in the history of salvation.... Hence when she is being preached and venerated, she summons the faithful to her Son and his sacrifice, and to love for the Father."[64] For this reason, Mary's faith, according to the Church's apostolic

---

64. Ibid., 65.

witness, in some way continues to become the faith of the pilgrim People of God: the faith of individuals and communities, of places and gatherings, and of the various groups existing in the Church. It is a faith that is passed on simultaneously through both the mind and the heart. It is gained or regained continually through prayer. Therefore, *"the Church* in her apostolic work also *rightly looks to her, who brought forth Christ,* conceived of the Holy Spirit and born of the Virgin, so that through the Church Christ *may be born and may increase in the hearts of the faithful also.* "[65]

Today, as on this pilgrimage of faith we draw near to the end of the second Christian millennium, the Church, through the teaching of the Second Vatican Council, calls our attention to her vision of herself, as the "one People of God...among all the nations of the earth." And she reminds us of that truth according to which all the faithful, though "scattered throughout the world, are in communion with each other in the Holy Spirit."[66] We can therefore say that in this union the mystery of Pentecost is continually being accomplished. At the same time, the Lord's apostles and disciples, in all the nations of the earth, "devote themselves to prayer *together with Mary, the mother of Jesus"* (Acts 1:14). As they constitute from generation to generation the "sign of the kingdom" which is not of his world,[67] they are also aware that in the midst of this world they must *gather around that King* to whom the nations have been given in heritage (cf. Ps 2:8), to whom the Father has given "the throne of David his father," so that he "will reign over the house of Jacob for ever, and of his kingdom there will be no end."

During this time of vigil, Mary, through the same faith which made her blessed, especially from the moment of the annunciation, is *present* in the Church's mission, *present* in the Church's work of introducing into the world *the kingdom of her Son.*[68]

This presence of Mary finds many different expressions in our day, just as it did throughout the Church's history. It also has a wide field of action: through the faith and piety of individual believers; through the traditions of Christian families or "domestic churches," of parish and

---

65. Ibid., 65.
66. Cf. ibid., 13.
67. Cf. ibid., 13.
68. Cf. ibid., 13.

missionary communities, religious institutes and dioceses; through the radiance and attraction of the great shrines where not only individuals or local groups, but sometimes whole nations and societies, even whole continents, seek to meet the Mother of the Lord, the one who is blessed because she believed, is the first among believers and therefore became the Mother of Emmanuel. This is the message of the land of Palestine, the spiritual homeland of all Christians because it was the homeland of the Savior of the world and of his Mother. This is the message of the many churches in Rome and throughout the world which have been raised up in the course of the centuries by the faith of Christians. This is the message of centers like Guadalupe, Lourdes, Fatima and the others situated in the various countries. Among them how could I fail to mention the one in my own native land, Jasna Gora? One could perhaps speak of a specific "geography" of faith and Marian devotion, which includes all these special places of pilgrimage where the People of God seek to meet the Mother of God in order to find, within the radius of the maternal presence of her, "who believed," a strengthening of their own faith. For *in Mary's faith,* first at the annunciation and then fully at the foot of the cross, an *interior space* was reopened within humanity which the eternal Father can fill "with every spiritual blessing." It is the space "of the new and eternal Covenant,"[69] and it continues to exist in the Church, which in Christ is "a kind of sacrament or sign of intimate union with God, and of the unity of all mankind."[70]

In the faith which Mary professed at the annunciation as the "handmaid of the Lord" and in which she constantly "precedes" the pilgrim People of God throughout the earth, the *Church "strives* energetically and constantly *to bring all humanity...back to Christ its Head* in the unity of his Spirit."[71]

2. The Church's journey and the unity of all Christians

29. "In all of Christ's disciples the Spirit arouses the desire to be peacefully *united,* in the manner determined by Christ, as one flock un-

---

69. Cf. *Roman Missal,* formula of the consecration of the chalice in the Eucharistic Prayers.

70. Second Vatican Ecumenical Council, Dogmatic Constitution on the Church *Lumen Gentium,* 1.

71. Ibid., 13.

der one shepherd."[72] The journey of the Church, especially in our own time, is marked by the sign of ecumenism: Christians are seeking ways to restore that unity which Christ implored from the Father for his disciples on the day before his passion: *"That they may all be one; even as you, Father, are in me, and I in you that they also may be in us, so that the world may believe* that you have sent me" (Jn 17:21). The unity of Christ's disciples, therefore, is a great sign given in order to kindle faith in the world while their division constitutes a scandal.[73]

The ecumenical movement, on the basis of a clearer and more widespread awareness of the urgent need to achieve the unity of all Christians, has found on the part of the Catholic Church its culminating expression in the work of the Second Vatican Council: Christians must deepen in themselves and each of their communities that "obedience of faith" of which Mary is the first and brightest example. And since she "shines forth on earth...as a sign of sure hope and solace for the pilgrim People of God," "it gives great joy and comfort to this most holy Synod that *among the divided brethren,* too, there are those who give due honor to the Mother of our Lord and Savior. This is especially so among the Easterners."[74]

30. Christians know that their unity will be truly rediscovered only if it is based on the unity of their faith. They must resolve considerable discrepancies of doctrine concerning the mystery and ministry of the Church, and sometimes also concerning the role of Mary in the work of salvation.[75] The dialogues begun by the Catholic Church with the Churches and ecclesial communities of the West[76] are steadily converging upon these *two inseparable aspects* of the same mystery of salvation. If the mystery of the Word made flesh enables us to glimpse the mystery of the divine motherhood and if, in turn, contemplation of the Mother of God brings us to a more profound understanding of the mys-

---

72. Ibid., 15.

73. Cf. Second Vatican Ecumenical Council, Decree on Ecumenism *Unitatis Redintegratio,* 1.

74. Dogmatic Constitution on the Church *Lumen Gentium,* 68, 69. On Mary Most Holy, promoter of Christian unity, and on the cult of Mary in the East, cf. Leo XIII, Encyclical Epistle *Adiutricem Populi* (September 5, 1895): *Acta Leonis,* XV, 300–312.

75. Cf. Second Vatican Ecumenical Council, Decree on Ecumenism *Unitatis Redintegratio,* 20.

76. Cf. ibid., 19.

tery of the Incarnation, then the same must be said for the mystery of the Church and Mary's role in the work of salvation. By a more profound study of both Mary and the Church, clarifying each by the light of the other, Christians who are eager to do what Jesus tells them—as their Mother recommends (cf. Jn 2:5)—will be able to go forward together on this "pilgrimage of faith." Mary, who is still the model of this pilgrimage, is to lead them to the unity which is willed by their one Lord and so much desired by those who are attentively listening to what "the Spirit is saying to the Churches" today (Rv 2:7, 11, 17).

Meanwhile, it is a hopeful sign that these Churches and ecclesial communities are finding agreement with the Catholic Church on fundamental points of Christian belief, including matters relating to the Virgin Mary. For they recognize her as the Mother of the Lord and hold that this forms part of our faith in Christ, true God and true man. They look to her who at the foot of the cross accepts as her son the beloved disciple, the one who in his turn accepts her as his mother.

Therefore, why should we not all together look to her as *our common Mother,* who prays for the unity of God's family and who "precedes" us all at the head of the long line of witnesses of faith in the one Lord, the Son of God, who was conceived in her virginal womb by the power of the Holy Spirit?

31. On the other hand, I wish to emphasize how profoundly the Catholic Church, the Orthodox Church and the ancient Churches of the East feel united by love and praise of the *Theotókos.* Not only "basic dogmas of the Christian faith concerning the Trinity and God's Word made flesh of the Virgin Mary were defined in ecumenical councils held in the East,"[77] but also in their liturgical worship "the Orientals pay high tribute, in very beautiful hymns, to Mary ever Virgin...God's Most Holy Mother."[78]

The brethren of these Churches have experienced a complex history, but it is one that has always been marked by an intense desire for Christian commitment and apostolic activity, despite frequent persecution, even to the point of bloodshed. It is a history of fidelity to the Lord, an authentic "pilgrimage of faith " in space and time, during which Eastern Christians have always looked with boundless trust to the Mother of the

---

77. Ibid., 14.
78. Ibid., 15.

Lord, celebrated her with praise and invoked her with unceasing prayer. In the difficult moments of their troubled Christian existence, "they have taken refuge under her protection,"[79] conscious of having in her a powerful aid. The Churches which profess the doctrine of Ephesus proclaim the Virgin as "true Mother of God," since "our Lord Jesus Christ, born of the Father before time began according to his divinity, in the last days, for our sake and for our salvation, was himself begotten of Mary, the Virgin Mother of God according to his humanity."[80] The Greek Fathers and the Byzantine tradition, contemplating the Virgin in the light of the Word made flesh, have sought to penetrate the depth of that bond which unites Mary, as the Mother of God, to Christ and the Church: the Virgin is a permanent presence in the whole reality of the salvific mystery.

The Coptic and Ethiopian traditions were introduced to this contemplation of the mystery of Mary by St. Cyril of Alexandria, and in their turn they have celebrated it with a profuse poetic blossoming.[81] The poetic genius of St. Ephrem the Syrian, called "the lyre of the Holy Spirit," tirelessly sang of Mary, leaving a still living mark on the whole tradition of the Syriac Church.[82]

In his panegyric of the *Theotókos,* St. Gregory of Narek, one of the outstanding glories of Armenia, with powerful poetic inspiration ponders the different aspects of the mystery of the Incarnation, and each of them is for him an occasion to sing and extol the extraordinary dignity and magnificent beauty of the Virgin Mary, Mother of the Word made flesh.[83]

It does not surprise us therefore that Mary occupies a privileged place in the worship of the ancient Oriental Churches with an incomparable abundance of feasts and hymns.

---

79. Second Vatican Ecumenical Council, Dogmatic Constitution on the Church *Lumen Gentium,* 66.

80. Ecumenical Council of Chalcedon, *Definitio fidei: Conciliorum Oecumenicorum Decreta,* Bologna 1973, 86 (*DS* 301).

81. Cf. *the Weddase Maryam* (Praises of Mary), which follows the Ethiopian Psalter and contains hymns and prayers to Mary for each day of the week. Cf. also the *Matshafa Kidana Mehrat (Book of the Pact of Mercy);* the importance given to Mary in the Ethiopian hymnology and liturgy deserves to be emphasized.

82. Cf. St. Ephrem, *Hymn. De Nativitate: Scriptores Syri,* 82, *CSCO,* 186.

83. Cf. St. Gregory of Narek, *Le livre de prieres: SCh.* 78, 160–163, 428–432.

32. In the Byzantine liturgy, in all the hours of the divine office, praise of the Mother is linked with praise of her Son and with the praise which, through the Son, is offered up to the Father in the Holy Spirit. In the Anaphora or Eucharistic Prayer of St. John Chrysostom, immediately after the epiclesis the assembled community sings in honor of the Mother of God: "It is truly just to proclaim you blessed, O Mother of God, who are most blessed, all pure and Mother of our God. We magnify you who are more honorable than the cherubim and incomparably more glorious than the seraphim, you who, without losing your virginity, gave birth to the Word of God, you who are truly the Mother of God."

These praises, which in every celebration of the Eucharistic liturgy are offered to Mary, have molded the faith, piety and prayer of the faithful. In the course of the centuries they have permeated their whole spiritual outlook, fostering in them a profound devotion to the "All Holy Mother of God."

33. This year there occurs the twelfth centenary of the Second Ecumenical Council of Nicaea (787). Putting an end to the well known controversy about the cult of sacred images, this council defined that, according to the teaching of the holy Fathers and the universal tradition of the Church, there could be exposed for the veneration of the faithful, together with the cross, also images of the Mother of God, of the angels and of the saints in churches and houses and at the roadside.[84] This custom has been maintained in the whole of the East and also in the West. Images of the Virgin have a place of honor in churches and houses. In them Mary is represented in a number of ways: as the throne of God carrying the Lord and giving him to humanity *(Theotókos);* as the way that leads to Christ and manifests him *(Hodegetria);* as a praying figure in an attitude of intercession and as a sign of the divine presence on the journey of the faithful until the day of the Lord *(Deësis);* as the protectress who stretches out her mantle over the peoples *(Pokrov),* or as the merciful Virgin of tenderness *(Eleousa).* She is usually represented with her Son, the child Jesus, in her arms: it is the relationship with the Son which glorifies the Mother.

---

84. Second Ecumenical Council of Nicaea: *Conciliorum Oecumenicorum Decreta,* Bologna 1973, 135–138 (*DS* 600–609).

Sometimes she embraces him with tenderness *(Glykophilousa);* at other times she is a hieratic figure, apparently rapt in contemplation of him, who is the Lord of history (cf. Rv 5:9–14).[85]

It is also appropriate to mention the icon of Our Lady of Vladimir, which continually accompanied the pilgrimage of faith of the peoples of ancient Rus'. The first millennium of the conversion of those noble lands to Christianity is approaching: lands of humble folk, of thinkers and of saints. The icons are still venerated in the Ukraine, in Byelorussia and in Russia under various titles. They are images which witness to the faith and spirit of prayer of that people, who sense the presence and protection of the Mother of God. In these icons the Virgin shines as the image of divine beauty, the abode of Eternal Wisdom, the figure of the one who prays, the prototype of contemplation, the image of glory: she who even in her earthly life possessed the spiritual knowledge inaccessible to human reasoning and who attained through faith the most sublime knowledge. I also recall the icon of the Virgin of the Cenacle, praying with the apostles as they awaited the Holy Spirit: could she not become the sign of hope for all those who, in fraternal dialogue, wish to deepen their obedience of faith?

34. Such a wealth of praise, built up by the different forms of the Church's great tradition, could help us to hasten the day when the Church can begin once more to breathe fully with her "two lungs," the East and the West. As I have often said, this is more than ever necessary today. It would be an effective aid in furthering the progress of the dialogue already taking place between the Catholic Church and the Churches and ecclesial communities of the West.[86] It would also be the way for the pilgrim Church to sing and to live more perfectly her "Magnificat."

3. The "Magnificat" of the pilgrim Church

35. At the present stage of her journey, therefore, the Church seeks to rediscover the unity of all who profess their faith in Christ, in order to show obedience to her Lord, who prayed for this unity before his passion.

---

85. Cf. Second Vatican Ecumenical Council, Dogmatic Constitution on the Church *Lumen Gentium,* 59.

86. Cf. Second Vatican Ecumenical Council, Decree on Ecumenism *Unitatis Redintegratio,* 19.

"Like a pilgrim in a foreign land, the Church presses forward amid the persecutions of the world and the consolations of God, announcing the cross and death of the Lord until he comes."[87] "Moving forward through trial and tribulation, *the Church is strengthened by the power of God's grace promised to her by the Lord,* so that in the weakness of the flesh she may not waver from perfect fidelity, but remain a bride worthy of her Lord; that moved by the Holy Spirit she may never cease to renew herself, until through the cross she arrives at the light which knows no setting."[88]

The Virgin Mother is constantly present on this journey of faith of the People of God toward the light. This is shown in a special way by *the canticle of the "Magnificat," which, having welled up from the depths of Mary's faith* at the visitation, ceaselessly reechoes in the heart of the Church down the centuries. This is proved by its daily recitation in the liturgy of Vespers and at many other moments of both personal and communal devotion.

> My soul magnifies the Lord,
> and my spirit rejoices in God my Savior,
> for he has looked on his servant in her lowliness.
> For behold, henceforth all generations will call me blessed;
> for he who is mighty has done great things for me,
> and holy is his name:
> And his mercy is from age to age
> on those who fear him.
> He has shown strength with his arm.
> he has scattered the proudhearted,
> he has cast down the mighty from their thrones,
> and lifted up the lowly;
> he has filled the hungry with good things,
> sent the rich away empty.
> He has helped his servant Israel,
> remembering his mercy,
> as he spoke to our fathers,
> to Abraham and to his posterity forever (Lk 1:46–55).

36. When Elizabeth greeted her young kinswoman coming from Nazareth, *Mary replied with the Magnificat.* In her greeting, Elizabeth

---

87. Second Vatican Ecumenical Council, Dogmatic Constitution on the Church *Lumen Gentium,* 8.

88. Ibid., 9.

first called Mary "blessed" because of "the fruit of her womb," and then she called her "blessed" because of her faith (cf. Lk 1:42, 45). These two blessings referred directly to the annunciation. Now, at the visitation, when Elizabeth's greeting bears witness to that culminating moment, Mary's faith acquires a new consciousness and a new expression. That which remained hidden in the depths of the "obedience of faith" at the annunciation can now be said to spring forth like a clear and lifegiving flame of the spirit. The words used by Mary on the threshold of Elizabeth's house are *an inspired profession of her faith,* in which *her response to the revealed word* is expressed with the religious and poetical exultation of her whole being toward God. In these sublime words, which are simultaneously very simple and wholly inspired by the sacred texts of the people of Israel,[89] Mary's personal experience, the ecstasy of her heart, shines forth. In them shines a ray of the mystery of God, the glory of his ineffable holiness, the eternal *love which, as an irrevocable gift, enters into human history.*

Mary is the first to share in this new revelation of God and, within the same, in this new "self-giving" of God. Therefore she proclaims: "For he who is mighty has done great things for me, and holy is his name." Her words reflect a joy of spirit which is difficult to express: "My spirit rejoices in God my Savior." Indeed, "the deepest truth about God and the salvation of man is made clear to us in Christ, who is at the same time the mediator and the fullness of all revelation."[90] In her exultation Mary confesses that she finds herself *in the very heart of this fullness* of Christ. She is conscious that the promise made to the fathers, first of all "to Abraham and to his posterity forever," is being fulfilled in herself. She is thus aware that concentrated within herself as the mother of Christ is *the whole salvific economy,* in which "from age to age" is manifested he who as the God of the Covenant, "remembers his mercy."

37. The Church, which from the beginning has modeled her earthly journey on that of the Mother of God, constantly repeats after her the words of the Magnificat. From the depths of the Virgin's faith at the annunciation and the visitation, the Church derives the truth about the God

---

89. As is well known, the words of the *Magnificat* contain or echo numerous passages of the Old Testament.

90. Second Vatican Ecumenical Council, Dogmatic Constitution on Divine Revelation *Dei Verbum,* 2.

of the Covenant: the God who is Almighty and does "great things" for man: "holy is his name." In the Magnificat the Church sees uprooted that sin which is found at the outset of the earthly history of man and woman, the sin of disbelief and of "little faith" in God. In contrast with the "suspicion" which the "father of lies" sowed in the heart of Eve the first woman, Mary, whom tradition is wont to call the "new Eve"[91] and the true "Mother of the living,"[92] boldly proclaims the *undimmed* truth about God: the holy and almighty God, who from the beginning is *the source of all gifts,* he who "has done great things" in her, as well as in the whole universe. In the act of creation God gives existence to all that is. In creating man, God gives him the dignity of the image and likeness of himself in a special way as compared with all earthly creatures. Moreover, in his desire to give, *God gives himself in the Son,* notwithstanding man's sin: "He so loved the world that he gave his only Son" (Jn 3:16). Mary is the first witness of this marvelous truth, which will be fully accomplished through "the works and words" (cf. Acts 1:1) of her Son and definitively through his cross and resurrection.

The Church, which even "amid trials and tribulations" does not cease repeating with Mary the words of the Magnificat, is sustained by the power of God's truth, proclaimed on that occasion with such extraordinary simplicity. At the same time, *by means of this truth about God,* the Church *desires to shed light upon* the difficult and sometimes tangled paths of man's earthly existence. The Church's journey, therefore, near the end of the second Christian millennium, involves a renewed commitment to her mission. Following him who said of himself: "[God] has anointed me *to preach good news to the poor"* (cf. Lk 4:18), the Church has sought from generation to generation and still seeks today to accomplish that same mission.

The Church's *love of preference for the poor* is wonderfully inscribed in Mary's Magnificat. The God of the Covenant, celebrated in the exultation of her spirit by the Virgin of Nazareth, is also he who "has cast down the mighty from their thrones, and lifted up the lowly...filled the hungry with good things, sent the rich away empty...scattered the

---

91. Cf., for example, St. Justin, *Dialogus cum Tryphone Iudaeo,* 100: Otto II, 358; St. Irenaeus, *Adversus Haereses* III, 22, 4: *SCh.* 211, 439–445; Tertullian, *De Carne Christi,* 17, 4–6: *CCL* 2, 904f.

92. Cf. St. Epiphanius, *Panarion,* III, 2; *Haer.* 78, 18: *PG* 42, 727–730.

proud hearted...and his mercy is from age to age on those who fear him." Mary is deeply imbued with the spirit of the "poor of Yahweh," who in the prayer of the psalms awaited from God their salvation, placing all their trust in him (cf. Pss 25; 31; 35; 55). Mary truly proclaims the coming of the "messiah of the poor" (cf. Is 11:4; 61:1). Drawing from Mary's heart, from the depth of her faith expressed in the words of the Magnificat, the Church renews ever more effectively in herself the awareness that *the truth about God who saves,* the truth about God who is the source of every gift, *cannot be separated from the manifestation of his love of preference for the poor and humble,* that love which, celebrated in the Magnificat, is later expressed in the words and works of Jesus.

The Church is thus aware—and at the present time this awareness is particularly vivid—not only that these two elements of the message contained in the Magnificat cannot be separated, but also that there is a duty to safeguard carefully the importance of "the poor" and of "the option in favor of the poor" in the word of the living God. These are matters and questions intimately connected with the *Christian meaning of freedom and liberation.* "Mary is totally dependent upon God and completely directed toward him, and at the side of her Son, she is *the most perfect image of freedom and of the liberation* of humanity and of the universe. It is to her as Mother and Model that the Church must look in order to understand in its completeness the meaning of her own mission."[93]

---

93. Congregation for the Doctrine of the Faith, *Instruction on Christian Freedom and Liberation* (March 22, 1986), 97.

PART III: MATERNAL MEDIATION

1. Mary, the Handmaid of the Lord

38. The Church knows and teaches with St. Paul that *there is only one mediator:* "For there is one God, and there is one mediator between God and men, the man Christ Jesus, who gave himself as a ransom for all" (1 Tm 2:5–6). "The maternal role of Mary toward people in no way obscures or diminishes the unique mediation of Christ, but rather shows its power":[94] it is mediation in Christ.

The Church knows and teaches that "all *the saving influences of the Blessed Virgin* on mankind originate...from the divine pleasure. They flow forth *from the superabundance of the merits of Christ,* rest on his mediation, depend entirely on it, and draw all their power from it. In no way do they impede the immediate union of the faithful with Christ. Rather, they foster this union."[95] This saving influence is sustained by the Holy Spirit, who, just as he overshadowed the Virgin Mary when he began in her the divine motherhood, in a similar way constantly sustains her solicitude for the brothers and sisters of her Son.

In effect, Mary's mediation *is intimately linked with her motherhood.* It possesses a specifically maternal character, which distinguishes it from the mediation of the other creatures who in various and always subordinate ways share in the one mediation of Christ, although her own mediation is also a shared mediation.[96] In fact, while it is true that "no

---

94. Second Vatican Ecumenical Council, Dogmatic Constitution on the Church *Lumen Gentium,* 60.

95. Ibid., 60.

96. Cf. the formula of mediatrix *"ad Mediatorem"* of St. Bernard, *In Dominica infra octavam Assumptionis Sermo,* 2: *Sancti Bernardi Opera,* V, 1968, 263. Mary as a pure mirror sends back to her Son all the glory and honor which she receives: St. Bernard, *In Nativitate Beatae Mariae Sermo, De Aquaeductu,* 12: *loc. cit.,* 283.

creature could ever be classed with the incarnate Word and Redeemer," at the same time "the unique mediation of the Redeemer does not exclude but rather gives rise among creatures to *a manifold cooperation* which is but a sharing in this unique source." And thus "the one goodness of God is in reality communicated diversely to his creatures."[97]

The teaching of the Second Vatican Council presents the truth of Mary's mediation as *"a sharing in the one unique source that is the mediation of Christ himself."* Thus we read: "The Church does not hesitate to profess this subordinate role of Mary. She experiences it continuously and commends it to the hearts of the faithful, so that, encouraged by this maternal help, they may more closely adhere to the Mediator and Redeemer."[98] This role is at the same time *special and extraordinary.* It flows from her divine motherhood and can be understood and lived in faith only on the basis of the full truth of this motherhood. Since by virtue of divine election Mary is the earthly Mother of the Father's consubstantial Son and his "generous companion" in the work of redemption, "she is a mother to us in the order of grace."[99] This role constitutes a real dimension of her presence in the saving mystery of Christ and the Church.

39. From this point of view we must consider once more the fundamental event in the economy of salvation, namely the Incarnation of the Word at the moment of the annunciation. It is significant that Mary, recognizing in the words of the divine messenger the will of the Most High and submitting to his power, says: *"Behold, I am the handmaid of the Lord;* let it be to me according to your word" (Lk 1:38). The first moment of submission to the one mediation "between God and men"—the mediation of Jesus Christ—is the Virgin of Nazareth's acceptance of motherhood. Mary consents to God's choice, in order to become through the power of the Holy Spirit the Mother of the Son of God. It can be said that a *consent to motherhood* is above all *a result of her total self-giving to God in virginity.* Mary accepted her election as Mother of the Son of God, guided by spousal love, the love which totally "consecrates" a human being to God. By virtue of this love, Mary wished to be always and in all things "given to God," living in virginity. The words

97. Second Vatican Ecumenical Council, Dogmatic Constitution on the Church *Lumen Gentium*, 62.

98. Ibid., 62.

99. Ibid., 61.

"Behold, I am the handmaid of the Lord" express the fact that from the outset she accepted and understood her own motherhood as a total *gift of self,* a gift of her person to the service of the saving plans of the Most High. And to the very end she lived her entire maternal sharing in the life of Jesus Christ, her Son, in a way that matched her vocation to virginity.

Mary's motherhood, completely pervaded by her spousal attitude as the "handmaid of the Lord," constitutes the first and fundamental dimension of that mediation which the Church confesses and proclaims in her regard[100] and continually "commends to the hearts of the faithful," since the Church has great trust in her. For it must be recognized that before anyone else it was God himself, the Eternal Father, who *entrusted himself to the Virgin of Nazareth,* giving her his own Son in the mystery of the Incarnation. Her election to the supreme office and dignity of Mother of the Son of God refers, on the ontological level, to the very reality of the union of the two natures in the person of the Word *(hypostatic union).* This basic fact of being the Mother of the Son of God is from the very beginning a complete openness to the person of Christ, to his whole work, to his whole mission. The words "Behold, I am the handmaid of the Lord" testify to Mary's openness of spirit: she perfectly unites in herself the love proper to virginity and the love characteristic of motherhood, which are joined and, as it were, fused together.

For this reason Mary became not only the "nursing mother" of the Son of Man but also the "associate of unique nobility"[101] of the Messiah and Redeemer. As I have already said, she advanced in her *pilgrimage* of faith, and in this pilgrimage to the foot of the cross there was simultaneously accomplished her maternal *cooperation* with the Savior's whole mission through her actions and sufferings. Along the path of this collaboration with the work of her Son, the Redeemer, Mary's motherhood itself underwent a singular transformation, becoming ever more imbued with "burning charity" toward all those to whom Christ's mission was directed. Through this "burning charity," which sought to achieve, in union with Christ, the restoration of "supernatural life to souls,"[102] Mary

---

100. Ibid., 62.
101. Ibid., 61.
102. Ibid., 61.

entered, in a way all her own, into the one mediation "between God and men" *which is the mediation of the man Christ Jesus.* If she was the first to experience within herself the supernatural consequences of this one mediation—in the annunciation she had been greeted as "full of grace"—then we must say that through this fullness of grace and supernatural life she was especially predisposed to cooperation with Christ, the one Mediator of human salvation. *And such cooperation* is *precisely this mediation subordinated* to the mediation of Christ.

In Mary's case we have a special and exceptional mediation, based upon her "fullness of grace," which was expressed in the complete willingness of the "handmaid of the Lord." In response to this interior willingness of his Mother, *Jesus Christ prepared her* ever more completely to become for all people their "mother in the order of grace." This is indicated, at least indirectly, by certain details noted by the synoptics (cf. Lk 11:28; 8:20–21; Mk 3:32–35; Mt 12:47–50) and still more so by the Gospel of John (cf. 2:1–12; 19:25–27), which I have already mentioned. Particularly eloquent in this regard are the words spoken by Jesus on the cross to Mary and John.

40. After the events of the resurrection and ascension Mary entered the upper room together with the apostles to await Pentecost, and was present there as the Mother of the glorified Lord. She was not only the one who "advanced in her pilgrimage of faith" and loyally persevered in her union with her Son "unto the cross," *but she was also the "handmaid of the Lord," left by her Son as Mother in the midst of the infant Church:* "Behold your mother." Thus there began to develop a special bond between this Mother and the Church. For the infant Church was the fruit of the cross and resurrection of her Son. Mary, who from the beginning had given herself without reserve to the person and work of her Son, could not but pour out upon the Church, from the very beginning, her maternal self-giving. After her Son's departure, her motherhood remains in the Church as maternal mediation: interceding for all her children, the Mother cooperates in the saving work of her Son, the Redeemer of the world. In fact the Council teaches that the "motherhood of Mary in the order of grace...*will last without interruption* until the eternal fulfillment of all the elect."[103] With the redeeming death of her

---

103. Ibid., 62.

Son, the maternal mediation of the handmaid of the Lord took on a universal dimension, for the work of redemption embraces the whole of humanity. Thus there is manifested in a singular way the efficacy of the one and universal mediation of Christ "between God and men." Mary's cooperation shares, in its subordinate character, *in the universality of the mediation of the Redeemer,* the one Mediator. This is clearly indicated by the Council in the words quoted above.

"For," the text goes on, "taken up to heaven, she did not lay aside this saving role, but by her manifold acts of intercession continues to win for us gifts of eternal salvation."[104] With this character of "intercession," first manifested at Cana in Galilee, Mary's mediation continues in the history of the Church and the world. We read that Mary "by her maternal charity, cares for the brethren of her Son who still journey on earth surrounded by dangers and difficulties, until they are led to their happy homeland."[105] In this way Mary's motherhood continues unceasingly in the Church as the mediation which intercedes, and the Church expresses her faith in this truth by invoking Mary "under the titles of Advocate, Auxiliatrix, Adjutrix and Mediatrix."[106]

41. Through her mediation, subordinate to that of the Redeemer, Mary contributes *in a special way to the union of the pilgrim Church* on earth with the eschatological and heavenly *reality* of the communion of saints, since she has already been "assumed into heaven."[107] The truth of the Assumption, defined by Pius XII, is reaffirmed by the Second Vatican Council, which thus expresses the Church's faith: "Preserved free from all guilt of original sin, the immaculate Virgin *was taken up body and soul into heavenly glory* upon the completion of her earthly sojourn. She was *exalted* by the Lord *as Queen of the Universe,* in order that she might be the more thoroughly conformed to her Son, the Lord

---

104. Ibid., 62.

105. Ibid., 62; in her prayer too the Church recognizes and celebrates Mary's "maternal role": it is a role "of intercession and forgiveness, petition and grace, reconciliation and peace" (cf. Preface of the Mass of the Blessed Virgin Mary, Mother and Mediatrix of Grace, in *Collectio Missarum de Beata Maria Virgine, editio typica* 1987, I, 120).

106. Ibid., 62.

107. Ibid., 62; cf. St. John Damascene, *Hom. in Dormitionem,* I, 11; II, 2, 14; III, 2: *SCh.* 80, 111f.; 127–131; 157–161; 181–185; St. Bernard, *In Assumptione Beatae Mariae Sermo,* 1–2: *Sancti Bernardi Opera,* V, 1968, 228–238.

of lords (cf. Rv 19:16) and the conqueror of sin and death."[108] In this teaching Pius XII was in continuity with Tradition, which has found many different expressions in the history of the Church, both in the East and in the West.

By the mystery of the Assumption into heaven there were definitively accomplished in Mary all the effects of the one mediation of *Christ the Redeemer of the world* and *risen Lord:* "In Christ shall all be made alive, but each in his own order: Christ the first fruits, then at his coming those who belong to Christ" (1 Cor 15:22–23). In the mystery of the Assumption is expressed the faith of the Church, according to which Mary is "united by a close and indissoluble bond" to Christ, for, if as Virgin and Mother she was singularly united with him *in his first coming,* so through her continued collaboration with him she will also be united with him in expectation of the second; "redeemed in an especially sublime manner by reason of the merits of her Son,"[109] she also has that specifically maternal role of mediatrix of mercy *at his final coming,* when all those who belong to Christ "shall be made alive," when "the last enemy to be destroyed is death" (1 Cor 15:26)."[110]

Connected with this exaltation of the noble "Daughter of Zion"[111] through her Assumption into heaven is the mystery of her eternal glory. For the Mother of Christ is glorified as "Queen of the Universe."[112] She who at the annunciation called herself the "handmaid of the Lord" remained throughout her earthly life faithful to what this name expresses. In this she confirmed that she was a true "disciple" of Christ, who strongly emphasized that his mission was one of service: "the Son of Man came not to be served but to serve, and to give his life as a ransom for many" (Mt 20:28). In this way Mary became the first of those who,

---

108. Dogmatic Constitution on the Church *Lumen Gentium,* 59; cf. Pope Pius XII, Apostolic Constitution *Munificentissimus Deus* (November 1, 1950): *AAS* 42 (1950) 769–771; St. Bernard presents Mary immersed in the splendor of the Son's glory: In *Dominica infra oct. Assumptionis Sermo,* 3; *Sancti Bernardi Opera,* V, 1968, 263f.

109. Dogmatic Constitution on the Church *Lumen Gentium,* 53.

110. On this particular aspect of Mary's mediation as *implorer of clemency* from the "Son as Judge," cf. St. Bernard, *In Dominica infra octavam Assumptionis Sermo,* 1–2: *Sancti Bernardi Opera,* V, 1968, 262f; Pope Leo XIII, Encyclical Epistle *Octobri Mense* (September 22, 1891): *Acta Leonis,* XI, 299–315.

111. Second Vatican Ecumenical Council, Dogmatic Constitution on the Church *Lumen Gentium,* 55.

112. Ibid., 59.

"serving Christ also in others, with humility and patience lead their brothers and sisters to that King whom to serve is to reign,"[113] and she fully obtained that "state of royal freedom" proper to Christ's disciples: to serve means to reign!

"Christ obeyed even at the cost of death, and was therefore raised up by the Father (cf. Phil. 2:8–9). Thus he entered into the glory of his kingdom. To him all things are made subject until he subjects himself and all created things to the Father, that God may be all in all (cf. 1 Cor 15:27–28)."[114] Mary, the handmaid of the Lord, has a share in this kingdom of the Son.[115] The *glory of serving* does not cease to be her royal exaltation: assumed into heaven, she does not cease her saving service, which expresses her maternal mediation "until the eternal fulfillment of all the elect."[116] Thus, she who here on earth "loyally persevered in her union with her Son unto the cross," continues to remain united with him, while now *"all things are subjected to him, until he subjects to the Father himself and all things."* Thus in her Assumption into heaven, Mary is as it were clothed by the whole reality of the communion of saints, and her very union with the Son in glory is wholly oriented toward the definitive fullness of the kingdom, *when "God will be all in all."*

In this phase too Mary's maternal mediation does not cease to be subordinate to him who is the one Mediator, *until the final realization of "the fullness of time,"* that is to say until "all things are united in Christ" (cf. Eph 1:10).

2. Mary in the life of the Church and of every Christian

42. Linking itself with Tradition, the Second Vatican Council brought new light to bear on the role of the Mother of Christ in the life of the Church. "Through the gift...of divine motherhood, Mary is united with her Son, the Redeemer, and with his singular graces and offices. By these, the Blessed Virgin is also intimately united with the Church: *the Mother of God is a figure of the Church* in the matter of faith, charity

---

113. Ibid., 36.

114. Ibid., 36.

115. With regard to Mary as Queen, cf. St. John Damascene, *Hom. in Nativitatem,* 6; 12; *Hom. in Dormitionem,* 1, 2, 12, 14; II, 11; III, 4: *SCh.* 80, 59f.; 77f.; 83f.; 113f.; 117; 151f.; 189–193.

116. Second Vatican Ecumenical Council, Dogmatic Constitution on the Church *Lumen Gentium,* 62.

and perfect union with Christ."[117] We have already noted how, from the beginning, Mary remains with the apostles in expectation of Pentecost and how, as "the blessed one who believed," she is present in the midst of the pilgrim Church from generation to generation through faith and as the model of the hope which does not disappoint (cf. Rm 5:5).

Mary believed in the fulfillment of what had been said to her by the Lord. As Virgin, she believed that she would conceive and bear a son: the "Holy One," who bears the name of "Son of God," the name "Jesus" (God who saves). As handmaid of the Lord, she remained in perfect fidelity to the person and mission of this Son. As Mother, *"believing and obeying...*she brought forth on earth the *Father's Son*. This she did, knowing not man but overshadowed by the Holy Spirit."[118]

For these reasons Mary is honored in the Church "with special reverence. Indeed, from most ancient times the Blessed Virgin Mary has been venerated under the title of 'God-bearer.' In all perils and needs, the faithful have fled prayerfully to her protection."[119] This cult is altogether special: it bears in itself and *expresses* the profound *link* which exists *between the Mother of Christ and the Church.*[120] As Virgin and Mother, Mary remains for the Church a "permanent model." It can therefore be said that especially under this aspect, namely as a model, or rather as a "figure," Mary, present in the mystery of Christ, remains constantly present also in the mystery of the Church. For the Church too is "called mother and virgin," and these names have a profound biblical and theological justification.[121]

43. The *Church "becomes* herself *a mother* by accepting God's word with fidelity."[122] Like Mary, who first believed by accepting the Word of God revealed to her at the annunciation and by remaining faithful to that word in all her trials even unto the cross, so too the Church becomes a mother when, *accepting with fidelity the Word of God,* "by

---

117. Ibid., 63.

118. Ibid., 63.

119. Ibid., 66.

120. Cf. St. Ambrose, *De Institutione Virginis,* XIV, 88–89: *PL* 16, 341, St. Augustine, *Sermo* 215, 4: *PL* 38, 1074; *De Sancta Virginitate,* II, 2; V, 5; VI, 6: *PL* 40, 397–398f.; 399; *Sermo* 191, II, 3: *PL* 38, 1010f.

121. Cf. Second Vatican Ecumenical Council, Dogmatic Constitution on the Church *Lumen Gentium,* 63.

122. Ibid., 64.

her preaching and by Baptism *she brings forth to a new and immortal life children* who are conceived *of the Holy Spirit* and born of God."[123] This "maternal" characteristic of the Church was expressed in a particularly vivid way by the apostle to the Gentiles when he wrote: "My little children, with whom I am again in travail until Christ be formed in you!" (Gal 4:19). These words of St. Paul contain an interesting sign of the early Church's awareness of her own motherhood, linked to her apostolic service to mankind. This awareness enabled and still enables the Church to see the mystery of her life and mission modeled *upon the example of the Mother of the Son,* who is "the first-born among many brethren" (Rm 8:29).

It can be said that from Mary the Church also learns her own motherhood: she recognizes the maternal dimension of her vocation, which is essentially bound to her sacramental nature, in "contemplating Mary's mysterious sanctity, imitating her charity and faithfully fulfilling the Father's will."[124] If the Church is the sign and instrument of intimate union with God, she is so by reason of her motherhood, because, receiving life from the Spirit, she "generates" sons and daughters of the human race to a new life in Christ. For, just as *Mary is at the service of the mystery of the Incarnation,* so *the Church* is always *at the service of the mystery of adoption to sonship* through grace.

Likewise, following the example of Mary, the Church remains the virgin faithful to her spouse: "The Church herself is a virgin who keeps whole and pure the fidelity she has pledged to her Spouse."[125] For the Church is the spouse of Christ, as is clear from the Pauline Letters (cf. Eph 5:21–33; 2 Cor 11:2), and from the title found in John: "bride of the Lamb" (Rv 21:9). If *the Church* as spouse "keeps the fidelity she *has pledged* to Christ," this fidelity, even though in the Apostle's teaching it has become an image of marriage (cf. Eph 5:23–33), also has value as a model of total self-giving to God in celibacy "for the kingdom of heaven," *in virginity consecrated to God* (cf. Mt 19:11–12; 2 Cor 11:2). Precisely such virginity, after the example of the Virgin of Nazareth, is the source of a special spiritual fruitfulness: *it is the source of motherhood in the Holy Spirit.*

---

123. Ibid., 64.
124. Ibid., 64.
125. Ibid., 64.

But *the Church* also preserves the faith *received from* Christ. Following the example of Mary, who kept and pondered in her heart everything relating to her divine Son (cf. Lk 2:19, 51), the Church is committed to preserving the Word of God and investigating its riches with discernment and prudence, in order to bear faithful witness to it before all mankind in every age.[126]

44. Given Mary's relationship to the Church as an exemplar, the Church is close to her and seeks to become like her: "Imitating the Mother of her Lord, and by the power of the Holy Spirit, she preserves with virginal purity an integral faith, a firm hope, and a sincere charity."[127] Mary is thus present in the mystery of the Church as a *model*. But the Church's mystery also consists in generating people to a new and immortal life: this is her motherhood in the Holy Spirit. And here Mary is not only the model and figure of the Church; she is much more. For *"with maternal love she cooperates in the birth and development"* of the sons and daughters of Mother Church. The Church's motherhood is accomplished not only according to the model and figure of the Mother of God but also with her "cooperation." The Church *draws* abundantly from this cooperation, that is to say from the maternal mediation which is characteristic of Mary, insofar as already on earth she cooperated in the rebirth and development of the Church's sons and daughters, as the Mother of that Son whom the Father "placed as the firstborn among many brethren."[128]

She cooperated, as the Second Vatican Council teaches, with a maternal love.[129] Here we perceive the real value of the words spoken by Jesus to his Mother at the hour of the cross: "Woman, behold your son" and to the disciple: "Behold your mother" (Jn 19:26–27). They are words which determine *Mary's place in the life of Christ's disciples* and they express—as I have already said—the new motherhood of the Mother of the Redeemer: a spiritual motherhood, born from the heart of the Paschal Mystery of the Redeemer of the world. It is a

---

126. Cf. Second Vatican Ecumenical Council, Dogmatic Constitution on Divine Revelation *Dei Verbum*, 8; St. Bonaventure, *Comment. in Evang. Lucae, Ad Claras Aquas,* VII, 53, no. 40, 68, no. 109.

127. Second Vatican Ecumenical Council, Dogmatic Constitution on the Church *Lumen Gentium*, 64.

128. Ibid., 63.

129. Cf. ibid., 63.

motherhood in the order of grace, for it implores the gift of the Spirit, who raises up the new children of God, redeems through the sacrifice of Christ: that Spirit whom, together with the Church, Mary too received on the day of Pentecost.

Her motherhood is particularly noted and experienced by the Christian people at the *Sacred Banquet*—the liturgical celebration of the mystery of the redemption—at which Christ, his true *body born of the Virgin Mary,* becomes present.

The piety of the Christian people has always very rightly sensed a *profound link* between devotion to the Blessed Virgin and worship of the Eucharist: this is a fact that can be seen in the liturgy of both the West and the East, in the traditions of the religious families, in the modern movements of spirituality, including those for youth, and in the pastoral practice of the Marian shrines. *Mary guides the faithful to the Eucharist.*

45. Of the essence of motherhood is the fact that it concerns the person. Motherhood always establishes a *unique and unrepeatable relationship* between two people: *between mother and child* and *between child and mother.* Even when the same woman is the mother of many children, her personal relationship with each one of them is of the very essence of motherhood. For each child is generated in a unique and unrepeatable way, and this is true both for the mother and for the child. Each child is surrounded in the same way by that maternal love on which are based the child's development and coming to maturity as a human being.

It can be said that motherhood "in the order of grace" preserves the analogy with what "in the order of nature" characterizes the union between mother and child. In the light of this fact it becomes easier to understand why in Christ's testament on Golgotha his Mother's new motherhood is expressed in the singular, in reference to one man: "Behold your son."

It can also be said that these same words fully show the reason *for the Marian dimension of the life of Christ's disciples.* This is true not only of John, who at that hour stood at the foot of the cross together with his Master's Mother, but it is also true of every disciple of Christ, of every Christian. The Redeemer entrusts his mother to the disciple, and at the same time he gives her to him as his mother. Mary's motherhood, which becomes man's inheritance, is a gift: *a gift which Christ himself makes* personally to every individual. The Redeemer entrusts Mary to

John because he entrusts John to Mary. At the foot of the cross there begins that special *entrusting of humanity to the Mother of Christ,* which in the history of the Church has been practiced and expressed in different ways. The same apostle and evangelist, after reporting the words addressed by Jesus on the cross to his Mother and to himself, adds: "And from that hour the disciple took her to his own home" (Jn 19:27). This statement certainly means that the role of son was attributed to the disciple and that he assumed responsibility for the Mother of his beloved Master. And since Mary was given as a mother to him personally, the statement indicates, even though indirectly, everything expressed by the intimate relationship of a child with its mother. And all of this can be included in the word "entrusting." Such entrusting is *the response* to a person's love, and in particular *to the love of a mother.*

The Marian dimension of the life of a disciple of Christ is expressed in a special way precisely through this filial entrusting to the Mother of Christ, which began with the testament of the Redeemer on Golgotha. Entrusting himself to Mary in a filial manner, the Christian, like the Apostle John, "welcomes" the Mother of Christ "into his own home"[130] and brings her into everything that makes up his inner life, that is to say into his human and Christian "I": he *"took her to his own home."* Thus the Christian seeks to be taken into that "maternal charity" with which the Redeemer's Mother "cares for the brethren of her Son,"[131] "in whose birth and development she cooperates"[132] in the measure of the gift proper to each one through the power of Christ's Spirit. Thus also is exercised that motherhood in the Spirit which became Mary's role at the foot of the cross and in the upper room.

46. This filial relationship, this self-entrusting of a child to its mother, not only has its *beginning in Christ* but can also be said to be *definitively directed toward him.* Mary can be said to continue to say to

---

130. Clearly, in the Greek text the expression *"eis ta idia"* goes beyond the mere acceptance of Mary by the disciple in the sense of material lodging and hospitality in his house; it indicates rather a *communion of life* established between the two as a result of the words of the dying Christ: cf. St. Augustine, *In Ioan. Evang. Tract.,* 119, 3: *CCL* 36, 659: "He took her to himself, not into his own property, for he possessed nothing of his own, but among his own duties, which he attended to with dedication."

131. Second Vatican Ecumenical Council, Dogmatic Constitution on the Church *Lumen Gentium,* 62.

132. Ibid., 63.

each individual the words which she spoke at Cana in Galilee: "Do whatever he tells you." For he, Christ, is the one Mediator between God and mankind; he is "the way, and the truth, and the life" (Jn 14:6); it is he whom the Father has given to the world, so that man "should not perish but have eternal life" (Jn 3:16). The Virgin of Nazareth became the first "witness" of this saving love of the Father, and she also wishes *to remain* its *humble handmaid always and everywhere.* For every Christian, for every human being, Mary is the one who first "believed," and precisely with her faith as Spouse and Mother she wishes to act upon all those who entrust themselves to her as her children. And it is well known that the more her children persevere and progress in this attitude, the nearer Mary leads them to the "unsearchable riches of Christ" (Eph 3:8). And to the same degree they recognize more and more clearly the dignity of man in all its fullness and the definitive meaning of his vocation, for "Christ...fully reveals man to man himself."[133]

This Marian dimension of Christian life takes on special importance in relation to women and their status. In fact, femininity has a *unique relationship* with the Mother of the Redeemer, a subject which can be studied in greater depth elsewhere. Here I simply wish to note that the figure of Mary of Nazareth sheds light on *womanhood as such* by the very fact that God, in the sublime event of the Incarnation of his Son, entrusted himself to the ministry, the free and active ministry, of a woman. It can thus be said that women, by looking to Mary, find in her the secret of living their femininity with dignity and of achieving their own true advancement. In the light of Mary, the Church sees in the face of women the reflection of a beauty which mirrors the loftiest sentiments of which the human heart is capable: the self-offering totality of love; the strength that is capable of bearing the greatest sorrows; limitless fidelity and tireless devotion to work; the ability to combine penetrating intuition with words of support and encouragement.

47. At the Council Paul VI solemnly proclaimed that *Mary is the Mother of the Church,* "that is, Mother of the entire Christian people, both faithful and pastors."[134] Later, in 1968, in the profession of faith known as the "Credo of the People of God," he restated this truth in an

---

133. Second Vatican Ecumenical Council, Pastoral Constitution on the Church in the Modern World *Gaudium et Spes,* 22.

134. Cf. Pope Paul VI, *Discourse of November 21, 1964: AAS* 56 (1964), 1015.

even more forceful way in these words: "We believe that the Most Holy Mother of God, the new Eve, the Mother of the Church, carries on in heaven her maternal role with regard to the members of Christ, cooperating in the birth and development of divine life in the souls of the redeemed."[135]

The Council's teaching emphasized that the truth concerning the Blessed Virgin, Mother of Christ, is an effective aid in exploring more deeply the truth concerning the Church. When speaking of the Constitution *Lumen Gentium,* which had just been approved by the Council, Paul VI said: "Knowledge of the true Catholic doctrine regarding the Blessed Virgin Mary will always be a key to *the exact understanding of the mystery of Christ and of the Church.* "[136] Mary is present in the Church as the Mother of Christ, and at the same time as that Mother whom Christ, in the mystery of the redemption, gave to humanity in the person of the Apostle John. Thus, in her new motherhood in the Spirit, Mary embraces each and every one *in* the Church, and embraces each and every one *through* the Church. In this sense Mary, Mother of the Church, is also the Church's model. Indeed, as Paul VI hopes and asks, the Church must draw "from the Virgin Mother of God the most authentic form of perfect imitation of Christ."[137]

Thanks to this special bond linking the Mother of Christ with the Church, there is further *clarified the mystery of that "woman"* who, from the first chapters of the Book of *Genesis* until the Book of *Revelation,* accompanies the revelation of God's salvific plan for humanity. For Mary, present in the Church as the Mother of the Redeemer, takes part, as a mother, in that "monumental struggle against the powers of darkness"[138] which continues throughout human history. And by her ecclesial identification as the "woman clothed with the sun" (Rv 12:1),[139] it can be said that "in the most Holy Virgin the Church has already reached that

135. Pope Paul VI, *Solemn Profession of Faith* (June 30, 1968), 15: *AAS* 60 (1968), 438f.

136. Pope Paul VI, *Address at the Closing of the Third Session of the Second Vatican Ecumenical Council* (November 21, 1964): *AAS* 56 (1964), 1015.

137. Ibid., 1016.

138. Cf. Second Vatican Ecumenical Council, Pastoral Constitution on the Church in the Modern World *Gaudium et Spes,* 37.

139. Cf. St. Bernard, *In Dominica infra octavam Assumptionis Sermo: Sancti Bernardi Opera* V, 1968, 262–274.

perfection whereby she exists without spot or wrinkle." Hence, as Christians raise their eyes with faith to Mary in the course of their earthly pilgrimage, they "strive to increase in holiness."[140] Mary, the exalted Daughter of Zion, helps all her children, wherever they may be and whatever their condition, *to find in Christ the path to the Father's house.*

Thus, throughout her life, the Church maintains with the Mother of God a link which embraces, in the saving mystery, the past, the present and the future, and venerates her as the spiritual mother of humanity and the advocate of grace.

3. The meaning of the Marian Year

48. It is precisely the special bond between humanity and this Mother which has led me to proclaim a Marian Year in the Church, in this period before the end of the second millennium since Christ's birth. A similar initiative was taken in the past, when Pius XII proclaimed 1954 as a Marian Year, in order to highlight the exceptional holiness of the Mother of Christ as expressed in the mysteries of her Immaculate Conception (defined exactly a century before) and of her Assumption into heaven.[141]

Now, following the line of the Second Vatican Council, I wish to emphasize the *special presence* of the Mother of God in the mystery of Christ and his Church. For this is a fundamental dimension emerging from the Mariology of the Council, the end of which is now more than twenty years behind us. The Extraordinary Synod of Bishops held in 1985 exhorted everyone to follow faithfully the teaching and guidelines of the Council. We can say that these two events—the Council and the synod—embody what the Holy Spirit himself wishes "to say to the Church" in the present phase of history.

In this context, the Marian Year is meant to promote a new and more careful reading of what the Council said about the Blessed Virgin Mary, Mother of God, in the mystery of Christ and of the Church, the topic to

---

140. Second Vatican Ecumenical Council, Dogmatic Constitution on the Church *Lumen Gentium,* 65.

141. Cf. Encyclical Letter *Fulgens Corona* (September 8, 1953): *AAS* 45 (1953) 577–592. Pius X with his Encyclical Letter *Ad Diem Illum* (February 2, 1904), on the occasion of the 50th anniversary of the dogmatic definition of the Immaculate Conception of the Blessed Virgin Mary, had proclaimed an extraordinary jubilee of a few months; Pius X, *P. M. Acta,* I, 147–166.

which the contents of this encyclical are devoted. Here we speak not only of the *doctrine of faith* but also of the *life of faith,* and thus of authentic "Marian spirituality," seen in the light of Tradition, and especially the spirituality to which the Council exhorts us.[142] Furthermore, Marian *spirituality,* like its corresponding *devotion,* finds a very rich source in the historical experience of individuals and of the various Christian communities present among the different peoples and nations of the world. In this regard, I would like to recall, among the many witnesses and teachers of this spirituality, the figure of St. Louis Marie Grignion de Montfort,[143] who proposes consecration to Christ through the hands of Mary, as an effective means for Christians to live faithfully their baptismal commitments. I am pleased to note that in our own time too new manifestations of this spirituality and devotion are not lacking.

There thus exist solid points of reference to look to and follow in the context of this Marian Year.

49. This Marian Year *will begin on the Solemnity of Pentecost, on June 7 next.* For it is a question not only of recalling that Mary "preceded" the entry of Christ the Lord into the history of the human family, but also of emphasizing, in the light of Mary, that from the moment when the mystery of the Incarnation was accomplished, human history entered "the fullness of time," and that the Church is the sign of this fullness. As the People of God, the Church makes her pilgrim way toward eternity through faith, in the midst of all the peoples and nations, beginning from the day of Pentecost. *Christ's Mother*—who was present at the beginning of "the time of the Church," when in expectation of the coming of the Holy Spirit she devoted herself to prayer in the midst of the apostles and her Son's disciples—constantly "precedes" *the Church in her journey* through human history. She is also the one who, precisely as the "handmaid of the Lord," cooperates unceasingly with the work of salvation accomplished by Christ, her Son.

Thus by means of this Marian Year *the Church is called* not only to remember everything in her past that testifies to the special maternal co-

---

142. Cf. Dogmatic Constitution on the Church *Lumen Gentium,* 66–67.

143. St. Louis Marie Grignion de Montfort, *Traite de la varie devotion a la Ste. Vierge.* This saint can rightly be linked with the figure of St. Alfonso Maria de' Liguori, the second centenary of whose death occurs this year; cf. among his works *Le glorie di Maria.*

operation of the Mother of God in the work of salvation in Christ the Lord, but also, on her own part, *to prepare* for the future the paths of this cooperation. For the end of the second Christian millennium opens up as a new prospect.

50. As has already been mentioned, also among our divided brethren many honor and celebrate the Mother of the Lord, especially among the Orientals. It is a Marian light cast upon ecumenism. In particular, I wish to mention once more that during the Marian Year there will occur the *millennium of the Baptism* of St. Vladimir, Grand Duke of Kiev (988). This marked the beginning of Christianity in the territories of what was then called Rus', and subsequently in other territories of Eastern Europe. In this way, through the work of evangelization, Christianity spread beyond Europe, as far as the northern territories of the Asian continent. We would therefore like, especially during this year, to join in prayer with all those who are celebrating the millennium of this Baptism, both Orthodox and Catholics, repeating and confirming with the Council those sentiments of joy and comfort that "the Easterners...with ardent emotion and devout mind concur in reverencing the Mother of God, ever Virgin."[144] Even though we are still experiencing the painful effects of the separation which took place some decades later (1054), we can say that *in the presence of the Mother of Christ we feel that we are true brothers and sisters* within that messianic People, which is called to be the one family of God on earth. As I announced at the beginning of the New Year, "We desire to reconfirm this universal inheritance of all the sons and daughters of this earth."[145]

In announcing the Year of Mary, I also indicated that it will end next year on the *Solemnity of the Assumption of the Blessed Virgin into heaven,* in order to emphasize the "great sign in heaven" spoken of by the *Apocalypse*. In this way we also wish to respond to the exhortation of the Council, which looks to Mary as "a sign of sure hope and solace for the pilgrim People of God." And the Council expresses this exhortation in the following words: "Let the entire body of the faithful pour forth persevering prayer to the Mother of God and Mother of mankind. Let them implore that she who aided the beginning of the Church by

---

144. Dogmatic Constitution on the Church *Lumen Gentium,* 69.
145. Homily on January 1, 1987.

her prayers may now, exalted as she is in heaven above all the saints and angels, intercede with her Son in the fellowship of all the saints. May she do so until all the peoples of the human family, whether they are honored with the name of Christian or whether they still do not know their Savior, are happily gathered together in peace and harmony into the one People of God, for the glory of the Most Holy and Undivided Trinity."[146]

146. Dogmatic Constitution on the Church *Lumen Gentium,* 69.

CONCLUSION

51. At the end of the daily Liturgy of the Hours, among the invocations addressed to Mary by the Church is the following:

"Loving Mother of the Redeemer,

gate of heaven, star of the sea,

assist your people who have fallen yet strive to rise again.

To the wonderment of nature you bore your Creator!"

"To the wonderment of nature"! These words of the antiphon express that *wonderment of faith* which accompanies the mystery of Mary's divine motherhood. In a sense, it does so in the heart of the whole of creation, and, directly, in the heart of the whole People of God, in the heart of the Church. How wonderfully far God has gone, the Creator and Lord of all things, in the "revelation of himself" to man![147] How clearly he has bridged all the spaces of that infinite "distance" which separates the Creator from the creature! If in himself he remains *ineffable and unsearchable,* still more *ineffable and unsearchable is he in the reality of the Incarnation* of the Word, who became man through the Virgin of Nazareth.

If he has eternally willed to call man to share in the divine nature (cf. 2 Pt 1:4), it can be said that he has matched the "divinization" of man to humanity's historical conditions, so that even after sin he is ready to restore at a great price the eternal plan of his love through the "humanization" of his Son, who is of the same being as himself. The whole of creation, and more directly man himself, cannot fail to be amazed at this gift in which he has become a sharer, in the Holy Spirit: "God so loved the world that he gave his only Son" (Jn 3:16).

---

147. Cf. Second Vatican Ecumenical Council, Dogmatic Constitution on Divine Revelation *Dei Verbum,* 2: "Through this revelation...the invisible God...out of the abundance of his love speaks to men as friends...and lives among them...so that he may invite and take them into fellowship with himself."

At the center of this mystery, in the midst of this wonderment of faith, stands Mary. As the loving Mother of the Redeemer, she was the first to experience it: "To the wonderment of nature you bore your Creator"!

52. The words of this liturgical antiphon also express *the truth of the "great transformation"* which the mystery of the Incarnation establishes for man. It is a transformation which belongs to his entire history, from that beginning which is revealed to us in the first chapters of *Genesis* until the final end, in the perspective of the end of the world, of which Jesus has revealed to us "neither the day nor the hour" (Mt 25:13). It is an unending and continuous transformation between falling and rising again, between the man of sin and the man of grace and justice. The Advent liturgy in particular is at the very heart of this transformation and captures its unceasing "here and now" when it exclaims: "Assist your people who have fallen yet strive to rise again"!

These words apply to every individual, every community, to nations and peoples, and to the generations and epochs of human history, to our own epoch, to these years of the millennium which is drawing to a close: "Assist, yes assist, your people who have fallen"!

This is the invocation addressed to Mary, the "loving Mother of the Redeemer," the invocation addressed to Christ, who through Mary entered human history. Year after year the antiphon rises to Mary, evoking that moment which saw the accomplishment of this essential historical transformation, which irreversibly continues: the transformation from "falling" to "rising."

Mankind has made wonderful discoveries and achieved extraordinary results in the fields of science and technology. It has made great advances along the path of progress and civilization, and in recent times one could say that it has succeeded in speeding up the pace of history. But the fundamental transformation, the one which can be called "original," constantly accompanies man's journey, and through all the events of history accompanies each and every individual. It is the transformation from "falling" to "rising," from death to life. It is also *a constant challenge* to people's consciences, a challenge to man's whole historical awareness: the challenge to follow the path of "not falling" in ways that are ever old and ever new, and of "rising again" if a fall has occurred.

As she goes forward with the whole of humanity toward the frontier between the two millennia, the Church, for her part, with the whole community of believers and in union with all men and women of good will, takes up the great challenge contained in these words of the Marian antiphon: "the people who have fallen yet strive to rise again," and she addresses both the Redeemer and his Mother with the plea: "Assist us." For as this prayer attests, the Church sees the Blessed Mother of God in the saving mystery of Christ and in her own mystery. She sees Mary deeply rooted in humanity's history, in man's eternal vocation according to the providential plan which God has made for him from eternity. She sees Mary maternally present and sharing in the many complicated problems which *today* beset the lives of individuals, families and nations; she sees her helping the Christian people in the constant struggle between good and evil, to ensure that it "does not fall," or, if it has fallen, that it "rises again."

I hope with all my heart that the reflections contained in the present encyclical will also serve to renew this vision in the hearts of all believers.

As Bishop of Rome, I send to all those to whom these thoughts are addressed the kiss of peace, my greeting and my blessing in our Lord Jesus Christ. Amen.

Given in Rome, at St. Peter's, on March 25, the Solemnity of the Annunciation of the Lord, in the year 1987, the ninth of my pontificate.

John Paul II

BEHOLD YOUR MOTHER: MARY IN THE LIFE OF THE PRIEST

Holy Thursday Letter of Pope John Paul II
March 25, 1988

INTRODUCTION

Historical Perspectives

Every year Pope John Paul II has written a Holy Thursday letter to priests. The 1988 letter reflected a theme in keeping with the Marian Year then being celebrated. The pope encouraged devotion to Mary in the life of the priest, especially in light of Mary's role.

In presenting some thoughts on celibacy, the pope drew on his "theology of the body," developed in a series of general audience talks from 1979 to 1984. In those catecheses John Paul had discussed the "nuptial meaning of redemption" in the context of marriage and celibacy.[1]

The Teaching

The letter states: "It is appropriate...to recall the reality of the Incarnation as it relates to the institution of the Eucharist and also to the institution of the sacrament of the priesthood." The document then quotes the ancient hymn: "Hail, true Body, born of the Virgin Mary: you truly suffered and were immolated on the cross for man" (*BYM* 1).

The Scriptures do not indicate that Mary was present at the Last Supper, but state that she was present at the foot of the cross. Acting in the person of Christ in celebrating the Eucharist, the priest "must not forget this suffering of his Mother." The priest is asked to constantly deepen his "spiritual bond with the Mother of God *who on the pilgrimage of faith 'goes before' the whole People of God. And in particular, when we celebrate the Eucharist and stand each day on Golgotha, we*

---

1. These talks are collected in one volume entitled *The Theology of the Body* (Boston: Pauline Books & Media, 1997).

need to have near us the one who through heroic faith carried to its zenith her union with her Son, precisely then on Golgotha" (*BYM* 2).

The priest is also to imitate John and take Mary into his home. By doing so, the priest accepts the grievous suffering of the heart of the mother. By recognizing and sharing Mary's suffering motherhood, and consequently her spiritual motherhood of the Church, the priest recognizes and exercises his spiritual fatherhood.

In reflecting on Mary as the Virgin Mother, the pope discusses the meaning of celibacy. He speaks of the "nuptial meaning of redemption," putting celibacy in the context of the theology of the body. In this context, the Holy Father also calls priests to seek "*a proper relationship with women and the attitude toward them shown by Jesus of Nazareth himself....* By reason of his vocation and service, the priest must discover in a new way *the question of the dignity and vocation of women* both in the Church and in today's world" (*BYM* 5).

Today

In this and in all the concerns of the priest, Mary will assist him in the spiritual struggles he faces, just as she has done throughout history (*BYM* 7).

TOPICAL OUTLINE

1. The Incarnation and Mary's role in it (1)

2. Mary's presence on Calvary (2)

3. Christ entrusted Mary to John (3)

4. Mary as a type of the Church, virgin and mother (4)

5. Celibacy and the priest's relationship with women (5)

6. Christ's friendship with the priest and Mary's role in it (6)

7. Mary's role in the spiritual struggles of the human race (7)

8. Thanksgiving for the gift of the priesthood (8)

BEHOLD YOUR MOTHER: MARY IN THE LIFE OF THE PRIEST

Promulgated by His Holiness Pope John Paul II
On March 25,1988

LETTER OF THE HOLY FATHER
POPE JOHN PAUL II
TO PRIESTS FOR HOLY THURSDAY 1988

Dear brothers in the priesthood,

1. Today we all return to the upper room. Gathering at the altar in so many places throughout the world, we celebrate in a special way the memorial of the Last Supper in the midst of the community of the People of God whom we serve. The words which Christ spoke on "the day before he suffered" reecho on our lips at the evening liturgy of Holy Thursday as they do every day; yet they do so in a particular way since they refer back to that special evening which is recalled by the Church *precisely today.*

Like our Lord, and at the same time *in persona Christi,* we say the words: "Take this, all of you, and eat it: *this is my body....* Take this, all of you, and drink from it: *this is the cup of my blood."* Indeed, the Lord himself commanded us to do so, when he said to the apostles: "Do this in memory of me" (Lk 22:19).

And as we do this, the *whole mystery of the Incarnation* must be alive in our minds and hearts. Christ, who on Holy Thursday announces that his body will be "given up" and his blood "shed," is the eternal Son, who "coming into the world," says to the Father: *"A body you prepared for me.... Behold, I come to do your will"* (cf. Heb 10:5–7).

It is precisely that Passover which is drawing near, when the Son of God, as Redeemer of the world, will fulfill the Father's will through the offering and *the immolation of his Body and Blood* on Golgotha. It is by means of this sacrifice that he "entered once for all into the Holy Place, taking...his own blood, thus securing an eternal redemption" (Heb 9:12). Indeed, this is the sacrifice of the "new and everlasting" covenant. See how it is intimately connected with the mystery of the Incarnation: the Word who became flesh (cf. Jn 1:14) immolates his humanity as *homo assumptus* in the unity of the divine Person.

It is appropriate during this year, being lived by the whole Church as a Marian Year, to recall the reality of the Incarnation as it relates to the institution of the Eucharist and also to the institution of the sacrament of the priesthood. The Incarnation was brought about by the Holy Spirit when he came down upon *the Virgin of Nazareth* and she spoke her *fiat* in response to the angel's message (cf. Lk 1:38).

Hail, true Body, born of the Virgin Mary: you truly suffered and were immolated on the cross for man.

Yes, the same Body! When we celebrate the Eucharist, through our priestly ministry there is made present the mystery of the incarnate Word, the Son who is of one being with the Father, who as a man "born of woman" is the Son of the Virgin Mary.

2. There is no indication that the Mother of Christ was present in the upper room at the Last Supper. *But she was present on Calvary,* at the foot of the cross, where as the Second Vatican Council teaches, "she stood, in accordance with the divine plan (cf. Jn 19:25), suffering grievously with her only-begotten Son, uniting herself with a maternal heart to his sacrifice, and lovingly consenting to the immolation of this victim which she herself had brought forth."[1] How far the *fiat* uttered by Mary at the annunciation had taken her!

---

1. Second Vatican Ecumenical Council, Dogmatic Constitution on the Church *Lumen Gentium,* 58.

When, acting *in persona Christi,* we celebrate the sacrament of the one same sacrifice of which Christ is and remains the only priest and victim, *we must not forget this suffering of his Mother,* in whom were fulfilled Simeon's words in the Temple at Jerusalem: "A sword will pierce through your own soul also" (Lk 2:35). They were spoken directly to Mary forty days after Jesus' birth. On Golgotha, beneath the cross, these words were completely fulfilled. When on the cross Mary's Son revealed himself fully as the "sign of contradiction," it was then that this immolation and mortal agony also reached her maternal heart.

Behold the agony of the heart of the Mother who suffered together with him, "consenting to the immolation of this victim which she herself had brought forth." Here we reach *the high point of Mary's presence in the mystery of Christ and of the Church* on earth. This high point is on the path of the "pilgrimage of faith" to which we make special reference in the Marian Year.[2]

Dear brothers: who more than we has an absolute need of a deep and unshakable faith—we, who by virtue of the apostolic succession begun in the upper room celebrate the sacrament of Christ's sacrifice? We must therefore constantly deepen our spiritual bond with the Mother of God *who on the pilgrimage of faith "goes before" the whole People of God.*

And in particular, when we celebrate the Eucharist and stand each day on Golgotha, we need to have near us the one who through heroic faith carried to its zenith her union with her Son, precisely then on Golgotha.

3. Moreover, has Christ not left us a special sign of this? See how during his agony on the cross he spoke the words which have for us the meaning of a testament: "When Jesus saw his mother, and the disciple whom he loved standing near, he said to his mother, 'Woman, behold, your son!' Then he said to the disciple, 'Behold, your mother!' And from that hour the disciple took her to his own home" (Jn 19:26–27).

That disciple, the Apostle John, was with Christ at the Last Supper. He was one of the "Twelve" to whom the Master addressed, together with the words instituting the Eucharist, the command: "Do this in memory of me." He received the power to celebrate the Eucharistic sacrifice instituted in the upper room on the eve of the passion, as the Church's most holy sacrament.

---

2. Cf. John Paul II, Encyclical Letter *Redemptoris Mater,* 33: *AAS* 79 (1987), 402.

At the moment of death, Jesus gives his own Mother to this disciple. John "took her to his own home." He took her as the first witness to the mystery of the Incarnation. And he, as an evangelist, expressed in the most profound yet simple way the truth about the Word who "became flesh and dwelt among us" (Jn 1:14), the truth about the Incarnation and the truth about Emmanuel.

And so, by taking "to his own home" the Mother who stood beneath her Son's cross, he also made his own *all that was within her on Golgotha:* the fact that she "suffered grievously with her only-begotten Son, uniting herself with a maternal heart in his sacrifice, and lovingly consenting to the immolation of this victim that she herself had brought forth." All this—the superhuman *experience of the sacrifice of our re- demption, inscribed in the heart of Christ the Redeemer's own Mother—* was entrusted to the man who in the upper room received the power to make this sacrifice present through the priestly ministry of the Eucharist.

Does this not have special eloquence for each of us? If John at the foot of the cross somehow represents every man and woman for whom the motherhood of the Mother of God is spiritually extended, how much more does this concern each of us, who are sacramentally called to the priestly ministry of the Eucharist in the Church!

The reality of Golgotha is truly an amazing one: the reality of Christ's sacrifice for the redemption of the world! Equally amazing is *the mystery of God of which we are ministers in the sacramental order* (cf. 1 Cor 4:1). But are we not threatened by the danger of being unworthy ministers? By the danger of not presenting ourselves with sufficient fidelity at the foot of Christ's cross as we celebrate the Eucharist?

Let us strive to be close to that Mother in whose heart is inscribed in a unique and incomparable way the mystery of the world's redemption.

4. The Second Vatican Council proclaims: "Through the gift and role of her divine motherhood, by which the Blessed Virgin is united with her Son...she is also intimately united with the Church. As St. Ambrose taught, *the Mother of God is a 'type' of the Church* in the matter of faith, charity and perfect union with Christ. For in the mystery of the Church, herself rightly called mother and virgin, the Blessed Virgin stands out in eminent and singular fashion as exemplar of both virginity and motherhood."[3]

---

3. Second Vatican Ecumenical Council, Dogmatic Constitution on the Church *Lumen Gentium,* 63.

The Council text goes on to develop this typological analogy: *"The Church,* moreover, contemplating Mary's mysterious sanctity, imitating her charity and faithfully fulfilling the Father's will, *becomes herself a mother* by faithfully accepting God's word. For by her preaching and by Baptism, she brings forth to a new and immortal life children who are conceived of the Holy Spirit and born of God. *The Church herself is a virgin,* who keeps whole and pure the fidelity she has pledged to her Spouse." The Church, therefore, "imitating the Mother of her Lord, and by the power of the Holy Spirit, preserves with virginal purity an integral faith, a firm hope and a sincere charity."[4]

At the foot of the cross on Golgotha, "the disciple took to his own home" Mary, whom Christ had pointed out to him with the words, "Behold, your mother." The Council's teaching demonstrates how much *the whole Church* has taken Mary into "the Church's own home," how profoundly the mystery of this Virgin Mother belongs to the mystery of the Church, to the Church's intimate reality.

All this is of fundamental importance for all the sons and daughters of the Church. *It has special significance for us* who have been marked with the sacramental sign of the priesthood which, while being "hierarchical," is at the same time "ministerial," in keeping with the example of Christ, the first servant of the world's redemption.

If everyone in the Church—the people who by Baptism participate in Christ's priestly function—possesses the common "royal priesthood" of which the Apostle Peter speaks (cf. 1 Pt 2:9), then all must apply to themselves the words of the Conciliar Constitution just quoted. But these words refer in a special way to us.

The Council sees *the Church's motherhood,* which is modeled on Mary's, *in the fact that the Church* "brings forth to a new and immortal life children who are conceived of the Holy Spirit and born of God." Here we find echoed St. Paul's words about "the children with whom I am again in travail" (cf. Gal 4:19), in the same way as a mother gives birth. When, in the Letter to the Ephesians, we read about Christ as the Spouse who "nourishes and cherishes" the Church as his body (cf. 5:29), we cannot fail to link this spousal solicitude on the part of Christ above all with the gift of Eucharistic food, similar to the many maternal concerns associated with "nourishing and cherishing" a child.

---

4. Ibid., 64.

It is worth recalling these scriptural references, so that the truth about the Church's motherhood, founded on the example of the Mother of God, may become more and more a part of our priestly consciousness. If each of us lives the equivalent of this *spiritual motherhood* in a manly way, namely, as a *"spiritual fatherhood,"* then Mary, as a "figure" of the Church, has a part to play in this experience of ours. The passages quoted show how profoundly this role is inscribed at the very center of our priestly and pastoral service. Is not Paul's analogy on "pain in childbirth" close to all of us in the many situations in which we too are involved in the spiritual process of *man's "generation" and "regeneration"* by the power of the Holy Spirit, the Giver of life? The most powerful experiences in this sphere are had by confessors all over the world—and not by them alone.

On Holy Thursday we need to deepen once again this mysterious truth of our vocation: this "spiritual fatherhood" which on the human level is similar to motherhood. Moreover, does not God himself, the Creator and Father, make the comparison between his love and the love of a human mother (cf. Is 49:15; 66:13)? Thus we are speaking of a characteristic of our priestly personality that expresses precisely *apostolic maturity and spiritual "fruitfulness."* If the whole Church "learns her own motherhood from Mary,"[5] do we not need to do so as well? Each of us, then, has to "take her to our own home" like the Apostle John on Golgotha, that is to say, each of us should allow Mary to dwell "within the home" of our sacramental priesthood, as mother and mediatrix of that "great mystery" (cf. Eph 5:32) which we all wish to serve with our lives.

5. *Mary is the Virgin Mother,* and when the Church turns to Mary, figure of the Church, she recognizes herself in Mary because the Church too is "called mother and virgin." The Church is virgin, because *"she guards whole and pure the faith given to the Spouse."* Christ, according to the teaching contained in the Letter to the Ephesians (cf. 5:32), is the Spouse of the Church. The nuptial meaning of redemption impels each of us to guard our fidelity to this vocation, by means of which we are made sharers of the saving mission of Christ, priest, prophet and king.

The analogy between the Church and the Virgin Mother has a special eloquence for us, who link our *priestly vocation to celibacy,* that is,

---

5. Cf. John Paul II, Encyclical Letter *Redemptoris Mater,* 43: *AAS* 79 (1987), 420.

to "making ourselves eunuchs for the sake of the kingdom of heaven." We recall the conversation with the apostles, in which Christ explained to them the meaning of this choice (cf. Mt 19:12), and we seek to understand the reasons fully. We freely renounce marriage and establishing our own family, in order to be better able to serve God and neighbor. It can be said that we renounce fatherhood "according to the flesh," in order that there may grow and develop in us fatherhood "according to the Spirit" (cf. Jn 1:13), which, as has already been said, possesses at the same time maternal characteristics. Virginal fidelity to the Spouse, which finds its own particular expression in this form of life, enables us to share in the intimate life of the Church, which, following the example of the Virgin, seeks to keep "whole and pure the fidelity she has pledged to her Spouse."

By reason of this model—yes, of the prototype which the Church finds in Mary—it is necessary that our *priestly choice of celibacy* for the whole of our lives *should also be placed within her heart.* We must have recourse to this Virgin Mother when we meet difficulties along our chosen path. With her help we must seek always a more profound understanding of this path, an ever more complete affirmation of it in our hearts. Finally, in fact, there must be developed in our life this fatherhood "according to the Spirit," which is one of the results of "making ourselves eunuchs for the sake of the kingdom of God."

From Mary, who represents the singular "fulfillment" of the biblical "woman" of the proto-evangelium (cf. Gn 3:15) and of the Book of Revelation (12:1), let us seek also *a proper relationship with women* and the attitude toward them *shown by Jesus of Nazareth himself.* We find this expressed in many passages of the Gospel. This theme is an important one in the life of every priest, and the Marian Year impels us to take it up again and to develop it in a special way. By reason of his vocation and service, the priest must discover in a new way *the question of the dignity and vocation of women* both in the Church and in today's world. He must understand thoroughly what Christ intended to say to all of us when he spoke to the Samaritan woman (cf. Jn 4:1–42), when he defended the adulteress threatened with stoning (cf. Jn 8:1–11), when he bore witness to her whose many sins were forgiven because she had loved much (cf. Lk 7:6–50), when he conversed with Mary and Martha at Bethany (cf. Lk 10:38–42; Jn 11:1–44), and finally, when he conveyed to the women, before others, "the Easter Good News" of his resurrection (cf. Mt 28:9–10).

The Church's mission, from apostolic times, was taken up in different ways *by men and by women.* In our own times, since the Second Vatican Council, this fact involves a new call addressed to each one of us, if the priesthood which we exercise in the different communities of the Church is to be truly ministerial and by this very fact effective and fruitful at the apostolic level.

6. Meeting today, on Holy Thursday, at the birthplace of our priesthood, we desire to read its fullest meaning through the prism of the Council teaching about the Church and her mission. The figure of the Mother of God belongs to this teaching in its entirety, as do the reflections of the present meditation.

Speaking from the cross on Golgotha, Christ said to the disciple: "Behold, your mother." And the disciple "took her to his own home" as Mother. Let us also *take Mary as Mother into the interior "home" of our priesthood.* For we belong to the "faithful in whose rebirth and development" the Mother of God "cooperates with a maternal love."[6] Yes, we have, in a certain sense, a special "right" to this love in consideration of the mystery of the upper room. Christ said: "No longer do I call you servants...but I have called you friends" (Jn 15:15). Without this "friendship" it would be difficult to think that, after the apostles, he *would entrust to us* the sacrament of his Body and Blood, the sacrament of his redeeming death and resurrection, in order that we might celebrate this ineffable sacrament in his name, indeed, *in persona Christi.* Without this special "friendship" it would also be difficult to think about Easter evening, when the risen Lord appeared in the midst of the apostles, saying to them: "Receive the Holy Spirit. Whose sins you forgive are forgiven them, and whose sins you retain are retained" (Jn 20:22–23).

Such a friendship involves a commitment. Such a friendship should instill a holy fear, a much greater sense of responsibility, a much greater readiness to give of oneself all that one can, with the help of God. In the upper room such a friendship has been profoundly sealed with the promise of the Paraclete: "He will teach you all things, and bring to your remembrance all that I have said to you.... He will bear witness to me, and you also are witnesses" (Jn 14:26; 15:26–27).

6. Cf. Second Vatican Ecumenical Council, Dogmatic Constitution on the Church *Lumen Gentium,* 63.

We always feel unworthy of Christ's friendship. But it is a good thing that we should have a holy fear of not remaining faithful to it.

The Mother of Christ knows all this. She herself has understood most completely the meaning of the words spoken to her during his agony on the cross: "Woman, behold, your son.... Behold, your mother." They referred to her and to the disciple—one of those to whom Christ said in the upper room: "You are my friends" (Jn 15:14); they referred to John and to all those who, through the mystery of the Last Supper, share in the same "friendship." *The Mother of God,* who (as the Council teaches) cooperates, with a mother's love, in the rebirth and the training of all those who become brothers of her Son—who become his friends—*will do everything in her power so that they may not betray this holy friendship,* so that they may be worthy of it.

7. Together with John, the apostle and evangelist, we turn the gaze of our soul *toward* that *"woman clothed with the sun,"* who appears on the eschatological horizon of the Church and the world in the Book of Revelation (cf. 12:1ff.). It is not difficult to recognize in her the same figure who, at the beginning of human history, after original sin, was foretold as the Mother of the Redeemer (cf. Gn 3:15). In the Book of Revelation we see her, on the one hand, as the exalted woman in the midst of visible creation, and on the other, as the one who continues to *take part in the spiritual battle for the victory of good over evil.* This is the combat waged by the Church in union with the Mother of God, her "model," "against the world rulers of this present darkness, against the spiritual hosts of wickedness," as we read in the Letter to the Ephesians (6:12). The beginning of this spiritual battle goes back to the moment when man "abused his liberty at the urging of personified Evil and set himself against God and sought to find fulfillment apart from God."[7] One can say that *man,* blinded by the prospect of being raised beyond the measure of the creature which he was (in the words of the tempter: "you will become as God"; (cf. Gn 3:5), has ceased to seek the truth of his own existence and progress in him who is "the first-born of all creation" (Col 1:15), and has ceased to give this creation and himself in Christ to God, from whom everything takes its origin. Man *has lost the*

---

7. Second Vatican Ecumenical Council, Pastoral Constitution on the Church in the Modern World *Gaudium et Spes,* 13.

awareness of being the priest of the whole visible world, turning the latter exclusively toward himself.

The words of the proto-evangelium at the beginning of the Scriptures and the words of the Book of Revelation at the end refer to the same battle in which man is involved. In the perspective of this spiritual battle which takes place in history, the Son of the woman is the Redeemer of the world. The redemption is accomplished through the sacrifice in which Christ—the Mediator of the new and eternal covenant—"entered once for all into the Holy Place...with his own blood," making room in the "house of the Father"—in the bosom of the Most Holy Trinity—for all "those who are called to the eternal inheritance" (cf. Heb 9:12, 15). It is precisely for this reason that the crucified and risen Christ is "the high priest of the good things to come" (Heb 9:11) and his *sacrifice means a new orientation of man's spiritual history toward God*—the Creator and Father, toward whom the first-born of all creation leads all in the Holy Spirit.

The priesthood, which has its beginning in the Last Supper, enables us to share in this essential transformation of man's spiritual history. For in the Eucharist we present the sacrifice of redemption, the same sacrifice which Christ offered on the cross "with his own blood." Through this sacrifice we too, as its sacramental dispensers, together with all those whom we serve through its celebration, *continually touch the decisive moment of that spiritual combat* which, according to the Books of Genesis and Revelation, is linked with the "woman." In this battle she is entirely united with the Redeemer. And therefore our priestly ministry too unites us with her: she who is the Mother of the Redeemer and the "model" of the Church. In this way all remain united with her in this spiritual battle which takes place throughout the course of human history. In this battle we have special part by virtue of our sacramental priesthood. We fulfill a special service in the work of the world's redemption.

The Council teaches that *Mary advanced in her pilgrimage of faith* through her perfect union with her Son unto the cross and goes before, presenting herself in an eminent and singular way to the whole People of God, which follows the same path, in the footsteps of Christ in the Holy Spirit. Should not we priests unite ourselves with her in a special way, we who as *pastors* of the Church must also lead the communities entrusted to us along the path which from the upper room of Pentecost follows Christ throughout human history?

8. Dear brothers in the priesthood: as we come together today with our bishops in so many different places on earth, it has been my wish to develop in this annual letter precisely the motif which also seems to me particularly linked with the subject of the Marian Year.

As we celebrate the Eucharist at so many altars throughout the world, *let us give thanks* to the Eternal Priest *for the gift* which he has bestowed on us in the sacrament of the priesthood. And in this thanksgiving may there be heard the words which the evangelist puts on Mary's lips on the occasion of her visit to her cousin Elizabeth: "The Almighty *has done great things for me,* and holy is his name" (Lk 1:49). Let us also give thanks to Mary for the indescribable gift of the priesthood, whereby we are able to serve in the Church every human being. *May gratitude also reawaken our zeal!* Is it not through our priestly ministry that there is accomplished what the next verses of Mary's Magnificat speak of? Behold, the Redeemer, the God of the cross and of the Eucharist, indeed "lifts up the lowly" and "fills the hungry with good things." He who was rich, yet for our sake became poor, so that by his poverty we might become rich (cf. 2 Cor 8:9), has entrusted to the humble Virgin of Nazareth the admirable *mystery of his poverty* which makes us rich. And he entrusts the same mystery to us too through the sacrament of the priesthood.

Let us unceasingly give thanks for this. Let us give thanks with the whole of our lives. Let us give thanks with all our strength. Let us give thanks together with Mary, the Mother of priests. *"How can I repay the Lord for his goodness to me?* The cup of salvation I will raise; I will call on the Lord's name" (Ps 115/116:12–13).

With fraternal charity I send to all my brothers in the priesthood and in the episcopate, for the day of our common celebration, my heartfelt greetings and my apostolic blessing.

From the Vatican, on March 25, the Solemnity of the Annunciation of the Lord, in the year 1988, the tenth of my pontificate.

John Paul II

THE VIRGIN MARY IN INTELLECTUAL AND SPIRITUAL FORMATION

Letter of the Congregation
for Catholic Education
March 25, 1988

INTRODUCTION

Combining Marian doctrine and pastoral perspectives, *The Virgin Mary in Intellectual and Spiritual Formation* addresses theological faculties, seminarians, and others engaged in ecclesiastical studies. The text builds on the major divisions of *Marialis Cultus* and follows the pastoral approach of *Redemptoris Mater,* presenting the essentials of post-Vatican II Marian theology up to 1988. While it refers to Sacred Scripture, the document does not directly build on it.

Historical Perspectives

The letter briefly traces the history of Marian doctrine from the creeds to the dogmas, and then considers the influence of "movements" within the Church before Vatican II. It summarizes the teaching of *Lumen Gentium,* comments on post-conciliar developments and discusses *Redemptoris Mater.* Finally, it delineates a method to approach and teach Mariology, indicating ways to implement this teaching on a pastoral level.

The Teaching

While it does not try to develop new aspects of Marian teaching, the letter has creatively synthesized previous documents in terms of Mary's active presence in the Church. It also points out *Lumen Gentium's* understanding of Mary as a member, figure, symbol and model of the Church.

The document draws attention to anthropology and speaks of Mary's human development: "The Virgin is both the highest historical realization of the Gospel, and the woman who, through her self-control, her sense of responsibility, her openness to others and to the spirit of service, her strength and her love, is the most completely realized on the human level" (*ISF* 15).

The text speaks of biblical exegesis as a new frontier for Mariology, concluding that "The study of the sacred Scriptures, therefore, must be the soul of Mariology" (*ISF* 24). The letter also refers to the post-conciliar interest in questions regarding Marian devotion in its historical context. It draws a link between liturgical expressions and popular devotions, and considers the problem of inculturation.

Regarding spirituality, the document notes that the study of Mariology ultimately aims to acquire a sound Marian spirituality, an essential aspect of Christian spirituality. As *Marialis Cultus* 21 stated, Mary is "Mother and teacher of the spiritual life" (*ISF* 35).

Today

The concluding articles of the document speak about the importance of teaching Marian theology. Such teaching should include study, devotion and lifestyle. As students learn the difference between true and false devotion to Mary, they will be able to distinguish authentic doctrine from aberrations. The students are asked to "nourish an authentic love for the Mother of the Savior…and develop the capacity to communicate such love to the Christian people through speech, writing and example, so that their Marian piety may be promoted and cultivated" (*ISF* 27–31).

The letter strongly insists on including Mary in theological studies, not only in seminaries but in "all centers of ecclesiastical studies." On the intellectual, spiritual and pastoral levels, such study will greatly benefit the Church.

TOPICAL OUTLINE

1. Introduction (1)

2. The Virgin Mary: An essential *datum* of the faith and the life of the Church

   A. The wealth of Marian doctrine (2–4)

   B. The Marian teaching of Vatican II (5)

      1. In relation to the Mystery of Christ (6–8)

      2. In relation to the mystery of the Church (9)

   C. Post-conciliar Marian developments (10–16)

   D. The Encyclical *Redemptoris Mater* of John Paul II (17)

   E. The contribution of Mariology to theological research (18–22)

3. The Virgin Mary in intellectual and spiritual formation

   A. Research in Mariology (23–26)

   B. The teaching of Mariology (27–31)

   C. Mariology and pastoral service (32–33)

   D. Conclusion (34–36)

THE VIRGIN MARY IN INTELLECTUAL AND SPIRITUAL FORMATION

Letter of the Congregation for Catholic Education
March 25, 1988

INTRODUCTION

1. The Second Extraordinary Assembly of the Synod of Bishops, which was held in 1985 for "the celebration, verification and promotion of Vatican Council II,"[1] affirmed that "special attention must be paid to the four major constitutions of the Council,"[2] in order to implement a program "having as its object a new, more extensive and deeper knowledge and reception of the Council."[3]

On his part, His Holiness Pope John Paul II has explained that the Marian Year is meant "to promote a new and more careful reading of what the Council said about the Blessed Virgin Mary, Mother of God, in the mystery of Christ and of the Church."[4]

---

1. Synod of Bishops, *Ecclesia sub Verbo Dei mysteria Christi celebrans pro salute mundi. Relatio finalis* (Vatican City, 1985), I, 2.

2. Ibid., I, 5.

3. Ibid., I, 6.

4. John Paul II, Encyclical Letter *Redemptoris Mater* (March 25, 1987) 48: *AAS* 79 (1987), 427.

In the light of these developments the Congregation for Catholic Education addresses this present circular letter to theological faculties, to seminaries and to other centers of ecclesiastical studies in order to offer some reflections on the Blessed Virgin and to emphasize that the promotion of knowledge, research and piety with regard to Mary of Nazareth is not to be restricted to the Marian Year, but must be permanent since the exemplary value and the mission of the Virgin are permanent. The Mother of the Lord is a "*datum* of divine revelation" and a "maternal presence" always operative in the life of the Church.[5]

---

5. Cf. *Redemptoris Mater,* 1, 25.

I

THE VIRGIN MARY: AN ESSENTIAL *DATUM* OF THE FAITH AND THE LIFE OF THE CHURCH

The wealth of Marian doctrine

2. The history of dogma and theology bears witness to the Church's faith about, and constant attention to, the Virgin Mary and to her mission in the history of salvation. Such attention is already evident in some of the New Testament writings and in a number of pages by authors in the sub-apostolic age.

The first symbols of the faith and, successively, the dogmatic formulas of the Councils of Constantinople (381), of Ephesus (431) and of Chalcedon (451) are evidence of the developing appreciation of the mystery of Christ, true God and true man, and at the same time of the progressive discovery of the role of Mary in the mystery of the Incarnation, a discovery which led to the dogmatic definition of Mary's divine and virginal motherhood.

The attention of the Church to Mary of Nazareth runs through the centuries, with many pronouncements about her being made. Without underestimating the blossoming which Mariological reflection produced in earlier periods of history, here we draw only on the more recent.

3. We recall the doctrinal importance of the dogmatic Bull *Ineffabilis Deus* (December 8, 1854) of Pius IX, the Apostolic Constitution *Munificentissimus Deus* (November 1, 1950) of Pius XII, and the Dogmatic Constitution *Lumen Gentium* (November 21, 1964), chapter eight of which is the fullest and most authoritative synthesis of Catholic doctrine about the Mother of the Lord ever to have been compiled by an ecumenical council. Also to be remembered for their theological and pastoral significance are other documents such as *Professio Fidei* (June 30, 1968), the Apostolic Exhortation *Signum Magnum* (May 13, 1967) and *Marialis Cultus* (February 2, 1974) of Paul VI, as well as the Encyclical *Redemptoris Mater* (March 25, 1987) of John Paul II.

4. It is also important to remember the influence of several "movements" which in several ways and from various points of view raised interest in the person of the Virgin and considerably influenced the composition of the Constitution *Lumen Gentium*: the biblical movement, which underlined the primary importance of the Sacred Scriptures for a presentation of the role of the Mother of the Lord, truly consonant with the revealed Word; the patristic movement, which put Mariology in contact with the thought of the Fathers of the Church so that its roots in Tradition could be more deeply appreciated; the ecclesiological movement, which contributed abundantly to the reconsideration and deepening appreciation of the relationship between Mary and the Church; the missionary movement, which progressively discovered the value of Mary of Nazareth, the first to be evangelized (cf. Lk 1:26–38) and the first evangelizer (cf. Lk 1:39–45), fount of inspiration in her commitment to the spreading of the Good News; the liturgical movement, which initiated a rich and rigorous study of the various liturgies and was able to document the way the rites of the Church testified to a heartfelt veneration toward Mary, the "ever Virgin Mother of Jesus Christ, our Lord and God";[6] the ecumenical movement, which called for a more exact understanding of the person of the Virgin in the sources of revelation, identifying more exactly the theological basis of Marian piety.

The Marian Teaching of Vatican II

5. The importance of chapter eight of *Lumen Gentium* lies in the value of its doctrinal synthesis and in its formulation of doctrine about the Blessed Virgin in the context of the mystery of Christ and of the Church. In this way the Council:

—allied itself to the patristic tradition which gives a privileged place to the history of salvation in every theological tract;

—stressed that the Mother of the Lord is not a peripheral figure in our faith and in the panorama of theology; rather, she, through her intimate participation in the history of salvation, "in a certain way unites and mirrors within herself the central truths of the faith";[7]

—formulated a common vision for the different positions about the way in which Marian matters are to be treated.

---

6. Roman Missal, Eucharistic Prayer I, *Communicantes*.
7. *Lumen Gentium*, 65.

A. In Relation to the Mystery of Christ

6. According to the doctrine of the Council, the relationship between Mary and God the Father derives from her role in relation to Christ. "When the time had fully come, God sent forth his Son, born of a woman...so that we might receive adoption as sons" (Gal 4:4–5).[8] Mary, therefore, who, by her condition, was the handmaid of the Lord (cf. Lk 1:38,48), "received the Word of God in her heart and in her body, and gave life to the world," becoming by grace the "Mother of God."[9] In view of this unique mission, God the Father preserved her from original sin, enriched her with an abundance of heavenly gifts and, in the plan of his Wisdom, "willed that consent of the predestined mother should precede the Incarnation."[10]

7. The Council, explaining the participation of Mary in the history of salvation, expounded, first of all, the multiple aspects of the relationship between the Virgin and Christ:

—She is "the most excellent *fruit* of the redemption,"[11] having been "redeemed in an especially sublime manner by reason of the merits of her Son";[12] thus the Fathers of the Church, the liturgy and the magisterium have called her "daughter of her Son"[13] in the order of grace.

—She is the *mother*, who, accepting with faith the message of the angel, conceived the Son of God in his human nature in her virginal womb through the action of the Holy Spirit and without the intervention of man; she brought him to birth, fed him, tended him and educated him.[14]

—She is the faithful *handmaid* who "devoted herself totally...to the person and work of her Son, serving under him and with him, the mystery of redemption."[15]

---

8. *Lumen Gentium,* 52.

9. Cf. *Lumen Gentium,* 53.

10. Cf. *Lumen Gentium,* 56.

11. *Sacrosanctum Concilium,* 103.

12. *Lumen Gentium,* 53.

13. Cf. *Concilium Toletanum XI,* 48: Denzinger-Schönmetzer, *Enchiridion Symbolorum definitionum et declarationum de rebus fidei et morum* (Barcinone 1976), 536.

14. Cf. *Lumen Gentium,* 57, 61.

15. *Lumen Gentium,* 56.

—She is the *cooperatrix* with the Redeemer: "She conceived, brought forth and nourished Christ. She presented him to the Father in the Temple, and was united with him in suffering as he died on the cross. In an utterly singular way she cooperated by her obedience, faith, hope and burning charity in the Savior's work of restoring supernatural life to souls."[16]

—She is the *disciple* who, during the preaching of Christ "received his praise when, in extolling a kingdom beyond the calculations of flesh and blood, he declared blessed (cf. Mk 3:35; Lk 11:27–28) those who heard and kept the word of God, as she was faithfully doing (cf. Lk 2:19, 51)."[17]

8. The relationship between Mary and the Holy Spirit is also to be seen in the light of Christ: "She is, at it were, fashioned and formed into a new creature"[18] by the Holy Spirit, and in a special way, is his temple;[19] through the power of the same Spirit (cf. Lk 1:35) she conceived in her virginal womb and gave Jesus Christ to the world.[20] During the visitation the gifts of the Messiah flowed through her: the outpouring of the Holy Spirit on Elizabeth, the joy of the future precursor (cf. Lk 1:41).

Full of faith in the promise of the Son (cf. Lk 24:49), the Virgin is present, praying in the midst of the community of disciples: persevering with them in one accord, we see Mary "prayerfully imploring the gift of the Spirit, who had already overshadowed her in the annunciation."[21]

B. In relation to the mystery of the Church

9. For Christ, and therefore also for the Church, God willed and predestined the Virgin from all eternity. Mary of Nazareth is:

—"hailed as a preeminent and altogether singular *member* of the Church"[22] because of the gifts of grace which adorn her and because of the place she occupies in the Mystical Body;

---

16. *Lumen Gentium,* 61. Cf. ibid., 56, 58.
17. *Lumen Gentium,* 58.
18. *Lumen Gentium,* 56.
19. Cf. *Lumen Gentium,* 53.
20. Cf. *Lumen Gentium,* 52, 63, 65.
21. *Lumen Gentium,* 59.
22. *Lumen Gentium,* 53.

—*mother* of the Church, since she is Mother of him who, from the first moment of the Incarnation in her virginal womb, unites to himself as Head his Mystical Body which is the Church;[23]

—*figure* of the Church, being virgin, spouse and mother, for the Church is virgin because its fidelity is whole and pure, spouse by its union with Christ, mother of the innumerable children of God;[24]

—virtuous *model* of the Church, which is inspired by her in the exercise of faith, hope and charity[25] and in apostolic work;[26]

—through her manifold acts of intercession, continuing to obtain the gifts of eternal salvation for the Church. By her maternal charity she cares for the brethren of her Son on their pilgrim way. Therefore the Blessed Virgin is invoked by the Church with the titles of *Advocate, Auxiliatrix, Adjutrix* and *Mediatrix*;[27]

—assumed body and soul into heaven, "the *eschatological* image and first flowering" of the Church[28] which sees and admires in her "that which she herself wholly desires and hopes to be"[29] finding in Mary "a sign of sure hope and solace."[30]

Post-Conciliar Marian Developments

10. During the years immediately following the Council, work by the Holy See, by many episcopal conferences, and by famous scholars, illustrating the teaching of the Council and responding to the problems that were emerging gradually, gave a new relevance and vigor to reflection on the Mother of the Lord.

The Apostolic Exhortation *Marialis Cultus* and the Encyclical *Redemptoris Mater* have made a particular contribution to this Mariological reawakening.

---

23. Paul VI, *Allocutio tertia SS. Concili periode exacta* (November 21, 1964): *AAS* 56 (1964), 1014–1018.

24. Cf. ibid., 64.

25. Cf. ibid., 53, 63, 65.

26. Cf. ibid., 65.

27. Cf. *Lumen Gentium,* 62.

28. Cf. *Lumen Gentium,* 68.

29. *Sacrosanctum Concilium,* 103.

30. *Lumen Gentium,* 68.

This is not the place to list completely all the various sectors of post-conciliar reflection on Mary. However, it seems useful to illustrate some of them in summary as example and stimulus to further research.

11. Biblical exegesis has opened new frontiers for Mariology, ever dedicating more attention to the inter-testamental literature. Some texts of the Old Testament, and especially the New Testament parts of Luke and Matthew on the infancy of Jesus, and the Johannine pericopes, have been the object of continuous and deep study, the results of which have reinforced the biblical basis of Mariology and considerably enriched its themes.

12. In the field of dogmatic theology, the study of Mariology has contributed in the post-conciliar debate to a more suitable illustration of dogmas brought about in: the discussion on original sin (dogma of the Immaculate Conception), on the Incarnation of the Word (dogma of the virginal conception of Christ, dogma of the divine maternity), on grace and freedom (doctrine of the cooperation of Mary in the work of salvation), on the ultimate destiny of man (dogma of the Assumption). This has required critical study of the historical circumstances in which these dogmas were defined, and of the language in which they were formulated, understanding them in the light of the insights of biblical exegesis, of a more rigorous understanding of Tradition, of the questions raised by the human sciences and with a refutation of unfounded objections.

13. The study of Mariology has taken great interest in the problems connected with devotion to the Blessed Virgin. There has been research into the historical roots of the devotion,[31] study of its doctrinal foundation, of its place in the "one Christian devotion,"[32] evaluation of its liturgical expression and its multiple manifestations of popular piety, and a deepening appreciation of their mutual relationship.

14. Mariology has also been especially considered in the field of ecumenism. With regard to the Churches of the Christian East, John Paul II has underlined "how profoundly the Catholic Church, the Orthodox Church and the ancient Churches of the East feel united by love and

---

31. Six International Marian Congresses, organized by the *Pontificia Accademia Mariana Internazionale,* held between 1967 and 1987, systematically studied manifestations of Marian piety from the first to the 20th centuries.

32. Paul VI, Apostolic Exhortation *Marialis Cultus* (February 2, 1974). Intr.: *AAS* 66 (1974), 114.

praise of the *'Theotókos'"*,[33] on his part, Dimitrios I, the Ecumenical Patriarch, has noted that "our two sister Churches have maintained throughout the centuries unextinguished the flame of devotion to the most venerated person of the all-holy Mother of God,"[34] and he went on to say that "the subject of Mariology should occupy a central position in the theological dialogue between our Churches...for the full establishment of our ecclesial communion."[35]

With regard to the Reformation Churches, the post-conciliar period has been characterized by dialogue and by the thrust toward mutual understanding. This has brought an end to the centuries-old mistrust, and has led to a better knowledge of respective doctrinal positions; it has also led to a number of common initiatives in research. Thus, at least in some cases, it has been possible to understand both the dangers in "obscuring" the person of Mary in ecclesial life, and also the necessity of holding to data of revelation.[36]

During these years, in the area of interreligious discourse, Mariology has studied Judaism, source of the "Daughter of Sion." It has also studied Islam, in which Mary is venerated as holy Mother of Christ.

15. Post-conciliar Mariology has given renewed attention to anthropology. The popes have repeatedly presented Mary of Nazareth as the supreme expression of human freedom in the cooperation of man with God, who "in the sublime event of the Incarnation of his Son, entrusted himself to the ministry, the free and active ministry of woman."[37]

In the convergence of the data of faith and the data of the anthropological sciences, when these turn their attention to Mary of Nazareth, one understands more clearly that the Virgin is both the highest historical realization of the Gospel,[38] and the woman who, through her self-control, her sense of responsibility, her openness to others and to the

---

33. *Redemptoris Mater,* 31.

34. Dimitrios I, *Homily given on December 7, 1987, during the celebration of Vespers at St. Mary Major (Rome): L'Osservatore Romano* (Eng. Ed. Dec. 21–28, 1987), p. 6.

35. Ibid., 6.

36. The *Ecumenical Directory* provides guidelines for a Mariological formation which is attentive to ecumenical needs: Secretariat for Promoting Christian Unity, *Spiritus Domini* (April 16, 1970): *AAS* 62 (1970), 705–724.

37. *Redemptoris Mater,* 46.

38. Cf. III Conferencia General del Episcopado Latino-Americano (Puebla, 1979), *La evangelizacion en el presente y en el futuro de America Latina* (Bogota, 1979), 282.

spirit of service, her strength and her love, is the most completely real-ized on the human level.

For example, the necessity has been noted:

—of drawing out the relevance of the human reality of the Virgin to people in our own time, stressing the fact that she is a historical person, a humble Jewish girl;

—of showing forth the permanent and universal human values of Mary in such a way that discourse about her throws light on discourse about man.

In this context, the subject of "Mary and women" has been treated many times, but it is susceptible of many different approaches; it is a long way from being exhausted and from yielding its finest fruits, and it awaits further developments.

16. New themes and treatments from new points of view have emerged in post-conciliar Mariology: the relationship between the Holy Spirit and Mary; the problem of inculturation of Marian doctrine and forms of Marian piety; the value of the *via pulchritudinis* for ad-vancing in knowledge of Mary and the capacity of the Virgin to stimu-late the highest expressions of literature and art; the discovery of the significance of Mary in relation to some urgent pastoral needs in our time (pro-life, the option for the poor, the proclamation of the Word...); the revaluation of the "Marian dimension of the life of a dis-ciple of Christ."[39]

The Encyclical "Redemptoris Mater" of John Paul II

17. In the wake of *Lumen Gentium* and of the magisterial documents which followed the Council comes the Encyclical *Redemptoris Mater* of John Paul II, which confirms the Christological and ecclesiological ap-proach to Mariology that clearly reveals the wide range of its contents.

Through a prolonged meditation on the exclamation of Elizabeth, "Blessed is she who believed" (Lk 1:45), the Holy Father thoroughly studies the multiple aspects of the "heroic faith" of the Virgin, which he considers "a kind of key which unlocks for us the innermost reality of Mary,"[40] and he illustrates the "maternal presence" of the Virgin in the

---

39. *Redemptoris Mater,* 45.
40. Ibid., 19.

pilgrimage of faith according to two lines of thought, one theological, the other pastoral and spiritual:

—the Virgin was actively present in the life of the Church—at its beginning (the mystery of the Incarnation), in its being set up (the mystery of Cana and of the cross) and in its manifestation (the mystery of Pentecost)—she is an "active presence" throughout the Church's history, being "at the center of pilgrim Church,"[41] performing a multiple function: of cooperation in the birth of the faithful in the life of grace, of exemplarity in the following of Christ, of "maternal mediation";[42]

—the deed by which Christ entrusted the disciple to the Mother and the Mother to the disciple (cf. Jn 19:25–27) has established the very closest relationship between Mary and the Church. The will of the Lord has been to assign a "Marian note" to the physiognomy of the Church, its pilgrimage, its pastoral activity; and in the spiritual life of each disciple, says the Holy Father, a "Marian dimension" is inherent.[43]

Redemptoris Mater as whole can be considered the encyclical of the "maternal and active presence" of Mary in the life of the Church:[44] in the pilgrimage of faith, in the worship of the Lord, in the work of evangelization, in progressive configuration to Christ, in ecumenical endeavor.

The Contribution of Mariology to Theological Research

18. The history of theology shows that an understanding of the mystery of the Virgin contributes to a more profound understanding of the mystery of Christ, of the Church and of the vocation of man.[45] Similarly, the close link of the Virgin with Christ, with the Church and man throws light on the truth about Mary of Nazareth.

19. In Mary, in fact, "everything is relative to Christ."[46] In consequence, "only in the mystery of Christ is her mystery fully made clear."[47] The more the Church deepens her appreciation of the mystery

---

41. Title of part II of the Encyclical *Redemptoris Mater.*
42. Title of part III of the Encyclical *Redemptoris Mater*.
43. Cf. *Redemptoris Mater,* 45–46.
44. Cf. ibid., 1, 25.
45. Cf. *Lumen Gentium,* 65.
46. *Marialis Cultus,* 25.
47. *Redemptoris Mater,* 4; cf. ibid., 19.

of Christ, the more it understands the singular dignity of the Mother of the Lord and her role in the history of salvation. But, in a certain measure, the contrary is also true: the Church, through Mary, that "exceptional witness to the mystery of Christ,"[48] has deepened its understanding of the mystery of the kenosis of the "Son of God" (Lk 3:38; cf. Phil 2:5–8) who became in Mary "Son of Adam" (Lk 3:38), and has recognized more clearly the historical roots of the "Son of David" (cf. Lk 1:32), his place among the Hebrew people, his membership in the "poor of Yahweh."

20. Everything about Mary—privileges, mission, destiny—is also intrinsically referable to the mystery of the Church. In the measure in which the mystery of the Church is understood the more distinctly does the mystery of Mary become apparent. Contemplating Mary, the Church recognizes its origins, its intimate nature, its mission of grace, its destiny to glory, and the pilgrimage of faith which it must follow.[49]

21. Finally, in Mary everything is referable to the human race, in all times and all places. She has a universal and permanent value. She is "our true sister,"[50] and "because she belongs to the offspring of Adam she is one with all human beings in their need for salvation."[51] Mary does not disappoint the expectations of contemporary man. Because she is the "perfect follower of Christ"[52] and the woman most completely realized as a person, she is a perennial source of fruitful inspiration.

For the disciples of the Lord the Virgin is a great symbol: a person who achieves the most intimate aspirations of her intellect, of her will and of her heart, being open through Christ in the Spirit to the transcendence of God in filial dedication, taking root in history through hardworking service of others.

As Paul VI wrote, "Contemplated in the episodes of the gospels and in the reality which she already possesses in the city of God, the Blessed Virgin Mary offers a calm vision and a reassuring word to modern man, torn as he often is between anguish and hope, defeated by the sense of his own limitations and assailed by limitless aspirations, troubled in his mind and divided in his heart, uncertain before the riddle of death, op-

---

48. Ibid., 27.
49. Cf. ibid., 2.
50. *Marialis Cultus,* 56.
51. *Lumen Gentium,* 53.
52. *Marialis Cultus,* 35.

pressed by loneliness while yearning for fellowship, a prey to boredom and disgust. She shows forth the victory of hope over anguish, of fellowship over solitude, of peace over anxiety, of joy and beauty over boredom and disgust, of eternal vision over earthly ones, of life over death."[53]

22. "Among all believers she is like a 'mirror' in which are reflected in the most profound and limpid way 'the mighty works of God' (Acts 2:11),"[54] which theology has the task of illustrating. The dignity and importance of Mariology, therefore, derive from the dignity and importance of Christology, from the value of ecclesiology and pneumatology, from the meaning of supernatural anthropology and from eschatology: Mariology is closely connected with these tracts.

---

53. Ibid., 57.
54. *Redemptoris Mater,* 25.

II

THE VIRGIN MARY IN INTELLECTUAL
AND SPIRITUAL FORMATION

Research in Mariology

23. The data expounded in the first part of this Letter show that Mariology is alive and active in relevant questions in matters doctrinal and pastoral. However, it is necessary that the study of Mariology, together with attention to the pastoral problems which are emerging gradually, attend to rigorous research, conducted according to scientific criteria.

24. The words of the Council apply: "Sacred theology rests on the written Word of God, together with sacred Tradition, as its primary and perpetual foundation. By scrutinizing in the light of faith all truth stored up in the mystery of Christ, theology is most powerfully strengthened and constantly rejuvenated by that word."[55] The study of the sacred Scriptures, therefore, must be the soul of Mariology.[56]

25. Further, the study of Tradition is essential to research in Mariology because, as Vatican II teaches, "sacred Tradition and sacred Scripture form one sacred deposit of the Word of God, which is committed to the Church."[57] The study of Tradition shows how particularly fruitful in quality and quantity is the Marian patrimony of the various liturgies and of the Fathers of the Church.

26. Research into Scripture and Tradition, conducted according to the most fruitful methods and with the most reliable instruments of critical enquiry, must be guided by the magisterium, since "the task of authentically interpreting the word God, whether written or handed on, has

---

55. *Dei Verbum,* 24.
56. Cf. ibid., 24; *Optatam Totius,* 16.
57. *Dei Verbum,* 10.

been entrusted exclusively to the living teaching office of the Church."[58] This research must also integrate and be strengthened by the more secure fruits of learning in anthropology and the human sciences.

The Teaching of Mariology

27. Considering the importance of the Virgin in the history of salvation and in the life of the People of God, and after promptings of Vatican Council II and of the popes, it would be unthinkable that the teaching of Mariology be obscured today. It is necessary, therefore, that it be given its just place in seminaries and theological faculties.

28. Such teaching, consisting of a "systematic treatment" will be:

a) organic, that is, inserted adequately in the program of studies of the theological curriculum;

b) complete, so that the person of the Virgin be considered in the whole history of salvation, that is, in her relation to God; to Christ, the Word incarnate, Savior and Mediator; to the Holy Spirit, the Sanctifier and Giver of life; to the Church, sacrament of salvation; to man—in his origins and his development in the life of grace, and his destiny to glory;

c) suited to the various types of institution (centers of religious culture, seminaries, theological faculties...) and to the level of the students: future priests and teachers of Mariology, animators of Marian piety in the dioceses, those who are responsible for formation in the religious life, catechists, those who give conferences, and the many who want to deepen their knowledge of Mary.

29. Teaching thus given will avoid one-sided presentations of the figure and mission of Mary, presentations which are detrimental to the whole vision of her mystery. Sound teaching will be a stimulus to deep research—in seminaries and through the writing of license and doctoral theses—into the sources of revelation and the documents. Mariological study can also profit from interdisciplinary teaching.

30. It is necessary, therefore, that every center of theological study—according to its proper physiognomy—plan that in its *Ratio studiorum* the teaching of Mariology be included, having the characteristics listed above, and, consequently, with the teachers of Mariology being properly qualified.

---

58. Cf. ibid., 10.

31. With regard to this latter point, we would draw attention to the norms of the Apostolic Constitution *Sapientia Christiana* which provide for licenses and doctorates in theology, specializing in Mariology.[59]

Mariology and Pastoral Service

32. Like every other theological discipline, Mariology has a precious contribution to make to pastoral life. *Marialis Cultus* affirms that "devotion to the Blessed Virgin, subordinated to worship of the divine Savior and in connection with it, also has great pastoral effectiveness and constitutes a force for renewing Christian living."[60] Also, Mariology is called to make its contribution to the work of evangelization.[61]

33. Mariological research, teaching and pastoral service tend to promotion of the authentic Marian piety which should characterize the life of every Christian, especially those who are dedicated to theological studies and who are preparing for the priesthood.

The Congregation for Catholic Education draws the attention of seminary educators to the necessity of promoting an authentic Marian piety among seminarians who will one day be principal workers in the pastoral life of the Church.

Vatican II, treating the necessity of seminarians having a profound spiritual life, recommended that seminarians "should love and honor the most Blessed Virgin Mary, who was given as a mother to his disciple by Christ Jesus as he hung dying on the cross."[62]

For its part, this Congregation, conforming to the thought of the Council, has underlined many times the value of Marian piety in the formation of seminarians:

---

59. This Congregation has been pleased to note the dissertations for the license or doctorate in theology which have treated Mariological themes. Persuaded of the importance of such studies and desiring their increase, in 1979 the Congregation instituted the "license or doctorate in theology with specialization in Mariology" (cf. John Paul II, Apostolic Constitution *Sapientia Christiana* (April 15, 1979), Appendix II ad art. 64 "Ordinationum," n. 12: *AAS* 71 (1979), 520. Two centers offer this specialization: the Pontifical "Marianum" Faculty of Theology in Rome, and the International Marian Research Institute, University of Dayton, Ohio, U.S.A. which is linked to the "Marianum."

60. *Marialis Cultus,* 57.

61. Cf. *Sapientia Christiana,* 3.

62. *Optatam Totius,* 8.

—in the *Ratio fundamentalis institutionis sacerdotalis,* the Congregation requests the seminarian "to have a fervent love for the Virgin Mary, Mother of Christ, who was in a special way associated with the work of redemption";[63]

—in the *circular letter concerning some of the more urgent aspects of spiritual formation in seminaries* the Congregation noted that "there is nothing better than true devotion to Mary, conceived as an ever more complete following of her example, to introduce one to the joy of believing,"[64] which is so important for anyone who will spend the rest of his life in the continual exercise of faith.

63. Congregatio Pro Institutione Catholica, *Ratio fundamentalis institutionis sacerdotalis* (Rome, 1985), 54 e.

64. Id., *Circular Letter Concerning Some of the More Urgent Aspects of Spiritual Formation in Seminaries,* II, 4.

CONCLUSION

The Code of Canon Law, treating of the formation of candidates for the priesthood, recommends devotion to the Blessed Virgin Mary so that, nourished by the exercises of piety, the students may acquire the spirit of prayer and be strengthened in their vocation.[65]

34. With this letter the Congregation for Catholic Education wishes to reaffirm the necessity of furnishing seminarians and students of all centers of ecclesiastical studies with Mariological formation which embraces study, devotion and lifestyle. They must:

a) acquire a *complete and exact knowledge* of the doctrine of the Church about the Virgin Mary, which enables them to distinguish between true and false devotion, and to distinguish authentic doctrine from its deformations arising from excess or neglect, and above all which discloses to them the way to understand and to contemplate the supreme beauty of the glorious Mother of Christ;

b) nourish an *authentic love* for the Mother of the Savior and Mother of mankind, which expresses itself in genuine forms of devotion and is led to "the imitation of her virtues,"[66] above all to a decisive commitment to live according to the commandments of God and to do his will (cf. Mt 7:21; Jn 15:14);

c) develop the *capacity to communicate* such love to the Christian people through speech, writing and example, so that their Marian piety may be promoted and cultivated.

35. There are numerous advantages to be derived from an adequate Mariological formation in which the ardor of faith and the commitment to study are harmoniously composed:

---

65. 5. Cf. *Code of Canon Law,* can. 246, par. 3.
66. *Lumen Gentium,* 67.

—on the *intellectual level,* so that the truth about God, about man, about Christ and about the Church are understood the more in understanding the "truth about Mary";

—on the *spiritual level,* so that such information will help a Christian to welcome the Mother of Jesus and "bring her into everything that makes up his inner life";[67]

—on the *pastoral level,* so that the Mother of the Lord may be strongly felt as a presence of grace among the Christian people.

36. The study of Mariology holds as its ultimate aim the acquisition of a sound Marian spirituality, an essential aspect of Christian spirituality. On his pilgrim way to the measure of the stature of the fullness of Christ (Eph 4:13), knowing the mission which God has entrusted to the Virgin in the history of salvation and in the life of the Church, the Christian takes her as "Mother and teacher of the spiritual life";[68] with her and like her, in the light of the Incarnation and of Easter, he impresses on his very existence a decisive orientation toward God through Christ in the Spirit, in order to express by his life in the Church the radical message of the Good News, especially the commandment of love (cf. Jn 15:12).

Your Eminence, Your Excellencies, Reverend Rectors of Seminaries, Reverend Presidents and Deans of Ecclesiastical Faculties, we trust that these brief guidelines will be responsibly received by teachers and students and will bring forth welcome fruits.

Wishing you the abundance of God's blessing, we remain,
Yours devotedly in Our Lord,

> William Cardinal Baum
> *Prefect*
>
> Antonio M. Javierre Ortas
> *Titular Archbishop of Meta*
> *Secretary*

---

67. *Redemptoris Mater,* 45.
68. Cf. *Marialis Cultus,* 21; *Collectio missarum de b. Maria Virgine,* form. 32.

ON THE DIGNITY AND VOCATION OF WOMEN

Mulieris Dignitatem

Apostolic Letter of Pope John Paul II
August 15, 1988

INTRODUCTION

Historical Perspectives

Pope John Paul II wrote this apostolic letter because of the importance of women's issues today. The pope points out that questions concerning the dignity and vocation of woman have been "a subject of constant human and Christian reflection" (*MD* 1). He refers to the efforts of Pius XII, John XIII and Paul VI to promote woman's dignity and responsibility. More recently, the 1987 synod of bishops took up issues relating to women in light of twenty years of post-Vatican II teaching. The synod had asked "for a further study of the anthropological and theological bases that are needed in order to solve the problems connected with the meaning and dignity of being a woman and of being a man" (*MD* 1).

The proclamation of the Marian Year lent itself to further study of woman, since Mary is the "woman" of the Bible in closest relationship to the Incarnation (cf. Gn 3:15; Jn 2:4; 19:16.). All elements converged: the study of the Church twenty years after Vatican II, the study of Mary within the Church, and the study of women in the Church and in the world.

Mulieris Dignitatem has nine major sections. It begins by situating the signs of the times and the Marian Year. It then focuses on the woman, Mary, Mother of God. By looking at Mary's union with God and the results of this union, it shows a basis for understanding what the human person can come to be.

This emphasis on the human person has been a hallmark of John Paul II's thought. From his days as a professor at the University of Lublin, he has developed a distinctive approach to this subject. It is based on a synthesis of Thomistic philosophy and the modern approach

361

to human experience known as phenomenology. As pope, he further developed this in his "theology of the body," presented in a series of general audience talks spanning five years.

In *Mulieris Dignitatem* the pope further develops this theology of the body. The document primarily treats the mystery of woman in this light, so the Marian elements are secondary. The pope brings them in to illustrate the great dignity of woman in light of Mary's unique vocation. In so doing, he also develops a deeper appreciation of Mary.

The Teaching

John Paul II's style of writing is more like a meditation than a statement of doctrine. This reflects his personalist approach, but does not diminish the teaching's magisterial character. He focuses on the human person in light of the mystery of Christ. In keeping with this emphasis, he points out that any discussion about woman first involves studying what it means to be a human being. He specifies, "This eternal *truth about the human being—* man and woman—a truth which is immutably fixed in human experience—*at the same time constitutes the mystery which only in 'the incarnate Word takes on light...* [since] Christ fully reveals man to himself and makes his supreme calling clear...' (*GS* 22)" (*MD* 2).

Most of the Marian content is found in chapters two and four. In chapter two, Mary is placed within the key event of the mystery of salvation: the Incarnation. "A woman is to be found at the center of this salvific event" (*MD* 3). Mary is seen in the context of the whole human family. She represents all humanity. Yet her union with God was totally unique, for she was the Mother of God. She accepted this vocation in full freedom, and in meditating on her consent, the pope's personalism comes to the fore. He says that the annunciation is "clearly interpersonal in character: it is a dialogue." In expressing her *fiat,* Mary "feels the need to express her personal relationship to the gift that has been revealed to her, saying: 'Behold, I am the handmaid of the Lord' (Lk 1:38)" (*MD* 5). John Paul then develops the idea that Mary's vocation was a vocation to service, in union with that of Christ. This is a favorite theme for him, which he spoke about in *Redemptor Hominis* (cf. n. 21).

In chapter four the pope develops the Eve-Mary parallel. This ancient theme, going back to St. Justin Martyr and especially St. Irenaeus, has a long history in the Catholic tradition. Yet it seems fair to say that John Paul has developed it in an even richer way by placing it within the context of the theology of the body. His rereading of the Book of Genesis shows that the tragedy of the first sin disturbed the original relationship between man and woman. Redemption overcomes this: "In Christ the mutual opposition between man and woman—which is the inheritance of original sin—is essentially overcome" (*MD* 11). The pope sees Mary as the expression of the fullness of womanhood, as God originally intended her to be, unmarred by sin. "In Mary, Eve discovers the nature of the true dignity of woman, of feminine humanity" (*MD* 11). The pope's reflections on this open up a new avenue of thought which deserves further study.

Mary is the fulfillment of the human person's creation in the image and likeness of God. The document presents the doctrine of creation, especially the creation of the human person, as person-communion-gift. The anthropomorphism of scriptural language is explained: "*God speaks in human language,* using human concepts and images..." (*MD* 8). The document states that the human person is "'like' God: created in his image and likeness. But then, *God too* is in some measure 'like man,' and precisely because of this likeness, he can be humanly known" (*MD* 8). The document goes on to speak about human relationality and how human generation compares to the relations in the Trinity.

John Paul II also speaks of the vocation of woman as mother and virgin. Mary unites both virginity and motherhood in her person. The pope discusses motherhood in relation to the covenant, stating that through Mary "God begins a New Covenant with humanity." This gives motherhood a certain universal aspect. "Each and every time that *motherhood* is repeated in human history, it is always *related to the covenant* which God established with the human race through the motherhood of the Mother of God" (*MD* 19).

The document also considers virginity for the sake of the kingdom as a motherhood according to the Spirit. It puts this in the context of the Church as Bride of Christ; this mystery, which is a gift, illumines our relationship to Christ.

Today

Ultimately, the divine and human mystery and the gift are love. Hence woman—in herself and in what she represents in and to the Church—in the context of this document, is an answer of love for the Church, the world, and for God.

TOPICAL OUTLINE

1. Introduction

    A. A sign of the times: new awareness of woman's dignity (1)

    B. The Marian Year (2)

2. Woman-Mother of God *(Theotókos)*

    A. The Incarnation as God's response to the human spirit's search for him; Mary's role (3)

    B. Mary as the Mother of God (4)

    C. Mary's place within Christ's messianic service (5)

3. The image and likeness of God

    A. Man and woman in the creation account of Genesis (6)

    B. Person—communion—gift (7)

        1. Human personhood involves relationships and reflects the Trinity

        2. Interpersonal communion *(communio)*

        3. The gift of oneself

    C. The fatherhood of God and human language (8)

4. Eve—Mary

    A. The "beginning" and the sin (9)

        1. The mystery of sin in relation to the human person as the image of God

ON THE DIGNITY
AND VOCATION OF WOMEN

Mulieris Dignitatem

Apostolic Letter of the Supreme Pontiff John Paul II
on the Occasion of the Marian Year, August 15, 1988

Venerable Brothers and dear Sons and Daughters,
Health and the Apostolic Blessing,

I

INTRODUCTION

A Sign of the Times

1. The dignity and the vocation of women—a subject of constant human and Christian reflection—have gained exceptional prominence in recent years. This can be seen, for example, *in the statements of the Church's Magisterium* present in various documents of the *Second Vatican Council,* which declares in its *Closing Message:* "The hour is coming, in fact has come, when the vocation of women is being acknowledged in its fullness, the hour in which women acquire in the world an influence, an effect and a power never hitherto achieved. That is why, at this moment when the human race is undergoing so deep a transformation, women imbued with a spirit of the Gospel can do so

much to aid humanity in not falling."[1] *This message* sums up what had already been expressed in the Council's teaching, specifically in the Pastoral Constitution *Gaudium et Spes*[2] and in the Decree on the Apostolate of the Laity *Apostolicam Actuositatem*.[3]

Similar thinking had already been put forth in the period before the Council, as can be seen in a number of Pope *Pius XII's* discourses[4] and in the Encyclical *Pacem in Terris* of Pope *John XXIII*.[5] After the Second Vatican Council, my predecessor *Paul VI* showed the relevance of this "sign of the times" when he conferred the title "Doctor of the Church" upon St. Teresa of Jesus and St. Catherine of Siena,[6] and likewise when, at the request of the 1971 Assembly of the Synod of Bishops, he set up *a special commission* for the study of contemporary problems concerning the *"effective promotion of the dignity and the responsibility of women."*[7] In one of his discourses Paul VI said: "Within Christianity, more than in any other religion, and since its very beginning, women have had a special dignity, of which the New Testament shows us many important aspects...; it is evident that women are meant to form part of the living and working structure of Christianity in so prominent a manner that perhaps not all their potentialities have yet been made clear."[8]

The Fathers of the recent Assembly of the Synod of Bishops (October 1987), which was devoted to "The Vocation and Mission of the Laity in the Church and in the World Twenty Years after the Second Vatican

---

1. The Council's Message to Women (December 8, 1965): *AAS* 58 (1966), 13–14.

2. Cf. Second Vatican Ecumenical Council, Pastoral Constitution on the Church in the Modern World *Gaudium et Spes,* 8, 9, 60.

3. Cf. Second Vatican Ecumenical Council, Decree on the Apostolate of the Laity *Apostolicam Actuositatem,* 9.

4. Cf. Pius XII, Address to Italian Women (October 21, 1945): *AAS* 37 (1945), 284–295; Address to the World Union of Catholic Women's Organizations (April 24, 1952): *AAS* 44 (1952), 420–424; Address to the participants in the XIV International Meeting of the World Union of Catholic Women's Organizations (September 29,1957): *AAS* 49 (1957), 906–922.

5. Cf. John XXIII, Encyclical Letter *Pacem in Terris* (April 11, 1963): *AAS* 55 (1963), 267–268.

6. Proclamation of St. Teresa of Jesus as a "Doctor of the Universal Church" (September 27, 1970): *AAS* 62 (1970), 590–596; Proclamation of St. Catherine of Siena as a "Doctor of the Universal Church" (October 4, 1970): *AAS* 62 (1970), 673–678.

7. Cf. *AAS* 65 (1973), 284f.

8. Paul VI, Address to participants at the National Meeting of the Centro Italiano Femminile (December 6, 1976): *Insegnamenti de Paolo VI,* XIV (1976), 1017.

Council," once more dealt with the dignity and vocation of women. One of their recommendations was for a further study of the anthropological and theological bases that are needed in order to solve the problems connected with the meaning and dignity of being a woman and of being a man. It is a question of understanding the reason for and the consequences of the Creator's decision that the human being should always and only exist as a woman or a man. It is only by beginning from these bases, which make it possible to understand the greatness of the dignity and vocation of women, that one is able to speak of their active presence in the Church and in society.

This is what I intend to deal with in this document. The Post-Synodal Exhortation, which will be published later, will present proposals of a pastoral nature on the place of women in the Church and in society. On this subject the Fathers offered some important reflections, after they had taken into consideration the testimonies of the lay auditors—both women and men—from the particular Churches throughout the world.

The Marian Year

2. The last Synod took place *within the Marian Year,* which gives special thrust to the consideration of this theme, as the Encyclical *Redemptoris Mater* points out.[9] This encyclical develops and updates the Second Vatican Council's teaching contained in Chapter VIII of the Dogmatic Constitution on the Church *Lumen Gentium.* The title of this chapter is significant: *"The Blessed Virgin Mary, the Mother of God, in the Mystery of Christ and of the Church."* Mary—the "woman" of the Bible (cf. Gn 3:15; Jn 2:4; 19:16)—intimately belongs to the salvific mystery of Christ, and is therefore also present in a special way in the mystery of the Church. Since "the Church is in Christ as a sacrament...of intimate union with God and of the unity of the whole human race,"[10] the special presence of the Mother of God in the mystery of the Church makes us think *of the exceptional link between this "woman" and the whole human family.* It is a question here of every man and woman, all

---

9. Cf. Encyclical Letter *Redemptoris Mater* (March 25, 1987), 46: *AAS* 79 (1987), 424f.

10. Second Vatican Ecumenical Council, Dogmatic Constitution on the Church *Lumen Gentium,* 1.

the sons and daughters of the human race, in whom from generation to generation a *fundamental inheritance* is realized, the inheritance that belongs to all humanity and that is linked with the mystery of the biblical "beginning": "God created man in his own image, in the image of God he created him; male and female he created them" (Gn 1:27).[11]

This eternal *truth about the human being*—man and woman—a truth which is immutably fixed in human experience—*at the same time constitutes the mystery which only in "the incarnate Word takes on light*...[since] Christ fully reveals man to himself and makes his supreme calling clear," as the Council teaches.[12] In this "revealing of man to himself," do we not need to find a special place for that "woman" who was the Mother of Christ? Cannot the *"message" of Christ,* contained in the Gospel, which has as its background the whole of Scripture, both the Old and the New Testament, say much to the Church and to humanity about the dignity of women and their vocation?

This is precisely what is meant to be the common thread running throughout the present document, which fits into the broader context of the Marian Year, as we approach the end of the second millennium after Christ's birth and the beginning of the third. And it seems to me that the best thing is to *give this text the style and character of a meditation.*

---

11. An illustration of the anthropological and theological significance of the "beginning" can be seen in the first part of the Wednesday general audience addresses dedicated to the "Theology of the Body," beginning September 5, 1979: *Insegnamenti* II, 2 (1979), 234–236.

12. Second Vatican Ecumenical Council, Pastoral Constitution on the Church in the Modern World *Gaudium et Spes,* 22.

II
WOMAN—MOTHER OF GOD
(THEOTÓKOS)

Union with God

3. "When the time had fully come, *God sent forth his son, born of woman.*" With these words of his Letter to the Galatians (4:4), the Apostle Paul links together the principal moments which essentially determine the fulfillment of the mystery "pre-determined in God" (cf. Eph 1:9). The Son, the Word, one in substance with the Father, becomes man, born of a woman, at "the fullness of time." This event leads *to the turning point* of man's history on earth, understood as salvation history. It is significant that St. Paul does not call the Mother of Christ by her own name "Mary," but calls her "woman": this coincides with the words of the proto-evangelium in the Book of Genesis (cf. 3:15). She is that "woman" who is present in the central salvific event which marks the "fullness of time": this event is realized in her and through her.

Thus there begins *the central event, the key event in the history of salvation:* the Lord's Paschal Mystery. Perhaps it would be worthwhile to reconsider it from the point of view of man's spiritual history, understood in the widest possible sense, and as this history is expressed through the different world religions. Let us recall at this point the words of the Second Vatican Council: *"People look to the various religions for answers* to those profound mysteries of the human condition which, today, even as in olden times, deeply stir the human heart: What is a human being? What is the meaning and purpose of our life? What is goodness and what is sin? What gives rise to our sorrows, and to what intent? Where lies the path to true happiness? What is the truth about death, judgment and retribution beyond the grave? What, finally, is *that ultimate and unutterable mystery which engulfs our being,* and from which we take our origin and toward which we move?"[13] From ancient times down to the present, there has existed among different peoples a certain perception of that hidden power which is present in the course of things and in the events of human life; at times, indeed, recognition can be found of a Supreme Divinity or even a Supreme Father."[14]

Against the background of this broad panorama, which testifies to the aspirations of the human spirit in search of God—at times as it were "groping its way" (cf. Acts 17:27)—the "fullness of time" spoken of in Paul's letter emphasizes *the response of God himself,* "in whom we live and move and have our being" (cf. Acts 17:28). This is the God who "in many and various ways spoke of old to our fathers by the prophets, but in these last days has spoken to us by a Son" (Heb 1:1–2). The sending of this Son, one in substance with the Father, as a man "born of woman," constitutes the culminating and *definitive point of God's self-revelation to humanity.* This self-revelation is *salvific in character,* as the Second Vatican Council teaches in another passage: "In his goodness and wisdom, God chose to reveal himself and to make known to us the hidden purpose of his will (cf. Eph 1:9) by which through Christ, the Word made flesh, man has access to the Father in the Holy Spirit and comes to share in the divine nature (cf. Eph 2:18; 2 Pt 1:4)."[15]

A woman is to be found at the *center of this salvific event.* The self-revelation of God, who is the inscrutable unity of the Trinity, is outlined *in the annunciation at Nazareth.* "Behold, you will conceive in your womb and bear a son, and you shall call his name Jesus. He will be great, and will be called the Son of the Most High...." "How shall this be, since I have no husband?" "The Holy Spirit will come upon you, and the power of the Most High will overshadow you; therefore the child to be born will be called holy, the Son of God.... For with God nothing will be impossible" (cf. Lk 1:31–37).[16]

---

13. Second Vatican Ecumenical Council, Declaration on the Relation of the Church to Non-Christian Religions *Nostra Aetate,* 1.

14. *Ibid.,* 2.

15. Second Vatican Ecumenical Council, Dogmatic Constitution on Divine Revelation *Dei Verbum,* 2.

16. Already according to the Fathers of the Church the first revelation of the Trinity in the New Testament took place in the annunciation. One reads in a homily attributed to St. Gregory Thaumaturgus: "You, O Mary, are resplendent with light in the sublime spiritual kingdom! In you the Father, who is without beginning and whose power has covered you, is glorified. In you the Son, whom you bore in the flesh, is adored. In you the Holy

It may be easy to think of this event *in the setting* of the *history of Israel,* the Chosen People of which Mary is a daughter, but it is also easy to think of it in the context of all the different ways in which humanity has always sought to answer the fundamental and definitive questions which most beset it. Do we not find in the annunciation at Nazareth the beginning of that definitive answer by which God *himself "attempts to calm people's hearts"?*[17] It is not just a matter here of God's words revealed through the prophets; rather with this response "the Word is truly made flesh" (cf. Jn 1:14). Hence *Mary* attains *a union with God that exceeds* all the expectations of the human spirit. It even exceeds the expectations of all Israel, in particular the daughters of this Chosen People, who, on the basis of the promise, could hope that one of their number would one day become the mother of the messiah. Who among them, however, could have imagined that the promised messiah would be "the Son of the Most High"? On the basis of the Old Testament's monotheistic faith such a thing was difficult to imagine. Only by the power of the Holy Spirit, who "overshadowed" her, was Mary able to accept what is "impossible with men, but not with God" (cf. Mk 10:27).

Theotókos

4. Thus the "fullness of time" manifests the extraordinary dignity of the "woman." On the one hand, this dignity consists *in the supernatural elevation to union with God* in Jesus Christ, which determines the ultimate finality of the existence of every person both on earth and in eternity. From this point of view, the "woman" is the representative and the archetype of the whole human race: she *represents the humanity* which belongs to all human beings, both men and women. On the other hand, however, the event at Nazareth highlights a form of union with the living God which can *only belong to the "woman,"* Mary: *the union between mother and son.* The Virgin of Nazareth truly becomes the Mother of God.

Spirit, who has brought about in your womb the birth of the great King, is celebrated. And it is thanks to you, O Full of grace, that the holy and consubstantial Trinity has been able to be known in the world" *(Hom. 2 in Annuntiat. Virg. Mariae: PG* 10, 1169). Cf. also St. Andrew of Crete, *In Annuntiat. B. Mariae: PG* 97, 909.

17. Cf. Second Vatican Ecumenical Council, Declaration on the Relation of the Church to Non-Christian Religions *Nostra Aetate,* 2.

This truth, which Christian faith has accepted from the beginning, was solemnly defined at the Council of Ephesus (431 A.D.).[18] In opposition to the opinion of Nestorius, who held that Mary was only the mother of the man Jesus, this Council emphasized the essential meaning of the motherhood of the Virgin Mary. At the moment of the annunciation, by responding with her *fiat,* Mary conceived a man who was the Son of God, of one substance with the Father. Therefore *she is truly the Mother of God, because motherhood concerns the whole person,* not just the body, nor even just human "nature." In this way the name *"Theotókos"*—Mother of God—became the name proper to the union with God granted to the Virgin Mary.

The particular union of the *"Theotókos"* with God—which fulfills in the most eminent manner the supernatural predestination to union with the Father which is granted to every human being *(filii in Filio)*—is a pure grace and, as such, *a gift of the Spirit.* At the same time, however, through her response of faith Mary exercises her free will and thus fully shares with her personal and feminine "I" in the event of the Incarnation. With her *fiat, Mary becomes the authentic subject* of that union with God which was realized in the mystery of the Incarnation of the Word, who is of one substance with the Father. All of God's action in human history at all times respects the free will of the human "I." And such was the case with the annunciation at Nazareth.

"To Serve Means to Reign"

5. This event is clearly *interpersonal in character:* it is a dialogue. We only understand it fully if we place the whole conversation between the angel and Mary in the context of the words: "full of grace."[19] The whole annunciation dialogue reveals the essential dimension of the event, namely, its *supernatural* dimension. Grace never casts nature aside or cancels it out, but rather perfects it and ennobles it *(kéchari-*

---

18. The theological doctrine on the Mother of God *(Theótokos),* held by many Fathers of the Church, and clarified and defined at the Council of Ephesus *(DS* 251) and at the Council of Chalcedon *(DS* 301), has been stated again by the Second Vatican Council in Chapter VIII of the Dogmatic Constitution on the Church *Lumen Gentium,* 52–69. Cf. Encyclical Letter *Redemptoris Mater,* 4, 31–32 and the notes 9, 78–83: *loc. cit.,* 365, 402–404.

19. Cf. Encyclical Letter *Redemptoris Mater,* 7–11 and the texts of the Fathers cited in note 21: *loc. cit.,* 367–373.

tôménê). Therefore *the "fullness of grace"* that was granted to the Virgin of Nazareth, with a view to the fact that she would become *"Theotókos,"* also *signifies the fullness of the perfection of "what is characteristic of woman,"* of *"what is feminine."* Here we find ourselves, in a sense, at the culminating point, the archetype, of the personal dignity of women.

When Mary responds to the words of the heavenly messenger with her *fiat,* she who is "full of grace" feels the need to express her personal relationship to the gift that has been revealed to her, saying: *"Behold, I am the handmaid of the Lord"* (Lk 1:38). This statement should not be deprived of its profound meaning, nor should it be diminished by artificially removing it from the overall context of the event and from the full content of the truth revealed about God and man. In the expression "handmaid of the Lord," one senses Mary's complete awareness of being a creature of God. The word "handmaid," near the end of the annunciation dialogue, is inscribed throughout the whole history of the Mother and the Son. In fact, this *Son,* who is the true and consubstantial "Son of the Most High," will often say of himself, especially at the culminating moment of his mission: "The Son of Man came not to be served but to serve" (Mk 10:45).

At all times Christ is aware of being "the servant of the Lord" according to the prophecy of Isaiah (cf. Is 42:1; 49:3, 6; 52:13) which includes the essential content of his messianic mission, namely, his awareness of being the Redeemer of the world. From the first moment of her divine motherhood, of her union with the Son whom "the Father sent into the world, that the world might be saved through him" (cf. Jn 3:17), *Mary takes her place within Christ's messianic service.*[20] It is precisely this service which constitutes the very foundation of that kingdom in which "to serve... means to reign."[21] Christ, the "Servant of the Lord," will show all people the royal dignity of service, the dignity which is joined in the closest possible way to the vocation of every person.

Thus, by considering the reality "Woman—Mother of God," we enter in a very appropriate way into this Marian Year meditation. *This reality* also *determines the essential horizon of reflection on the dignity and*

---

20. Cf. *ibid.,* 39–41: *loc. cit.,* 412–418.

21. Cf. Second Vatican Ecumenical Council, Dogmatic Constitution on the Church *Lumen Gentium,* 36.

the vocation of women. In anything we think, say or do concerning the dignity and the vocation of women, our thoughts, hearts and actions must not become detached from this horizon. The dignity of every human being and the vocation corresponding to that dignity find their definitive measure in *union with God.* Mary, the woman of the Bible, is the most complete expression of this dignity and vocation. For no human being, male or female, created in the image and likeness of God, can *in any* way attain fulfillment apart from this image and likeness.

III

THE IMAGE AND LIKENESS OF GOD

The Book of Genesis

6. Let us enter into the setting of the biblical "beginning." In it the revealed truth concerning man as "the image and likeness" of God constitutes the immutable *basis of all Christian anthropology.*[22] "God created man in his own image, in the image of God he created him; male and female he created them" (Gn 1:27). This concise passage contains the fundamental anthropological truths: man is the high point of the whole order of creation in the visible world; the human race, which takes its origin from the calling into existence of man and woman, crowns the whole work of creation; *both man and woman are human beings to an equal degree;* both are created *in God's image.* This image and likeness of God, which is essential for the human being, is passed on by the man and woman, as spouses and parents, to their descendants: "Be fruitful and multiply, and fill the earth and subdue it" (Gn 1:28). The Creator entrusts dominion over the earth to the human race, to all persons, to all men and women, who derive their dignity and vocation from the common "beginning."

In the Book of Genesis we find another description of the creation of man—man and woman (cf. 2:18–25)—to which we shall refer shortly. At this point, however, we can say that the biblical account puts forth the truth about the personal character of the human being. *Man is a person, man and woman equally so,* since both were created in the image and likeness of the personal God. What makes man like God is the fact

---

22. Cf. St. Irenaeus, *Adv. Haer;* V, 6, 1; V, 16, 2–3: *SCh.* 153, 72–81 and 216–221; St. Gregory of Nyssa, *De hom. op.* 16: *PG* 44, 180; *In Cant. Cant. Hom.* 2: *PG* 44, 805–808; St. Augustine, *In Ps.* 4, 8: *CCL* 38, 17.

that—unlike the whole world of other living creatures, including those endowed with senses *(animalia)*—man is also a rational being *(animal rationale).*[23] Thanks to this property, man and woman are able to "dominate" the other creatures of the visible world (cf. Gn 1:28).

The second description of the creation of man (cf. Gn 2:18–25) makes use of different language to express the truth about the creation of man, and especially of woman. In a sense the language is less precise, and, one might say, more descriptive and metaphorical—closer to the language of the myths known at the time. Nevertheless, we find no essential contradiction between the two texts. The text of Genesis 2:18–25 helps us to understand better what we find in the concise passage of Genesis 1:27–28. At the same time, if it is read together with the latter, it *helps us to understand even more profoundly* the fundamental *truth* which it contains *concerning man* created as man and woman in the image and likeness of God.

In the description found in Genesis 2:18–25, the woman is created by God "from the rib" of the man and is placed at his side as another "I"—as the companion of the man, who is alone in the surrounding world of living creatures and who finds in none of them a "helper" suitable for himself. Called into existence in this way, the woman is immediately recognized by the man as "flesh of his flesh and bone of his bones" (cf. Gn 2:23) and for this very reason she is called "woman." In biblical language this name indicates her essential identity with regard to man—'is-'issah—something which unfortunately modern languages in general are unable to express: "She shall be called woman *('issah)* because she was taken out of man *('is)"* (Gn 2:23).

The biblical text provides sufficient bases for recognizing the essential equality of man and woman from the point of view of their humanity.[24] From the very beginning, both are persons, unlike the other living beings in the world about them. *The woman is another "I" in a common humanity.* From the very beginning they appear as a "unity of the two":

---

23. "Persona est naturae rationalis individua substantia": Manlius Severinus Boethius, *Liber de persona et duabus naturis,* III: *PL* 64, 1343; cf. St. Thomas Aquinas, *Summa Theologiae,* Ia, q. 29, art. 1.

24. Among the Fathers of the Church who affirm the fundamental equality of man and woman before God cf. Origen, *In Iesu nave* IX, 9: *PG* 12, 878; Clement of Alexandria, *Paed.* 1, 4: *SCh.* 70, 128–131; St. Augustine, *Sermo* 51, II, 3: *PL* 38, 334–335.

and this signifies that the original solitude is overcome, the solitude in which man does not find "a helper fit for him" (Gn 2:20). Is it only a question here of a "helper" in activity, in "subduing the earth" (cf. Gn 1:28)? Certainly it is a matter of a life's companion, with whom, as a wife, the man can unite himself, becoming with her "one flesh" and for this reason leaving "his father and his mother" (cf. Gn 2:24). Thus in the same context as the creation of man and woman, the biblical account speaks of God's *instituting marriage* as an indispensable condition for the transmission of life to new generations, the transmission of life to which marriage and conjugal love are by their nature ordered: "Be fruitful and multiply, and fill the earth and subdue it" (Gn 1:28).

Person—Communion—Gift

7. By reflecting on the whole account found in Genesis 2:18–25, and by interpreting it in light of the truth about the image and likeness of God (cf. Gn 1:26–27), we can *understand* even *more fully what constitutes the personal character* of the human being, thanks to which both man and woman are like God. For every individual is made in the image of God, insofar as he or she is a rational and free creature capable of knowing God and loving him. Moreover, we read that man cannot exist "alone" (cf. Gn 2:18); he can exist only as a "unity of the two," and therefore *in relation to another human person*. It is a question here of a mutual relationship: man to woman and woman to man. Being a person in the image and likeness of God thus also involves existing in a relationship, in relation to the other "I." This is a prelude to the definitive self-revelation of the Triune God: a living unity in the communion of the Father, Son and Holy Spirit.

At the beginning of the Bible this is not yet stated directly. The whole Old Testament is mainly concerned with revealing the truth about the oneness and unity of God. Within this fundamental truth about God the New Testament will reveal the inscrutable mystery of God's inner life. *God,* who allows himself to be known by human beings through Christ, is the *unity of the Trinity:* unity in communion. In this way new light is also thrown on man's image and likeness to God, spoken of in the Book of Genesis. The fact that man "created as man and woman" is the image of God means not only that each of them individually is like God, as a rational and free being. It also means that man and woman, created as a "unity of the two" in their common humanity, are called to live in a communion of love, and in this way to mirror in the world the communion of love that is in God, through which the Three Persons love each other in the intimate mystery of the one divine life. The Father, Son and Holy Spirit, one God through the unity of the divinity, exist as persons through the inscrutable divine relationship. Only in this way can we understand the truth that God in himself is love (cf. 1 Jn 4:16).

The image and likeness of God in man, created as man and woman (in the analogy that can be presumed between Creator and creature), thus also expresses the "unity of the two" in a common humanity. This "unity of the two," which is a sign of interpersonal communion, *shows that the creation of man* is also marked by a certain likeness to the divine communion *("communio").* This likeness is a quality of the personal being of both man and woman, and is also a call and a task. The foundation of the whole *human "ethos"* is rooted in the image and likeness of God which the human being bears within himself from the beginning. Both the Old and New Testament will develop that "ethos," which reaches its apex in the *commandment of love.*[25]

In the "unity of the two," man and woman are called from the beginning not only to exist "side by side" or "together," but they are also called *to exist mutually "one for the other."*

This also explains the meaning of the "help" spoken of in Genesis 2:18–25: "I will make him *a helper fit for him."* The biblical context enables us to understand this in the sense that the woman must "help" the man—and in his turn he must help her—first of all by the very fact of their "being human persons." In a certain sense this enables man and woman to discover their humanity ever anew and to confirm its whole meaning. We can easily understand that—on this fundamental level—it is *a question of a "help" on the part of both, and at the same time a mutual "help."* To be human means to be called to interpersonal communion. The text of Genesis 2:18–25 shows that marriage is the first and, in a sense, the fundamental dimension of this call. But it is not the

---

25. St. Gregory of Nyssa states: "God is, above all, love and the fount of love. The great John says this: 'Love is of God' and 'God is love' (1 Jn 4:7–8). The Creator has impressed this character also on us. 'By this all men will know that you are my disciples, if you have love for one another' (Jn 13:35). Therefore, if this is not present, all the image becomes disfigured" *(De hom. op. 5: PG 44, 137).*

only one. The whole of human history unfolds within the context of this call. In this history, on the basis of the principle of mutually being "for" the other, in interpersonal "communion," there develops in humanity itself, in accordance with God's will, the integration of *what is "masculine" and what is "feminine."* The biblical texts, from Genesis onward, constantly enable us to discover the ground in which the truth about man is rooted, the solid and inviolable ground amid the many changes of human existence.

This truth also has to do with *the history of salvation.* In this regard a statement of the Second Vatican Council is especially significant. In the chapter on "The Community of Mankind" in the Pastoral Constitution *Gaudium et Spes,* we read: "The Lord Jesus, when he prayed to the Father 'that all may be one...as we are one' (Jn 17:21–22), opened up vistas closed to human reason. For he implied *a certain likeness* between the union of the divine Persons and the union of God's children in truth and charity. This likeness reveals that man, who is the only creature on earth which God willed for its own sake, cannot fully find himself except through a sincere gift of self."[26]

With these words, the council text presents a summary of the whole truth about man and woman—a truth which is already outlined in the first chapters of the Book of Genesis, and which is the structural basis of biblical and Christian anthropology. *Man*—whether man or woman—*is the only being among the creatures* of the visible world *that God the Creator "has willed for its own sake";* that creature is thus a person. Being a person means striving toward self-realization (the Council text speaks of self-discovery), which can only be achieved *"through a sincere gift of self."* The model for this interpretation of the person is God himself as Trinity, as a communion of Persons. To say that man is created in the image and likeness of God means that man is called to exist "for" others, to become a gift.

This applies to every human being, whether woman or man, who lives it out in accordance with the special qualities proper to each. Within the framework of the present meditation on the dignity and vocation of women, this truth about being human constitutes the *indispensable point of departure.* Already in the Book of Genesis we can discern,

---

26. Second Vatican Ecumenical Council, Pastoral Constitution on the Church in the Modern World *Gaudium et Spes,* 24.

in preliminary outline, the spousal character of the relationship between persons, which will serve as the basis for the subsequent development of the truth about motherhood, and about virginity, as two particular dimensions of the vocation of women in the light of divine revelation. These two dimensions will find their loftiest expression at the "fullness of time" (cf. Gal 4:4) in the "woman" of Nazareth: the Virgin-Mother.

The Anthropomorphism of Biblical Language

8. The presentation of man as "the image and likeness of God" at the very beginning of Sacred Scripture has *another significance too.* It is the key for understanding biblical revelation as God's word about himself. Speaking about himself, whether through the prophets, or through the Son (cf. Heb 1:1, 2) who became man, *God speaks in human language,* using human concepts and images. If this manner of expressing himself is characterized by a certain anthropomorphism, the reason is that man is "like" God: created in his image and likeness. But then, *God too* is in some measure "like man," and precisely because of this likeness, he can be humanly known. At the same time, the language of the Bible is sufficiently precise to indicate the limits of the "likeness," the limits of the "analogy." For biblical revelation says that, while man's "likeness" to God is true, the *"non-likeness"*[27] which separates the whole of creation from the Creator is *still more essentially true.* Although man is created in God's likeness, God does not cease to be for him the one "who dwells in unapproachable light" (1 Tm 6:16): he is the "Different One," by essence the "totally Other."

This observation on the limits of the analogy—the limits of man's likeness to God in biblical language—must also be kept in mind when, in different passages of Sacred Scripture (especially in the Old Testament), we find *comparisons that attribute to God "masculine" or "feminine" qualities.* We find in these passages an indirect confirmation of the truth that both man and woman were created in the image and likeness of God. If there is a likeness between Creator and creatures, it is understandable that the Bible would refer to God using expressions that attribute to him both "masculine" and "feminine" qualities.

---

27. Cf. Num 23:19; Hos 11:9; Is 40:18; 46:5; cf. also Fourth Lateran Council *(DS* 806).

We may quote here some characteristic passages from the prophet Isaiah: "But Zion said, 'The Lord has forsaken me, my Lord has forgotten me.' *Can a woman forget* her sucking child, that she should have no compassion on the son of her womb? Even these may forget, yet *I* will *not* forget you" (49:14–15). And elsewhere: *"As* one whom his *mother* comforts, so will I comfort you; you shall be comforted in Jerusalem" (66:13). In the Psalms too God is compared to a caring mother: "Like a child quieted at its mother's breast; like a child that is quieted is my soul. O Israel, hope in the Lord" (Ps 131:2–3). In various passages the love of God who cares for his people is shown to be like that of a mother: thus, *like a mother God* "has carried" humanity, and in particular, his Chosen People, within his own womb; he has given birth to it in travail, has nourished and comforted it (cf. Is 42:14; 46:3–4). In many passages God's love is presented as the "masculine" love of the bridegroom and father (cf. Hos 11:1–4; Jer 3:4–19), but also sometimes as the "feminine" love of a mother.

This characteristic of biblical language—its anthropomorphic way of speaking about God—*points* indirectly *to the mystery of the eternal "generating"* which belongs to the inner life of God. Nevertheless, in itself this "generating" has neither "masculine" nor "feminine" qualities. It is by nature totally divine. It is spiritual in the most perfect way, since "God is Spirit" (Jn 4:24) and possesses no property typical of the body, neither "feminine" nor "masculine." Thus even *"fatherhood" in God is completely divine* and free of the "masculine" bodily characteristics proper to human fatherhood. In this sense the Old Testament spoke of God as a Father and turned to him as a Father. Jesus Christ—who called God "Abba-Father" (Mk 14:36), and who as the only-begotten and consubstantial Son placed this truth at the very center of his Gospel, thus establishing the norm of Christian prayer—referred to fatherhood in this ultra-corporeal, superhuman and completely divine sense. He spoke as the Son, joined to the Father by the eternal mystery of divine generation, and he did so while being at the same time the truly human Son of his Virgin Mother.

Although it is not possible to attribute human qualities to the eternal generation of the Word of God, and although the divine fatherhood does not possess "masculine" characteristics in a physical sense, we must nevertheless seek in God the absolute *model* of all *"generation"* among human beings. This would seem to be the sense of the Letter to the

Ephesians: "I bow my knees before the Father, from whom every family in heaven and on earth is named" (3:14–15). All "generating" among creatures finds its primary model in that generating which in God is completely divine, that is, spiritual. All "generating" in the created world is to be likened to this absolute and uncreated model. Thus every element of human generation which is proper to man, and every element which is proper to woman, namely human *"fatherhood"* and *"motherhood,"* bears within itself a likeness to, or analogy with the divine "generating" and with that "fatherhood" which in God is "totally different" —that is, completely spiritual and divine in essence; whereas in the human order, generation is proper to the "unity of the two": both are "parents," the man and the woman alike.

IV

EVE—MARY

The "Beginning" and the Sin

9. "Although he was made by God in a state of justice, from the very dawn of history man abused his liberty, at the urging of the Evil One. Man set himself against God and sought to find fulfillment apart from God."[28] With these words the teaching of the last Council recalls the revealed doctrine about sin and in particular about that first sin, which is the "original" one. The biblical "beginning"—the creation of the world and of man in the world—*contains* in itself *the truth* about *this sin,* which can also be called the sin of man's "beginning" on the earth. Even though what is written in the Book of Genesis is expressed in the form of a symbolic narrative, as is the case in the description of the creation of man as male and female (cf. Gn 2:18–25), at the same time it reveals what should be called "the mystery of sin," and even more fully, "the mystery of evil" which exists in the world created by God.

It is not possible to read "the mystery of sin" without making reference to the whole truth about the "image and likeness" to God, which is the basis of biblical anthropology. This truth presents the creation of man as a special gift from the Creator, containing not only the foundation and source of the essential dignity of the human being—man and woman—in the created world, but also *the beginning of the call to both of them to share in the intimate life of God himself.* In the light of revelation, *creation likewise means the beginning of salvation history.* It is precisely in this beginning that sin is situated and manifests itself as opposition and negation.

---

28. Second Vatican Ecumenical Council, Pastoral Constitution on the Church in the Modern World *Gaudium et Spes,* 13.

It can be said, paradoxically, that the sin presented in the third chapter of Genesis confirms the truth about the image and likeness of God in man, since this truth means freedom, that is, man's use of free will by choosing good or his abuse of it by choosing evil, against the will of God. In its essence, however, sin is a negation of God as Creator in his relationship to man, and of what God wills for man, from the beginning and for ever. Creating man and woman in his own image and likeness, God wills for them the fullness of good, or supernatural happiness, which flows from sharing in his own life. *By committing sin man rejects this gift* and at the same time wills to become "as God, knowing good and evil" (Gn 3:5), that is to say, deciding what is good and what is evil independently of God, his Creator. The sin of the first parents has its own human "measure": an interior standard of its own in man's free will, and it also has within itself a certain "diabolic" characteristic,[29] which is clearly shown in the Book of Genesis (3:15). Sin brings about a break in the original unity which man enjoyed in the state of original justice: union with God as the source of the unity within his own "I," in the mutual relationship between man and woman *("communio personarum")* as well as in regard to the external world, to nature.

The biblical description of original sin in the third chapter of Genesis in a certain way "distinguishes the roles" which the woman and the man had in it. This is also referred to later in certain passages of the Bible, for example, Paul's Letter to Timothy: "For Adam was formed first, then Eve, and Adam was not deceived, but the woman was deceived and became a transgressor" (1 Tm 2:13–14). But there is no doubt that, independent of this "distinction of roles" in the biblical description, *that first sin is the sin of man,* created by God as male and female. It is also *the sin of the "first parents,"* to which is connected its hereditary character. In this sense we call it "original sin."

This sin, as already said, *cannot be properly understood without reference to the mystery of the creation* of the human being—man and woman—*in the image and likeness of God.* By means of this reference one can also understand the mystery of that "non-likeness" to God in which sin consists, and which manifests itself in the evil present in the history of the world. Similarly one can understand the mystery of that "non-likeness" to God, who "alone is good" (cf. Mt 19:17) and the full-

---

29. "Diabolic" from the Greek "dia-ballo" = "I divide, separate, slander."

ness of good. If sin's "non-likeness" to God, who is Holiness itself, presupposes "likeness" in the sphere of freedom and free will, it can then be said that for this very reason *the "non-likeness" contained in sin* is all the more tragic and sad. It must be admitted that God, as Creator and Father, is here wounded, "offended"—obviously offended—in the very heart of that gift which belongs to God's eternal plan for man.

At the same time, however, as the author of the evil of sin, *the human being—man and woman—is affected by it.* The third chapter of Genesis shows this with the words which clearly describe the new situation of man in the created world. It shows the perspective of "toil," by which man will earn his living (cf. Gn 3:17–19) and likewise the great "pain" with which the woman will give birth to her children (cf. Gn 3:16). And all this is marked by the necessity of death, which is the end of human life on earth. In this way man, as dust, will "return to the ground, for out of it he was taken...you are dust, and to dust you shall return" (cf. Gn 3:19).

These words are confirmed generation after generation. They do not mean that *the image and the likeness of God in the human being,* whether woman or man, has been destroyed by sin; they mean rather that it has been *"obscured"*[30] and in a sense "diminished." Sin in fact "diminishes" man, as the Second Vatican Council also recalls.[31] If man is the image and likeness of God by his very nature as a person, then his greatness and his dignity are achieved in the covenant with God, in union with him, in striving toward that fundamental unity which belongs to the internal "logic" of the very mystery of creation. This unity corresponds to the profound truth concerning all intelligent creatures and in particular concerning man, who among all the creatures of the visible world was *elevated* from the beginning through the eternal choice of God in Jesus: "He chose us in [Christ] before the foundation of the world.... He destined us in love to be his sons through Jesus Christ, according to the purpose of his will" (Eph 1:4–6). The biblical teaching taken as a whole enables us to say that predestination concerns all human persons, men and women, each and every one without exception.

---

30. Cf. Origen, *In Gen. hom.* 13, 4: *PG* 12, 234; St. Gregory of Nyssa, *De virg.* 12: *SCh.* 119, 404–419; *De beat.* VI: *PG* 44, 1272.

31. Cf. Second Vatican Ecumenical Council, Pastoral Constitution on the Church in the Modern World *Gaudium et Spes,* 13.

"He Shall Rule Over You"

10. The biblical description in the Book of Genesis outlines the truth about the consequences of man's sin, as it is shown by *the disturbance* of that original *relationship between man and woman* which corresponds to their individual dignity as persons. A human being, whether male or female, is a person, and therefore, "the only creature on earth which God willed for its own sake"; and at the same time this unique and unrepeatable creature "cannot fully find himself except through a sincere gift of self."[32] Here begins the relationship of "communion" in which the "unity of the two" and the personal dignity of both man and woman find expression. Therefore when we read in the biblical description the words addressed to the woman: *"Your desire shall be for your husband, and he shall rule over you"* (Gn 3:16), we discover a break and a constant threat precisely in regard to this "unity of the two" which corresponds to the dignity of the image and likeness of God in both of them. But this threat is more serious for the woman, since domination takes the place of "being a sincere gift" and therefore living "for" the other: "He shall rule over you." This "domination" indicates the disturbance and *loss of the stability* of that *fundamental equality* which the man and the woman possess in the "unity of the two": and this is especially to the disadvantage of the woman, whereas only the equality resulting from their dignity as persons can give to their mutual relationship the character of an authentic *"communio personarum."* While the violation of this equality, which is both a gift and a right deriving from God the Creator, involves an element to the disadvantage of the woman, at the same time it also diminishes the true dignity of the man. Here we touch upon *an extremely sensitive point in the dimension of that "ethos"* which was originally inscribed by the Creator in the very creation of both of them in his own image and likeness.

This statement in Genesis 3:16 is of great significance. It implies a reference to the mutual relationship of man and women *in marriage*. It refers to the desire born in the atmosphere of spousal love whereby the woman's "sincere gift of self" is responded to and matched by a corresponding "gift" on the part of the husband. Only on the basis of this principle can both of them, and in particular the woman, "discover

---

32. Cf. ibid., 24.

themselves" as a true "unity of the two" according to the dignity of the person. The matrimonial union requires respect for and a perfecting of the true personal subjectivity of both of them. *The woman cannot become the "object" of "domination" and male "possession."* But the words of the biblical text directly concern original sin and its lasting consequences in man and woman. Burdened by hereditary sinfulness, they bear within themselves the constant *"inclination to sin,"* the tendency to go against the moral order which corresponds to the rational nature and dignity of man and woman as persons. This tendency is expressed in *a threefold concupiscence,* which St. John defines as the lust of the eyes, the lust of the flesh, and the pride of life (cf. 1 Jn 2:16). The words of the Book of Genesis quoted previously (3:16) show how this threefold concupiscence, the "inclination to sin," will burden the mutual relationship of man and woman.

These words of Genesis refer directly to marriage, but indirectly *they concern the different spheres of social life:* the situations in which the woman remains disadvantaged or discriminated against by the fact of being a woman. The revealed truth concerning the creation of the human being as male and female constitutes the principal argument against all the objectively injurious and unjust situations which contain and express the inheritance of the sin which all human beings bear within themselves. The books of Sacred Scripture confirm in various places *the actual existence of such situations* and at the same time proclaim the need for conversion, that is to say, for purification from evil and liberation from sin: from what offends neighbor, what "diminishes" man, not only the one who is offended but also the one who causes the offense. This is the unchangeable message of the Word revealed by God. In it is expressed the biblical "ethos" until the end of time.[33]

In our times the question of "women's rights" has taken on new significance in the broad context of the rights of the human person. *The biblical and evangelical message* sheds light on this cause, which is the subject of much attention today, *by safeguarding the truth about the "unity" of the "two,"* that is to say, the truth about that dignity and

---

33. It is precisely by appealing to the divine law that the Fathers of the fourth century strongly react against the discrimination still in effect with regard to women in the customs and the civil legislation of their time. Cf. St. Gregory of Nazianzus, *Or.* 37, 6: *PG* 36, 290; St. Jerome, *Ad Oceanum ep.* 77, 3: *PL* 22, 691; St. Ambrose, *De instit. virg.* III, 16: *PL* 16, 309; St. Augustine, *Sermo* 132, 2: *PL* 38, 735; *Sermo* 392, 4: *PL* 39, 1711.

vocation that result from the specific diversity and personal originality of man and woman. Consequently, even the rightful opposition of women to what is expressed in the biblical words, "He shall rule over you" (Gn 3:16) must not under any condition lead to the "masculinization" of women. In the name of liberation from male "domination," women must not appropriate to themselves male characteristics contrary to their own feminine "originality." There is a well founded fear that if they take this path, women will not "reach fulfillment," but instead will *deform and lose what constitutes their essential richness.* It is indeed an enormous richness. In the biblical description, the words of the first man at the sight of the woman who had been created are words of admiration and enchantment, words which fill the whole history of man on earth.

The personal resources of femininity are certainly no less than the resources of masculinity: they are merely different. Hence a woman, as well as a man, must understand her "fulfillment" as a person, her dignity and vocation, on the basis of these resources, according to the richness of the femininity which she received on the day of creation and which she inherits as an expression of the "image and likeness of God" that is specifically hers. *The inheritance of sin* suggested by the words of the Bible—"Your desire shall be for your husband, and he shall rule over you"—*can be conquered* only by following this path. The overcoming of this evil inheritance is, generation after generation, the task of every human being, whether woman or man. For whenever man is responsible for offending a woman's personal dignity and vocation, he acts contrary to his own personal dignity and his own vocation.

Proto-evangelium

11. The Book of Genesis attests to the fact that sin is the evil at man's "beginning" and that, since then, its consequences weigh upon the whole human race. At the same time it contains *the first foretelling of victory* over evil, *over sin.* This is proved by the words which we read in Genesis 3:15, usually called the *"proto-evangelium":* "I will put enmity between you and the woman, and between your seed and her seed; he shall bruise your head, and you shall bruise his heel." It is significant that the foretelling of the Redeemer contained in these words refers to "the woman." She is assigned the first place in the proto-evangelium as the progenitrix of him who will be the Redeemer

of man.[34] And since the redemption is to be accomplished through a struggle against evil—through the "enmity" between the offspring of the woman and the offspring of him who, as "the father of lies" (Jn 8:44), is the first author of sin in human history—it is also *an enmity between him and the woman.*

These words give us a comprehensive view of the whole of revelation, first as a preparation for the Gospel and later as the Gospel itself. From this vantage point the two female figures, *Eve* and *Mary,* are joined under the *name of woman.*

The words of the proto-evangelium, reread in the light of the new Testament, express well the mission of woman in the Redeemer's salvific struggle against the author of evil in human history.

The comparison Eve-Mary constantly recurs in the course of reflection on the deposit of faith received from divine revelation. It is one of the themes frequently taken up by the Fathers, ecclesiastical writers and theologians.[35] As a rule, from this comparison there emerges at first sight a difference, a contrast. *Eve,* as "the mother of all the living" (Gn 3:20), is *the witness to the biblical "beginning,"* which contains the truth about the creation of man made in the image and likeness of God and the truth about original sin. *Mary is the witness to the new "beginning"* and the "new creation" (cf. 2 Cor 5:17), since she herself, as the first of the redeemed in salvation history, is "a new creation": she is "full of grace." It is difficult to grasp why the words of the proto-evangelium place such strong emphasis on the "woman," if it is not admitted that *in her the new and definitive covenant* of God with humanity *has its beginning,* the *covenant* in the redeeming blood of Christ. The covenant begins with a woman, the "woman" of the annunciation at Nazareth. Herein lies the

---

34. Cf. St. Irenaeus, *Adv. Haer.* III, 23, 7: *SCh.* 211, 462–465; V, 21, 1: *SCh.* 153, 260–265; St. Epiphanius, *Panar.* III, 2, 78: *PG* 42, 728–729; St. Augustine, *Enarr. in Ps.* 103, S. 4, 6: *CCL* 40, 1525.

35. Cf. St. Justin, *Dial. cum Tryph.* 100: *PG* 6, 709–712; St. Irenaeus, *Adv. Haer.* III, 22, 4: *SCh.* 211, 438–445; V, 19, 1: *SCh.* 153, 248–251; St. Cyril of Jerusalem, *Catech.* 12, 15: *PG* 33, 741; St. John Chrysostom, *In Ps.* 44, 7: *PG* 55, 193; St. John Damascene, *Hom. 2 in dorm. B.V.M.* 3: *SCh.* 80, 130–135; Hesychius, *Sermo 5 in Deiparam; PG* 93, 1464f.; Tertullian, *De carne Christi* 17: *CCL* 2, 904f.; St. Jerome, *Epist.* 22, 21: *PL* 22, 408; St. Augustine, *Sermo* 51, 2–3: *PL* 38, 335; *Sermo* 232, 2: *PL* 38, 1108; J. H. Newman, *A Letter to the Rev. E. B. Pusey,* Longmans, London 1865; M. J. Scheeben, *Handbuch der Katholischen Dogmatik,* V/1 (Freiburg 1954), 243–266; V/2 (Freiburg 306–499).

absolute originality of the Gospel: many times in the Old Testament, in order to intervene in the history of his people, God addressed himself to women, as in the case of the mothers of Samuel and Samson. However, to make his covenant with humanity, he addressed himself only to men: *Noah, Abraham and Moses.* At the beginning of the New Covenant, which is to be eternal and irrevocable, there is a woman: the Virgin of Nazareth. It is a *sign* that points to the fact that "in Jesus Christ" *"there is neither male nor female"* (Gal 3:28). In Christ the mutual opposition between man and woman—which is the inheritance of original sin—is essentially overcome. "For you are all *one* in Jesus Christ," St. Paul will write (Gal 3:28).

These words concern that original "unity of the two" which is linked with the creation of the human being as male and female, made in the image and likeness of God, and based on the model of that most perfect communion of Persons which is God himself. St. Paul states that the mystery of man's redemption in Jesus Christ, the son of Mary, resumes and renews that which in the mystery of creation corresponded to the eternal design of God the Creator. Precisely for this reason on the day of the creation of the human being as male and female "God saw everything that he had made, and behold, it was very good" (Gn 1:31). *The redemption restores,* in a sense, at its very root, *the good* that was essentially "diminished" by sin and its heritage in human history.

The "woman" of the proto-evangelium fits into the perspective of the redemption. The comparison Eve-Mary can be understood also in the sense that *Mary assumes* in herself and embraces the *mystery of the "woman"* whose beginning is Eve, "the mother of all the living" (Gn 3:20). First of all she assumes and embraces it within the mystery of Christ, "the new and the last Adam" (cf. 1 Cor 15:45), who assumed in his own person the nature of the first Adam. The essence of the New Covenant consists in the fact that the Son of God, who is of one substance with the eternal Father, becomes man: he takes humanity into the unity of the divine Person of the Word. The one who accomplishes the redemption is also a true man. The mystery of the world's redemption presupposes that *God the Son assumed humanity* as *the inheritance of Adam,* becoming like him and like every man in all things, "yet without sinning" (Heb 4:15). In this way he "fully reveals man to himself and makes man's supreme calling clear," as the Second Vatican Council teaches.[36] In a certain sense, he has helped man to discover "who he is" (cf. Ps 8:5).

In the tradition of faith and of Christian reflection throughout the ages, *the coupling Adam-Christ* is often linked with that of *Eve-Mary.* If Mary is described also as the "new Eve," what are the meanings of this analogy? Certainly there are many. Particularly noteworthy is the meaning which sees Mary as the full revelation of all that is included in the biblical word "woman": a revelation commensurate with the mystery of the redemption. *Mary* means, in a sense, a going beyond the limit spoken of in the Book of Genesis (3:16) and a return to that "beginning" in which one finds the "woman" as she was intended to be in *creation,* and therefore in the eternal mind of God: in the bosom of the Most Holy Trinity. Mary *is* "the new beginning" of the *dignity and vocation of women,* of each and every woman.[37]

A particular key for understanding this can be found in the words which the evangelist puts on Mary's lips after the annunciation, during her visit to Elizabeth: "He who is mighty has done great things for me" (Lk 1:49). These words certainly refer to the conception of her Son, who is the "Son of the Most High" (Lk 1:32), the "holy one" of God; but they can also signify *the discovery of her own feminine humanity. He "has done great things for me":* this is *the discovery of all the richness and personal resources of femininity,* all the eternal originality of the "woman," just as God wanted her to be, a person for her own sake, who discovers herself "by means of a sincere gift of self."

This discovery is connected with a clear awareness of God's gift, of his generosity. From the very "beginning" sin had obscured this awareness, in a sense had stifled it, as is shown in the words of the first temptation by the "father of lies" (cf. Gn 3:1–5). At the advent of the "fullness of time" (cf. Gal 4:4), when the mystery of redemption begins to be fulfilled in the history of humanity, this awareness bursts forth in all its power in the words of the biblical "woman" of Nazareth. *In Mary, Eve discovers* the nature of the true dignity of woman, of feminine humanity. This discovery must continually reach the heart of every woman and shape her vocation and her life.

---

36. Second Vatican Ecumenical Council, Pastoral Constitution on the Church in the Modern World *Gaudium et Spes,* 22.

37. Cf. St. Ambrose, *De instit. virg.* V, 33: *PL* 16, 313.

V

JESUS CHRIST

"They Marveled That He Was Talking with a Woman"

12. The words of the proto-evangelium in the Book of Genesis enable us to move into the context of the Gospel. Man's redemption, foretold in Genesis, now becomes a reality in the person and mission of Jesus Christ, in which we also recognize *what the reality of the redemption means* for the dignity and the vocation *of women*. This meaning becomes clearer for us from Christ's words and from his whole attitude toward women, an attitude which is extremely simple, and for this very reason extraordinary, if seen against the background of his time. It is an attitude marked by great clarity and depth. Various women appear along the path of the mission of Jesus of Nazareth, and his meeting with each of them is a confirmation of the evangelical "newness of life" already spoken of.

It is universally admitted—even by people with a critical attitude toward the Christian message—that *in the eyes of his contemporaries Christ became a promoter of women's true dignity* and of the *vocation* corresponding to this dignity. At times this caused wonder, surprise, often to the point of scandal. "They marveled that he was talking with a woman" (Jn 4:27), because this behavior differed from that of his contemporaries. Even Christ's own disciples "marveled." The Pharisee to whose house the sinful woman went to anoint Jesus' feet with perfumed oil "said to himself, 'If this man were a prophet, *he would have known who* and what sort of woman this is who is touching him, for she is a sinner'" (Lk 7:39). Even greater dismay, or even "holy indignation," must have filled the self-satisfied hearers of Christ's words. "The tax collectors and the harlots go into the kingdom of God before you" (Mt 21:31).

By speaking and acting in this way, Jesus made it clear that "the mysteries of the kingdom" were known to him in every detail. He also "knew what was in man" (Jn 2:25), in his innermost being, in his "heart." He was a witness of God's eternal plan for the human being, created in his own image and likeness as man and woman. He was also perfectly aware of the consequences of sin, of that "mystery of iniquity" working in human hearts as the bitter fruit of the obscuring of the divine image. It is truly significant that in his important discussion about marriage and its indissolubility, in the presence of "the scribes," who by profession were experts in the Law, Jesus *makes reference to the "beginning."* The question asked concerns a man's right "to divorce one's wife for any cause" (Mt 19:3) and therefore also concerns the woman's right, her rightful position in marriage, her dignity. The questioners think they have on their side the Mosaic legislation then followed in Israel: "Why then did Moses command one to give a certificate of divorce, and to put her away?" (Mt 19:7) Jesus answers: "For your hardness of heart Moses allowed you to divorce your wives, but from the beginning it was not so" (Mt 19:8). Jesus appeals to the "beginning"—to the creation of man as male and female and their ordering by God himself, which is based upon the fact that *both were created "in his image and likeness."* Therefore, when "a man shall leave his father and mother and is joined to his wife, so that the two become one flesh," there remains in force the law which comes from God himself: "What therefore God has joined together, let no man put asunder" (Mt 19:6).

The principle of this "ethos," which from the beginning marks the reality of creation, is now confirmed by Christ in opposition to that tradition which discriminated against women. In this tradition the male "dominated," without having proper regard for woman and for her dignity, which *the "ethos"* of creation made the basis of the mutual relationships of two people united in marriage. This "ethos" is *recalled and confirmed by Christ's words;* it is the "ethos" of the Gospel and of redemption.

Women in the Gospel

13. As we scan the pages of the Gospel, *many women, of different ages and conditions,* pass before our eyes. We meet women with illnesses or physical sufferings, such as the one who had "a spirit of infirmity for eighteen years; she was bent over and could not fully straighten herself" (Lk 13:11); or Simon's mother-in-law, who "lay sick with a fever" (Mk 1:30); or the woman "who had a flow of blood" (cf. Mk 5:25–

34)—who could not touch anyone because it was believed that her touch would make a person "impure." Each of them was healed, and the last-mentioned—the one with a flow of blood, who touched Jesus' garment "in the crowd" (Mk 5:27)—was praised by him for her great faith: "Your faith has made you well" (Mk 5:34). Then there is *the daughter of Jairus,* whom Jesus brings back to life, saying to her tenderly—"Little girl, I say to you, rise" (Mk 5:41). There is also *the widow of Naim,* whose only son Jesus brings back to life, accompanying his action by an expression of affectionate mercy—"He had compassion on her and said to her, 'Do not weep!'" (Lk 7:13). And finally there is the *Canaanite woman,* whom Christ extols for her faith, her humility and for that great-ness of spirit of which only a mother's heart is capable. "O woman, great is your faith! Be it done for you as you desire" (Mt 15:28). The Canaanite woman was asking for the healing of her daughter.

Sometimes the women whom Jesus met and who received so many graces from him, also accompanied him as he journeyed with the apostles through the towns and villages, proclaiming the Good News of the kingdom of God; and they "provided for them out of their means." The Gospel names Joanna, who was the wife of Herod's steward, Susanna and "many others" (cf. Lk 8:1–3).

Sometimes *women* appear *in the parables* which Jesus of Nazareth used to illustrate for his listeners the truth about the kingdom of God. This is the case in the parables of the lost coin (cf. Lk 15:8–10), the leaven (cf. Mt 13:33), and the wise and foolish virgins (cf. Mt 25:1–13). Particularly eloquent is the story of the widow's mite. While "the rich were putting their gifts into the treasury...a poor widow put in two cop-per coins." Then Jesus said: "This poor widow *has put in more than all of them....* She out of her poverty put in all the living that she had" (Lk 21:1–4). In this way Jesus presents her as a model for everyone and de-fends her, for in the socio-juridical system of the time widows were to-tally defenseless people (cf. also Lk 18:1–7).

In all of Jesus' teaching, as well as in his behavior, one can find nothing which reflects the discrimination against women prevalent in his day. On the contrary, *his words and works always express the respect and honor due to women.* The woman with a stoop is called a "daughter of Abraham" (Lk 13:16), while in the whole Bible the title "son of Abraham" is used only of men. Walking the *Via Dolorosa* to Golgotha, Jesus will say to the women: "Daughters of Jerusalem, do not weep for me" (Lk 23:28). This way of speaking to and about women, as well as his manner of treating them, clearly constitutes an "innovation" with respect to the prevailing custom at that time.

This becomes even more explicit in regard to women whom popular opinion contemptuously labeled sinners, public sinners and adulteresses. There is the Samaritan woman, to whom Jesus himself says: "For you have had five husbands, and he whom you now have is not your husband." And she, realizing that he knows the secrets of her life, recognizes him as the messiah and runs to tell her neighbors. The conversation leading up to this realization is one of the most beautiful in the Gospel (cf. Jn 4:7–27).

Then there is the public sinner who, in spite of her condemnation by common opinion, enters into the house of the Pharisee to anoint the feet of Jesus with perfumed oil. To his host, who is scandalized by this, he will say: "Her sins, which are many, are forgiven, for she loved much" (cf. Lk 7:37–47).

Finally, there is a situation which is perhaps the most eloquent: *a woman caught in adultery* is brought to Jesus. To the leading question: "In the law Moses commanded us to stone such. What do you say about her?" Jesus replies: "Let him who is without sin among you be the first to throw a stone at her." The power of truth contained in this answer is so great that "they went away, one by one, beginning with the eldest." Only Jesus and the woman remain. "Woman, where are they? Has no one condemned you?" "No one, Lord." "Neither do I condemn you; go, and do not sin again" (cf. Jn 8:3–11).

These episodes provide a very clear picture. Christ is the one who "knows what is in man" (cf. Jn 2:25)—in man and woman. He knows *the dignity of man,* his *worth in God's eyes.* He himself, the Christ, is the definitive confirmation of this worth. Everything he says and does is definitively fulfilled in the Paschal Mystery of the redemption. Jesus' attitude to the women whom he meets in the course of his Messianic service reflects the eternal plan of God, who, in creating each one of them, chooses her and loves her in Christ (cf. Eph 1:1–5). Each woman therefore is "the only creature on earth which God willed for its own sake." *Each of them from the "beginning" inherits as a woman the dignity of personhood.* Jesus of Nazareth confirms this dignity, recalls it, renews it, and makes it a part of the Gospel of the redemption for which he is sent into the world. Every word and gesture of Christ about women must therefore he brought into the dimension of the Paschal Mystery. In this way everything is completely explained.

The Woman Caught in Adultery

14. Jesus enters *into the concrete and historical situation of women,* a situation which is *weighed down by the inheritance of sin.* One of the ways in which this inheritance is expressed is habitual discrimination against women in favor of men. This inheritance is rooted within women too. From this point of view the episode of the woman "caught in adultery" (cf. Jn 8:3–11) is particularly eloquent. In the end Jesus says to her: *"Do not sin again,"* but first he *evokes an awareness* of sin in the men who accuse her in order to stone her, thereby revealing his profound capacity to see human consciences and actions in their true light. Jesus seems to say to the accusers: Is not this woman, for all her sin, above all a confirmation of your own transgressions, of your "male" injustice, your misdeeds?

This truth is *valid for the whole human race.* The episode recorded in the Gospel of John is repeated in countless similar situations in every period of history. A woman is left alone, exposed to public opinion with "her sin," while behind "her" sin there lurks a man—a sinner, guilty "of the other's sin," indeed equally responsible for it. And yet his sin escapes notice; it is passed over in silence: he does not appear to be responsible for "the other's sin"! Sometimes, forgetting his own sin, he makes himself the accuser, as in the case described. How often, in a similar way, *the woman pays* for her own sin (maybe it is she, in some cases, who is guilty of the "other's sin"—the sin of the man), but she alone pays and she pays *all alone!* How often is she abandoned with her pregnancy, when the man, the child's father, is unwilling to accept responsibility for it? And besides the many "unwed mothers" in our society, we also might consider all those who as a result of various pressures, even on the part of the guilty man, very often "get rid of" the child before it is born. "They get rid of it": but at what price? Public opinion today tries in various ways to "abolish" the evil of this sin. Normally a *woman's conscience does not let her forget* that she has taken the life of her own child, for she cannot destroy that readiness to accept life which marks her "ethos" from the "beginning."

The attitude of Jesus in the episode described in John 8:3–11 is significant. This is one of the few instances in which his power—the power of truth—is so clearly manifested with regard to human consciences. Jesus is calm, collected and thoughtful. As in the conversation with the Pharisees (cf. Mt 19:3–9), is Jesus not aware of being in contact with the mystery of the "beginning," when man was created male and female, and the woman was entrusted to the man with her feminine distinctiveness, and with her potential for motherhood? The man was also entrusted by the Creator to the woman—they were *entrusted to each other as persons* made in the image and likeness of God himself. This entrusting is the test of love, spousal love. In order to become "a sincere gift" to one another, each of them has to feel responsible for the gift. This test is meant for both of them—man and woman—from the "beginning." After original sin, contrary forces are at work in man and woman as a result of the threefold concupiscence, the "stimulus of sin." They act from deep within the human being. Thus Jesus will say in the sermon on the Mount: *"Every one who looks at a woman lustfully has already committed adultery with her in his heart"* (Mt 5:28). These words, addressed directly to man, show the fundamental truth of his responsibility vis-a-vis woman: her dignity, her motherhood, her vocation. But indirectly these words concern the woman. Christ did everything possible to ensure that—in the context of the customs and social relationships of that time—women would find in his teaching and actions their own subjectivity and dignity. On the basis of the eternal "unity of the two," *this dignity directly depends on woman herself, as a subject responsible for herself, and at the same time it is "given as a task" to man.* Christ logically appeals to man's responsibility. In the present meditation on women's dignity and vocation, it is necessary that we refer to the context which we find in the Gospel. The dignity and the vocation of women—as well as those of men—find their eternal source in the heart of God. And in the temporal conditions of human existence, they are closely connected with the "unity of the two." Consequently each man must look within himself to see whether she who was entrusted to him as a sister in humanity, as a spouse, has not become in his heart an object of adultery; to see whether she who, in different ways, is the co-subject of his existence in the world, has not become for him an "object": an object of pleasure, of exploitation.

Guardians of the Gospel Message

15. *Christ's way of acting, the Gospel of his words and deeds,* is a consistent *protest* against whatever offends the dignity of women. Consequently, the women who are close to Christ discover themselves in the truth which he "teaches" and "does," even when this truth concerns their

"sinfulness." They feel *"liberated" by this truth;* restored to themselves they feel loved with "eternal love," with a love which finds direct expression in Christ himself. In Christ's sphere of action their position is transformed. They feel that Jesus is speaking to them about matters which in those times one did not discuss with a woman. Perhaps the most significant example of this is the *Samaritan woman* at the well of Sychar. *Jesus*—who knows that she is a sinner and speaks to her about this—*discusses the most profound mysteries of God with her.* He speaks to her of God's infinite gift of love, which is like a "spring of water welling up to eternal life" (Jn 4:14). He speaks to her about God who is Spirit, and about the true adoration which the Father has a right to receive in spirit and truth (cf. Jn 4:24). Finally he reveals to her that he is the messiah promised to Israel (cf. Jn 4:26).

This is an event without precedent: that a *woman,* and what is more a "sinful woman," becomes a "disciple" of Christ. Indeed, once taught, she proclaims Christ to the inhabitants of Samaria, so that they too receive him with faith (cf. Jn 4:39–42). This is an unprecedented event, if one remembers the usual way women were treated by those who were teachers in Israel; whereas in Jesus of Nazareth's way of acting such an event becomes normal. In this regard, the sisters of Lazarus also deserve special mention: "Jesus loved Martha and her sister [Mary] and Lazarus" (cf. Jn 11:5). Mary "listened to the teaching" of Jesus; when he pays them a visit, he calls Mary's behavior "the good portion" in contrast to Martha's preoccupation with domestic matters (cf. Lk 10:38–42). On another occasion—*after the death of Lazarus*—Martha is the one who talks to Christ, and the conversation concerns the most profound truths of revelation and faith: "Lord, if you had been here, my brother would not have died." "Your brother will rise again." "I know that he will rise again in the resurrection at the last day." Jesus said to her: "I am the resurrection and the life; he who believes in me, though he die, yet shall he live, and whoever lives and believes in me shall never die. Do you believe this?" "Yes, Lord; I believe that you are the Christ, the Son of God, he who is coming into the world" (Jn 11:21–27). After this profession of faith Jesus raises Lazarus. *This conversation with Martha is one of the most important in the Gospel.*

Christ speaks to women about the things of God, and they understand them; there is a true resonance of mind and heart, a response of faith. Jesus expresses appreciation and admiration for this distinctly "feminine" response, as in the case of the Canaanite woman (cf. Mt 15:28). Sometimes he presents this lively faith, filled with love, as an example. *He teaches,* therefore, taking as *his starting point this feminine response of mind and heart.* This is the case with the "sinful" woman in the Pharisee's house, whose way of acting is taken by Jesus as the starting point for explaining the truth about the forgiveness of sins: "Her sins, which are many, are forgiven, for she loved much, but he who is forgiven little, loves little" (Lk 7:47). On the occasion of another anointing, Jesus defends the woman and her action before the disciples, Judas in particular: "Why do you trouble this woman? *For she has done a beautiful thing to me....* In pouring this ointment on my body she has done it to prepare me for burial. Truly, I say to you, wherever this Gospel is preached in the whole world, what she has done will be told in memory of her" (Mt 26:6–13).

Indeed, the Gospels not only describe what that woman did at Bethany in the house of Simon the Leper; they also highlight the fact that *women were in the forefront at the foot of the cross,* at the decisive moment in Jesus of Nazareth's whole messianic mission. John was the only apostle who remained faithful, but there were many faithful women. Not only the Mother of Christ and "his mother's sister, Mary the wife of Clopas and Mary Magdalene" (Jn 19:25) were present, but "there were also many women there, looking on from afar, who had followed Jesus from Galilee, ministering to him" (Mt 27:55). As we see, in this most arduous test of faith and fidelity the women proved stronger than the apostles. In this moment of danger, those who love much succeed in overcoming their fear. Before this there were the *women on the Via Dolorosa,* "who bewailed and lamented him" (Lk 23:27). Earlier still, there was *Pilate's wife,* who had warned her husband: "Have nothing to do with that righteous man, for I have suffered much over him today in a dream" (Mt 27:19).

First Witnesses of the Resurrection

16. From the beginning of Christ's mission, women show to him and to his mystery a special *sensitivity which is characteristic* of their *femininity.* It must also be said that this is especially confirmed in the Paschal Mystery, not only at the cross but also at the dawn of the resurrection. The women *are the first at the tomb.* They are the first to find it empty. They are the first to hear: "He is not here. *He has risen,* as he said" (Mt

28:6). They are the first to embrace his feet (cf. Mt 28:9). They are also the first to be called to announce this truth to the apostles (cf. Mt 28:1–10; Lk 24:8–11). The Gospel of John (cf. also Mk 16:9) emphasizes *the special role of Mary Magdalene*. She is the first to meet the risen Christ. At first she thinks he is the gardener; she recognizes him only when he calls her by name: "Jesus said to her, 'Mary.' She turned and said to him in Hebrew, 'Rabbouni' (which means Teacher). Jesus said to her, 'Do not hold me, for I have not yet ascended to the Father, but go to my brethren and say to them, I am ascending to my Father and to your Father, to my God and your God.' Mary Magdalene went and said to the disciples, 'I have seen the Lord'; and she told them that he had said these things to her" (Jn 20:16–18).

Hence she came to be called "the apostle of the apostles."[38] Mary Magdalene was the first eyewitness of the risen Christ, and for this reason she was also *the first to bear witness to him before the apostles*. This event, in a sense, crowns all that has been said previously about Christ entrusting divine truths to women as well as men. One can say that this fulfilled the words of the Prophet: *"I will pour out my spirit on all flesh; your sons and your daughters shall prophesy"* (Jl 3:1). On the fiftieth day after Christ's resurrection, these words are confirmed once more in the upper room in Jerusalem, at the descent of the Holy Spirit, the Paraclete (cf. Acts 2:17).

Everything that has been said so far about Christ's attitude to women confirms and clarifies, in the Holy Spirit, the truth about the equality of man and woman. One must speak of an essential "equality," since both of them—the woman as much as the man—are created in the image and likeness of God. Both of them are equally capable of receiving the outpouring of divine truth and love in the Holy Spirit. Both receive his salvific and sanctifying "visits."

The fact of being a man or a woman involves no limitation here, just as the salvific and sanctifying action of the Spirit in man is in no

---

38. Cf. Rabanus Maurus, *De vita beatae Mariae Magdalenae,* XXVII: "Salvator...ascensionis suae eam (=Mariam Magdalenam) ad apostolos instituit apostolam" *(PL* 112, 1474). "Facta est Apostolorum Apostola per hoc quod ei committitur ut resurrectionem dominicam discipulis annuntiet": St. Thomas Aquinas, *In Ioannem Evangelistam Expositio,* c. XX, 11. III, 6 *(Sancti Thomae Aquinatis Comment in Matthaeum et Ioannem Evangelistas),* Ed. Parmen. X, 629.

way limited by the fact that one is a Jew or a Greek, slave or free, according to the well-known words of St. Paul: "For you are all one in Christ Jesus" (Gal 3:28). *This unity does not cancel out diversity.* The Holy Spirit, who brings about this unity in the supernatural order of sanctifying grace, contributes in equal measure to the fact that "your sons will prophesy" and that "your daughters will prophesy." "To prophesy" means to express by one's words and one's life *"the mighty works of God"* (Acts 2:11), preserving the truth and originality of each person, whether woman or man. Gospel "equality," the "equality" of women and men in regard to the "mighty works of God"—manifested so clearly in the words and deeds of Jesus of Nazareth—constitutes the most obvious basis for the dignity and vocation of women in the Church and in the world. Every *vocation has* a profoundly *personal and prophetic meaning.* In "vocation" understood in this way, what is personally feminine reaches a new dimension: the dimension of the "mighty works of God," of which the woman becomes the living subject and an irreplaceable witness.

VI

MOTHERHOOD — VIRGINITY

Two Dimensions of Women's Vocation

17. We must now focus our meditation on virginity and motherhood as two particular dimensions of the fulfillment of the female personality. In the light of the Gospel, they acquire their full meaning and value in Mary, who as a virgin became the Mother of the Son of God. These *two dimensions of the female vocation* were united in her in an exceptional manner, in such a way that one did not exclude the other but wonderfully complemented it. The description of the annunciation in the Gospel of Luke clearly shows that this seemed impossible to the Virgin of Nazareth. When she hears the words: "You will conceive in your womb and bear a son, and you shall call his name Jesus," she immediately asks: "How can this be, since I have no husband?" (Lk 1:31, 34). In the usual order of things motherhood is the result of mutual "knowledge" between a man and woman in the marriage union. Mary, firm in her resolve to preserve her virginity, puts this question to the divine messenger, and obtains from him the explanation: *"The Holy Spirit will come upon you"*—your motherhood will not be the consequence of matrimonial "knowledge," but will be the work of the Holy Spirit; the "power of the Most High" will "overshadow" the mystery of the Son's conception and birth; as the Son of the Most High, he is given to you exclusively by God, in a manner known to God. Mary, therefore, maintained her virginal "I have no husband" (cf. Lk 1:34) and at the same time became a mother. *Virginity and motherhood coexist in her:* they do not mutually exclude each other or place limits on each other. Indeed, the person of the Mother of God helps everyone—especially women—to see how these two dimensions, these two paths in the vocation of women as persons, explain and complete each other.

Motherhood

18. In order to share in this "vision," we must once again *seek a deeper understanding of the truth about the human person* recalled by the Second Vatican Council. The human being—both male and female—is the only being in the world which God willed for its own sake. The human being is a person, a subject who decides for himself. At the same time, man "cannot fully find himself except through a sincere gift of self."[39] It has already been said that this description, indeed this definition of the person, corresponds to the fundamental biblical truth about the creation of the human being—man and woman—in the image and likeness of God. This is not a purely theoretical interpretation, nor an abstract definition, for it *gives an essential indication of what it means to be human,* while emphasizing *the value of the gift of self, the gift of the person.* In this vision of the person we also find the essence of that "ethos" which, together with the truth of creation, will be fully developed by the books of revelation, particularly the Gospels.

This truth about the person also opens up *the path to a full understanding of women's motherhood.* Motherhood is the fruit of the marriage union of a man and woman, of that biblical "knowledge" which corresponds to the "union of the two in one flesh" (cf. Gn 2:24). This brings about—on the woman's part—a special "gift of self " as an expression of that spousal love whereby the two are united to each other so closely that they become "one flesh." Biblical "knowledge" is achieved in accordance with the truth of the person only when the mutual self-giving is not distorted either by the desire of the man to become the "master" of his wife ("He shall rule over you") or by the woman remaining closed within her own instincts ("Your desire shall be for your husband"—Gn 3:16).

This *mutual gift of the person in marriage* opens to the gift of a new life, *a new human being,* who is also a person in the likeness of his parents. Motherhood implies from the beginning a special openness to the new person: and this is precisely the woman's "part." In this openness, in conceiving and giving birth to a child, the woman "discovers herself

---

39. Second Vatican Ecumenical Council, Pastoral Constitution on the Church in the Modern World *Gaudium et Spes,* 24.

through a sincere gift of self." The gift of interior readiness to accept the child and bring it into the world is linked to the marriage union, which—as mentioned earlier—should constitute a special moment in the mutual self-giving both by the woman and the man. According to the Bible, the conception and birth of a new human being are accompanied by the following words of the woman: *"I have brought a man into being with the help of the Lord"* (Gn 4:1). This exclamation of Eve, the "mother of all the living" is repeated every time a new human being comes into the world. It expresses the woman's joy and awareness that she is sharing in the great mystery of eternal generation. The spouses share in the creative power of God!

The woman's motherhood in the period between the baby's conception and birth is a biophysiological and psychological process which is better understood in our days than in the past, and is the subject of many detailed studies. Scientific analysis fully confirms that the very physical constitution of women is naturally disposed to motherhood—conception, pregnancy and giving birth—which is a consequence of the marriage union with the man. At the same time, this also corresponds to the psycho-physical structure of women. What the different branches of science have to say on this subject is important and useful, provided that it is not limited to an exclusively biophysiological interpretation of women and of motherhood. Such a *"restricted" picture* would go hand in hand with a materialistic concept of the human being and of the world. In such a case, what is truly essential would unfortunately be lost. Motherhood as a *human* fact and phenomenon is fully explained on the basis of the truth about the person. Motherhood *is linked to the personal structure of the woman and to the personal dimension of the gift:* "I have brought a man into being with the help of the Lord" (Gn 4:1). The Creator grants the parents the gift of a child. On the woman's part, this fact is linked in a special way to "a sincere gift of self." Mary's words at the annunciation—"Let it be to me according to your word"—signify the woman's readiness for the gift of self and her readiness to accept a new life.

The eternal mystery of generation, which is in God himself, the one and Triune God (cf. Eph 3:14–15), is reflected in the woman's motherhood and in the man's fatherhood. Human parenthood is something shared by both the man and the woman. Even if the woman, out of love for her husband, says: "I have given you a child," her words also mean: "This is our child." Although both of them together are parents of their child, *the woman's motherhood constitutes a special "part" in this shared parenthood,* and the most demanding part. Parenthood—even though it belongs to both—is realized much more fully in the woman, especially in the prenatal period. It is the woman who "pays" directly for this shared generation, which literally absorbs the energies of her body and soul. It is therefore necessary that *the man* be fully aware that in their shared parenthood he *owes a special debt to the woman.* No program of "equal rights" between women and men is valid unless it takes this fact fully into account.

Motherhood involves a special communion with the mystery of life, as it develops in the woman's womb. The mother is filled with wonder at this mystery of life, and "understands" with unique intuition what is happening inside her. In the light of the "beginning," the mother accepts and loves as a person the child she is carrying in her womb. This unique contact with the new human being developing within her gives rise to an attitude toward human beings—not only toward her own child, but every human being—which profoundly marks the woman's personality. It is commonly thought that *women* are more capable than men of paying attention *to another person,* and that motherhood develops this predisposition even more. The man—even with all his sharing in parenthood—always remains "outside" the process of pregnancy and the baby's birth; in many ways he has to *learn* his own *"fatherhood" from the mother.* One can say that this is part of the normal human dimension of parenthood, including the stages that follow the birth of the baby, especially the initial period. The child's upbringing, taken as a whole, should include the contribution of both parents: the maternal and paternal contribution. In any event, the mother's contribution is decisive in laying the foundation for a new human personality.

Motherhood in Relation to the Covenant

19. Our reflection returns to *the biblical exemplar of the "woman"* in the proto-evangelium. The "woman," as mother and first teacher of the human being (education being the spiritual dimension of parenthood), has a specific precedence over the man. Although motherhood, especially in the biophysical sense, depends upon the man, it places an essential "mark" on the whole personal growth process of new children. Motherhood *in the biophysical sense* appears to be passive: the formation process of a new life "takes place" in her, in her body, which is nevertheless profoundly

involved in that process. At the same time, motherhood *in its personal-ethical sense* expresses a very important creativity on the part of the woman, upon whom the very humanity of the new human being mainly depends. In this sense too the woman's motherhood presents a special call and a special challenge to the man and to his fatherhood.

The biblical exemplar of the "woman" finds its culmination *in the motherhood of the Mother of God.* The words of the proto-evangelium— "I will put enmity between you and the woman"—find here a fresh confirmation. We see that through Mary—through her maternal *fiat,* ("Let it be done to me")—God *begins a New Covenant with humanity.* This is the eternal and definitive covenant in Christ, in his body and blood, in his cross and resurrection. Precisely because this covenant is to be fulfilled "in flesh and blood," its beginning is in the Mother. Thanks solely to her and to her virginal and maternal *fiat,* the "Son of the Most High" can say to the Father: "A body you have prepared for me. Lo, I have come to do your will, O God" (cf. Heb 10:5, 7).

Motherhood has been introduced into the order of the covenant that God made with humanity in Jesus Christ. Each and every time that *motherhood* is repeated in human history, it is always *related to the covenant* which God established with the human race through the motherhood of the Mother of God.

Does not Jesus bear witness to this reality when he answers the exclamation of that woman in the crowd who blessed him for Mary's motherhood: "Blessed is the womb that bore you, and the breasts that you sucked!"? Jesus replies: "Blessed rather are those who hear the Word of God and keep it" (Lk 11:27–28). Jesus confirms the meaning of motherhood in reference to the body, but at the same time he indicates an even deeper meaning, which is connected with the order of the spirit: it is a sign of the covenant with God who "is spirit" (Jn 4:24). This is true above all for the motherhood of the Mother of God. The *motherhood* of every woman, understood in the light of the Gospel, is similarly not only "of flesh and blood": it expresses a profound *"listening to the Word of the living God"* and a readiness to "safeguard" this Word, which is "the Word of eternal life" (cf. Jn 6:68). For it is precisely those born of earthly mothers, the sons and daughters of the human race, who receive from the Son of God the power to become "children of God" (Jn 1:12). A dimension of the New Covenant in Christ's blood enters into human parenthood, making it a reality and a task for "new creatures" (cf. 2 Cor

5:17). The history of every human being passes through the threshold of a woman's motherhood; crossing it conditions "the revelation of the children of God" (cf. Rm 8:19).

"When a woman is in travail she has sorrow, because her hour has come; but when she is delivered of the child, *she no longer remembers the anguish,* for joy that a child is born into the world" (Jn 16:21). The first part of Christ's words refers to the "pangs of childbirth" which belong to the heritage of original sin; at the same time these words indicate *the link that exists between the woman's motherhood and the Paschal Mystery.* For this mystery also includes the Mother's sorrow at the foot of the cross—the Mother who through faith shares in the amazing mystery of her Son's "self-emptying": "This is perhaps the deepest 'kenosis' of faith in human history."[40]

As we contemplate this Mother, whose heart "a sword has pierced" (cf. Lk 2:35), our thoughts go to *all the suffering women in the world,* suffering either physically or morally. In this suffering a woman's sensitivity plays a role, even though she often succeeds in resisting suffering better than a man. It is difficult to enumerate these sufferings; it is difficult to call them all by name. We may recall her maternal care for her children, especially when they fall sick or fall into bad ways; the death of those most dear to her; the loneliness of mothers forgotten by their grown-up children; the loneliness of widows; the sufferings of women who struggle alone to make a living; and women who have been wronged or exploited. Then there are the sufferings of consciences as a result of sin, which has wounded the woman's human or maternal dignity: the wounds of consciences which do not heal easily. With these sufferings too we must place ourselves at the foot of the cross.

But the words of the Gospel about the woman who suffers when the time comes for her to give birth to her child, immediately afterward express *joy:* it is *"the joy that a child is born into the world."* This joy too is referred to the Paschal Mystery, to the joy which is communicated to the apostles *on the day of Christ's resurrection:* "So you have sorrow now" (these words were said the day before the Passion); "but I will see you again and your hearts will rejoice, and no one will take your joy from you" (Jn 16:22–23).

---

40. Encyclical Letter *Redemptoris Mater,* 18: *loc. cit.,* 383.

Virginity for the Sake of the Kingdom

20. In the teaching of Christ, *motherhood is connected with virginity*, but also *distinct from it.* Fundamental to this is Jesus' statement in the conversation on the indissolubility of marriage. Having heard the answer given to the Pharisees, the disciples say to Christ: "If such is the case of a man with his wife, it is not expedient to marry" (Mt 19:10). Independently of the meaning which "it is not expedient" had at that time in the mind of the disciples, *Christ* takes their mistaken opinion as a starting point for instructing them *on the value of celibacy.* He distinguishes celibacy which results from natural defects—even though they may have been caused by man—from *"celibacy for the sake of the kingdom of heaven."* Christ says, "and there are eunuchs who have made themselves eunuchs for the sake of the kingdom of heaven" (Mt 19:12). It is, then, a voluntary celibacy, chosen for the sake of the kingdom of heaven, in view of man's eschatological vocation to union with God. He then adds: "He who is able to receive this, let him receive it." These words repeat what he had said at the beginning of the discourse on celibacy (cf. Mt 19:11). Consequently, *celibacy for the kingdom of heaven* results not only from a free *choice* on the part of man, but also from a special *grace* on the part of God, who calls a particular person to live celibacy. While this is a special sign of the kingdom of God to come, it also serves as a way to devote all the energies of soul and body during one's earthly life exclusively for the sake of the eschatological kingdom.

Jesus' words are the answer to the disciples' question. They are addressed directly to those who put the question: in this case they were men. Nevertheless, Christ's answer, in itself, has a *value for men and for women.* In this context it indicates the evangelical ideal of virginity, an ideal which constitutes a clear "innovation" with respect to the tradition of the Old Testament. Certainly that tradition was connected in some way with Israel's expectation of the messiah's coming, especially among the women of Israel from whom he was to be born. In fact, the ideal of celibacy and virginity for the sake of greater closeness to God was not entirely foreign to certain Jewish circles, especially in the period immediately preceding the coming of Jesus. Nevertheless, celibacy for the sake of the kingdom, or rather virginity, is undeniably an innovation connected with the incarnation of God.

From the moment of Christ's coming, the expectation of the People of God has to be directed to the eschatological kingdom which is coming and to which he must lead "the new Israel." A new awareness of faith is essential for such a turnabout and change of values. Christ emphasizes this twice: "He who is able to receive this, let him receive it." Only "those to whom it is given" understand it (Mt 19:11). *Mary* is the first person in whom this *new awareness* is manifested, for she asks the angel: "How can this be, since I have no husband?" (Lk 1:34). Even though she is "betrothed to a man whose name was Joseph" (cf. Lk 1:27) she is firm in her resolve to remain a virgin. The motherhood which is accomplished in her comes exclusively from the "power of the Most High," and is the result of the Holy Spirit's coming down upon her (cf. Lk 1:35). This divine motherhood, therefore, is an altogether unforeseen response to the human expectation of women in Israel; it comes to Mary as a gift from God himself. This gift is the beginning and the prototype of a new expectation on the part of all. It measures up to the Eternal Covenant, to God's new and definitive promise: it is *a sign of eschatological hope.*

On the basis of the Gospel, the meaning of virginity was developed and better understood as a vocation for women too, one in which their dignity, like that of the Virgin of Nazareth, finds confirmation. The Gospel puts forward *the ideal of the consecration of the person,* that is, the person's exclusive dedication to God by virtue of the evangelical counsels: in particular, chastity, poverty and obedience. Their perfect incarnation is Jesus Christ himself. Whoever wishes to follow him in a radical way chooses to live according to these counsels. They are distinct from the commandments and show the Christian the radical way of the Gospel. From the very beginning of Christianity men and women have set out on this path, since the evangelical ideal is addressed to human beings without any distinction of sex.

In this wider context, *virginity* has to be considered *also as a path for women,* a path on which they realize their womanhood in a way different from marriage. In order to understand this path, it is necessary to refer once more to the fundamental idea of Christian anthropology. By freely choosing virginity, women confirm themselves as persons, as beings whom the Creator from the beginning has willed for their own sake.[41] At the same time they realize the personal value of their own

41. Cf. Second Vatican Ecumenical Council, Pastoral Constitution on the Church in the Modern World *Gaudium et Spes,* 24.

femininity by becoming "a sincere gift" for God who has revealed himself in Christ, a gift for Christ, the Redeemer of humanity and the spouse of souls: a "spousal" gift. *One cannot correctly understand virginity*—a woman's consecration in virginity—*without referring to spousal love.* It is through this kind of love that a person becomes a gift for the other.[42] Moreover, a man's consecration in priestly celibacy or in the religious state is to be understood analogously.

The naturally spousal predisposition of the feminine personality finds a response in virginity understood in this way. Women, called from the very "beginning" to be loved and to love, in a vocation to virginity *find Christ* first of all as the Redeemer who "loved until the end" through his total gift of self; and *they respond to this gift with a "sincere gift"* of their whole lives. They thus give themselves to the divine Spouse, and this personal gift tends to union, which is properly spiritual in character. Through the Holy Spirit's action a woman becomes "one spirit" with Christ the Spouse (cf. 1 Cor 6:17).

This is the evangelical ideal of virginity, in which both the dignity and the vocation of women are realized in a special way. In virginity thus understood the so-called *radicalism of the Gospel* finds expression: "Leave everything and follow Christ" (cf. Mt 19:27). This cannot be compared to remaining simply unmarried or single, because virginity is not restricted to a mere "no," but contains a profound "yes" in the spousal order: the gift of self for love in a total and undivided manner.

Motherhood according to the Spirit

21. Virginity according to the Gospel means *renouncing marriage and thus physical motherhood.* Nevertheless, the renunciation of this kind of motherhood, a renunciation that can involve great sacrifice for a woman, makes possible a different kind of motherhood: motherhood *"according to the Spirit"* (cf. Rm 8:4). For virginity does not deprive a woman of her prerogatives. Spiritual motherhood takes on many different forms. In the life of consecrated women, for example, who live according to the charism and the rules of the various apostolic institutes, it can express itself as concern for people, especially the most needy: the sick, the handicapped, the abandoned, orphans, the elderly, children,

---

42. Cf. John Paul II, Wednesday general audience addresses, April 7 and 21, 1982: *Insegnamenti* V, 1, (1982), 1126–1131 and 1175–1179.

young people, the imprisoned and, in general, people on the margins of society. *In this way a consecrated woman finds her Spouse,* different and the same in each and every person, according to his very words: "As you did it to one of the least of these my brethren, you did it to me" (Mt 25:40). Spousal love always involves a special readiness to be poured out for the sake of those who come within one's range of activity. In marriage this readiness, even though open to all, consists mainly in the love that parents give to their children. In virginity this readiness is open *to all people, who are embraced by the love of Christ the Spouse.*

Spousal love—with its maternal potential hidden in the heart of the woman as a virginal bride—when joined to Christ, the Redeemer of each and every person, is also predisposed to being open to each and every person. This is confirmed in the religious communities of apostolic life, and in a different way in communities of contemplative life, or the cloister. There exist still other forms of vocation to virginity for the sake of the kingdom; for example, the secular institutes, or the communities of consecrated persons which flourish within movements, groups and associations. In all of these *the same truth about the spiritual motherhood* of virgins is confirmed in various ways. However, it is not only a matter of communal forms but also of non-communal forms. In brief, virginity as a woman's vocation is always the vocation of a person—of a unique, individual person. Therefore the spiritual motherhood which makes itself felt in this vocation is also profoundly personal.

This is also the basis of a specific *convergence between the virginity* of the unmarried woman and *the motherhood* of the married woman. This convergence moves not only from motherhood toward virginity, as emphasized above; it also moves from virginity toward marriage, the form of woman's vocation in which she becomes a mother by giving birth to her children. The starting point of this second analogy is *the meaning of marriage.* A woman is "married" either through the sacrament of marriage or spiritually through marriage to Christ. *In both cases marriage* signifies the "sincere gift of the person" of the bride to the groom. In this way, one can say that the profile of marriage is found spiritually in virginity. And does not physical motherhood also have to be a spiritual motherhood, in order to respond to the whole truth about the human being who is a unity of body and spirit? Thus there exist many reasons for discerning in these two different paths—the two different vocations of women—a profound complementarity, and even a profound union within a person's being.

"My Little Children with Whom I Am Again in Travail"

22. The Gospel reveals and enables us to understand precisely this *mode of being of the human person.* The Gospel helps every woman and every man to live it and thus attain fulfillment. There exists a total equality with respect to the gifts of the Holy Spirit, with respect to the "mighty works of God" (Acts 2:11). Moreover, it is precisely in the face of the "mighty works of God" that St. Paul, as a man, feels the need to refer to what is essentially feminine in order to express the truth about his own apostolic service. This is exactly what Paul of Tarsus does when he addresses the Galatians with the words: *"My little children, with whom I am again in travail"* (Gal 4:19). In the First Letter to the Corinthians (7:38), St. Paul proclaims the superiority of virginity over marriage, which is a constant teaching of the Church in accordance with the spirit of Christ's words recorded in the Gospel of Matthew (19:10–12); he does so without in any way obscuring the importance of physical and spiritual motherhood. Indeed in order to illustrate the Church's fundamental mission, he finds nothing better than the reference to motherhood.

The same analogy—and the same truth—are present in the Dogmatic Constitution on the Church. *Mary is the "figure" of the Church:*[43] "For in the mystery of the Church, herself rightly called mother and virgin, the Blessed Virgin came first as an eminent and singular exemplar of both virginity and motherhood.... The Son whom she brought forth is he whom God placed as the firstborn among many brethren (cf. Rm 8:29), namely, among the faithful. In their birth and development she cooperates with a maternal love."[44] "Moreover, contemplating Mary's mysterious sanctity, imitating her charity, and faithfully fulfilling the Father's will, the Church *herself becomes a mother* by accepting God's word in faith. For by her preaching and by baptism she brings forth to a new and immortal life children who are conceived by the Holy Spirit

---

43. Cf. Second Vatican Ecumenical Council, Dogmatic Constitution on the Church *Lumen Gentium,* 63; St. Ambrose, *In Lc* II, 7: *SCh.* 45, 74; *De instit. virg.* XIV, 87–89: *PL* 16, 326–327; St. Cyril of Alexandria, *Hom.* 4: *PG* 77, 996; St. Isidore of Seville, *Allegoriae* 139: *PL* 83, 117.

44. Second Vatican Ecumenical Council, Dogmatic Constitution on the Church *Lumen Gentium,* 63.

and born of God."[45] This is motherhood "according to the Spirit" with regard to the sons and daughters of the human race. And this motherhood—as already mentioned—becomes the woman's "role" also in virginity. "The Church *herself is a virgin*, who keeps whole and pure the fidelity she has pledged to her Spouse."[46] This is most perfectly fulfilled in Mary. The Church, therefore, "imitating the Mother of her Lord, and by the power of the Holy Spirit...preserves with virginal purity an integral faith, a firm hope, and a sincere charity."[47]

The Council has confirmed that, unless one looks to the Mother of God, it is impossible to understand the mystery of the Church, her reality, her essential vitality. *Indirectly* we find here *a reference to the biblical exemplar of the "woman"* which is already clearly outlined in the description of the "beginning" (cf. Gn 3:15) and which proceeds from creation, through sin to the redemption. In this way there is a conformation of the profound union between what is human and what constitutes the divine economy of salvation in human history. The Bible convinces us of the fact that one can have no adequate hermeneutic of man, or of what is "human," without appropriate reference to what is "feminine." There is an analogy in God's salvific economy: if we wish to understand it fully in relation to the whole of human history, we cannot omit, in the perspective of our faith, the mystery of "woman": virgin-mother-spouse.

---

45. Ibid., 64.

46. Ibid., 64.

47. Ibid., 64. Concerning the relation Mary-Church which continuously recurs in the reflection of the Fathers of the Church and of the entire Christian Tradition, cf. Encyclical Letter *Redemptoris Mater,* 42–44 and notes 117–127: *loc. cit.,* 418–422. Cf. also: Clement of Alexandria, *Paed.* 1, 6: *SCh.* 70, 186f.; St. Ambrose, *In Lc* II, 7: *SCh.* 45, 74; St. Augustine, *Sermo* 192, 2: *PL* 38, 1012; *Sermo* 195, 2: *PL* 38, 1018; *Sermo* 25, 8: *PL* 46, 938; St. Leo the Great, *Sermo* 25, 5: *PL* 54, 211; *Sermo* 26, 2: *PL* 54, 213; St. Bede the Venerable, *In Lc* I, 2: *PL* 92, 330. "Both mothers"—writes Isaac of Stella, disciple of St. Bernard—"both virgins, both conceive through the work of the Holy Spirit...Mary...has given birth in body to her Head; the Church...gives to this Head her body. The one and the other are mothers of Christ: but neither of the two begets him entirely without the other. Properly for that reason...that which is said in general of the virgin mother Church is understood especially of the Virgin Mother Mary; and that which is said in a special way of the Virgin Mother Mary must be attributed in general to the virgin mother Church; and all that is said about one of the two can be understood without distinction of one from the other" *(Sermo* 51, 7–8: *SCh.* 339, 202–205).

VII

THE CHURCH—THE BRIDE OF CHRIST

The "Great Mystery"

23. Of fundamental importance here are the words of the Letter to the Ephesians:

> Husbands, love your wives, as Christ loved the Church and gave himself up for her, that he might sanctify her, having cleansed her by the washing of water with the word, that he might present the Church to himself in splendor, without spot or wrinkle or any such thing, that she might be holy and without blemish. Even so husbands should love their wives as their own bodies. He who loves his wife loves himself. For no man ever hates his own flesh, but nourishes and cherishes it, as Christ does the Church, because we are members of his body. "For this reason a man shall leave his father and mother and be joined to his wife, and the two shall become one flesh." *This mystery is a profound one,* and I am saying that *it refers to Christ and the Church* (5:25–32).

In this letter the author expresses the truth about the Church as the bride of Christ, and also indicates how this truth *is rooted in the biblical reality of the creation of the human being as male and female.* Created in the image and likeness of God as a "unity of the two," both have been called to a spousal love. Following the description of creation in the Book of Genesis (2:18–25), one can also say that this fundamental call appears in the creation of woman, and is inscribed by the Creator in the institution of marriage, which, according to Genesis 2:24, has the character of a union of persons *(communio personarum)* from the very beginning. Although not directly, the very description of the "beginning" (cf. Gn 1:27; 2:24) shows that the whole "ethos" of mutual relations between men and women has to correspond to the personal truth of their being.

All this has already been considered. The Letter to the Ephesians once again confirms this truth, while at the same time comparing the spousal character of the love between man and woman to the mystery of

Christ and of the Church. *Christ is the Bridegroom of the Church—the Church is the Bride of Christ.* This analogy is not without precedent; it transfers to the New Testament what was already contained *in the Old Testament,* especially in the prophets Hosea, Jeremiah, Ezekiel and Isaiah.[48] The respective passages deserve a separate analysis. Here we will cite only one text. This is how God speaks to his Chosen People through the Prophet:

> Fear not, for you will not be ashamed; be not confounded, for you will not be put to shame; for you will forget the shame of your youth, and the reproach of your widowhood you will remember no more. *For your Maker is your husband,* the Lord of hosts is his name; and the Holy One of Israel is *your Redeemer,* the God of the whole earth he is called. For the Lord has called you like a wife forsaken and grieved in spirit, like a wife of youth when she is cast off, says your God. For a brief moment I forsook you, but with great compassion I will gather you. In overflowing wrath for a moment I hid my face from you, but with everlasting love I will have compassion on you, says the Lord, your Redeemer.... For the mountains may depart and the hills be removed, *but my steadfast love shall not depart from you,* and my covenant of peace shall not be removed, says the Lord, who has compassion on you (Is 54:4–8, 10).

Since the human being—man and woman—has been created in God's image and likeness, God can speak about himself through the lips of the Prophet using language which is essentially human. In the text of Isaiah quoted above, the expression of God's love is *"human,"* but the *love* itself *is divine.* Since it is God's love, its spousal character is properly divine, even though it is expressed by the analogy of a man's love for a woman. The woman-bride is Israel, God's Chosen People, and this choice originates exclusively in God's gratuitous love. It is precisely this love which explains the covenant, a covenant often presented as a marriage covenant which God always renews with his Chosen People. On the part of God the covenant is a lasting "commitment"; he remains faithful to his spousal love even if the bride often shows herself to be unfaithful.

This *image of spousal love,* together with the figure of the divine Bridegroom—a very clear image in the texts of the prophets—finds crowning confirmation in the Letter to the Ephesians (5:23–32). *Christ is greeted as the bridegroom by John the Baptist* (cf. Jn 3:27–29). Indeed

---

48. Cf., for example, Hos 1:2; 2:16–18; Jer 2:2; Ezek 16:8; Is 50:1; 54:5–8.

Christ applies to himself this comparison drawn from the prophets (cf. Mk 2:19–20). The Apostle Paul, who is a bearer of the Old Testament heritage, writes to the Corinthians: "I feel a divine jealousy for you, for I betrothed you to Christ to present you as a pure bride to her one husband" (2 Cor 11:2). But the fullest expression of the truth about Christ the Redeemer's love, according to the analogy of spousal love in marriage, is found in the Letter to the Ephesians: *"Christ loved the Church and gave himself up for her"* (5:25), thereby fully confirming the fact that the Church is the bride of Christ: "The Holy One of Israel is your Redeemer" (Is 54:5). In St. Paul's text the analogy of the spousal relationship moves simultaneously in two directions which make up the whole of the "great mystery" *(sacramentum magnum)*. The covenant proper to spouses "explains" the spousal character of the union of Christ with the Church, and in its turn this union, as a "great sacrament," determines the sacramentality of marriage as a holy covenant between the two spouses, man and woman. Reading this rich and complex passage, which *taken as a whole is a great analogy,* we must *distinguish* that element which expresses the human reality of interpersonal relations from that which expresses in symbolic language the "great mystery" which is divine.

The Gospel "Innovation"

24. The text is addressed to the spouses as real women and men. It reminds them of the "ethos" of spousal love which goes back to the divine institution of marriage from the "beginning." Corresponding to the truth of this institution is the exhortation: *"Husbands, love your wives,"* love them because of that special and unique bond whereby in marriage a man and a woman become "one flesh" (Gn 2:24; Eph 5:31). In this love there is a fundamental *affirmation of the woman* as a person. This affirmation makes it possible for the female personality to develop fully and be enriched. This is precisely the way Christ acts as the bridegroom of the Church; he desires that she be "in splendor, without spot or wrinkle" (Eph 5:27). One can say that this fully captures the whole "style" of Christ in dealing with women. Husbands should make their own the elements of this style in regard to their wives; analogously, all men should do the same in regard to women in every situation. In this way both men and women bring about "the sincere gift of self."

The author of the Letter to the Ephesians sees no contradiction between an exhortation formulated in this way and the words: "Wives, be subject to your husbands, as to the Lord. For the husband is the head of the wife" (5:22–23). The author knows that this way of speaking, so profoundly rooted in the customs and religious tradition of the time, is to be understood and carried out in a new way: as *a "mutual subjection out of reverence for Christ"* (cf. Eph 5:21). This is especially true because the husband is called the "head" of the wife *as* Christ is the head of the Church; he is so in order to give "himself up for her" (Eph 5:25), and giving himself up for her means giving up even his own life. However, whereas in the relationship between Christ and the Church the subjection is only on the part of the Church, in the relationship between husband and wife the "subjection" is not one-sided but mutual.

In relation to the "old" this is evidently something "new": it is an innovation of the Gospel. We find various passages in which the apostolic writings express this innovation, even though they also communicate what is "old": what is rooted in the religious tradition of Israel, in its way of understanding and explaining the sacred texts, as for example the second chapter of the Book of Genesis.[49]

The apostolic letters are addressed to people living in an environment marked by that same traditional way of thinking and acting. The "innovation" of Christ is a fact: it constitutes the unambiguous content of the evangelical message and is the result of the redemption. However, the awareness that in marriage there is mutual "subjection of the spouses out of reverence for Christ," and not just that of the wife to the husband, must gradually establish itself in hearts, consciences, behavior and customs. This is a call which from that time onward does not cease to challenge succeeding generations; it is a call which people have to accept ever anew. St. Paul not only wrote: "In Christ Jesus...there is no more man or woman," but also wrote: "There is no more slave or freeman." Yet how many generations were needed for such a principle to be realized in the history of humanity through the abolition of slavery! And what is one to say of the many forms of slavery to which individuals and peoples are subjected, which have not yet disappeared from history?

But *the challenge presented by the "ethos" of the redemption* is clear and definitive. All the reasons in favor of the "subjection" of woman to man in marriage must be understood in the sense of a "mutual

---

49. Cf. Col 3:18; 1 Pt 3:1–6; Ti 2:4–5; Eph 5:22–24; 1 Cor 11:3–16; 14:33–35; 1 Tm 2:11–15.

subjection" of both "out of reverence for Christ." The measure of true spousal love finds its deepest source in Christ, who is the Bridegroom of the Church, his Bride.

The Symbolic Dimension of the "Great Mystery"

25. In the Letter to the Ephesians we encounter *a second dimension* of the analogy which, taken as a whole, serves to reveal the "great mystery." This is *a symbolic dimension*. If God's love for the human person, for the Chosen People of Israel, is presented by the Prophets as the love of the bridegroom for the bride, such an analogy expresses the "spousal" quality and the divine and non-human character of God's love: "For your Maker is your husband...the God of the whole earth he is called" (Is 54:5). The same can also be said of the spousal love of Christ the Redeemer: "For God so loved the world that he gave his only son" (Jn 3:16). It is a matter, therefore, of God's love expressed by means of the redemption accomplished by Christ. According to St. Paul's letter, this love is "like" the spousal love of human spouses, but naturally it is not "the same." For the analogy implies a likeness, while at the same time leaving ample room for non-likeness.

This is easily seen in regard to the person of the "bride." According to the Letter to the Ephesians, the bride *is the Church,* just as for the prophets the bride was Israel. She is therefore *a collective subject* and not *an individual person.* This collective subject is the People of God, a community made up of many persons, both women and men. "Christ has loved the Church" precisely as a community, as the People of God. At the same time, in this Church, which in the same passage is also called his "body" (cf. Eph 5:23), he has loved every individual person. For Christ has redeemed all without exception, every man and woman. It is precisely this love of God which is expressed in the redemption; the spousal character of this love reaches completion in the history of humanity and of the world.

Christ has entered this history and remains in it as the Bridegroom who "has given himself." "To give" means "to become a sincere gift" in the most complete and radical way: "Greater love has no man than this" (Jn 15:13). According to this conception, *all human beings—both women and men—are called* through the Church *to be the "Bride" of Christ, the Redeemer of the world.* In this way "being the bride," and thus the "feminine" element, becomes a symbol of all that is "human," according to the words of Paul: "There is neither male nor female; for you are all *one* in Christ Jesus" (Gal 3:28).

From a linguistic viewpoint we can say that the analogy of spousal love found in the Letter to the Ephesians links what is "masculine" to what is "feminine," since, as members of the Church, men too are included in the concept of "Bride." This should not surprise us, for St. Paul, in order to express his mission in Christ and in the Church, speaks of the "little children with whom he is again in travail" (cf. Gal 4:19). In the sphere of what is "human"—of what is humanly personal—*"masculinity" and "femininity" are distinct,* yet at the same time they *complete and explain each other.* This is also present in the great analogy of the "Bride" in the Letter to the Ephesians. In the Church every human being—male and female—is the "Bride," in that he or she accepts the gift of the love of Christ the Redeemer, and seeks to respond to it with the gift of his or her own person.

Christ is the Bridegroom. This expresses the truth about the love of God who "first loved us" (cf. 1 Jn 4:19) and who, with the gift generated by this spousal love for man, has exceeded all human expectations: "He loved them to the end" (Jn 13:1). The Bridegroom—the Son consubstantial with the Father as God—became the Son of Mary; he became the "son of man," true man, a male. *The symbol of the Bridegroom is masculine.* This masculine symbol represents the human aspect of the divine love which God has for Israel, for the Church, and for all people. Meditating on what the Gospels say about Christ's attitude toward women, we can conclude that *as a man,* a son of Israel, he *revealed* the dignity of the "daughters of Abraham" (cf. Lk 13:16), *the dignity belonging to women* from the very "beginning" on an equal footing with men. At the same time Christ emphasized the originality which distinguishes women from men, all the richness lavished upon women in the mystery of creation. Christ's attitude toward women serves as a model of what the Letter to the Ephesians expresses with the concept of "bridegroom." Precisely because Christ's divine love is the love of a bridegroom, it is the model and pattern of all human love, men's love in particular.

The Eucharist

26. Against the broad background of the "great mystery" expressed in the spousal relationship between Christ and the Church, it is possible

to understand adequately the calling of the "Twelve." *In calling only men as his apostles,* Christ *acted in a completely free and sovereign manner.* In doing so, he exercised the same freedom with which, in all his behavior, he emphasized the dignity and the vocation of women, without conforming to the prevailing customs and to the traditions sanctioned by the legislation of the time. Consequently, the assumption that he called men to be apostles in order to conform with the widespread mentality of his times, does not at all correspond to Christ's way of acting. "Teacher, we know that you are true, and teach the way of God truthfully, and care for no man; for *you do not regard the position of men"* (Mt 22:16). These words fully characterize *Jesus of Nazareth's behavior.* Here one also finds an explanation for the calling of the "Twelve." They are with Christ at the Last Supper. They alone receive the sacramental charge, "Do this in remembrance of me" (Lk 22:19; 1 Cor 11:24), which is joined to the institution of the Eucharist. On Easter Sunday night they receive the Holy Spirit for the forgiveness of sins: "Whose sins you forgive are forgiven them, and whose sins you retain are retained" (Jn 20:23).

We find ourselves at the very heart of the Paschal Mystery, which completely reveals the spousal love of God. Christ is the Bridegroom because "he has given himself": his body has been "given," his blood has been "poured out" (cf. Lk 22:19–20). In this way "he loved them to the end" (Jn 13:1). The "sincere gift" contained in the sacrifice of the cross gives definitive prominence to the spousal meaning of God's love. As the Redeemer of the world, Christ is the Bridegroom of the Church. *The Eucharist* is *the sacrament of our redemption.* It is *the sacrament of the Bridegroom and of the Bride.* The Eucharist makes present and realizes anew in a sacramental manner the redemptive act of Christ, who "creates" the Church, his body. Christ is united with this "body" as the bridegroom with the bride. All this is contained in the Letter to the Ephesians. The perennial "unity of the two" that exists between man and woman from the very "beginning" is introduced into this "great mystery" of Christ and of the Church.

Since Christ, in instituting the Eucharist, linked it in such an explicit way to the priestly service of the apostles, it is legitimate to conclude that he thereby wished to express the relationship between man and woman, between what is "feminine" and what is "masculine." It is a relationship willed by God both in the mystery of creation and in the mystery of redemption. It is *the Eucharist* above all that expresses *the redemptive act of Christ the Bridegroom toward the Church the Bride.* This is clear and unambiguous when the sacramental ministry of the Eucharist, in which the priest *acts "in persona Christi,"* is performed by a man. This explanation confirms the teaching of the Declaration *Inter Insigniores,* published at the behest of Paul VI in response to the question concerning the admission of women to the ministerial priesthood.[50]

The Gift of the Bride

27. The Second Vatican Council renewed the Church's awareness of the universality of the priesthood. In the New Covenant there is only one sacrifice and only one priest: Christ. *All the baptized share in the one priesthood of Christ,* both men and women, inasmuch as they must "present their bodies as a living sacrifice, holy and acceptable to God (cf. Rm 12:1), give witness to Christ in every place, and give an explanation to anyone who asks the reason for the hope in eternal life that is in them (cf. 1 Pt 3:15)."[51] Universal participation in Christ's sacrifice, in which the Redeemer has offered to the Father the whole world and humanity in particular, brings it about that all in the Church are "a kingdom of priests" (Rv 5:10; cf. 1 Pt 2:9), who not only share in the priestly mission but also in the prophetic and kingly mission of Christ the Messiah. Furthermore, this participation determines the organic unity of the Church, the People of God, with Christ. It expresses at the same time the "great mystery" described in the Letter to the Ephesians: *the Bride united to her Bridegroom;* united, because she lives his life; united, because she shares in his threefold mission *(tria munera Christi);* united *in such a manner as to respond* with a "sincere gift" of *self to the inexpressible gift of the love of the Bridegroom,* the Redeemer of the world. This concerns everyone in the Church, women as well as men. It obviously concerns those who share in the "ministerial priesthood,"[52] which

---

50. Cf. Congregation for the Doctrine of the Faith, Declaration Concerning the Question of the Admission of Women to the Ministerial Priesthood *Inter Insigniores* (October 15, 1976): *AAS* 69 (1977), 98–116.

51. Cf. Second Vatican Ecumenical Council, Dogmatic Constitution on the Church *Lumen Gentium,* 10.

52. Cf. ibid., 10.

is characterized by service. In the context of the "great mystery" of Christ and of the Church, all are called to respond—as a bride—with the gift of their lives to the inexpressible gift of the love of Christ, who alone, as the Redeemer of the world, is the Church's Bridegroom. The "royal priesthood," which is universal, at the same time expresses the gift of the Bride.

This is of *fundamental importance for understanding the Church in her* own *essence,* so as to avoid applying to the Church—even in her dimension as an "institution" made up of human beings and forming part of history—criteria of understanding and judgment which do not pertain to her nature. Although the Church possesses a "hierarchical" structure,[53] nevertheless this structure is totally ordered to the holiness of Christ's members. And holiness is measured according to the "great mystery" in which the Bride responds with the gift of love to the gift of the Bridegroom. She does this "in the Holy Spirit," since "God's love has been poured into our hearts through the Holy Spirit who has been given to us" (Rm 5:5). The Second Vatican Council, confirming the teaching of the whole of tradition, recalled that in the hierarchy of holiness it is *precisely the "woman,"* Mary of Nazareth, who is the "figure" of the Church. She "precedes" everyone on the path to holiness; in her person "the Church has already reached that perfection whereby she exists without spot or wrinkle (cf. Eph 5:27)."[54] In this sense, one can say that the Church is *both* "Marian" and "Apostolic-Petrine."[55]

---

53. Cf. ibid., 18–29.

54. Ibid., 65; cf. also 63; cf. Encyclical Letter *Redemptoris Mater,* 2–6; *loc. cit.,* 362–367.

55. "This *Marian profile* is also—even perhaps more so—fundamental and characteristic for the Church as is the *apostolic* and *Petrine* profile to which it is profoundly united.... The Marian dimension of the Church is antecedent to that of the Petrine, without being in any way divided from it or being less complementary. Mary Immaculate precedes all others, including obviously Peter himself and the apostles. This is so, not only because Peter and the apostles, being born of the human race under the burden of sin, form part of the Church which is 'holy from out of sinners,' but also because their triple *function* has no other purpose except to form the Church in line with the ideal of sanctity already programmed and prefigured in Mary. A contemporary theologian has rightly stated that Mary is 'Queen of the Apostles without any pretensions to apostolic powers: she has other and greater powers' (H. U. von Balthasar, *Neue Klarstellungen*)." Address to the Cardinal and Prelates of the Roman Curia (December 22, 1987); *L'Osservatore Romano,* December 23, 1987.

In the history of the Church, even from earliest times, there were side-by-side with men *a number of women,* for whom the response of the Bride to the Bridegroom's redemptive love acquired full expressive force. First we see those women who had personally encountered Christ and followed him. After his departure, together with the apostles, they "devoted themselves to prayer" in the upper room in Jerusalem until the day of Pentecost. On that day the Holy Spirit spoke through "the sons and daughters" of the People of God, thus fulfilling the words of the prophet Joel (cf. Acts 2:17). These women, and others afterward, played *an active and important role in the life of the early Church,* in building up from its foundations the first Christian community—and subsequent communities—*through their own charisms and their varied service.* The apostolic writings note their names, such as Phoebe, "a deaconess of the Church at Cenchreae" (cf. Rm 16:1), Prisca with her husband Aquila (cf. 2 Tm 4:19), Evodia and Syntyche (cf. Phil 4:2), Mary, Tryphaena, Persis and Tryphosa (cf. Rm 16:6, 12). St. Paul speaks of their "hard work" for Christ, and this hard work indicates the various fields of the Church's apostolic service, beginning with the "domestic Church." For in the latter, "sincere faith" passes from the mother to her children and grandchildren, as was the case in the house of Timothy (cf. 2 Tm 1:5).

The same thing is repeated down the centuries, from one generation to the next, as *the history of the Church* demonstrates. By defending the dignity of women and their vocation, the Church has shown honor and gratitude for those women who—faithful to the Gospel—have shared in every age in the apostolic mission of the whole People of God. They are the holy martyrs, virgins, and mothers of families, who bravely bore witness to their faith and passed on the Church's faith and tradition by bringing up their children in the spirit of the Gospel.

In every age and in every country we find many "perfect" women (cf. Prov 31:10) who, despite persecution, difficulties and discrimination, have shared in the Church's mission. It suffices to mention: Monica, the mother of Augustine, Macrina, Olga of Kiev, Matilda of Tuscany, Hedwig of Silesia, Jadwiga of Cracow, Elizabeth of Thuringia, Birgitta of Sweden, Joan of Arc, Rose of Lima, Elizabeth Ann Seton and Mary Ward.

The witness and the achievements of Christian women have had a significant impact on the life of the Church as well as of society. Even in the face of serious social discrimination, holy women have acted "freely," strengthened by their union with Christ. Such union and freedom rooted in God explain, for example, the great work of St. Catherine of Siena in the life of the Church, and the work of St. Teresa of Jesus in the monastic life.

In our own days too the Church is constantly enriched by the witness of the many women who fulfill their vocation to holiness. Holy women are an incarnation of the feminine ideal; they are also a model for all Christians, a model of the *"sequela Christi,"* an example of how the Bride must respond with love to the love of the Bridegroom.

VIII
"THE GREATEST OF THESE IS LOVE"

In the Face of Changes

28. "The Church believes that Christ, who died and was raised up for all, can through his Spirit offer man the light and the strength to respond to his supreme destiny."[56] We can apply these words of the Conciliar Constitution *Gaudium et Spes* to the present reflections. The particular reference to the dignity of women and their vocation, precisely in our time, can and must be received in the "light and power" which the Spirit grants to human beings, including the people of our own age, which is marked by so many different transformations. The Church "holds that in her Lord and Master can be found the key, the focal point, and the goal" of man and "of all human history," and she "maintains *that beneath all changes there are many realities which do not change and which have their ultimate foundation in Christ,* who is the same yesterday and today, yes and forever."[57]

These words of the Constitution on the Church in the Modern World show the path to be followed in undertaking the tasks connected with the dignity and vocation of women, against the background of the significant changes of our times. We can face these changes correctly and adequately only *if we go back* to the foundations which are to be found in Christ, to those *"immutable" truths and values* of which he himself remains the "faithful witness" (cf. Rv 1:5) and Teacher. A different way of acting would lead to doubtful, if not actually erroneous and deceptive results.

---

56. Cf. Second Vatican Ecumenical Council, Pastoral Constitution on the Church in the Modern World *Gaudium et Spes,* 10.

57. Ibid., 10.

The Dignity of Women and the Order of Love

29. The passage from the Letter to the Ephesians already quoted (5:21–33), in which the relationship between Christ and the Church is presented as the link between the Bridegroom and the Bride, also makes reference to the institution of marriage as recorded in the Book of Genesis (cf. 2:24). This passage connects the truth about marriage as a primordial sacrament with the creation of man and woman in the image and likeness of God (cf. Gn 1:27; 5:1). The significant comparison in the Letter to the Ephesians gives perfect clarity to *what is decisive for the dignity of women both in the eyes of God*—the Creator and Redeemer—*and in the eyes of human beings*—men and women. In God's eternal plan, woman is the one in whom the order of love in the created world of persons takes first root. The order of love belongs to the intimate life of God himself, the life of the Trinity. In the intimate life of God, the Holy Spirit is the personal hypostasis of love. Through the spirit, Uncreated Gift, love becomes a gift for created persons. *Love, which is of God, communicates itself to creatures:* "God's love has been poured into our hearts through the Holy Spirit who has been given to us" (Rm 5:5).

The calling of women into existence at man's side as "a helper fit for him" (Gn 2:18) in the "unity of the two," provides the visible world of creatures with particular conditions so that "the love of God may be poured into the hearts" of the beings created in his image. When the author of the Letter to the Ephesians calls Christ "the Bridegroom" and the Church "the Bride," he indirectly confirms through this analogy *the truth about woman as bride*. The Bridegroom is the one who loves. The Bride is loved: *it is she who receives love, in order to love in return.*

Rereading Genesis in light of the spousal symbol in the Letter to the Ephesians enables us to grasp a truth which seems to determine in an essential manner the question of women's dignity, and, subsequently, also the question of their vocation: *the dignity of women is measured by the order of love,* which is essentially the order of justice and charity.[58]

Only a person can love and only a person can be loved. This statement is primarily ontological in nature, and it gives rise to an ethical affirmation. Love is an ontological and ethical requirement of the person. The person must be loved, since love alone corresponds to what the

---

58. Cf. St. Augustine, *De Trinitate,* L. VIII, VII, 10–X, 14: *CCL* 50, 284–291.

person is. This explains *the commandment of love,* known already in the Old Testament (cf. Dt 6:5; Lv 19:18) and placed by Christ at the very center of the Gospel *"ethos"* (cf. Mt 22:36–40; Mk 12:28–34). This also explains the *primacy of love* expressed by St. Paul in the First Letter to the Corinthians: "The greatest of these is love" (cf. 13:13).

Unless we refer to this order and primacy we cannot give a complete and adequate answer to the question about women's dignity and vocation. When we say that the woman is the one who receives love in order to love in return, this refers not only or above all to the specific spousal relationship of marriage. It means something more universal, based on the very fact of her being a woman within all the interpersonal relationships which, in the most varied ways, shape society and structure the interaction between all persons—men and women. In this broad and diversified context, a *woman represents a particular value by the fact that she is a human person,* and, at the same time, this particular person, *by the fact of her femininity.* This concerns each and every woman, independently of the cultural context in which she lives, and independently of her spiritual, psychological and physical characteristics, as for example, age, education, health, work, and whether she is married or single.

The passage from the Letter to the Ephesians which we have been considering enables us to think of a special kind of "prophetism" that belongs to women in their femininity. The analogy of the Bridegroom and the Bride speaks of the love with which every human being—man and woman—is loved by God in Christ. But in the context of the biblical analogy and the text's interior logic, it is precisely the woman—the bride—who manifests this truth to everyone. This *"prophetic" character of women in their femininity* finds its highest expression in the Virgin Mother of God. She emphasizes, in the fullest and most direct way, the intimate linking of the order of love—which enters the world of human persons through a woman—with the Holy Spirit. At the annunciation Mary hears the words: "The Holy Spirit will come upon you" (Lk 1:35).

Awareness of a Mission

30. A woman's dignity is closely connected with the love which she receives by the very reason of her femininity; it is likewise connected *with the love which she gives in return.* The truth about the person and about love is thus confirmed. With regard to the truth about the person,

we must turn again to the Second Vatican Council: "Man, who is the only creature on earth that God willed for its own sake, cannot fully find himself except through a sincere gift of self."[59] This applies to every human being, as a person created in God's image, whether man or woman. This ontological affirmation also indicates the ethical dimension of a person's vocation. *Woman can only find herself by giving love to others.*

From the "beginning," woman—like man—was created and "placed" by God in this order of love. The sin of the first parents did not destroy this order, nor irreversibly cancel it out. This is proved by the words of the proto-evangelium (cf. Gn 3:15). Our reflections have focused on *the particular place occupied by the "woman"* in this key text of revelation. It is also to be noted how the same Woman, who attains the position of a biblical "exemplar," also appears within the eschatological perspective of the world and of humanity given in the Book of Revelation.[60] She is *"a woman clothed with the sun,"* with the moon under her feet, and on her head a crown of stars (cf. Rv 12:1). One can say she is a Woman of cosmic scale, on a scale with the whole work of creation. At the same time she is "suffering the pangs and anguish of childbirth" (Rv 12:2) like Eve "the mother of all the living" (Gn 3:20). She also suffers because "before the woman who is about to give birth" (cf. Rv 12:4) there stands "the great dragon...that ancient serpent" (Rv 12:9), already known from the proto-evangelium: the Evil One, the "father of lies" and of sin (cf. Jn 8:44). The "ancient serpent" wishes to devour "the child." While we see in this text an echo of the infancy narrative (cf. Mt 2:13, 16), we can also see that the struggle with evil and the Evil One marks the biblical exemplar of the "woman" from the beginning to the end of history. It is also *a struggle for man, for his true good, for his salvation.* Is not the Bible trying to tell us that it is precisely in the "woman"—Eve-Mary—that history witnesses a dramatic struggle for every human being, the struggle for his or her fundamental "yes" or "no" to God and God's eternal plan for humanity?

While the dignity of woman witnesses to the love which she receives in order to love in return, the biblical "exemplar" of the Woman also

---

59. Second Vatican Ecumenical Council, Pastoral Constitution on the Church in the Modern World *Gaudium et Spes,* 24.

60. Cf. in the Appendix to the works of St. Ambrose, *In Apoc.* IV, 3–4: *PL* 17, 876; St. Augustine, *De symb. ad. catech. sermo* IV: *PL* 40, 661.

seems to reveal *the true order of love which constitutes woman's own vocation.* Vocation is meant here in its fundamental, and one may say universal significance, a significance which is then actualized and expressed in women's many different "vocations" in the Church and the world.

The moral and spiritual strength of a woman is joined to her awareness that *God entrusts the human being to her in a special way.* Of course, God entrusts every human being to each and every other human being. But this entrusting concerns women in a special way—precisely by reason of their femininity—and this in a particular way determines their vocation.

The moral force of women, which draws strength from this awareness and this entrusting, expresses itself in a great number of figures of the Old Testament, of the time of Christ, and of later ages right up to our own day.

A woman is strong because of her awareness of this entrusting, strong because of the fact that God "entrusts the human being to her," always and in every way, even in the situations of social discrimination in which she may find herself. This awareness and this fundamental vocation speak to women of the dignity which they receive from God himself, and this makes them " strong" and strengthens their vocation. Thus the "perfect woman" (cf. Prov 31:10) becomes an irreplaceable support and source of spiritual strength for other people, who perceive the great energies of her spirit. These "perfect women" are owed much by their families, and sometimes by whole nations.

In our own time, the successes of science and technology make it possible to attain material well-being to a degree hitherto unknown. While this favors some, it pushes others to the margins of society. In this way, unilateral progress can also lead to a gradual *loss of sensitivity for man, that is, for what is essentially human.* In this sense, our time in particular *awaits the manifestation* of that "genius" which belongs to women, and which can ensure sensitivity for human beings in every circumstance: because they are human!—and because "the greatest of these is love" (cf. 1 Cor 13:13).

Thus a careful reading of the biblical exemplar of the Woman— from the Book of Genesis to the Book of Revelation—confirms that which constitutes woman's dignity and vocation, as well as that which is unchangeable and ever relevant in them, because it has its "ultimate foundation in Christ, who is the same yesterday and today, yes and forever."[61] If the human being is entrusted by God to women in a particular way, does not this mean that *Christ looks to them for the accomplishment of the "royal priesthood"* (1 Pt 2:9), which is the treasure he has given to every individual? Christ, as the supreme and only priest of the New and Eternal Covenant, and as the Bridegroom of the Church, does not cease to submit this same inheritance to the Father through the Spirit, so that God may be "everything to everyone" (1 Cor 15:28).[62]

Then the truth that "the greatest of these is love" (cf. 1 Cor 13:13) will have its definitive fulfillment.

---

61. Second Vatican Ecumenical Council, Pastoral Constitution on the Church in the Modern World *Gaudium et Spes,* 10.

62. Second Vatican Ecumenical Council, Dogmatic Constitution on the Church *Lumen Gentium,* 36.

IX
CONCLUSION

"If You Knew the Gift of God"

31. "If you knew the gift of God" (Jn 4:10), Jesus says to the Samaritan woman during one of those remarkable conversations which show his great esteem for the dignity of women and for the vocation which enables them to share in his messianic mission.

The present reflections, now at an end, have sought to recognize, within the "gift of God," what he, as Creator and Redeemer, entrusts to women, to every woman. In the Spirit of Christ, in fact, women can discover the entire meaning of their femininity and thus be disposed to making a "sincere gift of self" to others, thereby finding themselves.

During the Marian Year *the Church desires to give thanks to the Most Holy Trinity* for the "mystery of woman" and for every woman—for that which constitutes the eternal measure of her feminine dignity, for the "great works of God," which throughout human history have been accomplished in and through her. After all, was it not in and through her that the greatest event in human history—the Incarnation of God himself—was accomplished?

Therefore *the Church gives thanks for each and every woman:* for mothers, for sisters, for wives; for women consecrated to God in virginity; for women dedicated to the many human beings who await the gratuitous love of another person; for women who watch over the human persons in the family, which is the fundamental sign of the human community; for women who work professionally, and who at times are burdened by a great social responsibility; for *"perfect"* women and for "weak" women—for all women as they have come forth from the heart of God in all the beauty and richness of their femininity; as they have been embraced by his eternal love; as, together with men, they are pilgrims on this earth, which is the temporal "homeland" of all people and is transformed sometimes into a "valley of tears"; as they assume, together with men, *a common responsibility for the destiny of humanity* according to daily necessities and according to that definitive destiny which the human family has in God himself, in the bosom of the ineffable Trinity.

The Church gives thanks *for all the manifestations of the feminine "genius"* which have appeared in the course of history, in the midst of all peoples and nations, she gives thanks for all the charisms which the Holy Spirit distributes to women in the history of the People of God, for all the victories which she owes to their faith, hope and charity: she gives thanks for all *the fruits of feminine holiness.*

The Church asks at the same time that these invaluable "manifestations of the Spirit" (cf. 1 Cor 12:4 ff.), which with great generosity are poured forth upon the "daughters" of the eternal Jerusalem, may be attentively recognized and appreciated so that they may return for the common good of the Church and of humanity, especially in our times. Meditating on the biblical mystery of the "woman," the Church prays that in this mystery all women may discover themselves and their "supreme vocation."

May *Mary,* who "is a model of the Church in the matter of faith, charity, and perfect union with Christ,"[63] obtain for all of us *this same "grace,"* in the year which we have dedicated to her as we approach the third millennium from the coming of Christ.

With these sentiments, I impart the Apostolic Blessing to all the faithful, and in a special way to women, my sisters in Christ.

Given in Rome, at St. Peter's, on August 15, the Solemnity of the Assumption of the Blessed Virgin Mary, in the year 1988, the tenth of my pontificate.

John Paul II

---

63. Cf. ibid., 63.

GUARDIAN OF THE REDEEMER

Redemptoris Custos

Apostolic Exhortation of Pope John Paul II
August 15, 1989

INTRODUCTION

This document centers on St. Joseph, but is included in this volume because of Joseph's relation to Mary. The pope speaks of Joseph as the guardian of the Redeemer, thus connecting him to the mystery of the redemption and to Mary, the Mother of the Redeemer. *Redemptoris Custos* can be seen in relation to *Redemptoris Mater.*

Historical Perspectives

The pope draws on the Gospel portrait of Joseph, which is quite sparse, as well as the tradition of devotion to St. Joseph that has developed in the Church. In relation to Mary, the document focuses on a few key themes.

The Teaching

The first major section is on Joseph's marriage to Mary. It points out the parallel between the annunciation to Mary in Luke's Gospel with the annunciation to Joseph in Matthew's. *"The divine messenger introduces Joseph to the mystery of Mary's motherhood"* (*RC* 3). Confronted with this mystery, Joseph acted on the divine message. He showed a readiness to obey God just as Mary did.

The pope then stresses that *"the faith of Mary meets the faith of Joseph"* (RC 4). Just as Mary "advanced in her pilgrimage of faith," (*LG* 58), Joseph walked with her on the way of faith. Joseph became the "guardian of the mystery" and "together with Mary, and in relation to Mary, *he shares in this final phase of God's self-revelation in Christ"* (*RC* 5).

While affirming Mary's virginity, the document also affirms that Mary and Joseph had a true marriage. It was certainly a unique situation, but they were joined in a true spousal love. In speaking of the "'spousal gift of self' in receiving and expressing such a love" (*RC* 7), John Paul returns to ideas developed in his catechesis on the theology of the body. He speaks of Mary as a married woman, living this spousal love. He then makes applications to family life today.

Chapter three again speaks of Joseph as Mary's husband. Mary and Joseph were truly married, according to Jewish custom. Yet the mystery of grace was at work in Mary's heart, kindling in her a *"deep desire to give herself exclusively to God....* From the moment of the annunciation, Mary knew that *she was to fulfill her virginal desire* to give herself exclusively and fully to God precisely *by becoming the Mother of God's Son"* (*RC* 18). The pope here gives an insightful treatment to the question of Mary's desire for virginity. In her time and culture, which greatly valued marriage, it would be reading too much into the text to assert she had previously made a vow of virginity, as has sometimes been proposed. Yet we can think of the Holy Spirit at work in her, stirring up in her a desire to give herself to God, so that she was prepared to accept God's invitation at the annunciation.[1]

Today

The document thus presents Mary and Joseph as models of both kinds of love—spousal love and virginal love. Together, these two loves "represent the mystery of the Church—virgin and spouse" (*RC* 20). In the example of their love, Mary and Joseph have something to say to every generation of Christians.

---

1. For a fuller treatment of this question, based on an exegesis of Lk 1:34, see Ignace de la Potterie, *Mary in the Mystery of the Covenant* (New York: Alba House, 1992), 22–29.

TOPICAL OUTLINE

1. Introduction: occasion of the document (1)

2. The Gospel portrait of Joseph: Marriage to Mary

    A. The annunciation to Mary (2)

    B. The annunciation to Joseph (3)

3. The guardian of the mystery of God

    A. Joseph's way of faith (4–6)

    B. The marriage of Mary and Joseph (7)

    C. Joseph and the service of fatherhood (8)

    D. Joseph's share in the events of Jesus' childhood (9–16)

4. Joseph, the just man and the husband

    A. "Joseph's way": doing the will of God (17)

    B. The virginity of Mary and Joseph (18–19)

    C. Marriage and virginity as two ways of love (20)

    D. Joseph's fatherhood (21)

5. Work as an expression of love (22–24)

6. The primacy of the interior life (25–27)

7. Patron of the Church (28–32)

GUARDIAN OF THE REDEEMER

Redemptoris Custos

Promulgated by His Holiness Pope John Paul II
On August 15, 1989

*On the Person and Mission of Saint Joseph in the
Life of Christ and of the Church*

Introduction

1. "Joseph did *as the angel of the Lord commanded him and took his
wife"* (cf. Mt 1:24).

Inspired by the Gospel, the Fathers of the Church from the earliest
centuries stressed that just as St. Joseph took loving care of Mary and
gladly dedicated himself to Jesus Christ's upbringing,[1] he likewise
watches over and protects Christ's Mystical Body, that is, the Church, of
which the Virgin Mary is the exemplar and model.

On the occasion of the centenary of Pope Leo XIII's Encyclical
Epistle *Quamquam Pluries,*[2] and in line with the veneration given to St.
Joseph over the centuries, I wish to offer for your consideration, dear
brothers and sisters, some reflections concerning him "into whose cus-

---

1. Cf. St. Irenaeus, *Adversus Haereses,* IV, 23, 1: *SCh.* 100/2, 692–694.
2. Leo XIII, Encyclical Epistle *Quamquam Pluries* (August 15, 1889): *Leo XIII, P.M.
Acta,* IX (1890), 175–182.

tody God entrusted his most precious treasures."[3] I gladly fulfill this pastoral duty so that all may grow in devotion to the patron of the Universal Church and in love for the Savior whom he served in such an exemplary manner.

In this way the whole Christian people not only will turn to St. Joseph with greater fervor and invoke his patronage with trust, but also will always keep before their eyes his humble, mature way of serving and of "taking part" in the plan of salvation.[4]

I am convinced that by reflection upon the way that Mary's spouse shared in the divine mystery, the Church—on the road toward the future with all of humanity—will be enabled to discover ever anew her own identity within this redemptive plan, *which is founded on the mystery of the Incarnation.*

This is precisely the mystery in which Joseph of Nazareth "shared" like no other human being except Mary, the Mother of the incarnate Word. He shared in it with her; he was involved in the same salvific event; he was the guardian of the same love, through the power of which the eternal Father "destined us to be his sons through Jesus Christ" (Eph 1:5).

---

3. Sacror. Rituum Congreg., *Decr. Quemadmodum Deus* (December 8, 1870): Pius IX, *P.M. Acta,* pars I, vol. V, 282; Pius IX, Apostolic Letter *Inclytum Patriarcham* (July 7, 1871): *loc. cit.,* 331–335.

4. Cf. St. John Chrysostom, *In Matth. Hom.* V, 3: *PG* 57, 57f. The Fathers of the Church and the Popes, on the basis of their common name, also saw in Joseph of Egypt a prototype of Joseph of Nazareth, inasmuch as the former foreshadowed in some way the ministry and greatness of the latter, who was guardian of God the Father's most precious treasures—the incarnate Word and his most holy Mother: cf., for example, St. Bernard, *Super "Missus est," Hom.* II, 16: *Sancti Bernardi Opera,* Ed. Cist., IV, 33f.; Leo XIII, Encyclical Epistle *Quamquam Pluries* (August 15, 1889): *loc. cit.,* 179.

I

THE GOSPEL PORTRAIT

Marriage to Mary

2. "Joseph, Son of David, *do not fear to take Mary* your wife, for that which is conceived in her is of the Holy Spirit; she will bear a son, and you shall call his name Jesus, for he will save his people from their sins" (Mt 1:20–21).

In these words we find the core of biblical truth about St. Joseph; they refer to that moment in his life to which the Fathers of the Church make special reference.

The Evangelist Matthew explains the significance of this moment while also describing how Joseph lived it. However, in order to understand fully both its content and context, it is important to keep in mind the parallel passage in the *Gospel of Luke.* In Matthew we read: "Now the birth of Jesus Christ took place in this way. When his mother Mary had been betrothed to Joseph, before they came together she was found to be with child of the Holy Spirit" (Mt 1:18). However, the origin of Mary's pregnancy "of the Holy Spirit" is described more fully and explicitly in *what Luke tells us about the annunciation of Jesus' birth:* "The angel Gabriel was sent from God to a city of Galilee named Nazareth, to a virgin betrothed to a man whose name was Joseph, of the house of David; and the virgin's name was Mary" (Lk 1:26–27). The angel's greeting: "Hail, full of grace, the Lord is with you" (Lk 1:28) created an inner turmoil in Mary and also moved her to reflect. Then the messenger reassured the Virgin and at the same time revealed God's special plan for her: *"Do not be afraid, Mary, for you have found favor with God. And behold, you will conceive in your womb and bear a son,* and you shall call his name Jesus. He will be great, and will be called the Son of the Most High, and the Lord God will give to him the throne of his father David" (Lk 1:30–32).

A little earlier the Gospel writer had stated that at the moment of the annunciation, Mary was "betrothed to a man whose name was Joseph, of the house of David." The nature of this *"marriage"* is explained indirectly when Mary, after hearing what the messenger says about the birth of the child, asks, "How can this be, *since I do not know man?"* (Lk 1:34). The angel responds: "The Holy Spirit will come upon you, and the power of the Most High will overshadow you; therefore the child to be born will be called holy, the Son of God" (Lk 1:35). Although Mary is already "wedded" to Joseph, she will remain a virgin, because the child conceived in her at the annunciation was conceived by the power of the Holy Spirit.

At this point Luke's text coincides with Matthew 1:18 and serves to explain what we read there. If, after her marriage to Joseph, Mary "is found to be with child of the Holy Spirit," this fact corresponds to all that the annunciation means, in particular to Mary's final words: *"Let it be to me according to your word"* (Lk 1:38). In response to what is clearly the plan of God, with the passing of days and weeks Mary's "pregnancy" is visible to the people and to Joseph; she appears before them as one who must give birth and carry within herself the mystery of motherhood.

3. In these circumstances, "her husband Joseph, being a just man and unwilling to put her to shame, *resolved to send her away quietly"* (Mt 1:19). He did not know how to deal with Mary's "astonishing" motherhood. He certainly sought an answer to this unsettling question, but above all he sought a way out of what was for him a difficult situation. *"But as he considered this,* behold, an angel of the Lord appeared to him in a dream, saying, *'Joseph,* son of David, *do not fear to take Mary your wife,* for that which is conceived in her is of the Holy Spirit; she will bear a son, and you shall call his name Jesus, for he will save his people from their sins'"* (Mt 1:20–21).

There is a strict parallel between the "annunciation" in Matthew's text and the one in Luke. *The divine messenger introduces Joseph to the mystery of Mary's motherhood.* While remaining a virgin, she who by law is his "spouse" has become a mother through the power of the Holy Spirit. And when the Son in Mary's womb comes into the world, he must receive the name Jesus. This was a name known among the Israelites and sometimes given to their sons. In this case, however, *it is the*

Son who, in accordance with the divine promise, *will bring to perfect fulfillment the meaning of the name Jesus*—Yehos ua'—which means *"God saves."*

Joseph is visited by *the messenger* as "Mary's spouse," as the one who in due time must give this name to the Son to be born of the Virgin of Nazareth who is married to him. It is *to Joseph,* then, that the messenger turns, *entrusting to him the responsibilities of an earthly father with regard to Mary's Son.*

"When Joseph woke from sleep, he did as the angel of the Lord commanded him and took Mary as his wife" (Mt 1:24). He took her in all the mystery of her motherhood. He took her together with the Son who had come into the world by the power of the Holy Spirit. In this way *he showed a readiness of will like Mary's* with regard to what God asked of him through the angel.

II

THE GUARDIAN OF THE MYSTERY OF GOD

4. When, soon after the annunciation, Mary went to the house of Zechariah to visit her kinswoman Elizabeth, even as she offered her greeting she heard the words of Elizabeth, who was "filled with the Holy Spirit" (Lk 1:41). Besides offering a salutation which recalled that of the angel at the annunciation, Elizabeth also said: *"And blessed is she who believed that there would be a fulfillment of what was spoken to her from the Lord"* (Lk 1:45). These words were the guiding thought of the Encyclical *Redemptoris Mater,* in which I sought to deepen the teaching of the Second Vatican Council, which stated: *"The Blessed Virgin advanced in her pilgrimage of faith,* and faithfully preserved her union with her Son even to the cross,"[5] "preceding"[6] all those who follow Christ by faith.

Now at the beginning of this pilgrimage, *the faith of Mary meets the faith of Joseph.* If Elizabeth said of the Redeemer's Mother, "blessed is she who believed," in a certain sense this blessedness can be referred to Joseph as well, since he responded positively to the word of God when it was communicated to him at the decisive moment. While it is true that Joseph did not respond to the angel's "announcement" in the same way as Mary, he *"did as the angel of the Lord commanded him and took his wife." What he did is the clearest "obedience of faith"* (cf. Rm 1:5; 16:26; 2 Cor 10:5–6).

One can say that *what Joseph did* united him in an altogether special way to the faith of Mary. *He accepted* as truth coming from God *the very thing* that *she had already accepted* at the annunciation. The Council teaches: "'The obedience of faith' must be given to God as he reveals

---

5. Second Vatican Ecumenical Council, Dogmatic Constitution on the Church *Lumen Gentium,* 58.

6. Cf. ibid., 63.

himself. By this obedience of faith man freely commits himself entirely to God, making 'the full submission of his intellect and will to God who reveals,' and willingly assenting to the revelation given by him."[7] *This statement,* which touches the very essence of faith, *is perfectly applicable to Joseph of Nazareth.*

5. Therefore he became *a unique guardian of the mystery* "hidden for ages in God" (Eph 3:9), as did Mary, in that decisive moment which St. Paul calls *"the fullness of time,"* when "God sent forth his Son, born of woman...to redeem those who were under the law, so that we might receive adoption as sons" (Gal 4:4–5). In the words of the Council: "It pleased God, in his goodness and wisdom, to reveal himself and to make known the mystery of his will (cf. Eph 1:9). His will was that men should have access to the Father, through Christ, the Word made flesh, in the Holy Spirit, and become sharers in the divine nature (cf. Eph 2:18; 2 Pt 1:4)."[8]

Together with Mary, Joseph is the first guardian of this divine mystery. Together with Mary, and in relation to Mary, *he shares in this final phase of God's self-revelation in Christ* and he does so from the very beginning. Looking at the gospel texts of both Matthew and Luke, one can also say that Joseph is the first *to share in the faith of the Mother of God* and that in doing so he supports his spouse in the faith of the divine annunciation. He is also the first to be placed by God on the path of Mary's "pilgrimage of faith." It is a path along which—especially at the time of Calvary and Pentecost—Mary will precede in a perfect way.[9]

6. The path that was Joseph's—*his pilgrimage of faith—ended first,* that is to say, before Mary stood at the foot of the cross on Golgotha, and before the time after Christ returned to the Father, when she was present in the upper room on Pentecost, the day the Church was manifested to the world, having been born in the power of the Spirit of truth. Nevertheless, *Joseph's way of faith moved in the same direction:* it was totally determined by the same mystery, of which he, together with Mary, had been the first guardian. The Incarnation and

---

7. Second Vatican Ecumenical Council, Dogmatic Constitution on Divine Revelation *Dei Verbum,* 5.

8. Ibid., 2.

9. Cf. Second Vatican Ecumenical Council, Dogmatic Constitution on the Church *Lumen Gentium,* 63.

redemption constitute an organic and indissoluble unity, in which "the plan of revelation is realized by words and deeds which are intrinsically bound up with each other."[10] Precisely because of this unity, Pope John XXIII, who had a great devotion to St. Joseph, directed that Joseph's name be inserted in the Roman Canon of the Mass—which is the perpetual memorial of redemption—after the name of Mary and before the apostles, popes and martyrs.[11]

The Service of Fatherhood

7. As can be deduced from the gospel texts, Joseph's marriage to Mary is the juridical basis of his fatherhood. It was to assure fatherly protection for Jesus that God chose Joseph to be Mary's spouse. It follows that Joseph's fatherhood—a relationship that places him as close as possible to Christ, to whom every election and predestination is ordered (cf. Rm 8:28–29)—comes to pass through marriage to Mary, that is, through the family.

While clearly affirming that Jesus was conceived by the power of the Holy Spirit, and that virginity remained intact in the marriage (cf. Mt 1:18–25; Lk 1:26–38), the evangelists refer to Joseph as Mary's husband and to Mary as his wife (cf. Mt 1:16, 18–20, 24; Lk 1:27; 2:5).

And while it is important for the Church to profess *the virginal conception of Jesus,* it is no less important to uphold *Mary's marriage to Joseph,* because juridically Joseph's fatherhood depends on it. Thus one understands why the generations are listed according to the genealogy of Joseph: "Why," St. Augustine asks, "should they not be according to Joseph? Was he not Mary's husband?... Scripture states, through the authority of an angel, that he was her husband. *Do not fear,* says the angel, *to take Mary your wife, for that which is conceived in her is of the Holy Spirit.* Joseph was told to name the child, although not born from his seed. *She will bear a son,* the angel says, *and you will call him Jesus. Scripture recognizes that Jesus is not born of Joseph's seed, since in his concern about the origin of Mary's pregnancy, Joseph is told that it is of the Holy Spirit.* Nonetheless, he is not

---

10. Second Vatican Ecumenical Council, Dogmatic Constitution on Divine Revelation *Dei Verbum,* 2.

11. Sacred Congregation of Rites, *Decree Novis Hisce Temporibus* (November 13, 1962): *AAS* 54 (1962), p. 873.

deprived of his fatherly authority from the moment that he is told to name the child. Finally, even the Virgin Mary, well aware that she has not conceived Christ as a result of conjugal relations with Joseph, still calls him *Christ's father.*"[12]

The *Son of Mary* is also *Joseph's Son* by virtue of the marriage bond that unites them: "By reason of their faithful marriage *both of them* deserve to be called Christ's parents, not only his mother, but also his father, who was a parent in the same way that he was the mother's spouse: *in mind,* not in the flesh."[13] In this marriage none of the requisites of marriage were lacking: "In Christ's parents all the goods of marriage were realized—offspring, fidelity, the sacrament: the *offspring* being the Lord Jesus himself; *fidelity,* since there was no adultery: *the sacrament,* since there was no divorce."[14]

Analyzing the nature of marriage, both St. Augustine and St. Thomas always identify it with an "indivisible union of souls," a "union of hearts," with "consent."[15] These elements are found in an exemplary manner in the marriage of Mary and Joseph. At the culmination of the history of salvation, when God reveals his love for humanity through the gift of the Word, it is precisely *the marriage of Mary and Joseph* that brings to realization in full "freedom" the "spousal gift of self" in receiving and expressing such a love.[16] "In this great undertaking which is the renewal of all things in Christ, marriage—it too purified and renewed—becomes a new reality, a sacrament of the New Covenant. We see that at the beginning of the New Testament, as at the beginning of the Old, there is a married couple. But whereas Adam and Eve were the source of evil which was unleashed on the world, Joseph and Mary arc the summit from which holiness spreads all over the earth. The Savior began the work of salvation by this virginal and

---

12. St. Augustine, *Sermo* 51, 10, 16: *PL* 38, 342.

13. St. Augustine, *De Nuptiis et Concupiscentia,* I, 11, 12: *PL* 44, 421; cf. *De Consensu Evangelistarum,* II, 1, 2: *PL* 34, 1071; *Contra Faustum,* III, 2: *PL* 42, 214.

14. St. Augustine, *De Nuptiis et Concupiscentia,* I, 11, 13: *PL* 44, 421; cf. *Contra Iulianum,* V, 12, 46: *PL* 44, 810.

15. Cf. St. Augustine, *Contra Faustum,* 23, 8: *PL* 42, 470f.; *De Consensu Evangelistarum,* II, 1, 3: *PL* 34, 1072; *Sermo* 51, 13, 21: *PL* 38, 344f.; St. Thomas, *Summa Theol.,* III, q. 29, a. 2 in conclus.

16. Cf. *Discourses* of January 9, 16, February 20, 1980: *Insegnamenti,* III/I (1980), pp. 88–92; 148–152; 428–431.

holy union, wherein is manifested his all-powerful will to *purify and sanctify the family*—that sanctuary of love and cradle of life."[17]

How much the family of today can learn from this! "The essence and role of the family are in the final analysis specified by love. Hence the family has *the mission to guard, reveal and communicate love,* and this is a living reflection of and a real sharing in God's love for humanity and the love of Christ the Lord for the Church his bride."[18] This being the case, it is in the Holy Family, the original "Church in miniature *(Ecclesia domestica),*"[19] that every Christian family must be reflected. "Through God's mysterious design, it was in that family that the Son of God spent long years of a hidden life. It is therefore the prototype and example for all Christian families."[20]

8. St. Joseph was called by God to serve the person and mission of Jesus directly *through the exercise of his fatherhood.* It is precisely in this way that, as the Church's liturgy teaches, he "cooperated in the fullness of time in the great mystery of salvation" and is truly a "minister of salvation."[21] His fatherhood is expressed concretely "in his having made his life a service, a sacrifice to the mystery of the Incarnation and to the redemptive mission connected with it; in having used the legal authority which was his over the Holy Family in order to make a total gift of self, of his life and work; in having turned his human vocation to domestic love into a superhuman oblation of self, an oblation of his heart and all his abilities into love placed at the service of the Messiah growing up in his house."[22]

In recalling that "the beginnings of our redemption" were entrusted

---

17. Paul VI, *Discourse to the "Equipes Notre-Dame" Movement* (May 4, 1970), 7: *AAS* 62 (1970), p. 431. Similar praise of the Family of Nazareth as a perfect example of domestic life can be found, for example, in Leo XIII, Apostolic Letter *Neminem Fugit* (June 14, 1892); Leo XIII, *P.M. Acta,* XII (1892), 149f.; Benedict XV, Motu Proprio *Bonum Sane* (July 25, 1920): *AAS* 12 (1920), pp. 313–317.

18. Apostolic Exhortation *Familiaris Consortio* (November 22, 1981), 17: *AAS* 74 (1982), 100.

19. Ibid., 49: *loc. cit.,* 140; cf. Second Vatican Ecumenical Council, Dogmatic Constitution on the Church *Lumen Gentium,* 11; Decree on the Apostolate of the Laity *Apostolicam Actuositatem,* 11.

20. Apostolic Exhortation *Familiaris Consortio* (November 22, 1981), 85: *loc. cit.,* 189f.

21. Cf. St. John Chrysostom, *In Matth. Hom.* V, 3: *PG* 57, 57f.

22. Paul VI, *Discourse* (March 19, 1966): *Insegnamenti,* IV (1966), p. 110.

"to the faithful care of Joseph,"[23] the liturgy specifies that "God placed him at the head of his family, as a faithful and prudent servant, so that with fatherly care he might watch over his only-begotten Son."[24] Leo XIII emphasized the sublime nature of this mission: "He among all stands out in his august dignity, since by divine disposition he was guardian, and according to human opinion, father of God's Son. Whence it followed that the Word of God was subjected to Joseph; he obeyed him and rendered to him that honor and reverence that children owe to their father."[25]

Since it is inconceivable that such a sublime task would not be matched by the necessary qualities to adequately fulfill it, we must recognize that Joseph showed Jesus "by a special gift from heaven, all the natural love, all the affectionate solicitude that a father's heart can know."[26]

Besides fatherly authority over Jesus, God also gave Joseph a share in the corresponding love, the love that has its origin in the Father "from whom every family in heaven and on earth is named" (Eph 3:15).

The Gospels clearly describe the fatherly responsibility of Joseph toward Jesus. For salvation—which comes through the humanity of Jesus—is realized in actions which are an everyday part of family life, in keeping with that "condescension" which is inherent in the economy of the Incarnation. The gospel writers carefully show how in the life of Jesus nothing was left to chance, but how everything took place according to God's predetermined plan. The oft-repeated formula, "This happened, so that there might be fulfilled..." in reference to a particular event in the Old Testament, serves to emphasize the unity and continuity of the plan which is fulfilled in Christ.

With the Incarnation, the "promises" and "figures" of the Old Testament become "reality": places, persons, events and rites interrelate according to precise divine commands communicated by angels and received by creatures who are particularly sensitive to the voice of

---

23. Cf. *Roman Missal,* Collect for the Solemnity of St. Joseph, Husband of the Blessed Virgin Mary.

24. Cf. ibid., Preface for the Solemnity of St. Joseph, Husband of the Blessed Virgin Mary.

25. Leo XIII, Encyclical Epistle *Quamquam Pluries* (August 15, 1889): *loc. cit.,* p. 178.

26. Pius XII, *Radio Message to Catholic School Students in the United States of America* (February 19, 1958): *AAS* 50 (1958), p. 174.

God. Mary is the Lord's humble servant, prepared from eternity for the task of being the Mother of God. Joseph is the one whom God chose to be the "overseer of the Lord's birth,"[27] the one who has the responsibility to look after the Son of God's "ordained" entry into the world, in accordance with divine dispositions and human laws. All of the so-called "private" or "hidden" life of Jesus is entrusted to Joseph's guardianship.

The Census

9. Journeying to Bethlehem for the census in obedience to the orders of legitimate authority, Joseph fulfilled for the child the significant task of officially inserting the name "Jesus, son of Joseph of Nazareth" (cf. Jn 1:45) in the registry of the Roman Empire. This registration clearly shows that Jesus belongs to the human race as a man among men, a citizen of this world, subject to laws and civil institutions, but also *"savior of the world."* Origen gives a good description of the theological significance, by no means marginal, of this historical fact: "Since the first census of the whole world took place under Caesar Augustus, and among all the others Joseph too went to register together with Mary his wife, who was with child, and since Jesus was born before the census was completed: to the person who makes a careful examination it will appear that a kind of mystery is expressed in the fact that at the time when all people in the world presented themselves to be counted, Christ too should be counted. By being registered with everyone, he could sanctify everyone; inscribed with the whole world in the census, he offered to the world communion with himself, and after presenting himself he wrote all the people of the world in the book of the living, so that as many as believed in him could then be written in heaven with the saints of God, to whom be glory and power for ever and ever. Amen."[28]

The Birth at Bethlehem

10. As guardian of the mystery "hidden for ages in the mind of God," which begins to unfold before his eyes "in the fullness of time," *Joseph, together with Mary,* is a privileged witness to the birth of the

---

27. Origen, *Hom. XIII in Lucam,* 7: *SCh.* 87, 214f.
28. Origen, *Hom. XI in Lucam,* 6: *SCh.* 87, 196f.

Son of God into the world *on Christmas night in Bethlehem.* Luke writes: *"And while they were there, the time came for her to be delivered. And she gave birth to her first-born son* and wrapped him in swaddling cloths, and laid him in a manger, because there was no place for them in the inn" (Lk 2:6–7).

Joseph was an eyewitness to this birth, which took place in conditions that, humanly speaking, were embarrassing—a first announcement of that "self-emptying" (cf. Phil 2:5–8) which Christ freely accepted for the forgiveness of sins. Joseph also *witnessed the adoration of the shepherds* who arrived at Jesus' birthplace after the angel had brought them the great and happy news (cf. Lk 2:15–16) . Later he also *witnessed the homage of the magi who came from the East* (cf. Mt 2:11).

The Circumcision

11. A son's circumcision was the first religious obligation of a father, and with this ceremony (cf. Lk 2:21) Joseph exercised his right and duty with regard to Jesus.

The principle which holds that all the rites of the Old Testament are a shadow of the reality (cf. Heb 9:9 f.; 10:1) serves to explain why Jesus would accept them. As with all the other rites, circumcision too is "fulfilled" in Jesus. God's covenant with Abraham, of which circumcision was the sign (cf. Gn 17:13), reaches its full effect and perfect realization in Jesus, who is the "yes" of all the ancient promises (cf. 2 Cor 1:20).

Conferral of the Name

12. At the circumcision Joseph names the child "Jesus." This is the only name in which there is salvation (cf. Acts 4:12). Its significance had been revealed to Joseph at the moment of his "annunciation": "You shall call the child Jesus, for he will save his people from their sins" (cf. Mt 1:21). In conferring the name, Joseph declares his own legal fatherhood over Jesus, and in speaking the name he proclaims the child's mission as Savior.

The Presentation of Jesus in the Temple

13. This rite, to which Luke refers (2:22 ff.), includes the ransom of the first-born and sheds light on the subsequent stay of Jesus in the Temple at the age of twelve.

The *ransoming of the first-born* is another obligation of the father, and it is fulfilled by Joseph. Represented in the firstborn is the people of the covenant, ransomed from slavery in order to belong to God. Here too, Jesus—who is the true "price" of ransom (cf. 1 Cor 6:20; 7:23; 1 Pt 1:19)—not only "fulfills" the Old Testament rite, but at the same time transcends it, since he is not a subject to be redeemed, but the very author of redemption.

The gospel writer notes that "his father and his mother marveled at what was said about him" (Lk 2:23), in particular at *what Simeon said* in his canticle to God, when he referred to Jesus as the "salvation which you have prepared in the presence of all peoples, a light for revelation to the Gentiles, and for glory to your people Israel" and as a "sign that is spoken against" (cf. Lk 2:30–34).

The Flight into Egypt

14. After the presentation in the Temple the Evangelist Luke notes: "And when they had performed everything according to the law of the Lord, *they returned to Galilee,* to their own city, Nazareth. And the child grew and became strong, filled with wisdom, and the favor of God was upon him" (Lk 2:39–40).

But *according to Matthew's text,* a very important event took place before the return to Galilee, an event in which divine providence once again had recourse to Joseph. We read: "Now when [the magi] had departed, behold, an angel of the Lord appeared to Joseph in a dream and said, *'Rise, take the child and his mother, and flee to Egypt,* and remain there till I tell you; for Herod is about to search for the child, to destroy him'" (Mt 2:13). Herod learned from the magi who came from the East about the birth of the "king of the Jews" (Mt 2:2). And when the magi departed, he "sent and killed all the male children in Bethlehem and in all that region who were two years old or under" (Mt 2:16). By killing them all, he wished to kill the newborn "king of the Jews" whom he had heard about. And so, Joseph, having been warned in a dream, "took the child and his mother by night, and *departed to Egypt,* and remained there *until the death of Herod.* This was to fulfill what the Lord had spoken by the prophet, 'Out of Egypt have I called my son'" (Mt 2:14–15; cf. Hos 11:1).

And so Jesus' way back to Nazareth from Bethlehem passed through Egypt. Just as Israel had followed the path of the exodus "from the condition of slavery" in order to begin the Old Covenant, so *Joseph, guardian and cooperator in the providential mystery of God,* even in exile watched over the one who brings about the New Covenant.

Jesus' Stay in the Temple

15. From the time of the annunciation, both Joseph and Mary found themselves, in a certain sense, *at the heart of the mystery* hidden for ages in the mind of God, a mystery which had taken on flesh: *"The Word became flesh and dwelt among us"* (Jn 1:14). He dwelt among men, within the surroundings of *the Holy Family of Nazareth*—one of many families in this small town in Galilee, one of the many families of the land of Israel. There Jesus "grew and became strong, filled with wisdom, and the favor of God was upon him" (Lk 2:40). The Gospels summarize in a few words the *long period of the "hidden" life,* during which Jesus prepared himself for his messianic mission. Only one episode from this "hidden time" is described in the *Gospel of Luke: the Passover in Jerusalem when Jesus was twelve years old.* Together with Mary and Joseph, Jesus took part in the feast as a young pilgrim. "And when the feast was ended, as they were returning, the boy Jesus stayed behind in Jerusalem. His parents did not know it" (Lk 2:43). After a day's journey, they noticed his absence and began to search "among their kinsfolk and acquaintances." "After three days *they found him in the temple,* sitting among the teachers, listening to them and asking them questions, and all who heard him were amazed at his understanding and his answers" (Lk 2:47). Mary asked: "Son, why have you treated us so? *Behold, your father and I have been looking for you anxiously"* (Lk 2:48). The answer Jesus gave was such that "they did not understand the saying which he spoke to them." He had said, "How is it that you sought me? Did you not know *that I must be in my Father's house?"* (Lk 2:49–50).

Joseph, of whom Mary had just used the words "your father," heard this answer. That, after all, is what all the people said and thought: "Jesus was the son (as was supposed) of Joseph" (Lk 3:23). Nonetheless, the reply of Jesus in the Temple brought once again to the mind of his "presumed father" what he had heard on that night twelve years earlier: "Joseph...do not fear to take Mary your wife, for *that which is conceived in her is of the Holy Spirit."* From that time onward he knew that he was a guardian of the mystery of God, and it was *precisely this mystery* that the twelve-year-old *Jesus brought to mind:* "I must be in my Father's house."

The Support and Education of Jesus of Nazareth

16. The growth of Jesus "in wisdom and in stature, and in favor with God and man" (Lk 2:52) took place within the Holy Family under the eyes of Joseph, who had the important task of "raising" Jesus, that is, feeding, clothing and educating him in the Law and in a trade, in keeping with the duties of a father.

In the Eucharistic Sacrifice, the Church venerates the memory of Mary, the ever Virgin Mother of God, and the memory of St. Joseph,[29] because "he fed him whom the faithful must eat as the bread of eternal life."[30]

For his part, Jesus "was obedient to them" (Lk 2:51), respectfully returning the affection of his "parents." In this way he wished to sanctify the obligations of the family and of work, which he performed at the side of Joseph.

---

29. Cf. *Roman Missal,* Eucharistic Prayer I.

30. Sacror. Rituum Congreg., *Decr. Quemadmodum Deus* (December 8, 1870): *loc. cit.,* 282.

III
A JUST MAN, A HUSBAND

17. In the course of that pilgrimage of faith which was his life, Joseph, like Mary, remained faithful to God's call until the end. While Mary's life was the bringing to fullness of that *fiat* first spoken at the annunciation, *at the moment of Joseph's own "annunciation"* he said nothing; instead he simply *"did* as the angel of the Lord commanded him" (Mt 1:24). And *this first "doing" became the beginning of "Joseph's way."* The Gospels do not record any word ever spoken by Joseph along that way. But *the silence of Joseph* has its own special eloquence, for thanks to that silence we can understand the truth of the Gospel's judgment that he was "a just man" (Mt 1:19).

One must come to understand this truth, for it contains *one of the most important testimonies concerning man and his vocation.* Through many generations the Church has read this testimony with ever greater attention and with deeper understanding, drawing, as it were, "what is new and what is old" (Mt 13:52) from the storehouse of the noble figure of Joseph.

18. Above all, the "just" man of Nazareth possesses the clear characteristics of a husband. Luke refers to Mary as "a virgin betrothed to a man whose name was Joseph" (Lk 1:27). Even before the "mystery hidden for ages" (Eph 3:9) began to be fulfilled, the Gospels set before us *the image of husband and wife.* According to Jewish custom, marriage took place in two stages: first, the legal, or true marriage was celebrated, and then, only after a certain period of time, the husband brought the wife into his own house. Thus, before he lived with Mary, Joseph was already her "husband." *Mary, however, preserved her deep desire to give herself exclusively to God.* One may well ask how this desire of Mary's could be reconciled with a "wedding." The answer can only come from the saving events as they unfold, from the special action of God himself. From the moment of the annunciation, Mary knew that *she was to fulfill*

her virginal desire to give herself exclusively and fully to God precisely *by becoming the Mother of God's Son.* Becoming a mother by the power of the Holy Spirit was the form taken by her gift of self: a form which God himself expected of the Virgin Mary, who was "betrothed" to Joseph. Mary uttered her *fiat.* The fact that Mary was "betrothed" to Joseph *was part of the very plan of God.* This is pointed out by Luke and especially by Matthew. The words spoken to Joseph are very significant: "Do not fear to take Mary *your wife,* for that which has been conceived in her is of the Holy Spirit" (Mt 1:20). These words explain the mystery of Joseph's wife: In her motherhood Mary is a virgin. In her, "the Son of the Most High" assumed a human body and became "the Son of Man."

Addressing Joseph through the words of the angel, God speaks to him *as the husband of the Virgin of Nazareth.* What took place in her through the power of the Holy Spirit also *confirmed in a special way the marriage bond* which already existed between Joseph and Mary. God's messenger was clear in what he said to Joseph: "Do not fear to take Mary *your wife* into your home." Hence, what had taken place earlier, namely, Joseph's marriage to Mary, happened in accord with God's will and was meant to endure. In her divine motherhood Mary had to continue to live as "a virgin, the wife of her husband" (cf. Lk 1:27).

19. In the words of the "annunciation" by night, Joseph not only heard the divine truth concerning his wife's indescribable vocation; he *also heard once again the truth about his own vocation.* This "just" man, who, in the spirit of the noblest traditions of the Chosen People, loved the Virgin of Nazareth and was bound to her by a husband's love, was once again called by God to this love.

"Joseph did as the angel of the Lord commanded him; he took his wife" into his home (Mt 1:24); what was conceived in Mary was "of the Holy Spirit." From expressions such as these are we not to suppose that his *love as a man was also given new birth by the Holy Spirit?* Are we not to think that the love of God which has been poured forth into the human heart through the Holy Spirit (cf. Rm 5:5) molds every human love to perfection? This love of God also molds—in a completely unique way—the love of husband and wife, deepening within it everything of human worth and beauty, everything that bespeaks an exclusive gift of self, a covenant between persons, and an authentic communion according to the model of the Blessed Trinity.

"Joseph...took his wife; *but he knew her not,* until she had borne a son" (Mt 1:24–25). These words indicate *another kind of closeness in marriage.* The deep spiritual closeness arising from marital union and the interpersonal contact between man and woman have their definitive origin in the Spirit, the Giver of Life (cf. Jn 6:63). *Joseph, in obedience to the Spirit, found in the Spirit the source of love,* the conjugal love which he experienced as a man. And this love proved to be greater than this "just man" could ever have expected within the limits of his human heart.

20. In the liturgy, Mary is celebrated as "united to Joseph, the just man, by a bond of marital and virginal love."[31] There are really two kinds of love here, both of which *together* represent the mystery of the Church—virgin and spouse—as symbolized in the marriage of Mary and Joseph. "Virginity or celibacy for the sake of the kingdom of God not only does not contradict the dignity of marriage but presupposes and confirms it. Marriage and virginity are two ways of expressing and living the one mystery of the covenant of God with his people,"[32] the covenant which is a communion of love between God and human beings.

Through his complete self-sacrifice, Joseph expressed his generous love for the Mother of God, and gave her a husband's "gift of self." Even though he decided to draw back so as not to interfere in the plan of God which was coming to pass in Mary, Joseph obeyed the explicit command of the angel and took Mary into his home, while respecting the fact that she belonged exclusively to God.

On the other hand, it was from his marriage to Mary that Joseph derived his singular dignity and his rights in regard to Jesus. "It is certain that the dignity of the Mother of God is so exalted that nothing could be more sublime; yet because Mary was united to Joseph by the bond of marriage, there can be no doubt that *Joseph approached as no other person ever could* that eminent dignity whereby the Mother of God towers above all creatures. Since marriage is the highest degree of association and friendship involving by its very nature a communion of goods, it follows that God, by giving Joseph to the Virgin, did not give him to her only as a companion for life, a witness of her virginity and protector of her honor; he also gave Joseph to Mary in order that *he might share,* through the marriage pact, in her own sublime greatness."[33]

---

31. *Collectio Missarum de Beata Maria Virgine,* 1, "Sancta Maria de Nazareth," Praefatio.

32. Apostolic Exhortation *Familiaris Consortio* (November 22, 1981), 16: *loc. cit.,* 98.

33. Leo XIII, Encyclical Epistle *Quamquam Pluries* (August 15, 1889): *loc. cit.,* 177 f.

21. This *bond of charity was the core of the Holy Family's life,* first in the poverty of Bethlehem, then in their exile in Egypt, and later in the house of Nazareth. The Church deeply venerates this family, and proposes it as the model of all families. Inserted directly in the mystery of the Incarnation, the family of Nazareth has its own special mystery. And in this mystery, as in the Incarnation, one finds a true fatherhood: *the human form of the family of the Son of God,* a true human family, formed by the divine mystery. *In this family, Joseph is the father: his fatherhood* is not one that derives from begetting offspring, but neither is it an "apparent" or merely "substitute" fatherhood. Rather, it is one that *fully shares in authentic human fatherhood* and the mission of a father in the family. This is a consequence of the hypostatic union: humanity taken up into the unity of the Divine Person of the Word-Son, Jesus Christ. Together with human nature, *all that is human, and especially the family*—as the first dimension of man's existence in the world—*is also taken up* in Christ. Within this context, Joseph's human fatherhood was also "taken up" in the mystery of Christ's Incarnation.

On the basis of this principle, the words which Mary spoke to the twelve-year-old Jesus in the Temple take on their full significance: *"Your father and I...*have been looking for you." This is no conventional phrase: Mary's words to Jesus show the complete reality of the Incarnation present in the mystery of the family of Nazareth. From the beginning, *Joseph accepted with the "obedience of faith"* his human fatherhood over Jesus. And thus, following the light of the Holy Spirit who gives himself to human beings through faith, he certainly came to discover ever more fully *the indescribable gift that was his human fatherhood.*

IV
WORK AS AN EXPRESSION OF LOVE

22. *Work was the daily expression of love in the life of the family of Nazareth.* The Gospel specifies the kind of work Joseph did in order to support his family: he was a carpenter. This simple word sums up Joseph's entire life. For Jesus, these were hidden years, the years to which Luke refers after recounting the episode that occurred in the Temple: "And he went down with them and came to Nazareth, and was obedient to them" (Lk 2:51). This *"submission"* or obedience of Jesus in the house of Nazareth should be *understood as a sharing in the work of Joseph.* Having learned the work of his presumed father, he was known as "the carpenter's son." If the family of Nazareth is an example and model for human families, in the order of salvation and holiness, so too, by analogy, is Jesus' work at the side of Joseph the carpenter. In our own day, the Church has emphasized this by instituting the liturgical memorial of St. Joseph the Worker on May 1. *Human work,* and especially manual labor, *receive special prominence in the Gospel.* Along with the humanity of the Son of God, work too has been taken up in the mystery of the Incarnation, *and has also been redeemed in a special way.* At the workbench where he plied his trade together with Jesus, Joseph brought human work closer to the mystery of the redemption.

23. In the human growth of Jesus "in wisdom, age and grace," the *virtue of industriousness* played a notable role, since "work is a human good" which "transforms nature" and makes man "in a sense, more human."[34]

---

34. Cf. Encyclical Letter *Laborem Exercens* (September 14, 1981), 9: *AAS* 73 (1981), 599 f.

The importance of work in human life demands that its meaning be known and assimilated in order to "help all people to come closer to God, the Creator and Redeemer, to participate in his salvific plan for man and the world, and to deepen...friendship with Christ in their lives, by accepting, through faith, a living participation in his threefold mission as Priest, Prophet and King."[35]

24. What is crucially important here is the sanctification of daily life, a sanctification which each person must acquire according to his or her own state, and one which can be promoted according to a model accessible to all people: "St. Joseph is the model of those humble ones that Christianity raises up to great destinies...he is the proof that in order to be a good and genuine follower of Christ, there is no need of great things—it is enough to have the common, simple and human virtues, but they need to be true and authentic."[36]

---

35. Ibid., 24: *loc. cit.,* 638. The Popes in recent times have constantly presented St. Joseph as the "model" of workers and laborers; cf., for example, Leo XIII, Encyclical Epistle *Quamquam Pluries* (August 15, 1889): *loc. cit.,* 180; Benedict XV, Motu Proprio *Bonum Sane* (July 25, 1920)*: loc. cit.,* 314–316; Pius XII, *Discourse* (March 11, 1945), 4: *AAS* 37 (1945), 72; *Discourse* (May 1, 1955): *AAS* 47 (1955), 406; John XXIII, *Radio Address* (May 1, 1960): *AAS* 52 (1960), 398.

36. Paul VI, *Discourse* (March 19, 1969): *Insegnamenti,* VII (1969), 1268.

V

THE PRIMACY OF THE INTERIOR LIFE

25. The same aura of silence that envelops everything else about Joseph also shrouds his work as a carpenter in the house of Nazareth. It is, however, *a silence that reveals in a special way the inner portrait* of the man. The Gospels speak exclusively of what Joseph "did." Still, they allow us to discover in his "actions"—shrouded in silence as they are—an aura of *deep contemplation.* Joseph was in daily contact with the mystery "hidden from ages past," and which "dwelt" under his roof. This explains, for example, why St. Teresa of Jesus, the great reformer of the Carmelites, promoted the renewal of veneration to St. Joseph in Western Christianity.

26. The total sacrifice, whereby Joseph surrendered his whole existence to the demands of the Messiah's coming into his home, becomes understandable only in the light of his profound interior life. It was from this interior life that "very singular commands and consolations came, bringing him also the logic and strength that belong to simple and clear souls, and giving him the power of making great decisions—such as the decision to put his liberty immediately at the disposition of the divine designs, to make over to them also his legitimate human calling, his conjugal happiness, to accept the conditions, the responsibility and the burden of a family, but, through an incomparable virginal love, to renounce that natural conjugal love that is the foundation and nourishment of the family." [37]

This submission to God, this readiness of will to dedicate oneself to all that serves him, is really nothing less than that *exercise of devotion* which constitutes one expression of the virtue of religion. [38]

---

37. Ibid.: *loc. cit.,* 1267.
38. Cf. St. Thomas, *Summa Theol.,* II–IIae, q. 82, a. 3, *ad* 2.

27. The communion of life between Joseph and Jesus leads us to consider once again the mystery of the Incarnation, precisely in reference to the humanity of Jesus as the efficacious instrument of his divinity for the purpose of sanctifying man: "By virtue of his divinity, Christ's human actions were salvific for us, causing grace within us, either by merit or by a certain efficacy."[39]

Among those actions, the gospel writers highlight those which have to do with the Paschal Mystery, but they also underscore the importance of physical contact with Jesus for healing (cf. for example, Mk 1:41), and the influence Jesus exercised upon John the Baptist when they were both in their mothers' wombs (cf. Lk 1:41–44).

As we have seen, the apostolic witness did not neglect the story of Jesus' birth, his circumcision, his presentation in the Temple, his flight into Egypt and his hidden life in Nazareth. It recognized the "mystery" of grace present in each of these saving "acts," inasmuch as they all share the same source of love: the divinity of Christ. If through Christ's humanity this love shone on all mankind, the first beneficiaries were undoubtedly those whom the divine will had most intimately associated with itself: Mary, the Mother of Jesus, and Joseph, his presumed father.[40]

Why should the "fatherly" love of Joseph not have had an influence upon the "filial" love of Jesus? And vice versa, why should the "filial" love of Jesus not have had an influence upon the "fatherly" love of Joseph, thus leading to a further deepening of their unique relationship? Those souls most sensitive to the impulses of divine love have rightly seen in Joseph a brilliant example of the interior life.

Furthermore, in Joseph, the apparent tension between the active and the contemplative life finds an ideal harmony that is only possible for those who possess the perfection of charity. Following St. Augustine's well known distinction between the love of the truth *(caritas veritatis)* and the practical demands of love *(necessitas caritatis),*[41] we can say that Joseph experienced both *love of the truth*—that pure contemplative love of the divine Truth which radiated from the humanity of Christ— and *the demands of love*—that equally pure and selfless love required for his vocation to safeguard and develop the humanity of Jesus, which was inseparably linked to his divinity.

---

39. Ibid., III, q. 8, a. 1, *ad* 1.

40. Cf. Pius XII, Encyclical Letter *Haurietis Aquas* (May 15, 1956), III: *AAS* 48 (1956), 329f.

41. Cf. St. Thomas, *Summa Theol.,* II–IIae, q. 182, a. 1, *ad* 3.

VI

PATRON OF THE CHURCH IN OUR DAY

28. At a difficult time in the Church's history, Pope Pius IX, wishing to place her under the powerful patronage of the holy patriarch Joseph, declared him "Patron of the Catholic Church."[42] For Pius IX this was no idle gesture, since by virtue of the sublime dignity which God has granted to his most faithful servant Joseph, "the Church, after the Blessed Virgin, his spouse, has always held him in great honor and showered him with praise, having recourse to him amid tribulations."[43]

What are the reasons for such great confidence? Leo XIII explained it in this way: "The reasons why St. Joseph must be considered the special patron of the Church, and the Church in turn draws exceeding hope from his care and patronage, chiefly arise from his having been the husband of Mary and the presumed father of Jesus.... Joseph was in his day the lawful and natural guardian, head and defender of the Holy Family.... It is thus fitting and most worthy of Joseph's dignity that, in the same way that he once kept unceasing holy watch over the family of Nazareth, so now does he protect and defend with his heavenly patronage the Church of Christ."[44]

29. This patronage must be invoked as ever necessary for the Church, not only as a defense against all dangers, but also, and indeed primarily, as an impetus for her renewed commitment to evangelization in the world and to re-evangelization in those lands and nations where— as I wrote in the Apostolic Exhortation *Christifideles Laici*— "religion and the Christian life were formerly flourishing and...are now put to a

---

42. Cf. Sacror. Rituum Congreg., Decr. *Quemadmodum Deus* (December 8, 1870): *loc. cit.,* 283.

43. Ibid.: *loc. cit.,* 282f.

44. Leo XIII, Encyclical Epistle *Quamquam Pluries* (August 15, 1889): *loc. cit.,* 177–179.

hard test."[45] In order to bring the first proclamation of Christ, or to bring it anew wherever it has been neglected or forgotten, the Church has need of special "power from on high" (cf. Lk 24:49; Acts 1:8): a gift of the Spirit of the Lord, a gift which is not unrelated to the intercession and example of his saints.

30. Besides trusting in Joseph's sure protection, the Church also trusts in his noble example, which transcends all individual states of life and serves as a model for the entire Christian community, whatever the condition and duties of each of its members may be.

As the *Constitution on Divine Revelation* of the Second Vatican Council has said, the basic attitude of the entire Church must be that of "hearing the Word of God with reverence,"[46] an absolute readiness to serve faithfully God's salvific will revealed in Jesus. Already at the beginning of human redemption, after Mary, we find the model of obedience made incarnate in St. Joseph, the man known for having faithfully carried out God's commands.

Pope Paul VI invited us to invoke Joseph's patronage "as the Church has been wont to do in these recent times, for herself in the first place, with a spontaneous theological reflection on the marriage of divine and human action in the great economy of the redemption, in which economy the first—the divine one—is wholly sufficient unto itself, while the second—the human action which is ours—though capable of nothing (cf. Jn 15:5), is never dispensed from a humble but conditional and ennobling collaboration. The Church also calls upon Joseph as her protector because of a profound and ever present desire to reinvigorate her ancient life with true evangelical virtues, such as shine forth in St. Joseph."[47]

31. The Church transforms these needs into prayer. Recalling that God wished to entrust the beginnings of our redemption to the faithful care of St. Joseph, she asks God to grant that she may faithfully cooperate in the work of salvation, that she may receive the same faithfulness and purity of heart that inspired Joseph in serving the incarnate Word,

---

45. Post-Synodal Apostolic Exhortation *Christifideles Laici* (December 30, 1988), 34: *AAS* 81 (1989), 456.

46. Second Vatican Ecumenical Council, Dogmatic Constitution on Divine Revelation *Dei Verbum,* 1.

47. Paul VI, *Discourse* (March 19, 1969): *Insegnamenti,* VII (1969), 1269.

and that she may walk before God in the ways of holiness and justice, following Joseph's example and through his intercession.[48]

One hundred years ago, Pope Leo XIII had already exhorted the Catholic world to pray for the protection of St. Joseph, patron of the whole Church. The Encyclical Epistle *Quamquam Pluries* appealed to Joseph's "fatherly love...for the child Jesus" and commended to him, as "the provident guardian of the divine family," "the beloved inheritance which Jesus Christ purchased by his blood." Since that time—as I recalled at the beginning of this Exhortation—*the Church has implored the protection of St. Joseph* on the basis of "that sacred bond of charity which united him to the Immaculate Virgin Mother of God," and the Church has commended to Joseph all of her cares, including those dangers which threaten the human family.

Even *today* we have *many reasons to pray in a similar way:* "Most beloved father, dispel the evil of falsehood and sin...graciously assist us from heaven in our struggle with the powers of darkness...and just as once you saved the Child Jesus from mortal danger, so now defend God's holy Church from the snares of her enemies and from all adversity."[49] Today we still have *good reason to commend everyone to St. Joseph.*

32. It is my heartfelt wish that these reflections on the person of St. Joseph will renew in us the prayerful devotion which my Predecessor called for a century ago. Our prayers and *the very person of Joseph have renewed significance for the Church in our day* in light of the Third Christian Millennium.

The Second Vatican Council made all of us sensitive once again to the "great things which God has done," and to that *"economy of salvation"* of which St. Joseph was a special minister. Commending ourselves, then, to the protection of him to whose custody God "entrusted his greatest and most precious treasures,"[50] *let us at the same time learn from him how to be servants of the "economy of salvation."* May St.

---

48. Cf. *Roman Missal,* Collect, Prayer over the Gifts for the Solemnity of St. Joseph, Husband of the Blessed Virgin Mary; Prayer after Communion from the Votive Mass of St. Joseph.

49. Cf. Leo XIII, *"Oratio ad Sanctum Iosephum,"* contained immediately after the text of the Encyclical Epistle *Quamquam Pluries* (August 15, 1889), Leo XIII, *P.M. Acta,* IX (1890), 183.

50. Sacror Rituum Congreg., *Decr. Quemadmodum Deus* (December 8 1870): *loc. cit.,* 282.

Joseph become for all of us an exceptional teacher in the service of *Christ's saving mission,* a mission which is the responsibility of each and every member of the Church: husbands and wives, parents, those who live by the work of their hands or by any other kind of work, those called to the contemplative life and those called to the apostolate.

This just man, who bore within himself the entire heritage of the Old Covenant, was also *brought into the "beginning" of the New and Eternal Covenant in Jesus Christ.* May he show us the paths of this saving covenant as we stand at the threshold of the next millennium, in which there must be a continuation and further development of the "fullness of time" that belongs to the ineffable mystery of the Incarnation of the Word.

May St. Joseph obtain for the Church and for the world, as well as for each of us, the blessing of the Father, Son and Holy Spirit.

Given at Rome, in St. Peter's, on August 15—the Solemnity of the Assumption of the Blessed Virgin Mary—in the year 1989, the eleventh of my pontificate.

John Paul II

THE SPLENDOR OF TRUTH

Veritatis Splendor

Encyclical Letter of Pope John Paul II

INTRODUCTION

Historical Perspectives

A relatively long span of time elapsed between *Guardian of the Redeemer* (1989), and *Veritatis Splendor* (1993). The pope's Marian emphasis continued. During his trips to various nations, he often offered an act of entrustment of the people to Mary.[1] He frequently concluded various documents with a Marian reflection and prayer. However, this Marian content seldom reflected new dimensions. *Veritatis Splendor* picks up and develops a theme John Paul had touched on in *Dives in Misericordia,* that is, Mary's share in Christ's mercy.

The Teaching

Veritatis Splendor develops the theme of Mary's mercy within the context of morality and the new evangelization. The document begins with the theme of light: Jesus Christ is the true light that enlightens everyone (Jn 1:9). Three main chapters cover the material on morality. Chapter one establishes relationship to Christ as the basis for morality. Chapter two focuses on questions fundamental to morality: law; freedom and law, conscience and truth, fundamental choice, and the moral act. Chapter three returns to a Christological theme and speaks of evangelization as a decision-making point. We do what we do for the sake of Christ and our relationship to him.

---

1. See Arthur B. Calkins, *Totus Tuus* (Libertyville, IL: Academy of the Immaculate, 1992).

Then, almost as a surprise, the final chapter turns to Mary, Mother of Mercy. Even though she does not know sin, "she is able to have compassion on every kind of weakness" (*VS* 120). She is rich in love because she is filled with grace. The document states: "Mary experiences, in perfect docility to the Spirit, the richness and the universality of God's love, which opens her heart and enables it to embrace the entire human race" (*VS* 120). The Church invites believers "to seek and to find in the saints, and above all in the virgin Mother of God 'full of grace' and 'all-holy,' the model, the strength and the joy needed to live a life in accordance with God's commandments and the beatitudes of the Gospel" (*VS* 107). The document goes on to say: "Mary is the radiant sign and inviting model of the moral life. As St. Ambrose put it, 'The life of this one person can serve as a model for everyone'"[2] (*VS* 120). The document links Mary's spiritual motherhood to the moral life:

> She understands sinful man and loves him with a mother's love. Precisely for this reason she is on the side of truth and shares the Church's burden in recalling always and to everyone the demands of morality. Nor does she permit sinful man to be deceived by those who claim to love him by justifying his sin, for she knows that the sacrifice of Christ her Son would thus be emptied of its power (*VS* 120).

Today

By her words at Cana, "Do whatever he tells you" (Jn 2:5), Mary continues to ask us to exercise our moral freedom.

Veritatis Splendor concludes with an act of entrustment of the moral life of the People of God to Mary, Mother of Mercy. The last paragraph consists of a prayer to Mary under this title.

---

2. *De Virginibus,* Bk II, Chap. II, 15: *PL* 16, 222.

THE SPLENDOR OF TRUTH

Veritatis Splendor

Promulgated by His Holiness Pope John Paul II
On August 6, 1993

MARY, MOTHER OF MERCY

118. At the end of these considerations, let us entrust ourselves, the sufferings and the joys of our life, the moral life of believers and people of good will, and the research of moralists, to Mary, Mother of God and Mother of Mercy.

Mary is Mother of Mercy because her Son, Jesus Christ, was sent by the Father as the revelation of God's mercy (cf. Jn 3:16–18). Christ came not to condemn but to forgive, to show mercy (cf. Mt 9:13). And the greatest mercy of all is found in his being in our midst and calling us to meet him and to confess with Peter that he is "the Son of the living God" (Mt 16:16). No human sin can erase the mercy of God, or prevent him from unleashing all his triumphant power, if we only call upon him. Indeed, sin itself makes even more radiant the love of the Father who, in order to ransom a slave, sacrificed his Son:[1] his mercy toward us is redemption. This mercy reaches its fullness in the gift of the Spirit who

---

1. *"O inaestimabilis dilectio caritatis: ut servum redimeres, Filium tradidisti!"* *Missale Romanum, In Resurrectione Domini, Praeconium Paschale.*

bestows new life and demands that it be lived. No matter how many and great the obstacles put in his way by human frailty and sin, the Spirit, who renews the face of the earth (cf. Ps 104:30), makes possible the miracle of the perfect accomplishment of the good. This renewal, which gives the ability to do what is good, noble, beautiful, pleasing to God and in conformity with his will, is in some way the flowering of the gift of mercy, which offers liberation from the slavery of evil and gives the strength to sin no more. Through the gift of new life, Jesus makes us sharers in his love and leads us to the Father in the Spirit.

119. Such is the consoling certainty of Christian faith, the source of its profound humanity and *extraordinary simplicity*. At times, in the discussions about new and complex moral problems, it can seem that Christian morality is in itself too demanding, difficult to understand and almost impossible to practice. This is untrue, since Christian morality consists, in the simplicity of the Gospel, in *following Jesus Christ*, in abandoning oneself to him, in letting oneself be transformed by his grace and renewed by his mercy, gifts which come to us in the living communion of his Church. St. Augustine reminds us that "he who would live has a place to live, and has everything needed to live. Let him draw near, let him believe, let him become part of the body, that he may have life. Let him not shrink from the unity of the members."[2] By the light of the Holy Spirit, the living essence of Christian morality can be understood by everyone, even the least learned, but particularly those who are able to preserve an "undivided heart" (Ps 86:11). On the other hand, this evangelical simplicity does not exempt one from facing reality in its complexity; rather, it can lead to a more genuine understanding of reality, inasmuch as following Christ will gradually bring out the distinctive character of authentic Christian morality, while providing the vital energy needed to carry it out. It is the task of the Church's Magisterium to see that the dynamic process of following Christ develops in an organic manner, without the falsification or obscuring of its moral demands, with all their consequences. The one who loves Christ keeps his commandments (cf. Jn 14:15).

120. Mary is also Mother of Mercy because it is to her that Jesus entrusts his Church and all humanity. At the foot of the cross, when she accepts John as her son, when she asks, together with Christ, forgive-

---

2. *In Iohannis Evangelium Tractatus*, 26, 13: *CCL*, 36, 266.

ness from the Father for those who do not know what they do (cf. Lk 23:34), Mary experiences, in perfect docility to the Spirit, the richness and the universality of God's love, which opens her heart and enables it to embrace the entire human race. Thus Mary becomes Mother of each and every one of us, the Mother who obtains for us divine mercy.

Mary is the radiant sign and inviting model of the moral life. As St. Ambrose put it, "The life of this one person can serve as a model for everyone."[3] And while speaking specifically to virgins but within a context open to all, he affirmed: "The first stimulus to learning is the nobility of the teacher. Who can be more noble than the Mother of God? Who can be more glorious than the one chosen by Glory Itself?"[4] Mary lived and exercised her freedom precisely by giving herself to God and accepting God's gift within herself. Until the time of his birth, she sheltered in her womb the Son of God who became man; she raised him and enabled him to grow, and she accompanied him in that supreme act of freedom which is the complete sacrifice of his own life. By the gift of herself, Mary entered fully into the plan of God who gives himself to the world. By accepting and pondering in her heart events which she did not always understand (cf. Lk 2:19), she became the model of all those who hear the Word of God and keep it (cf. Lk 11:28), and merited the title of "Seat of Wisdom." This Wisdom is Jesus Christ himself, the Eternal Word of God, who perfectly reveals and accomplishes the will of the Father (cf. Heb 10:5–10). Mary invites everyone to accept this Wisdom. To us too she addresses the command she gave to the servants at Cana in Galilee during the marriage feast: "Do whatever he tells you" (Jn 2:5).

Mary shares our human condition, but in complete openness to the grace of God. Not having known sin, she is able to have compassion on every kind of weakness. She understands sinful man and loves him with a mother's love. Precisely for this reason she is on the side of truth and shares the Church's burden in recalling always and to everyone the demands of morality. Nor does she permit sinful man to be deceived by those who claim to love him by justifying his sin, for she knows that the sacrifice of Christ her Son would thus be emptied of its power. No absolution offered by beguiling doctrines, even in the areas

---

3. *De Virginibus,* Bk. II, Chap. II, 15: *PL* 16, 222.

4. Ibid., Bk. II, Chap. II, 7: *PL* 16, 220.

of philosophy and theology, can make man truly happy: only the cross and the glory of the risen Christ can grant peace to his conscience and salvation to his life.

O Mary,
Mother of Mercy,
watch over all people,
that the cross of Christ
may not be emptied of its power,
that man may not stray
from the path of the good
or become blind to sin,
but may put his hope ever more fully in God
who is "rich in mercy" (Eph 2:4).
May he carry out the good works
prepared by God beforehand (cf. Eph 2:10)
and so live completely
"for the praise of his glory" (Eph 1:12).

ON PREPARATION
FOR THE JUBILEE
OF THE YEAR 2000

Tertio Millennio Adveniente

Apostolic Letter of Pope John Paul II
November 10, 1994

INTRODUCTION

Historical Perspectives

The Marian Year in 1987–88 had emphasized the time of preparation before the turn of the millennium. In a symbolic sense, the year was chosen to represent Mary's birth. With the advent of Mary's life, the world approached the Incarnation. Pope John Paul II called for spiritual renewal in preparation for the coming of the third millennium since the birth of Christ. What had started with Mary was to continue hand in hand with her.

Tertio Millennio has five major parts:

1) *"Jesus Christ is the same yesterday and today..."*

2) *The Jubilee of the Year 2000*

3) *Preparation for the Great Jubilee*

4) *Immediate Preparation* with two phases leading to the celebration of the jubilee. The second phase was to be divided into three periods: the first year was dedicated to Jesus Christ; the second, to the Holy Spirit; and the third, to God the Father.

5) The final chapter, *"Jesus Christ is the same...forever."*

The Teaching

Each of the three years preceding the millennium emphasized a different aspect of Mary in relationship to the Trinity. 1997, the year of Christ, focused in a special way on Mary's divine motherhood. The Church looked to Mary as a model of faith. In the Year of the Holy Spirit, 1998, Mary's attentiveness to the Spirit, her prayerful attitude of meditating on God's word, became the focus. In the year of God the Father, 1999, the Church contemplated Mary as the beloved daughter of the Father.

The final year, the year 2000, was meant to give glory to the Trinity. The year was to be intensely Eucharistic, ecumenical and universal. Mary, who gave the incarnate Word his flesh, will play her ongoing supporting role in the new millennium.

Today

The Marian perspective in *Tertio Millennio Adveniente* sees her as supporting us today and offering a model for us to imitate. Mary had a major part to play in the Incarnation of the Word of God; she continues to stand by us as we move forward through time. John Paul II entrusts the Church to Mary's maternal intercession. She, the Mother of the Redeemer, is the Mother of Fairest Love. She is the Star who safely guides Christians to the Lord (cf. *TM* 59).

ON PREPARATION FOR THE JUBILEE OF THE YEAR 2000

Tertio Millennio Adveniente

Promulgated by His Holiness Pope John Paul II
On November 10, 1994

First year of preparation for the millennium: the year of Christ

43. *The Blessed Virgin* who will be as it were "indirectly" present in the whole preparatory phase, will be contemplated in this first year especially in the mystery of her divine motherhood. It was in her womb that the Word became flesh! The affirmation of the central place of Christ cannot therefore be separated from the recognition of the role played by his Most Holy Mother. Veneration of her, when properly understood, can in no way take away from "the dignity and efficacy of Christ the one Mediator."[1] Mary in fact constantly points to her divine Son and she is proposed to all believers as the *model of faith* which is put into practice. "Devotedly meditating on her and contemplating her in the light of the Word made man, the Church with reverence enters more intimately into the supreme mystery of the Incarnation and becomes ever increasingly like her Spouse."[2]

---

1. Second Vatican Ecumenical Council, Dogmatic Constitution on the Church *Lumen Gentium,* 62.
2. Ibid., 65.

Second year of preparation for the millennium: the year of the Holy Spirit

48. *Mary,* who conceived the incarnate Word by the power of the Holy Spirit and then in the whole of her life allowed herself to be guided by his interior activity, will be contemplated and imitated during this year above all as the woman who was docile to the voice of the Spirit, a woman of silence and attentiveness, a woman of hope who, like Abraham, accepted God's will "hoping against hope" (cf. Rom 4:18). Mary gave full expression to the longing of the poor of Yahweh and is a radiant model for those who entrust themselves with all their hearts to the promises of God.

Third year of preparation for the millennium: the year of the Father

54. In this broad perspective of commitments, *Mary Most Holy,* the highly favored daughter of the Father, will appear before the eyes of believers as the perfect model of love toward both God and neighbor. As she herself says in the Canticle of the Magnificat, great things were done for her by the Almighty, whose name is holy (cf. Lk 1:49). The Father chose her for a *unique mission* in the history of salvation: that of being the Mother of the long-awaited Savior. The Virgin Mary responded to God's call with complete openness: "Behold, I am the handmaid of the Lord" (Lk 1:38). Her motherhood, which began in Nazareth and was lived most intensely in Jerusalem at the foot of the cross, will be felt during this year as a loving and urgent invitation addressed to all the children of God, so that they will return to the house of the Father when they hear her maternal voice: "Do whatever Christ tells you" (cf. Jn 2:5).

59. I entrust this responsibility of the whole Church to the maternal intercession of Mary, Mother of the Redeemer. She, the Mother of Fairest Love, will be for Christians on the way to the Great Jubilee of the Third Millennium the Star which safely guides their steps to the Lord. May the unassuming young woman of Nazareth, who two thousand years ago offered to the world the incarnate Word, lead the men and women of the new millennium toward the One who is "the true light that enlightens every man" (Jn 1:9).

With these sentiments I impart to all my blessing.

INDEX

A

Pauline
BOOKS & MEDIA

The Daughters of St. Paul operate book and media centers at the following addresses. Visit, call or write the one nearest you today, or find us on the World Wide Web, www.pauline.org

California
3908 Sepulveda Blvd., Culver City, CA 90230; 310-397-8676
5945 Balboa Ave., San Diego, CA 92111; 858-565-9181
46 Geary Street, San Francisco, CA 94108; 415-781-5180

Florida
145 S.W. 107th Ave., Miami, FL 33174; 305-559-6715

Hawaii
1143 Bishop Street, Honolulu, HI 96813; 808-521-2731
Neighbor Islands call: 800-259-8463

Illinois
172 North Michigan Ave., Chicago, IL 60601; 312-346-4228

Louisiana
4403 Veterans Memorial Blvd., Metairie, LA 70006; 504-887-7631

Massachusetts
Rte. 1, 885 Providence Hwy., Dedham, MA 02026; 781-326-5385

Missouri
9804 Watson Rd., St. Louis, MO 63126; 314-965-3512

New Jersey
561 U.S. Route 1, Wick Plaza, Edison, NJ 08817; 732-572-1200

New York
150 East 52nd Street, New York, NY 10022; 212-754-1110
78 Fort Place, Staten Island, NY 10301; 718-447-5071

Ohio
2105 Ontario Street, Cleveland, OH 44115; 216-621-9427

Pennsylvania
9171-A Roosevelt Blvd., Philadelphia, PA 19114; 215-676-9494

South Carolina
243 King Street, Charleston, SC 29401; 843-577-0175

Tennessee
4811 Poplar Ave., Memphis, TN 38117; 901-761-2987

Texas
114 Main Plaza, San Antonio, TX 78205; 210-224-8101

Virginia
1025 King Street, Alexandria, VA 22314; 703-549-3806

Canada
3022 Dufferin Street, Toronto, Ontario, Canada M6B 3T5; 416-781-9131
1155 Yonge Street, Toronto, Ontario, Canada M4T 1W2; 416-934-3440

¡También somos su fuente para libros, videos y música en español!